Happy reading darling.

Mum x

THE SCOTS IN GERMANY.

ILLVSTRIS·GENEROSVS·DOMINVS DOMINVS IACOBVS·RAMSAY·SCOTVS·EQVES·AVRATVS·GEN·MAI·ANNO ÆTAT·47·1636·

Continuò ORAndo feliciter omnia cedunt,
Adde, LABORAndo memorabile nomen habebis

GENERAL RAMSAY

THE

SCOTS IN GERMANY:

BEING A CONTRIBUTION TOWARDS

THE HISTORY OF THE SCOT ABROAD

BY

TH. A. FISCHER

TRANSLATOR OF " SARTOR RESARTUS "

AUTHOR OF

" DAS LEBEN CARLYLE'S "; " LEBEN UND WERKE ALFRED LORD TENNYSON'S ";
" DREI STUDIEN ZUR ENGLISCHEN LITERATURGESCHICHTE."

JOHN DONALD PUBLISHERS LTD

EDINBURGH

PREFACE.

WHEN I several years ago commenced to write this book, voices were not wanting advising me to abandon the idea, chiefly on account of the vast area from which the material had to be gathered and the almost total want of preparatory inquiry into this particular branch of Scottish History.

When I nevertheless persevered in my task, though experiencing to the full the truth of those Cassandra voices, it was owing not only to an interest which warmed with the increasing difficulties, but to the very kind and active help that friends of historical research both in Scotland and in Germany have afforded me in supplying copies of records or other sources of information, or in reading proofs, or in acting as guides through the labyrinths of their libraries. It would be too long to mention their names; my thanks are due to them all, in particular to the librarians and keepers of records in Edinburgh, Glasgow, Aberdeen, St Andrews, Fort Augustus, Dundee, and in half a hundred places in Sweden, Germany and Austria.

That notwithstanding this kind co-operation the present book is still far from complete, I am only too painfully aware.

There is more than enough of material to be found among the Records of Königsberg and Danzig alone for a contemplated second volume, to be devoted to the Scottish settlements in Prussia only, of which we have given a sketch in the First Part of the present work. Such a volume ought to be written.

Perhaps some Society like the Scottish History Society or the Society of Antiquaries would think it worth its while to originate and stimulate research in this direction. So many old barrows have been ransacked, so many old Ogham stones been read, so many old Charter Chests been examined at their expense and instigation. Here then is a new field; quite as interesting to the Scottish historian, a field altogether neglected hitherto, but full of the promise of the most interesting and surprising results!

It must be left to the future with more or less confidence to point out and smooth the way towards the happy consummation of a task, towards which the present volume only forms a contribution.

I regret very much that my search for the portraits of Alesius and Durie has hitherto proved fruitless.

To the courtesy of Baron Johnston in Silesia, of the "Historische Verein" at Hanau, and of the Rev. King Hewison at Rothesay I am indebted for the three portraits reproduced.

In conclusion, let me say that I am still collecting the likenesses of famous Scots in Germany and that I shall be grateful for the direct communication of any criticisms or alterations concerning the form or the substance of the present, as well as for any suggestion or help towards the writing of the contemplated second volume.

THE AUTHOR.

20 SOUTH FREDERICK STREET,
EDINBURGH, *February* 1902.

CONTENTS.

PART I.

COMMERCE AND TRADE.

COMMERCE AND TRADE.

THE COMMERCIAL INTERCOURSE OF SCOTLAND WITH GERMANY AND POLAND.

THE commercial intercourse of Scotland with Germany dates almost, if not quite, as far back as that with Flanders, where already in the commencement of the XIIIth Century a Scotch Settlement at Bruges was known under the name of "Scottendyk."[1] The oldest document relative to Scotch-German trade is the famous letter of William Wallace, the national Hero and champion of his country's liberty, which was discovered in 1829 by the German Scholar and Antiquarian Dr. Lappenberg among the archives of the Free City of Lübeck, the renowned chief of the Hanseatic league. It bears the date of 1297 and runs as follows:[2] " Andrew Moray and William Wallace, leaders of the Scotch army, and the commonwealth of the same kingdom send to the prudent and discreet men, our good friends, the Senate and the commoners of Lübeck and of Hamburg greeting and a continuous increase of sincere affection. We have been informed by trustworthy merchants of the said kingdom of Scotland, that you on your own behalf have been friendly and helpful in counsel and deed in all things and enterprises concerning us and our merchants, though our own merits did not occasion this. We are therefore the more beholden to you, and wishing to prove our gratitude in a worthy manner we ask you to make it known among your merchants that they can now have a safe access with their merchandize to all harbours of the Kingdom of

[1] A House called " Scotland " existed at Bruges in 1367; a street " Scotland " since 1291.
[2] See the Latin original in the Appendix.

Scotland, because the Kingdom of Scotland has, thanks
be to God, by war been recovered from the power of the
English. Farewell. Given at Hadsington (Haddington)
in Scotland on the eleventh day of October in the Year
of Grace one thousand two hundred and ninety seven."
 " We also pray you to be good enough to further the
business of John Burnet and John Frere, our merchants,
just as you might wish that we should further the business
of your merchants. Farewell. Given as above."
 As will be seen, the letter was written immediately
after the victorious battle of the Scots near Stirling and
the advance of the army into Northumberland.[1]
 Previous to this date we can scarcely speak of a
regular trade between the two countries; and even up
to a much later date the development of commercial
intercommunication is slow. This is but natural, when we
consider that piracy and the almost ceaseless wars between
England and Scotland, and later between the Hanseatic
League and the Kingdoms of the North, must be added
to the already universal want of safety of the traffic on
land and sea.
 England had during the XIVth and XVth Centuries issued
repeatedly strict orders against providing the "rebellious
Scots" with arms, flour or victuals of any kind by way
of the sea. King Henry IV had even tried to persuade
the Master[2] of the Teutonic Order at Marienburg
Konrad von Jungingen, to cease from trading with the
Scots altogether, but had only received the dignified
answer, that the Order lived in peace with all Christians
and could not forbid the King of Scotland to trade
with its territories.[3] Thereupon the English out of
revenge burn a ship from Stralsund " because it had
sided with the enemy,"[4] and repeatedly raise complaints

[1] See *Hansisches Urkundenbuch*, i. 422, and the Wallace Papers.
[2] Called in German "Hochmeister." Originally a religious Institution
for the Suppression of the heathens in Prussia, the Order was in the early
Middle Ages engaged in extensive trading operations with England,
Sweden, Scotland, etc.
[3] Cp. *Hanserecesse*, v. pp. 64, 65.   [4] *Hans. Urk. Buch*, ii. 84.

on account of the alleged contravening of their trade-prohibitions.[1]

As to the piracy of those days, almost all seafaring nations were guilty of it   The Frisians however and the Scots seem to have enjoyed the worst reputation.   The complaints of the suffering shipowners are very frequent. In Scotland as in other countries men of the highest rank took part not only in trading beyond the seas,[2] but also in the more fascinating enterprise of procuring booty at sea by force, an enterprise, which they considered, as their forefathers did before them, a legitimate field of knightly prowess and adventure.   Prominent in this respect is the Earl of Mar in the beginning of the XVth Century. Once he had with his companion Davidson taken a Prussian "Kraier" (small ship) on her voyage to Flanders and later on tried to sell the goods at Harfleur, where, however, they had been arrested by Hanseatic merchants.   The Parliament of Paris refused the handing over of these goods to the proper owners on account of letters of safe-conduct granted to the Scotsman.   More-over, the Earl of Mar, Alexander Stuart, excuses himself in a letter written at Aberdeen and addressed to Danzig, saying that not he, but Dutch fishermen had committed the deed (1410).   He even threatened a feud and did not hesitate in the following year to put his threats into execution.   Again the inhabitants of Danzig, or Danskin as it is invariably written, had to suffer most.   One of their skippers, named Claus Belleken, who was about to carry a load of salt, flour and beer from Rostock to Scotland, was attacked by the people of the Pirate-Earl on the 6th of June 1412 near Cape Lindesnaes.   They

---

[1] In 1315, for instance, a merchant of Lübeck called Witte is accused of having carried provision to the Scots.   See *Hans. Urk. Buch*, ii. 110.

[2] Even royalty did not disdain trading, and in the *Hanserecesse*, v. 21, we read : " Item Adam Balon, eyme Schotten, wart syn schiff genommen do hatte ynne eyn ritter, her Johan von Abernethyn 100 nobeles und William Fawkonere 100 gulden und 60 nobeles." Anno 1391. (Likewise the ship of Adam Balon, a Scot, was taken, in which a knight Sir John Abernethy [had a share to the extent] of 100 nobles, William Faulconer 100 guldens and 60 nobels.")

threatened to throw him overboard, but relented and finally permitted him to escape in a boat with three of his men. The rest of the crew were taken prisoners and carried to Scotland, where they were employed in carrying stones for the building of a castle in the interior of the country. Two men, Tideman v. d. Osten and Hanneke Schole made good their flight and arrived home safely by way of Flanders.[1]

On the other hand the captain of a sloop from Hamburgh sells the cargo of a plundered ship consisting of wax and other goods in Scotland (1309). In the year 1316 a citizen of Berwick complains, that on a "Tuesday before Easter" a ship of his destined for Berwick, with a cargo of victuals had been seized by vessels from Lübeck, Rostock and Stralsund. He himself had been taken prisoner, his men killed; only by paying the sum of 50 marks as a ransom had he been able to procure his liberty. He now prays the King for power to bring the miscreants to justice.[2]

In the month of December 1462 a citizen of Danzig called Kilekanne is accused of piracy before the Scotch Admiral Sir Alexander Napier. Thereupon the Danzig Magistrates address a long Latin letter to Edinburgh and send a certain Letzke to assist the accused in his trial.[3] Examples of this kind could easily be adduced in great number for centuries afterwards. In the public accounts of the city of Aberdeen in the year 1596 we find an accurate statement of the expense of executing four pirates who had plundered a ship from Danzig.[4]

If one adds to this a great many taxes and heavy duties of export, especially on wool and skins, the bad construction of ships, etc., all of which tended to cripple and delay a satisfactory development of trade: it is not to be wondered at, that the best and most liberal intentions

---

[1] See Theodor Hirsch, *Handelsgeschichte Danzigs unter der Herrschaft des deutschen Ordens.* Leipzig, 1858, p. 117 ff.

[2] *Calendar of Documents rel. to Scotland,* ed. by Bain, iii. 104.

[3] *Hans. Urk. Buch,* viii. 672.

[4] See Turreff, *Antiquarian Gleanings from Aberdeen Records,* 1859.

of the Scotch rulers as to the commercial intercourse of
Scotland with other countries were only partially realised.
And no doubt some of the best Kings of Scotland had
the trade and the shipping of their country very near at
heart. William the Lion (1165-1214) granted "liberum
ansum" to the northern towns of his kingdom and Robert
Bruce, the great patron of shipping and ship-building,
towering high above the men of his time by his far-
reaching intelligence and his practical genius as he excelled them in martial accomplishments, in a letter to the
Magistrates of Lübeck, dated April 22nd, 1321, promises
all merchants of this or any other city of "Alemannia,"
who "wish to visit Scotland on account of trade, favour,
assistance and protection of the customs and liberties
granted to them by former Kings of Scotland.[1]

The Earl of March desires the Magistrates of Danzig
to make efforts for the revival of the trade between
Prussia and Scotland, which had been interrupted by
the emprisonment of a certain Caspar Lange. The letter
is undated but belongs very probably to the end of the
XIVth Century.[2]

King James II, so well known by his own energy and
public spirit, takes the merchants of Bremen with their
servants and ships under his protection and asks his
friends and allies to treat them well.[3] (Feb. 14, 1453).
This letter secured for Bremen a direct trade with
Scotland and was particularly useful because France was
one of the allies spoken of in the recommendation.

Queen Mary commanded several Scottish men-of-war
to put an end to the nuisance of piracy in Scottish
waters and to look after the safety of the vessels from
Danzig, Emden and Hamburg as well as those from
France and Sweden (1550).

But these good intentions and efforts of single in-

[1] See the original in the Appendix. Cp. *Lübecker Urk. Buch*, iii. 68.
[2] This was very likely not the well known warrior Patrick, Earl of
March, in the commencement of the XIVth Cent. ; but probably a later
Earl of the same name. See Hirsch, *l.c.*, *note* i. and Appendix.
[3] See *Hans. Urk. Buch*, viii. 167, and Appendix.

dividuals were not able to cope with the general insecurity of the law and trade of which we have spoken. After these premises we shall now examine what German and Scottish documents tell us concerning the commercial intercourse of both countries. Of the greatest importance in Germany are the Baltic cities, above all Danzig, then Königsberg, Stralsund, Elbing, Lübeck and Greifswald;[1] but Hamburg, Bremen, Rostock and Wismar are also mentioned. In Scotland, Aberdeen and Leith take the first place, followed by Perth, Dundee, St, Andrews and—up to 1333—Berwick-on-Tweed.

Beginning with the XIVth Century we have a short, French letter of the year 1302, announcing the arrestment of a certain Gregoire de Gorton (Gordon), a merchant: "en une nief de Lubyk Dalemeygne, fretté d'aler (aller) vers Aberdeen en Escoce."[2] A little later a ship of Lübeck brings iron for the King's castles to Scotland.[3] A ship from Stralsund to Scotland is burned at Berwick by the English Admiral John Butetort in the reign of Edward I. The money contained in it is taken as a lawful prize, because the crew had joined the Scotch enemies. King Edward II writes with regard to these facts more than five years later (March 13th, 1312) to the Magistrates of Stralsund, demanding the release of English goods which had been arrested to the amount of 1100 marks.[4] In the year 1316 we read of the capture of a ship from Berwick by the Lübeckers;[5] 1319 the goods belonging to merchants of Stralsund and Lübeck are restored by the King's command after having been seized unlawfully. The cities of "Hildernesse" (Inverness), Edinburgh, St Andries (Andrews) and Cupar,

---

[1] Königsberg is often called Keenesburgh or Queenisburgh, and has for this reason been confused with Quedlinburg, which is an inland town at the foot of the Harz mountains. Stralsund becomes Trailsound, Trallesund, etc., in Scotch documents, Greifswald Grippiswold, Lübeck Lupky, etc.

[2] *Documents resp. Scotland,* printed for the Maitland Club, 1842, p. 82.

[3] *Calendar of Documents relating to Scotland,* Bain, vol. ii.

[4] *Hans. Urk. Buch,* ii. 84.

[5] *Calendar of Documents relating to Scotland,* Bain, vol. iii.

after much bickering and reproachful correspondence
declare themselves ready for a compromise with the
German merchants (1348) at Bruges.[1] In the year 1382
a vessel from Rostock to Scotland is mentioned and the
skippers Snidewindt, Marquart Vrese and others of
Lübeck are freighting a ship with "mail armour, ropes,
anchors and victuals" to the same country.[2] Frequent
mention is made in this and the next century of Danzig,
which was then rapidly growing in prosperity, and of
Königsberg, the chief trading centre of the Teutonic
Order. A ship from Danzig to Scotland is seized by
the French (1382); and the "Groszschäffer" of the
Teutonic Knights, who occupied much the same position
in the commercial branch of the Order as the Hochmeister
did in its military and religious enterprises, towards the
end of the century employed Factors or "Lieger" at
Glasgow (Lettecowe) and Edinburgh, whose business it
was to sell the goods forwarded to them for their
employers. The only other Liegers employed by the
Order were those of Flanders. The factor's name at
Edinburgh was Hermann Gral, where he is mentioned
till 1406.[3]

About the same time we are told in the accounts of
the Exchequer of Scotland anent certain expenditures at
Perth, that he paid the sum of 194 pounds 6 shillings
and 8 pence to Prussian merchants for: "miremio
(timber) emto, pro machinis construendis et pro instru-
mentis pro castris" (1382-3).[4] How much we should
like now to hear more about these war-engines and
instruments for the king's castles, even at the expense
of a diffuse accuracy! Equally interesting is the notice
in the same Exchequer Rolls that Prussian sailors "in

---

[1] *Hans. Urk. Buch,* iii. 62, 64, where also the names of the two
accredited messengers are given, viz. Adam Thor from Edinburgh, and
William Feth from Dundee.

[2] *Ibid.* iv.

[3] *Handelsrechnungen des deutschen Ordens,* von C. Sattler. The name
of the Factor of Danzig was Nicolaus Rodau ; he died at Edinburgh in
1420.

[4] *Exchequer Rolls,* iii. 659.

their ignorance" carried away skins from Leith without
paying the necessary duty.[1]

In the year 1386 Telchten, a skipper from Danzig, is
attacked by French pirates on his voyage to Scotland,
whilst another citizen of the same town obtains letters of
safe-conduct to Glasgow, where he goes on account of
some property left by his father.[2]
The next centuries offer us more abundant information.
The towns of Danzig and Aberdeen still maintain their
prominent position.   In 1402 one Gercke Veusan sends
a cargo of flour from Königsberg to Scotland, but his
ship was lost, being taken by the English.[3]   The same
account-books of the Teutonic Order also tell us that
two years later several ships containing wheat, flour,
rye, malt and wainscot to the value of 2800 marks
were sent to Edinburgh.[4]   Aberdeen in a letter dated
Dec. 1, 1410, reminds the magistrates of Danzig of
the old friendship existing between Prussia and Scotland
and puts her seal, as being sufficiently well known at
Danzig, to a letter of neighbouring noblemen, whilst the
magistrates of the latter place point to the privileges of
their citizens at Edinburgh "juxta ritum ab evo"[5] (1452).
In the Rotuli Scotiæ a letter of safe-conduct is printed
in 1406 for two skippers and the servants of the Bishop
of St Andrews, who were to fetch wood from Prussia
(Spruce) for the building of their church; a similar letter
is granted at about the same time to one "John de
Camford of Danskin" for ship and passengers.   It is in
this century that we hear first of Scotch merchants settled

[1] *Exchequer Rolls*, iii. 168.   [2] *Hans. Urk. Buch*, v.
[3] Cp. Sattler, *Handelsrechnungen*, p. 269. "Item Gercke Veusan,
unser dyner, verlos uns 100 nobilen an mel, das namen im die Engelschen
in der see als er gegen Schottland segilte "=Likewise G. V. our servant
lost us 100 nobels in flour, which the English took from him on the
sea, when he sailed towards Scotland.
[4] Sattler, p. 20.
[5] See Hirsch, *l.c.*, p. 118, *notes* 5 and 6.   According to the *Annals
of Aberdeen* (1818), the citizens there had to pay 5 marks for the
right of trading with Danzig.

at Danzig. The trade between this port and Scotland assumes considerable proportions. The cargo of the vessels is either addressed to German Factors in Scotland or accompanied by a special Factor. Here also the nobility of the country take part in trading operations. The names of John and George von Baysen are mentioned as such, and above all the Family of the "von dem Walde" or "van dem Wolde." A certain Henry of this ilk, so Hirsch tells us, together with two other merchants of Danzig, sends a ship loaded with a variety of goods to Scotland, commissioning his relative Reinhold to sell them; but his trouble is great, when this factor commits suicide at Edinburgh. Hans von dem Walde employs two other factors called Zegebad and Resen, in this city.[1] We also read of a certain Nicolaus or Claus Jerre (1421-1444), who took part in extensive commercial enterprises and had dealings with King James I of Scotland and his favourite Lord William Crichton at Edinburgh. At one time he furnishes the King with a splendid beaver-hat, ornamented with pearls to the value of seven Pounds, and the Queen with an inlaid table valued at five Pounds.[2] But he received no payment. The King was murdered in 1437, and, his son and successor James II (1437-1460) refusing to pay his father's debts, the Diet of Hansetowns at Danzig takes the matter in hand and threatens to arrest all Scotch goods in Prussia[3] (1443).

In the year 1428 a Prussian merchant delivers iron "ad usum regis" to Edinburgh;[4] 1438 Beer from Hamburg is sent to Lord Crichton for the coronation-festivities; 1435 a payment occurs for wood and beams for the castle of Stirling; 1444 a ship of Aberdeen

[1] Cp. Letter of Danzig to Edinburgh (21st and 24th April 1444). *Danz. Miss.* iii. 77. Hennig van ye Walde occurs in the list of six Prussian merchants to whom certain payments were made (1430). *Exchequer Rolls of Scot.* iv. 514.
[2] See Hirsch, *l.c.*, p. 119 ff.
[3] *Ibid.*, note 17. Letter of Danzig to the King of Scotland, 8th of July 1444. *Hanserecesse, neue Folge*, iii. 72.
[4] *Exchequer Rolls of Scot.* iv. 437.

brings rye from Stralsund. During the years 1449-1456 other payments for wood, beer and timber for Edinburgh Castle are made. The demand for German beer, especially that of Wismar, Rostock and Danzig, is on the increase, though chiefly used by the rich. It was called "cerevisia Almanniæ" or "beer" to distinguish it from the homebrewed article "ale."

Now and afterwards a long time is often taken up to settle between the merchants of the different towns those quarrels that had their rise in piracy. Take for instance the case of James Lauder (Jacobus de Lawdre), who writes to the Hochmeister von Erlichhausen in the month of August 1452 on account of the arrestment of Scotch goods. The greater part of them had been released, but a certain Schönau of Danzig still held his part. In the autumn of the same year he writes again complaining that hitherto his efforts to obtain his property from Schönau had been fruitless. He had no other way but to apply to Erlichhausen because his predecessor in office, the late Hochmeister, had ordered the arrestment. Finally on March 27th, 1453, the following judgment is given: "The public notary Armeknecht testifies, that the members of the council, assembled by the Hochmeister to settle the quarrel between the Scotch merchant Lauder, from Edinburgh, representative of the Scotch merchants Robert Ross, John Tuke, Patrick Ramsan (!) and others on the one side and Schönau, a citizen of Danzig on the other, concerning certain merchandise, have decided that the documents of the parties are unreliable and have to be sent to a higher court." In the meantime Schönau was to pay Lauder 140 merks, "that is 20 Merks down and 20 Merks every following Whitsunside till the amount be reached." The report adds: "Presentibus ibidem honorabilibus viris Willielmus Kant de Dondy (Dundee) et Thomas Wilhelmsson (Williamson) mercatoribus de prefato regno Scotie.[1])" About this time mention is made for the first time of the city of Thorn as trading with Scotland. A ship loaded

---

[1] Cp. *Hans. Urk. Buch,* viii. 173.

there with goods of various description to the value of
500 merks and destined for certain Scotch ports, is
plundered at Newcastle by the English.[1] In Leith we find
the name of Jan Law, a skipper, who sailed to and from
the "Eastlands," and in Edinburgh those of the merchants
William Halyburton of Haddington and John Collen;[2]
whilst the skippers Herman Bar and John Pape seem to
have sailed with fair regularity from Danzig to Scotland.
These voyages were however not always successful.
Twice, in 1463 and 1490,[3] their cargo, consisting of wool
and rabbit-skins, is taken. Sometimes losses like these are
voluntarily made good: Aberdeen, for instance, in a letter
to Danzig (1487) declares her willingness to repair any
losses caused and proved to be caused by the Scots,[4]
and Edinburgh pays sixty-six pounds to the merchants
of Danzig for damage done to their ships.[5] (1459). Not
long after this we read of a vessel from Rostock, which on
her way to Scotland is driven by adverse winds to Bergen.
In the year 1462 Danzig sends, as we have seen, a long
letter to the Scotch Admiral "Napare" (Napier) in
support of her citizen Kilekanne, who had been accused
of piracy.[6] Another citizen named Lentzke will attend
the trial on behalf of the accused.

Thus again we perceive the paralysing effect and the
grave consequences of piracy throughout this century.
Indeed so frequent were the complaints of the merchants
particularly against the Scots[7] that the Hanse Towns were
at last driven to extreme measures.

The dreaded Earl of Mar did, as we have seen, threaten
war, when taken to account for his many outrages upon
German vessels. The Diet of the Hanse Towns at
Lüneburg therefore proposed to interdict all commerce
of the Baltic cities with Scotland (1412). The cities

---

[1] *Hans. Urk. Buch,* viii. 60.   [2] *Lüb. Urk. Buch,* ix. 197.
[3] *Extracts from the Burgh Records of Aberdeen,* p. 235.
[4] *Ibid.* p. 235.
[5] *Hans. Urk. Buch,* viii. 512.   [6] *Ibid.* viii. 672.
[7] Complaints against the English were raised in 1482 and afterwards,
but they had the pretext of being at war with Scotland.

of Danzig and Stralsund, however, refuse to support a measure of so sweeping a character. Finally, it was agreed to prohibit for a time the importation of Scotch wool and woollen cloths. But even this prohibition failed to have the desired effect. It was the German staple at Brügge (Bruges), where the cloths of Scotch wool were manufactured, that suffered most severely under it. After continued exhortations not to remain satisfied with half-hearted measures such as these, and after renewed acts of piracy on the part of the Scots, Danzig at last consents, and on the 31st of August 1415 at the Hanseatic Diet at Elbing the resolution is passed to interdict all trade with Scotland especially in woollens in the Prussian cities also. Then the Scots gave in. Already in the following year a truce was entered upon between Flanders and the Regent (King James being a prisoner in England), during which further deliberations were to take place. But the Scotch ambassadors never arrived. The Hanse Diets of 1418 and 1421 renewed the prohibition; again Flanders acts as mediator, and finally a treaty with Scotland is concluded according to which Flanders undertakes to compensate the Hanse merchants. Tacitly the law was allowed to become a dead letter and trade was formally restored in 1436.[1] During this period protests from Scotland had not been wanting. Thus Robert, the Regent, in the early twenties writes from Falkirk to the Hochmeister of the Teutonic Order complaining bitterly of the restrictions on Scotch exportation of wool, and expressing astonishment that the merchants of the Order should be prohibited from sailing to Scotland. At the same time the Scots and English settled in Prussia likewise complained of oppression. It appears that the Prussian cities had not accepted the terms of the treaty of 1437 which promised to the Scots and English the same privileges as those enjoyed by the Hanse merchants or Easterlings in England; on the contrary, Scotch and English merchants at Stralsund and Danzig were treated worse than other nations. "No Scotsman nor any other

---

[1] Cp. *Hanserecesse*, new issue, i. *n.* 542.

man outside the Hansa shall keep an open shop" says an old law of Stralsund (1442),[1] whilst at Danzig they were refused a separate house and the liberty of trading and bartering among one another. Burdensome taxes were imposed on them.[2] On account of these and similar "great wickedness" of the Magistrates they address long letters of complaint to the King of Scotland (*e.g.* in the year 1423), but matters do not seem to have improved much.

It was with an ill-concealed jealousy that the Baltic cities observed the merchant-vessels of the West spread their sails on Baltic waters. They were sure to put obstacles in the way of trade and did not even shrink from open acts of violence.[3] Fair commercial rivalry was unknown, undesired and a thing to be suppressed with the utmost rigour of the law. Envy and jealousy filled the citizen at the success of the immigrant stranger. This commercial polity, which found an early expression with regard to the pedlar's trade in Scotch cloth in the following prohibition of Danzig: "henceforward shall no Scotchman nor Englishman trade in country-districts, be he who he may be"[4]—ruled all trade for centuries afterwards and was sanctioned in a more or less narrow manner by all trading nations. Only now and then, when the spirit of oppression became too palpably mischievous, a warning voice was raised.

An instance of this occurs at the Hanse Diet of Lübeck on the 28th of May 1498, when the Burgo-master of Danzig replied to his colleague of Hamburg, who had recommended the refusal of citizenship to strangers, more especially to the Scotch and English, in the following terms: "Dear Sirs, if we were to expel all our citizens that are not born within the hanse, our city would well nigh become a desert,"[5]

---

[1] *Hans. Rec.*, new issue, ii. 514.
[2] *Hans. Rec.*, new issue, iii. 72.   [3] *Hans. Rec.*, 2nd div. xi.
[4] *Hans. Urk. Buch*, iv. 137. Or, "vortmer zo schal nen (no) Schotte edder (or) Engelsman varen zu de lant he zy (be) we he zy."
[5] *Hans. Rec.*, 3rd div. iv.134.

indicating not only a more liberal frame of mind but also the great number of Scots that must have been settled at Danzig about this time. Similarly the Scots, compelled by the famine of their country, issue a decree according to which all strangers bringing victuals to their shore should have free access and be certain of a friendly reception.[1] But these were exceptions, passing moods so to speak, which in no way affected the general tendency of the times.

Next to the dangers on sea, bad debts proved a very grave obstacle in the way of trade-development. It was bad debts among other reasons that caused the trade of the Teutonic Order with Scotland to languish. Following the example of their King many Scots in the beginning of the XIVth Century do not seem to have troubled themselves much about the payment of their debts. In 1417 we find in the account-books of the Order a long list of "bad debts,"[2] that is those that could not be recovered. The city of Glasgow and the 'Customers of Edinburgh' are high up in the list with fifteen pounds and twenty pounds respectively; and there are other high-sounding names like that of the Earl of Agues (Angus), Lord Dalkeith, Archibald Stuart, Sir John Seaton, and the Earl Duclos (Douglas),[3] the latter owing the large sum of 216 pounds.

Now and then we find in the documents amidst dry or seemingly dry details, traces of unintentional humour; for example, when in the year 1489 Heinrich Polseyne, a merchant of Stralsund, sends the request to the Magistrates of Aberdeen to inquire into the state and the habits of the so-called St Cuthbert's geese of the Orkney Islands.[4] The matter is entered into with laudable and most obliging thoroughness. Witnesses are called and they relate the most wonderful stories. The birds, it appears, build their nests under the altar of the church in the island of Farne, walk forth when mass is being

[1] *Sc. Acts of Parliament*, ii. 36, 41, 119, 144.
[2] See Sattler, *l.c.*, and Appendix.   [3] Sattler, *l.c.*, p. 75 f.
[4] *Spalding Club Publications*, vol. iv., Miscellanies.

read and pluck the officiating priest by his gown. They seek their food in the sea and are quite unfit for cooking or roasting. A stone-weight of feathers is valued at a gold "rosenoble." Among the witnesses are Hans Skele (Scheele) and Heinrich Worbosse, citizens of Greifswald and probably seafaring men.

Very likely Polseyne was a man of a far-reaching mind. He wanted to make the geese better known in Aberdeen, or, in modern phraseology, to create a market for the feathers. The odour of sanctity once being established, a thriving trade was sure to follow. Or did Polseyne wish to palm off the feathers of his native Pommeranian geese for those of the famous Eiderduck?

But we must pass on to the sketch of the Scottish-German trade during the XVIth Century, premising, as we did before, a few general remarks relative to the political aspects of the time.

For James IV, King of Scotland, the war of the Hanseatic League against Denmark was fraught with dangers and difficulties. He was applied to and urged on from two sides, by his uncle, the Danish King, who repeatedly and most pressingly demanded men and ships, advising him at the same time to imprison all Hanseatic traders in Scotland, especially those of Lübeck; and by the German Emperor Maximilian, who had written to him and to the King of France in favour of his cities, requesting that no help should be given to Denmark. Under these harassing circumstances James did what a wise man would have done: he contented himself with the resources of diplomacy. In 1508 he sent an ambassador to the Cities of Lübeck, Hamburg and Danzig advising them not to support the Swedes against his uncle. Danzig replied that her relations with both Kingdoms were of a friendly nature; if the King wanted to assist the Danes, he might leave the ships of Danzig unmolested and above all try to abolish those commercial restrictions that were still in use at Edinburgh.[1] In another

[1] *Epist. Regum. Scot.* i. 112 f.

B

letter addressed to the Emperor, James complains of the boldness of the Lübeckers and of the unjustified attacks and cruelties his merchants had to suffer from them on the high seas. Fond of moralising, as he always is, he adds, that the blood of Christians should much rather be spilt in fighting against the common enemies of Christ.[1] Again in 1512 he exhorts the cities to keep the peace,[2] or rather to conclude it; which was done in the same year at Malmö.

Important for the development of Scottish trade during this period was the order of Margaret of Parma, prohibiting under the pretext of danger from the plague the importation of wool from Scotland into Flanders (1564). The staple for cloth was consequently transferred from Bruges to Emden, a small but rising port in Friesland.

Equally important was the foundation of the "Fellowship of Eastland Merchants" by Queen Elizabeth, who were to control and manage the whole trade with the Baltic cities by means of factors or "liegers," and to compete with the still powerful association of the Hanseatic League. In almost all cities on the coast of Prussia settlements of English and Scottish merchants were now established.[3] Trade with England and Scotland flourished, all the more since the direct communication between one port and the other without the intermediate stage of a "staple," became more and more usual.

On the other hand great obstructions to trade were still experienced in the insecurity of the water-ways, most of all, however, in the terrible scourge of the Middle Ages, the Plague. In the very year 1500 we find a ship of Danzig, suspected of the plague at Aberdeen. The cargo is burned; the sailors are for fifteen days confined in certain houses.[4] Edinburgh also adopts strict measures

---

[1] *Ep. Reg. Scot.* i. 66.   [2] *Hanserecesse,* 3rd ser. iv. 476.

[3] There is an English-Scotch Trading Company in Elbing since 1578; a brotherhood of Scotch traders is founded at Greifswald in 1590 by citizens of that town, who were of Scotch origin. A street called Schottenstrasse in Elbing; two suburbs in Danzig named *Alt-* and *Neu-*Schottland bear witness of these old settlements.

[4] *Extracts from Burgh Records of Aberdeen,* p. 428.

with regard to ships coming from the plague-stricken
Danzig (1564). Their crews are being isolated on a
small island in the Firth of Forth, ship and cargo are
disinfected.[1] The landing of either crew or goods is forbidden on pain of death in 1569.[2] Two brothers, Robert
and Nicolaus Liclos, Scotsmen, died of the plague at
Danzig in 1564 and two of their friends are commissioned
from Edinburgh to look after their property. In 1566,
Queen Mary writes to the magistrates of the same city in
favour of a certain David Melville who goes to Danzig
on a similar errand.[3] This danger from the plague is
threatening till far into the XVIIth and XVIIIth Century.
As late as 1653 a vessel from Königsberg is stopped at
Dundee as suspected.[4]

Complaints concerning piracy are still frequent and
somewhat monotonous. They are, however, important
as affording an idea of the extent of the trade between
Germany and Scotland. In the year 1512, a Scotsman
accuses natives of Lübeck before the King of Denmark
for having seized his ship and its freight of timber on the
voyage to Scotland; Lübeck, on the other hand, complains
of the capture of two of her ships [5] and demands—"mindful of the old friendship between the two peoples"—restitution. She also asks that her vessels be not molested on the
voyage to Bergen, the great emporium of the northern
trade in those days; she even uses threats and announces
her fleet ready to protect her trade in the northern regions
against all comers, French or Scotch alike.[6] A similar
case happened in the year 1591, when the good ship
"Noah's Ark" of Danzig was shipwrecked on the coast
of Unst in the stormy month of October. The owners
sent one Conrad von Bobbert to lay their claims before
the Scotch authorities.[7] Better and more effective was

---

[1] *Reg. of Privy Council of Sc.* i. 280, ii. 279, vi. 289, 441.
[2] *Edinburgh Burgh Records*, iii. 182 ff., 263.
[3] *Reg. of Privy Council of Sc.* xiv. 219, 254.
[4] Maxwell, *History of Dundee*, p. 509.
[5] *Hanse Rec.* 3rd ser. vi. 436 ff.   [6] *Ibid.* vi. 624.
[7] Original in the Gen. Reg. House, Edinburgh.

the resolution of Lübeck and Rostock henceforward to arm their boats to Bergen and only to sail in company.

Whilst a tolerable security of trade was thus being enforced in these regions by the energetic action of the Hanse Cities, the trouble broke out in another quarter. The Scots complain of the Eastland captains for disturbing the fishing off the Orkney and Shetland islands, and the Hanse merchants of cruelty and atrocities committed against their skippers on the part of the natives. Many letters are exchanged on this subject. King James V writes to Bremen in 1540[1] and the Magistrates of Bremen address a long Latin letter, written in strong terms, to Queen Mary, in which the pirates are called "Harpyas."[2]   A certain Earl of Orkney seems to have taken a prominent part in these acts of piracy.

Nor are the "deditissimi consules et senatus Imperialis civitatis Lubece" behindhand.   A letter of theirs to the Regent of Scotland (1557) tells the woeful tale of a ship taken by French "classionarii" (pirates) and brought into the port of "Monrosse" (Montrose).   The writers urge the release of the vessel (Oct. 8) since there was no war between Her Majesty and the Hanse Towns.   Another letter, dated Oct. 23rd, follows, praying for expedition of the matter as well as for compensation.[3]   At last, in the year 1559 the aggrieved merchants of the said cities and the owners of the plundered vessel, the "Saint Martin," resolve to send Joachim Halspag as their delegate to Scotland with full powers to demand final satisfaction.[4]

In August 1564 Danzig writes to Edinburgh in favour of a certain H. Biers, who had travelled to Scotland on a

[1] *Epist. Regum Scot.*, ii. 81.
[2] *Privy Council Rec.* xiv. 270 ff.   It seems as if the Scots had often to suffer for the transgressions of the English.   The Germans were inclined to consider them one nation as they spoke one language.   English pirates attack ships of Bremen and Hamburg off the Shetlands, see *Rec. of Privy C. of Sc.* ii. 653.
[3] *Cal. of State Papers rel. to Scotland,* Bain, p. 202 ff.
[4] Original in the Gen. Reg. House, Edinburgh.

like errand. He succeeds in obtaining a decree for compensation, the goods having been taken unjustly.[1]

Nor are other causes for complaints wanting. Thus
Queen Mary's Regent in 1545 writes to the Magistrates of
Lübeck anent the conduct of a certain Bockard Cloch,
who, whilst a law-suit was pending, had absconded with his
ship causing great loss to the city of Edinburgh, but more
especially to a citizen of Malmö, who claimed the fourth
part of the cargo.[2] Worse still is the case of John
Knape, a skipper from Wismar in Mecklenburg, on
whose account the Duke Ulrich writes a long Latin letter
to Edinburgh in 1566. It appears that this Knape had
sailed to Scotland three years ago in a vessel belonging
to two merchants of Wismar. Since then no news had
been received from him. His wife and family were living
in poverty in his native place.[3] In the meantime it
transpired that he had sold the cargo on his own account
and had taken service under the Queen of a foreign
country. In February of the same year the Magistrates
of Wismar likewise addressed the Queen praying that
their agent might be permitted to bring ship and cargo to
Danzig, or to load coal in case of its being empty.[4]

There is quite a modern flavour in the account of some
sailors from Hamburg who are tried and fined at
Aberdeen in 1549 for fighting and assault.[5]

Of greater importance is the prolongation of a treaty
between Countess Anna of Oldenburg and Delmenhorst
and the Scottish Crown, which had been concluded
one hundred years previous in 1447.

As to the regular shipping trade during this century
the names of the same cities occur again that we met
with in the preceding century. But Lübeck and Hamburg
have lost somewhat of their proud position compared

---

[1] *Cal. of State Documents,* i.   [2] *Epist. Reg. Sc.* ii. 254.
[3] Legitissima sua, honestissima et pudicissima conjux et liberi aliquot."
Reg. of Privy C. of Sc. xiv. 242 ff.
[4] One of the earliest instances of the export of coal (" carbo lapideus ")
from Scotland.
[5] *Extracts from the Rec. of Aberdeen,* p. 300.

with the growing importance of the Baltic cities of Prussia and Poland.

In 1508 we find the importation of salt from Stralsund (Trailsound) recorded;[1] in 1510 that of masts for King's ships from Danzig. Macpherson in his *Annals of Commerce* talks of "many Scotch ships in the East-Seas." In 1522-23 several vessels from Königsberg and Danzig to Dundee are mentioned, one from Greifswald (Grippiswold) in 1513. During the years 1539-1542 a great danger threatened the commercial relations between Scotland and Pommerania. Two skippers, Hans Knake and Hans Steffen from Anclam, which in the documents is called Tanglunen, complain that the cargo of their ship after having been brought into the port of Aberdeen by French pirates had been arrested there. The King of Scotland refers the matter to his highest court of justice and the plaintiffs appear in person. But although they return home after due decision, "multo locupletiores," as the report has it, yet they are not satisfied, but succeed by turning and twisting of their case to persuade the magistrates and the Duke of Pommerania that they have suffered grievous wrong. Letters are consequently issued by these authorities commanding the arrestments of the goods of the Scottish merchants in Stralsund. It needed the dignified, clear and convincing epistles of King James V, who encloses a copy of the court's sentence to the Duke to set matters right.[2]

About the same time the King writes to the Magistrates of Hamburg recommending his messenger Murray, who was to buy horses trained for tournaments (1538).[3]

In 1524 a citizen of Edinburgh, Edward Crawford, who is about to travel to Danzig for the purpose of buying grain, obtains a letter of safe-conduct from the Scottish Regent,[4] whilst Lord Douglas, on the 16th of

[1] *Edinb. Burgh Rec.* i. 115.
[2] Letters to Duke Bogislaus (March 6th, 1539); to Duke Philipp and the Magistrates of Anclam (May 24th, 1542) and to Duke George and Stettin (1542). See *Epis. Reg. Scot.* ii. 322 ff.
[3] *Epist. Reg. Scot.* ii. 37   [4] *Epist. Reg. Scot.* ii.

COMMERCE AND TRADE. 23

March 1542, writes to the English Admiral Lisle asking him to extend his protection to a certain William Fehn, the master of a ship of 40 tons, about to sail for Danzig, thence to return with victuals so that he "might remain unmolested by English ships."[1] In a deed of purchase dated May 5, 1533, mention is made of the trade between Edinburgh and Danzig. A ship from the latter port lies in the harbour of Leith in 1544. It is the same which is afterwards wrongfully taken by Patrick Bothwell, who has to compensate the Danzig owner and his factor Fanholf in Edinburgh by making over to them certain properties in land.[2]

About this time there seems also to have been some commerce between Glasgow and Danzig or Poland. It was chiefly in the hands of the rich house of Archibald Lyon. After his death, his son-in-law George Morison became the head of the firm. He and his ship perished on a voyage to Danzig.[3]

In 1546 a vessel from Dundee sails to the same city;[4] three years later a ship from Hamburg brings soap to Edinburgh.[5] Beer is imported from Stralsund and wood for the repair of a church from Rostock to Dundee, the beams to be sixteen yards in length.[6]

It is in this century that we find the first indications of a gradually increasing emigration from Scotland to the Baltic cities and to Poland.[7] The captain of a ship from Edinburgh named Dawson receives permission to carry five merchants to Danskin, and James Foular six, hailing from Peebles, Glasgow, Edinburgh and Dumfries[8] (1555). In 1589 two citizens of Edinburgh become security for six "Polish Cramers," that is Scotsmen who were going

---

[1] Fraser, *Douglas* Book iv. 148.
[2] *Reg. Magni Sig. Sc.*, sub dato 1533 and 1549.
[3] See Macure, *Hist. of Glasgow*, p. 103, 115.
[4] *Extracts from Burgh Rec. of Aberdeen*, p. 300.
[5] *Edinb. Burgh Rec.* ii. 145. Only in the XVIIth Century attempts were made to manufacture soap in Scotland.
[6] Maxwell, *History of Dundee*, p. 140.
[7] *Edinb. Burgh Records*, ii. 217 f.
[8] *Ibid.* iv. 543.

to Poland as pedlars.[1] Their names are : John Knox, James Hunter, Macmillan, Carwood, Gilchrist and Muir. They sail for Königsberg.

James Gowan and Robert Jack, Scotch merchants, dwelt in Trailsound (Stralsund) ; the brothers Ancroft in Greifswald (Grippiswold).

The chief share in the trade with the East-lands is still claimed by Aberdeen. Gilbert Menzies, a native of this town, imports grain from Danzig in 1563, and in the following year several ships are freighted with victuals from the Baltic port to the same place.[2] One of the ships is called the " Andrew "; another one boasts of the curious name of " Ly-by-the-fire "[3] (1556). Indeed the commerce between the two cities had by this time become so profitable, that a special duty was imposed on all goods imported from Danzig to Aberdeen, a duty which was large enough to pay for the expense of the great light in the gable of the church of St Ninians on the Castle Hill.[4]

Of the last quarter of the century and the first thirty years of the next we are particularly well informed through the invaluable entries of Wedderburne of the " Compt Buik " fame.[5] The list of ships sailing from Dundee extends from the year 1580 to 1618. We reproduce the latter in tabular form as far as it refers to Baltic Ports, omitting only those vessels, the destination of which—though apparently German—could not with certainty be deciphered.[6] It must also be borne in mind that the entries from 1584-1588 as well as those from 1589-1612 are wanting.

---

[1] The beginnings of this emigration date back to the commencement of the XVth Century.

[2] *Reg. of Privy Council of Sc.* xiv. 191, 198.

[3] *Extracts from the Burgh Rec. of Aberdeen,* ii.

[4] W. Watt, *History of Aberdeen,* p. 312 f.

[5] *The Compt Buik of David Wedderburne,* ed. by Millar, 1898. See also *The Ledger of Andr. Halyburton in the Rec. Public,* 1867.

[6] For instance : Troseck, Ludholm, Wairdberye.

Year	Name of Ship	Destination	Cargo taken home
1581	Falcon	Overdansk (?)	...
,,	Unicorn	Queenisbrig	...
,,	Harry	Danskin	...
,,	Ship	,,	...
1582	Hund	,,	Iron, Pitch, Tar
,,	Little Pink	Lupke (Lübeck)	Wood
,,	Grace of God	Danskin	Wood, Boards
,,	Ship	,,	Iron, Hemp, Wood
,,	George	,,	2000 Boards
1583	Swan	,,	Wood, Spars
,,	Mary Gallant	,,	...
,,	Ship	,,	Iron, Hemp, Copper kettles
,,	,,	,,	Wood
,,	Klinkbellis	,,	Iron, Hemp, Soap, etc.
,,	Grace of God	,,	...
,,	Ship	Lubkey	Salt, Boards
,,	,,	Danskin	...
1588	Thomas	,,	...
,,	Expeditioun	,,	...
,,	James	,,	Hemp, Lint, etc.
,,	Dragon	,,	Pitch, Tar, Iron, Lint
,,	Engyll	,,	...
,,	Ship	Crailsund	Beer
1589	,,	Trailsound	Beer, etc.
,,	,,	Danskin	Soap, Wood
1612	Dow	Crailsund	Beer
,,	Ship	Danskin	Wood, Iron
,,	Elspet	,,	Iron, Lint, Ropes, etc.
,,	Gift of God	,,	...
,,	Margaret	Queenisbrig	Hemp, Iron, Wood, Lint, etc.
1613	Swift	Prussia	"Danzig Ware"
,,	Jonas	Queenisbrig	Rye, Wax, Rigging
,,	Mary Jahne	,,	Lint, Wax
1614	Angell	Grippiswold	Beer
,,	Good Fortune	Queenisbrig	Wood, Iron nails, etc.
,,	Elspet	,,	Wood, Wax, Pitch
1615	Ship	Trailsound	Grain, Boards
,,	Grace of God	Danskin	...
,,	Margaret	,,	Iron, Pitch, Glass, Lint, Flour, etc.
,,	Ship	Queenisbrig	Pitch, Tar
,,	Gift of God	Danskin	Iron, Lint, Lead

Year	Name of Ship	Destination	Cargo taken home
1616	Thomas	Poill (Poland)[1]	Iron, Pitch
,,	Fox	Danskin	Powder, Window glass, etc.
,,	Good Fortune	Poille	...
,,	Jonas	Lubke	...
1617	Robert	Danskin	...
,,	Roebuck	Trailsund	Beer
1618	Hope of Grace	Queenisbrig	Lint, Pitch
,,	Elspet	Danskin	...

We have therefore in the years 1581-1584 eighteen ships of Dundee, fifteen of which sail to Danzig, one to Königsberg, two to Lübeck. In 1588 four ships sail to Danzig, two to Stralsund, and during the period 1612-1618 twelve to Danzig, six to Königsberg, three to Stralsund, one to Greifswald and one to Lübeck. Altogether Dundee kept a fleet of about twenty to thirty ships[2] to trade with the Baltic ports. If we remember that Dundee with regard to shipping, only takes the second place,[3] we can form an adequate idea of the extent of the Scottish trade with the Baltic cities.

Nor are the two books of Wedderburne and Halyburton less interesting concerning the manner of trade in bygone days. The skipper, it appears, was at the same time the salesman of his goods, unless a special personage was sent along with him for this purpose. Sometimes the merchant would himself travel with the ship that contained his merchandise. Thus Wedderburne sends one Patrick Gordon in William Fyfe's ship to Danzig in 1597, and entrusts him among other things with two old rose nobles,[4] one new one, and two double ducats " to be warit

[1] Poill = Poland, here for Danzig.
[2] The number cannot be given exactly as many ships in the above list are unnamed and might be identical with ships already mentioned.
[3] In 1692 Leith possessed twenty-four ships, Dundee twenty-one, Montrose eighteen, Glasgow fifteen.
[4] A gold coin, first issued by Edward III. It bears its name from the five-leaved English rose on the reverse.

on rye gif it be within 48 gudlenis [1] and falzeing thereof on lynt, a part thereof to be shippit in any ship that hapins to be frauchtit." Or he sends fifty reals "in a pocket" "to wair on wax and if it be extraordiner deir forby the waunted prices at his discretioune to wair on coper." And when he goes himself to Königsberg in 1596 he takes with him amongst a multitude of foreign coins, a gold chain weighing fourteen crowns. Thus we still see the remnants of primitive barter in the XVIth Century.

During the last quarter of it Scotland is visited by famine of a particularly aggravated character. We hear complaints of it in 1572 and in 1595.[2] King James VI writes to his ambassador at the court of Denmark, Sir P. Waus, and Peter Young to try and get the duties remitted at Elsinore for the numerous Scotch vessels ready to sail for Danzig for the purpose of buying victuals; and this not only on account of the "great scarcitie and famine at home" but also in order to prevent them selling their freight elsewhere, and falling an easy prey to English ships.[3]

To the many cases of piracy already mentioned we add the following: a merchant of Emden accuses the Earl of Orkney of having plundered his ship laden with rye from Danzig, off the coast of Norway.[4] A skipper named Ogilvie of Dundee is sentenced to pay damages to a Danzig merchant.[5] Three years later in 1594 the same man stands his trial against Thomas Stalker, a Scotsman settled at Danzig, who accuses him of having plundered the ship "Grite Jonas." Part of the cargo, strange to say, belonged to the Grand Duke of Toscana. When driven by the stress of weather to the Orkney islands the governor and two citizens of Dundee arrested the goods

---

[1] Probably "gulden." There was no silver gulden till the middle of the XVIIth Century.
[2] *Reg. of Privy Council of Sc.* ii. 148, and Birrell's *Diary.*
[3] *Correspondence of Sir P. Waus,* p. 401.
[4] *Reg. of Privy Council of Scot.* iv. 331.
[5] *Ibid.* iv. 627.

as " papistical." [1] Ogilvie is sentenced to pay compensation to the Grand Duke.

Finally we may mention as interesting that in 1572 cannons and ammunition for the castle of Edinburgh are imported from Hamburg; [2] and that a certain captain William Rentoun receives permission to levy and transport one hundred and fifty men for the service of the city of Danzig which had just then entered upon a disastrous war against the King of Poland, Stephan Bathory [3] (1577).

The XVIIth Century, of which we had a glimpse already in the Dundee ship-list, commences with a trial for fighting and manslaughter in broad daylight among the Scottish settlers of Danzig. [4] Then again we hear of precautionary measures against the introduction of the plague through German ships. [5]

In the year 1603 David Smart claims before the magistrates of Dundee the inheritance of his brother, who died at Danzig and left about 600 pounds. The authorities in Germany acknowledge his claim and send the money. [6]

In the same year the following new ships occur : the " Fortune " and " Neptune " from Emden, " Mary " and " Pelican " from Stralsund to Scotland. [7] One ship from Flemisberry, very probably Flensburg, is mentioned in 1616.

About this time (1606) the ruinous state of their church causes much anxiety to the City Fathers of Aberdeen. They resolve therefore to send a trustworthy person in " William Meason's ship " to Danzig

[1] *Reg. of Privy Council of Scot.* v. 214. Thirty-nine books formed a part of the cargo, one of them bears the title : *Description of the History of Poland.*

[2] *Cal. of State Papers rel. to Scot.*, Thorpe, vol. i. 330.

[3] See above. There is a discrepancy in the statement of the *Reg. of Privy Council of Scotland* and Hartknoch, the German historian. The latter mentions 700 men. Probably the Scottish source only refers to the first draught of soldiers, as the difficulties of levying were great.

[4] *Reg. of Privy Council of Scot.* vi. 856 f.

[5] *Ibid.* vi. 289, 441, and often.

[6] Maxwell, *Hist. of Old Dundee,* p. 344 f.

[7] See *Ledger of Andr. Halyburton.*

in order to buy lead to the value of 105 Pound Scots for the repair of the sacred building. In 1619 the Castle of Edinburgh again runs short of ammunition, and a vessel is despatched to Danzig to bring over " 200 stane " of gunpowder.[1] To the common articles of import from Germany, such as wood and timber, wainscot, lint, wax, flour, grain, iron, etc. is now added glass (1610-12).[2] But no sooner has notice been taken of this fact than an order against its importation is issued (1621). Salt is being imported in 1656-1658 to the value of 1100 Pounds. The trade in skins seems to have been particularly brisk. Two small boats from Aberdeen carry 8000 lamb-skins in 1617 and in 1650 no less than 30,000 lamb-fells are exported to Danzig. The old articles of export are increased by knitted wool-wares, especially stockings.[3]

Seven ships sail from Leith to Königsberg in 1622 and mention is made of one ship from Bremen and one from Königsberg in 1625-26; the former had to seek shelter in Tynemouth. Two vessels from Leith are lying in the harbour of Danzig towards the end of July 1626.[4]

A dangerous voyage was that of Henry Dinklaff with his ship the " Pruss Mayden " from Kneiphovia (a part of Königsberg). It was attacked by the rebellious Scottish Clan Jan and would have been plundered but for the assistance of a royal vessel.[5] Finally Montrose and Kirkcaldy send a ship each to Königsberg and Danzig in 1688 and 1692.

A great obstacle in the way of trade was the war between Great Britain, Spain and France during this century. A long story is told of a certain Captain Robertson, who, fortified by letters of marque from the King of Scotland, had attacked ships from Lübeck,

---

[1] *Reg. of Privy Council of Scot.* xi. 563.   [2] Halyburton, *l.c.*
[3] Kennedy, *Annals of Aberdeen*, p. 258 ff.   Scotch wool was famous all through the Middle Ages. In early centuries (about 1250) it wa manufactured in the monasteries of the Cistercian monks at Culross, Maros (Melrose), Cupar and Glenluce.
[4] *Reg. of Privy Council of Scot.* second ser. i. 47, 199, 669.
[5] *Ibid.* p. 119.

because of their carrying ammunition and other prohibited freight. His own vessel, however, had suffered
so much in the fight, that it had to seek refuge in a
Norwegian port to get repaired. But no sooner had it
arrived there, than German sailors, mostly hailing from
Hamburg, board the ship, ill-treat the crew and abuse
the Scottish flag. Afterwards the Court at Hamburg
refuses to acknowledge the statements of the witnesses
made before the Scottish Admiral, and the King sees
himself compelled to renew the letters of reprisal to
Robertson.[1]

Another time a ship of Danzig sailing to Spain is
driven by stress of weather to the coast of the Shetland
isles, and there saved by Scottish sailors, only to be
carried as a lawful prize into the harbour of Leith, where
it has to lie six weeks until the captain, one Edward
Jansen, complains before the authorities at Edinburgh,
that he had no longer any means to feed his crew. An
order is then given to sell part of the cargo, consisting
of wax. Finally the Danzig skipper gets his rights, and
ship and cargo are restored.[2]

Again Danzig complains in 1672 with regard to the
unlawful seizure of three vessels, two of which, the " Sun "
and the " Crown," had been brought into Scottish ports
suspected of carrying contraband-goods.[3]

With the XVIIIth Century Scotland lost the last
remnant of independence. Her trade became the trade of
Great Britain. After the last fierce death struggle of a
lost cause the neighbour south of the Tweed gradually
learned, if not to love his neighbour in the north, at
least not to slay him. Gradually the pirates hide in story-
books, and the grim spectre of the plague keeps at a
respectful distance ; gradually a more enlightened commercial policy gains the day, and the full profit of a
rational working of the resources of the country is earned
by the people. The export also changes in kind. Coal,

[1] *Acts of Parliament of Scot.*, 1641, c. 65, v. 386, 430 a.
[2] *Reg. of Privy Council of Scot.*, second ser. I. lxxii.
[3] See originals in the possession of the Marquis of Bath.

the black jewel of the land, and the herring the silvery treasure of the sea, take the place of rabbit-skins and coarse wool.

But our sketch of the commercial relations between Germany and Scotland during the period of the independence of the latter would be incomplete without considering that curious German and Polish inland traffic—a pedlar-trade —carried on by Scotsmen during the XVth, XVIth and XVIIth Centuries. The origin of this remarkable historical fact is to be found in a very large Scotch emigration to Danzig, Königsberg and Poland from the end of the XVth Century and earlier, gradually increasing until the end of the XVIIth, an emigration which makes Poland the America of those days. Some writers have tried to explain this fact from one cause only. They have tried in vain. It was not religious persecution alone, not the well-known roaming disposition of the Scotch alone, which drove them across the sea in thousands. It was the result of many causes working together. First and chiefly: the hunger and the distress of their country. We have already mentioned the letter of King James VI dated 1587 in which the great "scarcitie" and famine is spoken of and the hope of alleviating it by a speedy importation of "viveris" from Germany. But already in the year 1572 famine had been so severe that the King saw himself compelled to take the extraordinary step of commanding emigration by solemn proclamation at Leith.[1] Birrell notices a great famine in 1595 in his diary, and the chronicles of the Scotch towns are full of the distressful state of the country.[2] Further reasons we find in the never-ending religious and political wars at home, the hardships of the law of primogeniture, in the love of martial adventure and in the pronounced clannishness of the people. The first thing a Scotsman did who had emigrated to Danzig or Königsberg or had settled at Krakaw was, to invite other members of his family, who perhaps found it difficult to

---

[1] *Reg. of Privy Council of Scot.* ii. 148.

[2] "Distress and wars drove us out of Scotland," say the Scots in a trial held at Breslau towards the end of the XVth Century. See Appendix.

make their way at home, owing to the disturbed and poverty-stricken condition of their native land.

But why—one might ask—was distant Poland chosen of all other countries as the goal of emigration? The answer is not far to seek. The English were the enemies of Scotland: all trade with them partly restricted, partly prohibited altogether. Holland was already full of the Scotch;[1] and France, eldorado as it proved to be to the Scottish soldier and scholar, did not offer the same facilities for trade as a country did, where the middle and trading class between the noble and the serf was actually non-existing. All trading in Poland on the other hand was done by Jews and foreigners;[2] here then was a field for the enterprising Scot: a wide country with plenty of room to travel about, an excellent seaport, Danzig, visited since the days of old by many a Scotch trading vessel; a luxurious and magnificent royal court and little competition in business. In a book of the time Poland is called the heaven for the nobility, the paradise for the Jews, the hell for the peasant, and the gold mine for the stranger; and a famous Scotch traveller, named Lithgow, who on his journeyings over Europe had also visited Krakaw and Lublin and found many of his countrymen there, calls Poland the "mother and nurse of the youths and younglings of Scotland, clothing, feeding and enriching them with the fatness of her best things, besides 30,000 Scots families that live incorporate in her bowels. And certainlie Poland may be termed in this kind the mother of our commerce and the first commencement of all our best merchants' wealth, or at least most part of them."[3]

This statement has been doubted. But it agrees with other contemporaneous information. Sir James Cochrane, the Scotch Ambassador at the Court of Poland, "tells of

---

[1] Steevens, *Hist. of the Scotch Church at Rotterdam.*

[2] Stanislas Tomkowicz: *Przyczynek do historyi Skotów w Krakowie i w Polsce.*

[3] William Lithgow, *The totall Discourse of the rare adventures and painfull peregrinations of long nineteen yeares travailes.* London, 1640.

many thousand Scots in the country besides women, children
and servants"; [1] and in a letter of the English Statesman
Chamberlain to his friend Carlton (1621)[2] we read:
'The Polish Ambassador had an audience of the King
. . . there are about 30,000 Scots in Poland.'
Sir John Skene, the celebrated Scotch lawyer, who
had travelled far and wide on the continent, confirms in
his book, " De verborum significatione " sub verbo
"pedlar" that he had met a vast multitude of them,
his countrymen, in Krakau (1569).

To this may be added long lists of names of Scotch
settlers in Poland and Prussia, which have been handed
down to us in the archives of these countries.

Scotch emigration then, having been proved to be
extremely large and to affect all classes of society and
all ages, it is not to be wondered at, that many went,
who were utterly unable and unfit to make their own
living, or who finally turned out a disgrace to their
country. It is quite surprising how many young Scotch
boys not older than fifteen or seventeen years sought
their fortune at that time in Danzig.[3] Naturally enough
complaints of rowdyism were frequent. Patrick Gordon,
then Scotch Consul at Danzig, a man who will engage
our notice again, draws the attention of King James
VI to the miserable and disorderly state of many of the
emigrants, and adds that the Scotch settlers themselves
wished to get rid of them. It is in consequence of this
letter that the King in 1625 issues the following
proclamation : —

" Whereas the grite number of young boyes uncapable
of service and destitute of meanis of liveing yearlie
transported out of that our kingdome to the East-seas
and specially to the town of Dantzik and there manie
tymes miserablie in grite numbers dyeing in the streets

---

[1] See Thurloe's *State Papers.*
[2] *Calendar of State Papers,* Dom. Ser., 38.
[3] The hardships of such a youth in a foreign country are well depicted
in the four letters of young Francis Craw, dating 1671-1681, given in
the Appendix.

have given quite scandall to the people of those countries
and laid one foull imputation on that our kingdome, to
the grite hinderance and detriment of those our subjects
of the better, who traffique in the saidis countreyis : it
is our pleasour, that by oppin proclamatioun ye cause
prohibite all maisters of shippis to transport anie youthes
of either sex to the said easterne countreyis bot such as
either salbe sent for by their friendis dwelling there, or
then, sall carrie with them sufficient meanis of meantenance at least for ane yeare under the pane of fyfe
hundreth markis monie of that our kingdome, toties
quoties they sall offend in that kind." [1]

After this edict the emigration, though it did not
cease, took a different channel; the people emigrating
often having some means of their own, or intending, if
they were cadets of a lord or laird of the country, to enter
the military service of Poland or, finally, wishing to visit
their many friends in Germany. [2]

Most of the Scotsmen settled in Poland were
pedlars. [3] They sold tin utensils, a kind of woollen stuff
called " Scotch," and linen kerchiefs, often decorated with
pictures of the Turkish wars. Those that lived in towns
had small shops ('institutae Scotorum'), where one could
buy iron goods and scissors and knives and cloths of
every description, or they kept booths at the large fairs
all over the country.

In many respects the great expectations of these
Scotch emigrants were not realised. It is true, there
was religious tolerance in Poland since 1573, and we
never hear of any religious persecution; but Poland
as well as Germany was always ready to invent new
obstacles and burdens in the way of the free exercise of
their trade. Of two trading restrictions of Stralsund and
Danzig in the first half of the XVth Century we have
already spoken. [4] Later on, in the year 1564, a tax was

---

[1] *Reg. of Privy Council of Scot.* xiii. 702 f.   [2] Tomkowicz, *l.c.*
[3] The expression " A Scotch Pedlar's Pack in Poland " became
proverbial. Cp. Howel, *Epist. Ho-Elianae*, p. 316 (1633).
[4] See page 14 f.

imposed on the Scots of Poland, a poll-tax, in common with the Jews and Gipsies. If a pedlar went on foot, he had to pay one florin; if he kept a horse, he had to pay for it in addition. 1578 one florin for the man, two florins for the horse were raised; 1613 two florins for the man and fifteen groschens for the horse. But this was only an apparent relaxation : for now a tax is imposed on the goods also. At last the influential Scotsmen by their united efforts succeeded in mitigating these hardships. First of all they appealed to the King of Scotland, complaining at the same time of the inactivity of the Scotch Consul Gordon at Danzig.[1] The King wrote in strong words to his representative in return and possibly also to his friend the King of Poland. Anyhow the terms of the law by which they were placed on a level with the Jews, terms that had chiefly caused the irritation, were expunged, and an edict of 1629 promised them the same treatment as other " foreign merchants."[2]

Other restrictions for other Polish towns followed, chiefly caused and called forth by the jealousy of the native merchants. King Sigismund II Augustus issued an edict on the 17th of Sept. 1568, which was to check the influx of Scotsmen into Bromberg. It was chiefly directed against the pedlars or small shopkeepers ('revenditores'). Merchants, who sell, not by the ell and the pound, but in whole pieces or by stone-weight, are exempt, and special mention is made of four Scottish merchants already members of the guild. It is therefore to be assumed that the Scots tried to evade the restrictions of the law by becoming citizens and members of the merchant fraternity. In 1673 one Gasparus Wolson (Wilson) is the president of the guild; town councillors, aldermen, even burgo-masters of Scottish birth or parentage, occur in old Brom-

---

[1] About Gordon and Stercovius, the Pole, see Appendix.
[2] Stan. Tomkowicz, *l.c.* Still we read that an edict against the Scots of 1552 was renewed, 1636, in Western-Prussia, then belonging to Poland. "Vagrant Scots" was a term often used in those days in official documents. See S. Sembritzki, *Die Schotten und Engländer in Ostpreussen, Altpreuss. Monatsschrift*, Bd. xxix. Heft 3, p. 232.

berg documents. Especially frequent are the names of
Watson, Wilson, Wallace, Hutton, Herin (Heron) and
M'Kean. In 1733, a Joseph Wilson is provost, in 1823
one Makkien " Archivarius."[1]
Nor were the laws against the Scots in other countries
less strict. The town of Breslau issued an edict on the
2nd of July 1533 against pedlars, Scots, gipsies, beggars,
etc. In 1558 Markgraf Albrecht of Brandenburg, Duke
of Prussia, gave an order not to allow Scotch " vagabonds," to roam about in the country, "because they are the
ruin of our own poor subjects, taking away their living and
reducing them to beggary." He also accuses them of
using false weights and measures and strictly limits their
trade to the annual fairs appointed by law.[2] Thirty-one
years later his son Georg Friedrich repeats his father's
prohibition in much the same words.[3]
Greater still was the hostility shown to the strangers
by the native tradespeople. The cutler-guild at Krakau
accuses the " cunning" Scots before the court, "that they
did not content themselves with one shop but had several
at each end of the town, and would moreover send a boy
to sell their wares from house to house."[4] Similarly the
united guild of " Krämer " of Prussia, in the year 1569,
Nov. 11th, present a supplication to the Markgraf, in which
they state that their business is spoiled by the travelling
Scots, that nobody cared to come into the town to buy, if he
could get the goods brought to his own house; that the
orders issued as far back as 1545 were disobeyed; that there
was a Scotsman, called Ventour, who said he was a citizen
of Zinten, but he did not live up to it, but kept boys,
who in his name travelled all over Samlandt, doing
great harm to the whole country; they (*i.e.* the Scots)

---

[1] *Jahrbuch des Bromberger histor. Vereins*, 1888, p. 31 f. and
Appendix.
[2] Original in the Archives of Königsberg.
[3] Original likewise in Königsberg. Date Sept. 22, 1589.
[4] Abraham Grabowski Altertümliche Nachrichten von Krakau (1852).
A proverb of Lithuania says : " su Szotù bey Kunningù ne bylinek," *i.e.*
" with a Scotsman and a priest don't begin a law-suit." See Chr.
Gottlieb Mielke's *Dictionary*, Königsberg, 1800, p. 423.

probably 'bought beaver and marten skins and amber in Prussia and sold them in Lublin (Poland)'; not content with that they brought "false (adulterated) ware" into the country, such as pepper, saffron, silk spoiled by water. ('versoffene Seide'). "Let alone that they are cheats," continues the indictment, " bribing the custom officers and, it is to be feared, acting as spies to betray the conntry (!) which may God prevent." The petitioners finally express the charitable wish that His Serene Highness would deliver the Scots and their goods into their hands, and that then they would make over the value of the goods taken from them to some hospital.[1]

Now, we will not for a moment deny that among the 30,000 Scottish pedlars there were some that did not always act up to the dictates of conscience, and that many of them lived a life of misery and privation,[2] but this document of the "gantze Krämerzunft von Preussen" bears on the face of it only too clearly the ill-concealed inability to withstand a sudden, keen competition of trade.

Against these insinuations the Scots defend themselves in many supplications addressed to the Duke of Prussia In 1599 they sign as "the honorable Company of the honorable Scottish Nation," at other times as the "elders of the Scots in the districts of Holland,[3] Riesenburg and the Prussian Mark" or as the "Scots of the district Rastenburg and Barten" (1628).

They state first of all that they "the poor foreigners have been 'very exceedingly' grieved ('mit fast hochbetrübtem gemüthe') at the order of the Duke commanding them to cease their journeyings as pedlars in the country except to the duly ordained public fairs, "as if we, the poor strangers, were the worst of all." Then they explain that they were not newly-arrived

---

[1] Original in the Archives of Königsberg.
[2] This seems to have been the case particularly with the Scots pilgrims, who returned from Rome across Germany to Danzig and thence home. See Appendix.
[3] Town and district about 60 miles to S.W. of Königsberg.

"juvenales" but mostly "fellows well up in years" ('ziemlich betagte gesellen"), who had been travelling about for many years in this country and against whom there never was any complaint raised as to "false measure," etc. "Why is it," they continue, "that we Scots alone should be singled out for such excessively severe measures, seeing there are so many other stranger-merchants in the land? We are the most humble and faithful subjects of the Duke and have at all times paid 'duty and contribution.' We shall continue to do so, nay to serve Y.R.H. 'to the risk of our body and blood' ('mit Aufsetzung Leibes und Bludts').

"That we have not been made use of hitherto, is not our fault; but it may yet come to pass, and though we are at the present time not domiciled or owners of houses ('heuszlich angesessen'), the good God can in his own gracious time bring it about that we settle in the dominions of Y.R.H. as the rightful owners of property."[1]

Finally, they offer to pay an annual tax of two Thaler, and urgently requesting again a withdrawal of the order and measures to prevent the violent seizure ('Auffgreiffer') of their persons, they sign in dutiful submission as subjects of H.R.H.

The Scots of the districts of Barten and Rastenburg complain moreover, that there was no distinction made in the imposing of their 'contributions,' though their trade-earnings were very different. They also, very properly, request that a central comptroller should be appointed of the whole province, who would make a list of their names and receive their taxes at stated times; instead of having this tax gathered, as now, by magistrates, collectors of the duty on grain, burgomasters and town-clerks.[2]

It strikes one as very curious in these hostile trade-

---

[1] Original Supplication, 4th of Oct. 1599, in the Royal Archives at Königsberg. Another specimen is given in the Appendix.

[2] Supplication of the year 1628. A similar census had already been made in 1615 by a Scotsman named Jacob Koch (Cook). See further on.

manifestations against the Scots that the Jews are constantly coupled with them; and yet the fact is easily explained by the consideration that previous to the arrival of the Scots the whole retail traffick in Poland lay almost exclusively in the hands of the Jews. The Scottish strangers stepped into the Jewish inheritance with all its advantages *and burdens.* Remembering this, and also bearing in mind that large money transactions were carried on by the Scots, we need no longer be astonished at the prejudices and groundless reproaches of injured competitors: they were gratuitously transferred from the Jewish to the Scottish pedlar.

For the Scots, however, these and similar manifestations of ill-will served the good end of accelerating their acquiring the rights of citizenship in the towns of Prussia and Poland, and of making them band themselves together for mutual protection in a large union (Brüderschaft) with laws regulating their traffick, such as their own King James had recommended and the German and Polish authorities acquiesced in. This they did, and we possess very interesting accounts of their constitution. One comes from Krakau. In the year 1603 the Polish Government had commissioned Abraham Young (Jung), a captain in the Scotch regiment of the King, with full judicial power to make inquiries into the organisation of his countrymen in Poland. The depositions of a witness named Richard Tamson, a merchant of Posen, have been preserved, and from them it appears that the Scottish Brotherhood in Poland had twelve branches with their own elders and judges. The latter had power not only to impose fines, but also, with the consent of the elders, to pronounce the sentence of banishment. On each fair-day they held their meetings and a general court of appeal met at Thorn on the Feast of Epiphany, when each Scotsman could produce his grievances. There was no appeal to the King. The "decreta" or decrees were entered into a special book. The duty of the elders was to do everything necessary for the protection of the guild and its privileges, and to receive every newly arrived Scotsman into the brotherhood. The clergymen, who collected a tax every year for the building of their own Presbyterian churches, belonged to the number of the elders *ex officio*. Each guild had its own books, some of which showed a hostile feeling towards the Roman Catholics.[1] Guilelmus Forbes, Gilbert King, Peter Orem, Guilelmus Henderson and John Forbes, rich Scotch merchants in Krakau, were for many years judges. The new member of the guild had to swear an oath, to observe the laws and regulations and to submit to the decisions of the court. He wrote his name with his own hand into a book.[2]

Other witnesses add, that the Scots in Poland elected four judges every year, who issued decrees and were at once accusers and judges. Very often the punishment inflicted was a kind of proscription, so that nobody was allowed to speak, eat or drink with the person in question. Criminal cases however did not come under the jurisdiction of this court.[3] Fines paid were again lent out at a high rate of interest. As their highest judge the Scots acknowledged, according to a privilege granted them by King Stephen Bathory, the Royal Marshall only. They even disputed Captain Young's right to meddle in their affairs until King Sigismund III made him the chief of all Scotch merchants living in Poland (March 20th, 1604).[4] Now they had to obey him and to enter their names into *his* books "in order that they might be found easier if required for the defence of the country"; as the order significantly adds. From this blow, and a necessary blow it seems to have been, the Scotch autonomy never recovered.

We are still more accurately informed of the constitution of the Scotch Brotherhood in Brandenburg and

[1] Some of the decrees were directed against the Roman Catholics. It is related of one John Ramsay in Posen, that he escaped the sentence of banishment by his flight.

[2] Tomkowicz, *l.c.*, p. 164.   [3] Tomkowicz, *l.c.*, p. 165.

[4] As a reason for this appointment is adduced : " cum inter alias Scoticæ nationis hominum magnum hic esse numerum nobis constet et plerosque licentiose vivere ut neque judices neque jurisdictionem neque leges neque superiorem ullum agnoscant." Tomkowicz, *l.c.*, 166.

Preussen. There in 1615 a certain Jacob Koch (Kock or Cook), a Scotsman, made at the command of the Kurfürst (Elector) a complete list of the Scotch Krämers in the dominions of His Serene Highness. This list contains 410 names.[1] Prefixed are certain recommendations of Koch's as to taxation, and his own travelling expenses. At the end he adds the twenty articles which constituted the Scotch Guild or Nation or Brotherhood. This curious and important document, literally translated from the German, runs as follows :—

"In the name of the holy and inseparable Trinity. As a great number of the Scottish nation in this Dukedom of Prussia, scattered here and there, seek their living, and many of them not capable of a fixed abode or a certain jurisdiction, and since on that account frequent disorders have taken place, the Oberburggraf of this country many years ago did graciously permit them, to establish certain rules and articles amongst themselves, so as to prevent much bothering of the magistrates, cheating and other excesses and irregularities for the maintenance of good order, lest they might be considered, as has been done most unjustly and untruly, mere fugitives and vagabonds. They have therefore constituted 'unanimo et successivo consensu' a certain brotherhood amongst themselves, and ordered that their meetings should take place four times in the year: at Martinmas, Candlemas, Whitsuntide and Bartholomew's Day (Aug. 24th), when it is the duty of the youngest brother to invite the others to be present without fail. After prayer all their names are called by the secretary, and he who is not there before prayer, must pay five groschen into the poor-fund. But those who stay away altogether without sufficient excuse, shall incur the penalty the elders may deem proper to inflict."

Besides this there are contributions and collections for the poor, sick and needy according to the means of each one; there is also something given to the hospital out of the collected fines. The other articles are as follows :—

[1] Original in the Archives of Königsberg.

1. "*Of the Sabbath.*

Nobody shall without grave reasons miss the service and the sermon in this Duchy of Prussia in whatever place it may be. This is the will of all and the duty of a Christian. Neither shall he profane the Sabbath by gluttony, drinking and gambling and such like misdeeds, but keep it holy with love towards God and his neighbour according to the rule of God's Word. He shall also partake four times a year as a token of his Christianity, of the supper of the Lord, in which He offers us His true body and His true blood spilt on the cross, and shall not withdraw himself from the table of the Lord. He who purposely offends this order shall after due warning, if it occur again, be expelled from the Brotherhood.

2. *Of duty towards those in authority.*

In the next place everyone shall pray for those in authority, show himself obedient and reverent, and in case of necessity be ready to serve it even unto death. He shall also pay the due rent for his stall in the fairs and as the Brethren have settled before, contribute an annual tax to the rulers for their gracious protection and the hoped-for confirmation of our articles. Neither shall any of us refuse to pay if a tax should eventually be imposed upon us.

3. *Of our elders.*

Those that the Brotherhood esteems most worthy shall be chosen for elders by a majority of votes, and they shall then be reminded of their duties out of God's Word.

4. *Oath of the elders.*

We the elders do swear with hands uplifted before God and the whole Brotherhood, that we will not, according to our best knowledge and that power which God has given us, do ought or allow it to be done against any body, that goes against justice and is the outcome of mere partiality for the preservation of the Brotherhood. So help us God and His holy Word.

5. *Of the appeal from the decision of the elders to that of the whole Brotherhood and from it again to the German municipal Court.*

If anyone should feel himself aggrieved by the sentence of the elders, he is free to appeal to the united Brotherhood. But if the united Brotherhood confirm the sentence of the elders and the appellant be not content yet, he may go to the judges in the cities. Two of our elders however shall be in duty bound to defend their decision before the German Court. If the sentence be approved of as just by the presiding judge, the appellant must pay, if otherwise, the elders ought to pay damages to the appealer.

If it should so happen, that clearly one or the other of the elders from envy or favour should try to obtain an unjust decree, he shall, if convicted, be fined and dismissed from office.

6. *Of those that withstand the elders.*

They shall without delay and with one accord be punished.

7. *Of false measure, weight and wares.*

Concerning this point, it has been resolved by common consent of the Brotherhood, that nobody, be he rich or poor, shall use false measure, weight or goods against God's written law: Thou shalt not steal. He who does not desist shall be handed over to the presiding judge, that he may be sentenced as a thief or be expelled the country, or punished with imprisonment as the occasion requires, if he should not be able to pay. Or if a brother sell to the other brother or to anybody else adulterated goods, the seller shall not only have no price, but also refund the damages that may have accrued to the buyer hereby, and submit to the decree of the elders. But this is to be done only upon condition, that the buyer can prove his case, for otherwise many might come and use this subterfuge adducing unheard of things, even those that never entered a man's mind. And he who tries to dispose of false goods knowingly shall be punished without delay, and the value of the goods be paid into the poor-fund.

8. *Of those who are consulted concerning a sale and give false account.*

They shall be punished according to the verdict of the elders, and in case of the offence being repeated twice or three times be considered untrustworthy witnesses and expelled the Brotherhood.

9. *Of those who outside the fairs sell their goods to the detriment of the towns.*

They shall be severely punished according to the verdict of the elders. Likewise nobody shall be permitted to keep more than one shop in the country. Offenders to be duly punished.

10. *Of those who know something of others that is against our rule, and yet do not reveal it.*

Everyone shall at our regular meeting according to his conscience tell everything that he can prove of anybody, wherein an excess or crime has been committed. If he conceal it and it should come out afterwards through others, both shall be duly punished.

11. *Of moving into decent lodgings.*

It has been ordered that all Brethren of our guild shall take up their lodgings in honest houses. He who stays in suspected places shall not go unpunished. He shall also dress decently and suitably to his station, and shall invariably be present at the funeral of a deceased brother at the time appointed to assist in burying him honorably.

12. *Those who abstract anything in peasants' houses or farms, or from other people, be it ever so trifling, shall first settle with the party and afterwards be punished by the Brethren.*

13. *Of those who at meetings draw daggers, knives or the like.*

They shall be punished severely and be handed over to the municipal Court.

14. *Of those who use nicknames instead of Christian names.*

Let them be punished without delay.

15. *Of Brethren, who have been murdered by evil-doers.*

We pledge ourselves to seek and pursue the evil-doer, who without provocation murdered one of our Brethren or did him any other wrong, until he has been seized, and after he has been put in prison to proceed against him until he has either been executed or liberated by the judge. But if one of our Brethren be killed secretly or injured, we will pursue the evil-doer at his expense, if he has means; if not, we will raise money according to our power so that we may carry out our purpose. As to the property of him that was murdered or robbed, we shall only use it 'pendente lite.' Whatever may be left after the execution of justice, our elders shall hand it over to the murdered man's relations when claimed, on condition, however, that the fourth Pfennig go to the prince. And in case the late man had relations in the country, if they be spendthrifts, the money shall not be handed over to them, but be retained for his other friends in Scotland for a year. If the right heirs do not claim the property within the space of a year, the assets shall be distributed among the poor.

16. *Of those who have for some time stayed abroad.*

We have resolved, that those of our Brethren, who hire a servant-man from elsewhere or make an agreement with him in the country . . . . shall be punished, especially if the said man or boy did not complete his time, but ran away from his master or was mixed up with other crimes. . . .[1]

17. *Of stiff-necked and wilful servants.*

They shall be expelled and lose their wages unless they improve.

18. Because every year some of our nation are brought here by skippers and others, who turn out badly and refuse to do well, having already before they arrived here, as experience has taught us, misbehaved, which tends to the disgrace of the whole Scottish nation, and more especially causes unmerited disrespect, contempt and injury to our Brotherhood in this place: we have resolved, that if a skipper or other person do bring or procure such servants, he should place them with friends, if such there are, giving sufficient proof of their honesty

[1] The whole of this paragraph is anything but clear.

and find security of well-known people; but if the new-comer cannot be lodged in this way, he shall take him home again. He who trespasses any of these rules shall be punished by the Brotherhood.

Item, if anyone hire a servant who has been living here for some time, yet owes his former master still something, the new master shall pay this debt. Nobody is to keep more than one servant for four years.

If the master wrong the servant, he shall be punished after due consideration of the case. . .

19. Not to hire any strange man, unless he can give honest proof of having served his master faithfully for four years.

20. If any one of our Brethren, be he free man or serving, be found squandering his own or goods entrusted to him by card-playing, dice, laziness or other evil and useless doings by which the Brotherhood suffer injury: if this should happen in the country he shall have power to hold the offender till help arrives or bring him to the magistrate, lest he do squander the remaining property also, and from this remaining money shall he be satisfied who found him out and perhaps spent some money in doing so, though he be only a serving man. But if he be a free man but carries other people's wares, and is admittedly in debt: he shall fare likewise.

All the Brethren have solemnly sworn to observe the above articles in all particulars as far as possible, so help them God![1]"

After this most excellent constitution had been ratified by the authorities, though with many alterations, complaints against the lawlessness of the Scotch cease.

But then trouble arose from political causes.

In Scotland in the meantime the thundercloud had burst over the heads of the unfortunate Stuarts. Charles I having been found guilty of treason had been beheaded in front of his own palace, and Charles II as a fugitive in France needed money for the maintenance of his semi-royal state, money again for his

---

[1] Original in the Stadt Archiv at Königsberg

far-reaching political intrigues. In his necessity he wrote to a number of foreign princes, nay he even recollected his beloved subjects settled in Poland, of whose thriving state, rumour—ever increasing in wonder with the increasing distance — had perhaps reached his ears. As a proof of their loyalty these Scots were now to pay a tax amounting to no less than the tenth part of their possessions. This was the meaning and the message of the King's ambassador, Sir J. Cochrane, to Hamburg, Danzig and Poland. The fourth paragraph of his instructions ran : "If you finde it to be true that our said good brother, the King of Poland, hath endeavoured to bring all our Scotch subjects in that kingdome to a just acknowledgment of us and of our power and authority as their lawfull king, you shall from us thankfully acknowledge his friendship and justice therein and intreate him to continue and improve his kindness to us in that particular so farr, that none of them be permitted to enjoy the libertie they have in that kingdome, but such as shall approve their loyaltie and good affection to us by some supply of money or other assistance according to their abilitie in this time of our great necessitie. To which end you shall intreat our said good brother to authorize and encourage our loane of money or other assistance that our said subjects can be induced to give us."[1]

A further duty of the ambassador was to assemble the most prominent Scotsmen in Poland, to acquaint them with all the circumstances of the "abominable" murder of his father and to persuade them to assist their lawful monarch with a sum of money collected among themselves.

The consequence of this embassy and this request was a decree of the "good royal brother," the King of Poland, dated 1650, which, in recognition of the friendship of the King of England's grandfather "tempore necessitatis belli Turcici," and in order to assist him in his present distress, commanded all the Scotch settled in

[1] *Hist. MSS. Commission Report*, xiii. 2, 26.

Poland to assess personally their fortunes and to deposit within two months ten per cent of it with the local magistrates. This edict was approved of by the parliament in December of the same year. It was, however, but slowly and almost unwillingly, it appears, carried into effect. Poland herself was about this time implicated in a frightful war against the Cossacks and her means were straitened. Finally, towards the end of January 1651, John Cazimir commanded Henry Drioss, secretary to the Royal Exchequer, to enforce this tribute to the King of England "ratione subsidii" with all energy.[1]

On the 28th of February four of the wealthiest and most influential Scotsmen of the city of Krakau, Carmichael, Fraser, Blackhal and George Cruikshank, are cited before the Burgomaster. There they had on oath to tell the amount of their property and to bind themselves to inform their countrymen of the decree of the Polish parliament. But the payment of the tax took place only on the 3rd of March. The four mentioned above paid down large amounts varying from two to six hundred dollars; others less. Andrew Dixon, a Scotch merchant of Krakau, refused altogether to pay on the plea that he, having lived in Poland for the last fifty-seven years, ought to be exempt from being taxed. His case was postponed for a closer examination of the circumstances. A like plea is brought forward by James Cramer of Brady, Richard Gordon of Leopol, and others. The loyalty does not seem to have been quite as great as King Charles II presumed or was led to presume. Nevertheless a sum of £10,000 was collected, of which sum, however, only £600 or £800 reached the King.[2]

Nor were the political troubles on the Continent less disastrous to the Scotch settlers. In the year 1656 Danzig had declared war against Sweden and the greatest possible efforts were made for the defence of the town. Men and money were urgently needed, and, knowing that

---

[1] Tomkowicz, *l.c.* Krakau, Volumina legum. Johnson's *Lives of the Poets*, ed. Napier, 1890, Appendix.

[2] Clarendon, *Hist. of the Rebellion*, v. 255.

Oliver Cromwell favoured the Swedes, the magistrates resolved to compel the Scotch and English settlers either to submit—

(1) To the administration of the oath of fidelity;
(2) To military service ;
(3) To a war-tax ;
or to quit the country.

The Scots unanimously refused these three points; whereupon the expulsion of them, not even the asked-for delay of a few months being granted, finally took effect on the 12th July 1656.[1] The banishment, however, cannot have lasted long, for we find Scotch merchants in Danzig mentioned very soon afterwards.

In the meantime, thanks to their industry and their superior intelligence, many of the Scotch merchants in Poland had earned great riches and obtained influential positions at court. If they did not return to Scotland, they acquired landed property in the country of their adoption. Eight of the richest were made " mercatores aulici" or "curiales," purveyors to the Court.[2] As such they enjoyed very great trading privileges. They were also bankers. Many of them were ennobled. The names of Scott, who lived in the castle, Orem, Dixon and Fergusson are mentioned as such. How important their position was, is evident from an edict issued by King Stephan in the year 1585. "Beloved subjects," it runs, "the Scots who always follow our court and who are at liberty in all places, where We and our Royal Council stay, to exhibit their wares and to sell them, complain that they are prevented by our faithful subjects from exercising their privileges granted by us, in Krakau likewise. Now we command you to put nothing in their way in this business, especially not to hinder those to whom we have given liberty of trading and assigned a certain district. For if they on account of the failure of their trade should leave

[1] Thurloe's *State Papers*, v. 88, 107, 176, 195.
[2] They were appointed for life ; the last time by King Augustus II in 1697. Since that time nothing more is heard of the Scots as a " nation " or " corporation " in Poland proper.

our court, none of you indeed will follow us into Lithuania and other places. Our court cannot be without them, that supply us with all that is necessary. It is just, therefore, that they should enjoy the same privileges in Krakau as elsewhere. They have also supplied us well in former times of war. Let a certain district be assigned to them. This we command our faithful subjects.[1]—Niplomice, the 7th of May 1585."

From this document it would appear that the trading-liberty of the Scots was bound by certain local limits. However this may be, taken as a whole, their situation in the country was tolerable. It was nothing extraordinary that they should be taxed as pedlars: the pedlars in England at that time paid a similar tax; it was nothing extraordinary that they should meet with trade opposition: the times were not ripe yet for the blessings of an un-fettered competition. On the other hand we read of no religious persecution; they enjoyed many privileges; they occupied high positions at various times in the town council, and the luxurious Royal Court, not being willing to miss those who had furnished supplies in money and otherwise in times of war and peace, plainly preferred them to its own trading subjects.

It is, however, not in Warsaw and Krakau and surrounding districts only that we meet with the trading Scot. He spreads over the whole of Eastern and Western Prussia, Brandenburg, Pommern and Mecklenburg. Andrew Spalding emigrates in the beginning of the XVIIth Century from Scotland and settles in the small town of Plau in Mecklenburg, which had at that time a considerable cloth-manufacture and trade with England. In time he becomes a senator of the place. A branch of the family was ennobled in Prussia in 1834.[2] In Wismar the Scots appear about the middle of the XVIth Century; they were small traders. The names of William and Th.

---

[1] *Acta Hist. Polon.* viii. lib. i. i. See Johnson's *Lives of the Poets,* ed. Napier, in the Appendix referring to Denham.

[2] *Der Deutsche Herold,* " The German Herald," vol. xxx. p. 120 f. Cp. also Birth-Brieves of Dundee in the Appendix and Supplement.

Donatzen (Donaldson) 1571; Jacob Mackay (1579-1592); Andreas Jack (about 1600), who married Mackay's widow; Thomas Dumasson (Tompson? 1577); and Hans (John) Selby (1597-1602) are preserved in the records. The name of Watson also occurs, though it is not expressly stated that its bearer was of Scottish origin.[1] A Scotsman, John Grinlis (Greenlees?), buys a shop "under the town-hall" at Strasburg in Western Prussia for the high price of 110 Marks.[2] (1573.) Burgomaster and Councillors of Mewe in the same province are commanded by a rescript of Sigismund III, dated 1588, to admit the Scotsman Andrew Herve, who had been settled in the place for the last ten years, without delay to the freedom of the city.[3] In Tilsit Scotch merchants are first mentioned in 1592, in Memel about 1607,[4] in Stuhm 1594.[5] In Barten (Eastern Prussia) an old epitaph may be seen in the church erected by Thomas Gordon for one Alexander Schant (?) from Aberdeen, who died in 1637, fifty-five years old. In Marggrabowa lived about 1670 a Scotch merchant called John Birrell; in Angerburg occur the names of Daniel Wilson, Thomas Hamilton, George Wilson and William Anderson as owners of breweries.[6] The last-named became a town councillor. His son and grandson obtained the dignity of burgomaster. Other names of Scotch people occur in Christburg and Strasburg.[7] Even as far as Lithuania and Masuren, in Ragnit, Stallupönen, Goldap and Lyck and Insterburg did they settle and find a home.[8]

Of the Scots that settled in Memel since the commencement of the XVIIth Century, the Ogilvies, Muttrays and Simpsons were most successful and rose to high distinctions. Thomas and John Ogilvie founded a potash

---

[1] Communicated.
[2] Plehn, *Geschichte des Kreises Strasburg*, Leipzig, 1900, p. 178.
[3] Joh. Sembritzki in *Altpreuss. Monats Schrift*, Band xxx. Heft 3 and 4.
[4] Sembritzki, *Geschichte Memels*, 1900.
[5] The names, 'David Trumb and Steinson (?).
[6] Sembritzki, *die Schotten und Engländer*, p. 228.
[7] The names given for Christburg and Strasburg: Donalson and Donellson, are probably identical.
[8] Sembritzki, *l.c.*, p. 351 f.

factory there in 1771. John Simpson († 1774) as well as W. Muttray obtained the dignity of "Bürgermeister," the latter in 1813. Thomas Ogilvie became a member of the Town Council. All three distinguished themselves by their truly noble liberality and their constant efforts for the benefit of their fellow-citizens. John Simpson and his cousin Ludwig became the chief founders of the Lodge Memphis (1776) and left many valuable gifts and donations especially to the Reformed, i.e. Calvinistic, Church, of which they were members. When Muttray resigned his official dignity as Mayor in 1815, he expended almost the whole of the salary that had been attached to it, on charitable purposes, giving to the Elementary Schools a donation of 1000 Thaler,[1] to the Institute for the education of the Poor 600 Thaler, and for the purchase of books, instruments, etc., 250. He also deserves the chief credit for considerable sums collected in 1815 and sent to the King of Prussia at Paris, who expended them for the comfort of the wounded during the great war against Napoleon. Thomas Ogilvie at his death in 1811 left a considerable legacy to the poor of Memel.

Other names of Scotsmen residing in this town are : Littlejohn (1616), Pesaller (1616), G. Wölssel (?) (1620), A. Smith, the three last named from Aberdeen. Also Arrot, Adam, Barclay, Durham, Irwing, Marschall, Minorgam (?), Mitchel, Mitchelhill, Murray, Palmer, Ramsay, Ritchie, Scrumseour (Scrimgeour): all of the XVIIth Century. Later on we find a rope-maker James Duncan mentioned; indeed the emigration to Memel seems never to have ceased, since as late as the beginning of the XIXth Century Scotsmen were enrolled as citizens, notably one Robert Pitcairn from Perth in 1807.[2]

In the town of Elbing—the seat of the Swedish Governor-General for the Baltic coast from Memel to

[1] Six Thaler = One Pound.

[2] Johannes Sembritzki, *Geschichte Memels* (*History of Memel*), Memel, 1900, pp. 110, 152, 210, 231, 241, 246 f., 295. About Scottish Officers at this town and the affairs of the Church see in its proper place.

Elbing during the Thirty Years' War, and strongly garrisoned by Scotch troops—the following names are rescued out of many: 1. Thomas Achenwall (Auchinvale) (born 1581, died 1653).[1] His birthbrief is still preserved and is issued by the "Praefectus et consules et senatores civitatis Sterlinensis" on the 24th of February 1614. 2. William Lamb de Aberton, whose son William is born at Elbing on the 7th of December 1586. 3. Alexander Nisbet from Edinburgh, who died in 1617. 4. Charles Ramsay, born 1576 at Dundee, died at Elbing in February 1650. His birthbrief (1611) tells us that he was the son of Charles Ramsay at Deidonum "urbis nostrae olim consiliarius," and of Janeta Duncan. His family existed at Elbing up to 1863.[2]

The earliest settlement of the Scots took place in Danzig, as we have seen; but the exact date of the foundation of the suburb, called 'Alt-Schottland' (Old Scotland), so called after a colony of Scottish weavers, is difficult to ascertain. We shall not go wrong, however, if we fix the year of the first arrival of the colonists at about 1380. With this the historian Goldbeck agrees, and adds, that the place must have been tolerably well cultivated in the XIVth Century, for it was burnt to the ground in 1520, when the Poles had engaged upon a war of two years' duration with Albrecht, the head or 'Hochmeister' of the Teutonic Order and afterwards first Duke of Prussia. The Carthusian Prior Schwengel (*ca.* 1720) relates, that Alt-Schottland was inhabited originally by so-called "gardiners," *i.e.* small peasant-proprietors, and that not till later on tradespeople, especially Scottish linen-weavers and tanners, had settled there. According to him the place was already known as "Alt-Schottland" in 1433, when it was burned by the Hussites. He further tells us, that on account of the growing prosperity of the place, the people of Danzig procured the privilege, that within a radius of five miles no town was to be built and no trade to be established

---

[1] Cp. Part iv.
[2] Kindly communicated by Prof. Dr Neubaur at Elbing.

that was commonly carried on in townships only.   But already in 1526 the Bishop takes the part of the linen-weavers.   This is to be explained from the fact, that 'Schottland' and other small places in the neighbourhood of Danzig belonged to the so-called 'liberties of the Church,' that is to say, to the property of the Bishop of Leslau and the Monastery of Pelplin.   These 'liberties' became Prussian possessions at the first division of Poland in 1772, whilst the town of Danzig itself obtained the dignity of a 'free City.'

Here as elsewhere the Scottish settlers held together very closely; a Scottish factor, or 'resident' as he was called afterwards, looked after their interests.   Numerous Scottish names, such as Murray, Muttray, Simpson, Nesbit, Maclean (Macklin), still current in or about Danzig, testify to the extent of the former colony. Some rich Scottish merchants there we shall have to mention in due course.

In the town of Posen, then belonging to Poland, the records of a number of Scotch families date back to the middle of the XVIth Century.   They were mostly engaged in trade; some of them, however, were handicraftsmen. King Stephan Bathory tried to make them permanent citizens by directing the Magistrate of Posen in 1567 to remove those Scotsmen out of the town, who had no house-property.   The strangers now endeavoured to fulfil the necessary conditions.   They were an active, intelligent and cautious race, some of them well-to-do.   Their number, however, decreased in the following century, chiefly on account of heavy taxation.   The Forbeses and Watsons are especially named as very rich.   The then (XVIth Century) famous merchant and shipowner Ryd (=Reid) in Danzig and Posen, is very probably also of Scotch origin.   He was a banker too and supplied large sums to the needy Polish aristocracy.[1]   Here as elsewhere, the hostility of the native trade-unions was

---

[1] In 1605 there are twenty Scotch merchants and about as many craftsmen in Posen; in 1651 only eleven, the richest of them Al. Smart, who had to assess his income on the occasion of the subsidy for the King

great. • Thus there is a passage in the Statutes of the
Purse-maker guild saying: "It shall not be permitted
to merchants, be they Scotch or Jews, to sell purses
singly, but only by the dozen. Offenders to lose their
goods" (1675). And the shoemakers received a constitution from the magistrates, in which the nineteenth
paragraph runs: "No master or any other person shall
make so bold as to bring boots and shoes from elsewhere
for sale in Posen, least of all the Jews, Scots, Armenians,
Lithuanians and others that are not members of the
guild." A similar rule obtained with the tinsmiths.[1]

Whilst this trade-opposition was common enough all
over Poland and Prussia, in Posen an event happened,
which in the midst of religious intolerance could not
fail to render the Scotch settlers hated. It was in the
year 1652 that a drunk Scot, in a public-house and in
the presence of several people, uttered some blasphemous
remarks against the Virgin Mary. A great uproar and
tumult arose and he barely escaped with his life. But
not content with that, the offender had to stand his trial,
the three classes of the representatives of the inhabitants
assembled in the town-house, and resolved to petition the
King, "feria tertia in crastino festi natalis Sancti Joannis
Baptistae," to defend the honour of the most holy Virgin,
and to have the culprit punished most severely.[2]

Thus it came to pass that in the XVIIIth Century
only a few Scotch families, such as the Watsons, Fergussons
and Forbeses were settled in Posen.

In the town of Deutsch-Krone (Polish = Walcz)
a Scotchman with the name of Wolson (Wilson or
Watson?) is made a sort of honorary member of the
guild of cloth-makers (1617). It must have been an
exceptional act, since, in general, 'Jews, Scots and
Heretics, i.e. Protestants,' were refused admission.

It was here that a curious action, for sumptuous
apparel, in contravention of the laws against luxury

of England, possessed only 6000 gulden. S. Lukaszewicz, *Historisch
statistisches Bild der Stadt Posen*, i. 79 f.

[1] S. Lukaszewicz, *l.c.*, p. 80.   [2] *Ibid., l.c.*, p. 80.

frequently promulgated in Poland during the first quarter of the XVIIth Century, was preferred against the strangers. They were said to have dressed in robes of blue silk, richly trimmed with costly fur and that they had even assumed the distinctive sign of the nobility, the shoes of yellow morocco leather. The plaintiff was a Polish nobleman, named Ostrowski, and amongst the accused were the two richest merchants of Krone, Wolson and Lawson. Now the Scots being proverbially known to be inclined to thrift and parsimony rather than to sumptuousness in the way of silk and morocco leather, the complaint seems on the face of it absurd; there were other reasons, probably, which induced the plaintiff to prefer this charge. Wolson as well as Lawson had both acquired a large fortune; both were money-lenders, and the Polish nobility of the surrounding district seem to have been pretty well at their mercy by reason of their debts. Thus we read, that in 1617 the nobleman John v. der Golz and Barbara v. Walda mortgaged their share of the estate of Klausdorf to Wolson, the Scot, for 1000 Guldens. and some years later (1630) another member of the Golz family, not finding the magistrates of Krone inclined to assist him in his law-suit against Wolson, attacked him at night 'and maltreated him.' But he is himself brought to book in 1635 and 1639 for a debt to the Scotchman amounting to 736 Guldens.

In a similar manner Sophia Lawson, the widow of the above-named Lawson, and her son Christoph hold a bond of one Bernhard von Blankenburg; and when Christoph dies in 1641 and his property comes to be divided, we are told that five noblemen, whose names are given, owe him a debt of nearly 6000 Gulden. May not also a case like this have been the reason of Ostrowski's charges? Be this as it may, the important position of the Scottish settlers as money-lenders and bankers receives additional and interesting confirmation by these events in the history of Deutsch-Krone.

Another settlement of the Scots was at Putzig, not far from Danzig. In the records of this town we read of several actions for insult preferred by them, against the inhabitants for calling them "Scottish rogues." A long law-suit of this description against one called George Ratzke in 1620 ends with his being sentenced to pay a fine and costs, and when he is unable to do this, he is banished out of the town "for a year and a day." [1]

Most of these immigrants were, as we have seen, of the reformed faith; yet the Roman Catholics were not wanting. They showed a predilection for the Catholic province of Ermeland or visited, as far as they did not belong to the trading fraternity, the school of the Jesuits at Braunsberg. Speaking of the foundation of St Rochus' Chapel at Arnsdorf the author [2] relates: "Once upon a time when a merchant from abroad, a Scot, drove from Guttstedt to Wormditt, where in those days much trade was done, he heard near Arnsdorf a ploughman ploughing near the road sing a Scotch tune. He wondered and stopped, called the ploughman and being questioned as to what brought him to this country the latter told his countryman, that his name was Maier (probably Mayor), that he had been forced to leave his native place during the religious persecutions of Queen Elizabeth, and that he and many others had at last arrived in Ermeland, where he, owing to his poverty, had to hire himself out as a farm-labourer. The merchant, who from the manner in which the tale was told, recognised Maiers' great capacities, took him with him and left him with the Jesuits at Braunsberg for further education. Later on the former ploughman became a rich merchant. Out of gratitude towards God for the fortunate turn of his life he in the year 1617 built a chapel dedicated to St Rochus at Arnsdorf with eight windows, a small steeple and a bell. On a slab of black marble on the eastern wall we read the following inscription:

---

[1] Similar charges are brought forward in 1624 and 1641. Sometimes the Scottish took the law into their own hands and retaliated with blows.

[2] Prof. Dittrich in *Zeitschrift für d. Gesch. und Altertumskunde Ermlands*, ix. 432 ff.

I. M. I.

Famatus Joann Maier, natione
Scotus, Civis Brunob; in pueris
Ahrensdorfii et Lauterwaldii serviens
ex voti causa hoc sacellum
ad Dei Omnipotentis gloriam
fundavit et exstruxit. Anno
Salutis humanae 1617.

i.e. the famous John Mayor, a Scot, citizen of Braunsberg
in his youth serving at Ahrensdorf and Lauterwald,
founded and built this chapel according to a vow, in
honour of the Almighty God. In the year of grace
1617."[1]

Finally it deserves mention, that many of the im-
migrated Scotch merchants, who in not a few cases
belonged to the class of "lairds" at home, became
founders of noble families in the land of their adoption.
There is a close connection between the Austrian Barons
von Skene,[2] who own large cloth-manufactories and sugar-
refineries in Prerau and Brünn, and David Skene, a native
of Aberdeen, who was made a citizen of Posen in 1586
and whose second son married the daughter of a Scotch
merchant in Danzig, named Chalmers.

Nathaniel Gordon left Scotland, fourteen years old, in
1701, and went to Krakau to seek his fortune. He
succeeded so well that he became the ancestor of the
Polish noble family of Gordon now living at Ycon, their
family seat to the north of Krakau. Two brothers
Gibson, who came to Danzig in or about 1600, amassed
a great fortune. A descendant of theirs received the
title of "Baron" from Frederick the Great.[3] Many of
the Ogilvies, who are met with throughout Poland,
obtained high military titles and dignities.[4] The Bonars,
of an ancient and very numerous Scotch clan, emigrated
to Poland as early as the XVth Century. Upon them
also were conferred the highest honours. One John

---

[1] Cp. Sembritzki, *l.c.*, p. 230 ff.
[2] Now represented by A. von Skene, Freiherr and Member of the
Austrian Parliament. As to the Edle von Ramsays see Supplement.
[3] See Appendix.   [4] See Part ii., *The Army*.

de Bonar, became Burggraf Krakau, and Baron of the German Empire; a second one Theobald was made Franciscan-General; whilst a third St John Isaiah de Bonar was even canonised by the church in 1483.

Especially numerous among Scotch emigrants were the Fergussons and Frasers. In the year 1662 there died in Poland the merchant John Fergusson. He had encouraged two nephews George and William to emigrate also (1703). One of these, the eldest, married Catharina Concordia Tepper of Posen, a sister of a rich Banker Tepper in Warsaw. Their son Peter became the successor and heir of his uncle, was chosen a member of the legislative assembly and was granted permission to add the name Tepper to his own. He died in 1794. His son again Philipp Bernhard von Fergusson-Tepper, called the "second banker of Europe," was made honorary citizen of Edinburgh. He possessed a splendid house in Warsaw and built a Protestant Church next to it; besides being a large land-owner in the Kingdom of Prussia.[1] In spite of his Protestant faith he was a Knight of the Order of Malta. His children intermarried with noble Russian and Prussian families.[2]

As to the noble family of Johnston of Craigieburn near Moffat, now of Rathen in Silesia, the reader will find the necessary information in Parts II. and IV.

In Krakau we find mention made incidentally to some money-transaction, of one Jacob Drummond who is further styled: "ex familia magnifici baronis de Borlandt oriundus"; and in the beginning of the XVIIth Century of one William Lindsay, whose son Jacob wrote for a certificate of his noble birth.[3]

[1] He bought estates to the value of £85,000 and received a letter from the King of Prussia, expressing pleasure at his becoming a Prussian subject.

[2] The Scotch have always shown special aptitude for banking. In Paris there lived a Scotch merchant Mercer in the reign of Charles II, who was a kind of Fugger in his days; in Stockholm another Scotsman, Seton, acted the same part, providing the always needy Gustav III with the necessary moneys.

[3] He belonged to the Lindsays of Fesdo. See *Lives of the Lindsays*, i. 444.

It often happened, that these young Scots, who were at first perhaps only known by their Christian names, afterwards when success smiled on them or when they claimed an inheritance or applied for a situation, wrote home for their birth-certificates or birth-briefs, elaborate genealogical statements most of them according to Scotch predilections in that special branch of domestic history. A large collection of these is to be found in the so-called Propinquity Books at Aberdeen.

Of the rich Scotch merchants abroad, many made a noble use of their prosperity. Besides the founder of the Chapel of St Rochus, let another Roman Catholic be mentioned, who in the documents is erroneously called Portius instead of Porteous.[1] He lived at Krosna in Poland and was engaged in a very flourishing trade in Hungarian wines. He rebuilt the church of his adopted home, which had been destroyed by fire, endowed it with rich vestments, altar-vessels, a baptismal font and beautiful bells. At his death he left legacies to the King and to the place of his birth, besides a large amount of money to his heirs. In the writing on a picture of him in Krosna he is called " generosus."

Another Scotsman, better known than Porteous, Robert Gordon of Aberdeen, spent the wealth which he had accumulated at Danzig in founding Gordon's Hospital in Aberdeen. John Turner, also a Scotch merchant of Danzig left at his death in 1680 four hundred Marks annually for the maintenance of four poor students, and legacies for the Scotch school, the Elisabeth Hospital and the "Pockenhaus" at Danzig. Patrick Forbes and William Lumsden witness the will.[2]

Among the Scots who emigrated to Danzig during the first half of the XVIIth Century was a certain Cockburn, whose name, according to the dialect of the district, became Kabrun. Orginally no doubt a merchant, he soon succeeded in buying a small landed property near the city

---

[1] He is called of "Lanxeth," a name which I could not identify with any Scotch place, and signs "H. M. Factor." Cp. Tomkowicz, *l.c.*, p. 154, *note*.

[2] *Records of Marischal College of Aberdeen.*

and in obtaining the rights of a citzen. A grandson of this first Kabrun acquired great wealth, owing chiefly to his superior and uncommon technical abilities. He started the first sugar-refining works at Danzig, had an extensive trade with Poland and was engaged in other factory-enterprise. His son James born on the ninth of January 1759, became one of the most philanthropic and public spirited merchants Danzig ever possessed. His youth was passed in a time full of political oppression and suffering. The hard measures of Frederick the Great against the town, which after three centuries of thriving growth and privileges under the sovereignty of Poland, resisted his desires of incorporation and especially the heavy duties levied in all the suburbs and surrounding districts occupied by the Prussians on all goods imported into Danzig from the side of the sea or that of Poland, completely paralysed the trade. But Kabrun's business suffered besides that for private reasons. His partner had incautiously become surety for a strange firm, and a great flood occurring in 1775 had destroyed a considerable part of his goods and stores. Thus it came to pass, that the father failed, and the youth, then scarcely seventeen, was thrown back on his own energy and resources. Matters mended, however, soon. An uncle took him into his business, where he in a short time completely gained the confidence of his employer by his untiring application, and his commercial ability. He undertook successful travels in Holland and England and was fortunate also in some small commercial undertakings of his own. After acting for a time as partner of the firm, he in 1800 after his uncle's death became the sole representative of it and rapidly acquired the envied and enviable position as one of the wealthiest and most generous merchants of Danzig. Not satisfied with the great revival of trade after the final incorporation into Prussia, he tried to start new branches of industry by settling in his native town a colony of silk-weavers from the South of Germany, granting them dwellings and guaranteeing them fair wages. He also extended his shipping trade, by sending one of his vessels to the distant port of Buenos Ayres. Fond of travelling his large collection of paintings and prints was constantly added to, whilst in his leisure hours he composed essays on the science of Financing or wrote other books, notably his "Life of a Merchant," an autobiography, which after the great model of Goethe, he called: "Wahrheit ohne Dichtung" (Truth without Fiction). It was through him also that the plan of erecting an Opera-House was successfully carried out at the cost of about £4000. In short, Kabrun proved besides being an enterprising merchant, a munificent patron of all that contributed to the mental development of his fellow-citizens. Unfortunately he had to abandon his favourite scheme of establishing a commercial academy at Danzig owing to the indolence of the inhabitants and the threatening aspect of the times. The sufferings of the town during the reign of Napoleon are well known. It was twice besieged, once by the French in 1807 from the 24th of April to the 24th of May and again by the Russians and Germans in 1814 before the final retreat of the French. Kabrun's energy found ample scope for work. He acted as a true helper in distress and a father of the poor and suffering; displaying everywhere a total disregard of his own health and comfort in his desire to ameliorate the terrible consequences of war and privation. Not only did he collect a large sum of money from his friends in Germany, which he conscientiously distributed chiefly amongst working men, who wanted to purchase new tools or buy material to rebuild their houses, but he also wrote to his business-connections in London, and originated a collection in the City in aid of the sufferers of Danzig, which amounted to the large sum of £5000. Not being a man of a strong physical constitution it was not to be wondered at, that this ceaseless strain accelerated his death. Occupied with the plans for his new country house, and with the erection of dwellings for the families of poor artizans on an estate lately purchased by him and partly intended for mercantile and technical purposes, he was struck by paralysis on October 24th, 1814. By his will he left his whole library, his pictures, drawings and prints and the sum of 100,000 Gulden for the foundation of a Commercial Academy at Danzig.[1] The two sons of Kabrun, both dying without male heirs, increased this bequest of their father by rich legacies and the gift of further art-treasures. Owing to adverse circumstances the Commercial Establishment was not opened till July 2nd, 1832; but since then it has exercised a very beneficent and widespread influence over the youths of the town and district, and the name of Kabrun, who although of Scottish origin, had become the prototype of a public-spirited, far-seeing German patriot, will be unforgotten.

Finally mention must be made of William Brown of Angus in Scotland, who went to Danzig about 1693, and returned to England in 1699 after having acquired great wealth. He was made a Baronet.[2]

Very various indeed were the claims that were made upon the liberality of these Scotch merchants abroad. It will be remembered, how thoroughly Charles II took advantage of his faithful subjects in Poland in the year 1651. Towards the end of that century it happened that the buildings of Marischal College became dilapidated, and again the Scot abroad, especially at Königsberg and Danzig, must come to the rescue. The Rector and the Professors of Aberdeen, after having received contributions some sixteen years ago, address a new letter to their distant countrymen with the prayer to assist them still further in procuring the necessary building funds. Nor was this appeal in vain. Very considerable sums were contributed by fifty-four members of the Scotch Brotherhood in Königsberg, by twenty-one at Warsaw, and many others at Danzig, Elbing and other places. John Turner above named had already in 1685 subscribed over 600 pounds; Postmaster Low in Danzig 290, Patrick Forbes at Danzig 280 pounds. The latter wrote on the 6th of September 1684 to the Rector and the Professors of Aberdeen as follows:—

---

[1] Völkel, *Life of Kabrun* and Appendix.
[2] *Memorials of the Browns of Fordell*, by R. R. Stodart, p. 19 f., 202 f.

"Right honorabell Sirs,
        Through this bearer Baylie Alexander Gordone,
your acceptabell letter I reseawed and heawing respect to
such worthie persones, your good desinges and rasonabell
demands, I wold not be refractive bot heaw (for hes
discharg) delyvred to the forsaid Baylie Gordone ane
hundred Crossdollers in specie which I intreat yee will
accept and registrat in yor books for the building of the
Marischall Colleg. I wish it be onlly imployed to that
use, and it shall be allwayes my earnest wish to heyr, gif
not to see, Learneing may increas in my native, which is
the speciall mean to uphold both church and stait, which
God allmightie mantin in hes fear, love and unyformetie
to the end.
        Commiteing you and your desing to the directyone of
the allmighty and myselff to your favor, I subscrybe
                Sir, yours in observaunc
                        PATRICK FORBES."

Low and Miller write in a similar strain in 1700 and
1701; the latter holding out no hope of collecting more,
for "times are so very hard in this country and so little
trade."[1]

Another Scotch merchant established a bursary for a
Polish student at Edinburgh and Patrick Aikenhead, who
died at Danzig in 1693, left a legacy of 3500 pounds to
the same city, "ad pios usus."[2]

Of the contributions towards the building of a new
Church at Danzig for the united "British Nation" as
well as of the Davidson Bequest in the same town, we
have already spoken.

In short, the saying "blood is thicker than water"
may be applied to these Scotch merchants abroad with
the same propriety as it applies to the emigrants in
Australia: their blood remains their blood, their home
their home.

[1] *Records of the Marischall College of Aberdeen*, i. 356-360. See
Appendix.
[2] Robert Chambers, *Edinburgh Merchants*, p. 24.

But in the land of their adoption also the Scots have left, though in the times when drums of war did not cease beating, hundreds of them perished and left no trace behind, the grateful recollections of a new race. They have founded families which flourish to this day in Germany, Russia, Sweden, Holland, Austria and France; they have proved their industry and their intelligence, their bravery and their strength of religious conviction amidst many dangers and calumnies, and by sacrificing the results of their labour, nay their lives, shown their gratitude towards a country, which had in times of dearth and persecution become a refuge for them.

PART II.

THE ARMY.

THE ARMY.

SCOTTISH bravery and Scottish loyalty have been rendered immortal by the historian and the poet not only in their motherland. Kings and Emperors of the Continent have acknowledged these sterling qualities from time immemorial. In France,—a country led by the common hatred of England into an alliance, which for centuries formed the central fact of English history,—there existed a Royal Bodyguard composed of Scotsmen since very early times. Its duty was to accompany the sovereign wherever he went and to answer for his safety. In the hands of its officers were the keys of the royal bedchamber and private chapel; they protected the royal barge, when the King had to cross a river or lake, and the sedan chair in which he was being carried. On state occasions three of this Bodyguard stood on each side of His Majesty, their halberds decorated with silk of the royal colour, white. As a military regiment the guard appears since 1425, in order to fight henceforth in all the great battles at the head of the French army.

In Poland, where king and nobles alike used to surround their persons with a bodyguard, it was the Scots again of whom by preference it was composed. In Denmark and Holland, Scotch regiments have for centuries acquired honour and glory on many a battlefield. More than once Scottish officers have held the fate of colossal Russia in their hands, and Gustavus Adolfus, "the Lion and the Bulwark of the North," would without his Scotch regiments and leaders hardly have gained his victories and saved the cause of Protestantism in Germany.

It is not our task here to follow the glorious career of the Scottish Guard in France. He who desires information on this interesting chapter of French history, will find in

English as well as in French literature works full of
diligent research and fascinating detail.[1] We have to do
with the deeds of Scotch warriors and officers in Germany
and for a German cause.

It is commonly taken for granted that Scotch officers
and mercenaries did not appear on German soil before
the Thirty Years' War (1618-1648). This is however
erroneous. Already three centuries earlier, at the time
when the Order of the Teutonic Knights proclaimed a
crusade against the heathen in the far east of Prussia, the
knights of Scotland also prepared for such a pious and
warlike expedition. In England the powerful Earl of
Derby, afterwards King Henry IV, and many other nobles
of many Christian nations had set the example, during the
years 1389-1391. Indeed so popular had these Prussian
crusades become, that not only was the German word
" reysa "—a journey, an expedition—adopted as the
technical term for them in English, but they were made
the final proof and seal of the perfection of a Christian
knight. Thus Chaucer in the Prologue to the Canterbury
Tales describes his knight—

> " Full often tyme he hadde the bord bygonne
> Above alle naciouns in Pruce :
> In Lettowe hadde he reysed and in Ruce
> Ne Christian man so ofte of his degree " ;

and already in 1356 we find that the brothers Walther and
Norman de Lesselyn obtain safe-conduct to Prussia. Six
years later a certain David de Berclay—scutifer—applies
for similar letters for himself, twelve knights and twelve
horses, bound for Prussia. The same application is made
in 1378 by Adam de Heburn who sails for Prussia with
ten knights.[2]

But the most celebrated " reyse " of all, was that of
Lord William Douglas of Nithisdale, called Black

---

[1] Michel, *Francisque : Les Ecossais en France et les Francais en
Ecosse.* London, Trübner & Co., 2 vols. 1862.
    Burton, J. H., *The Scot Abroad.* Edinburgh 1898. The first
volume contains the History of the Scottish Guard in France.
[2] *Rotuli Scotiae*, 37 *Edw. III* and *I*, 797.

Douglas. It is mentioned by German, French, English and Scotch writers; by the last named not without a touch of the legendary.

William Douglas was the natural son of Archibald Douglas. He was as famous for his knightly virtues as for his prodigious bodily strength. King Robert II of Scotland had given him his daughter Egidia in marriage in acknowledgment of his many deeds of valour, and the united knights of England and Scotland, who after the battle of Otterburne in August 1388 agreed to terminate their incessant feuds by an armistice of three years duration, had, according to Scotch sources, made him commander of a fleet of 240 ships. Shortly after his arrival at Danzig (Danskin) he excited the jealousy of some English warriors of rank, who as friends of his mortal enemy Clifford did not scruple to assassinate him. It appears that this Clifford had in Scotland challenged Douglas to fight him in single combat and, when Douglas went to Paris to procure armour, spread the slanderous rumour, that fear had prompted him to flight.[1] But when his opponent returned in due time for the duel, it was Clifford himself who had absconded. We are not told that he went to Prussia also, but his friends acted for him, hired assassins, waylaid Douglas on his way home from church and killed him and one of his servants near the end of a bridge after a most stubborn resistance.[2] Most probably this was the bridge, or more correctly the quay, of the Mottlau river, called then as now the "long bridge." One of its gates, the Frauenthor, was near the High Altar of the Church of St Mary.

A crime so atrocious could not fail to produce the greatest indignation among the French and Scottish knights. The table of honour at Königsberg at which the Teutonic Knights desired to welcome their foreign guests, was deferred until the arrival in the enemy's country. Boucicault, the far-famed French warrior, who was present at an expedition into Prussia

---

[1] Hirsch, *Scriptores Rerum Prussicarum,* ii. 644.
[2] Douglas fell fighting "lyke ane lyon."

for the fourth time, openly and vehemently blamed the English for their foul crime, and challenged every one of them to single combat that would call the deed by another name. But the English refused to give an account except to the Scottish knights.[1]

Two points remain unsettled in this affair, so well authenicated in its main features: the place and the time. The French author of the Adventures of Boucicault and one of the German chroniclers place the scene of the murder at Königsberg, whilst the Scotch and English sources as well as the other German Chronicler mention Danzig as such.[2] The time is variously given as 1390 or 1391; but Douglas seems to have been alive as late as 1392.[3]

However this may be, the old writers are perfectly consistent in the relation of the fact itself; we know even the companions-in-arms of Douglas with tolerable certainty. Their names have curiously enough come to us in an old bill of obligation, written by James Douglas of Dalkeith at Danzig for Sir Robert Stuart of Durisdeer, who lived at the end of the XIVth Century.[4]

After this time we hear almost nothing of Scottish mercenaries in Germany for two centuries; nor is this to be wondered at considering the great draining of warlike youths to France and Holland.

It is not till 1577 that the City of Danzig, then waging war against the King of Poland, Stephan Bathory, hired a regiment of 700 Scots. They were permitted to take their own clergymen with them.

Some thirty or forty years later during an armistice in the Netherlands several Scottish regiments of the Dutch Brigade under Sir E. Cecil were sent to assist the Protest-

[1] *Le livre des faicts du Mareschal Boucicault*, in Michaud and Pougoulat's *Nouvelle Collection des Mémoires*, Paris, 1836, Tome ii. See also Appendix.

[2] Hirsch in his edition of *Prussian Chroniclers* rightly inclines to Danzig.

[3] *Dictionary of Nat. Biography*, vol. 15.

[4] See Report of the Historical MSS. Commission, xi. and Appendix.

ant Elector of Brandenburg in his war against the Emperor Leopold and Wolfgang William of the Bavarian Palatinate for the possession of the principality of Jülich.[1] A colonel Henderson is mentioned particularly as having shown great bravery in the capture of the strong fortress of that name.

But only when the bloody torch of the Thirty Years' War (1618-1648) shed its lurid light over the whole of Europe and when Gustavus Adolfus' fame, not only as that of a saviour of the cause of Protestantism, but also as that of an unusually brilliant general and strategist, rapidly spread over the civilised world, a great number of Scottish officers, many of them of noble rank, enlisted in the Swedish Army, to go, as it were, through the high school of military training, and Scotland became the country in which by far the most numerous levies of soldiers for the " Lion of the North," were raised. Between twenty and thirty thousand men made the cause of the Swedes and of German Protestantism their own.

How deeply this fact, denuding whole tracts of country of its young men, was felt in the domestic life of Scotland, may be read in the dusty records of history. It has found a more eloquent and a more touching expression in the songs of the people.

> He's brave as brave can be ;
> He wad rather fa' than flee ;
> But his life is dear to me,
> Send him hame, send him hame.
>
> Your love ne'er learnt to flee
> But he fell in Germanie ;
> Fighting brave for loyaltie :
> Mournfu' dame, mournfu' dame !

Or in another place :

> Oh, woe unto these cruell wars
> That ever they began !
> For they have reft my native isle
> Of many a pretty man.

---

[1] This was the so-called War of Succession of Jülich. Duke William had died in 1609 without leaving a direct heir. It ended by a division which gave the Brandenburger the lion's share (1614).

> First they took my brothers twain
> Then wiled my love frae me :
> Oh, woe unto these cruell wars
> In low Germanie!

Even in the language of the Gaels the fact stands recorded. There we have a proverb referring to the levies by Colonel Mackay for the Swedes—

> Na h-uile fear a theid a dhollaidh
> Gheibh a dolar bho Mhac Aoidh.

'He who is down in luck, can still get a dollar (recruiting money) from Mackay.'

On the whole the report of these Scottish mercenaries is a good one. R. Cannon, the well-known military author, says of them : "No troops could be better fitted, morally as well as physically, for desperate undertakings, than these Scots. They proved hardy, frugal and sober soldiers." The same praise is bestowed upon them by an old wood-engraving preserved in the British Museum. It represents four Highlanders, three in kilts, the fourth in a sort of trunk-hose. Above it are the German words : "In solchem Habit gehen die 800 in Stettin angekommenen Irrländer oder Irren ";[1] *i.e.,* "In such dress the 800 Highlanders (lately) arrived at Stettin walk (about)." Under it we read : "Es ist ein starkes, dauerhafftiges Volk, behilft sich mit geringer Speis, hat es nicht Brod, so essen sie Wurzeln, wenn's auch die Nothdurfft erfordert, konnen des Tags über die 20 teutsche meil' lauffen, haben neben Muskeden ihre Bogen und Köcher und lange Messer "; *i.e.,* "They are a strong, hardy race, contenting themselves with little food, if they have no bread, they eat roots and carrots ; in case of necessity they are able to walk twenty German miles in a day ;[2] they have besides muskets, their bows and quivers and long knives."

What raised the position of the Scottish soldier in the

---

[1] Erse (Highlanders).

[2] This would be a prodigious feat indeed calculating the distance as between 80 and 100 English miles.

Thirty Years' War above that of the common mercenary, was the feeling of loyalty towards the unfortunate King of Bohemia, whose wife was a daughter of their own King James VI. They saw in the cause of the Scottish princess their own.

Moreover they mostly descended from decent, if poor, families, and were led by the sons of the lower and higher nobility, often chiefs of the clans. These officers excelled in bravery, pride and a certain "perfervidum ingenium," which is ascribed to the Scots from times immemorial. When the King of Denmark at first refused to let them retain their silk flag with the cross of St Andrew on it, they all threatened instant departure, and when Gustavus Adolfus quizzed brave Colonel Hepburn on account of the splendour of his armour and of his being a Roman Catholic, he at once sheathed his sword and left the Swedish service. The Emperor Charles V of Germany had already recognized the sensitive pride of these high-minded men and wisely recommended: "qu'on n'irritast les Ecossois, sachant bien que les Ecossois estaient pauvres mais gens vaillants";[1] and it would have been better if the Swedish king had followed his advice.[2]

To say, however, that these mercenaries of Scotland had all been animated by a religious or even a political motive, would mean to ignore the spirit of the time. Granted that these motives played a conspicuous and noble part in many of the officers, yet with the bulk of them the military training under so famous a King was the first consideration, and with the rank and file of the men— pay and hope of booty.

Walter Scott has in his *Legend of Montrose* added the sketch of the Scottish soldier of fortune in the Thirty Years' War to his long and magnificent picture-gallery illustrative of the history of Scotland. For artistic reasons, however, he made our friend Dugald Dalgetty, who changes his masters, after some nice reasoning to

---

[1] Meteren, fol. 310.
[2] As a weapon the Scottish soldiers mostly used the pike, " la senora y reina de los armas " as it is called.

comfort his conscience, almost with the same ease as one
changes one's gloves; who performs wonders of valour
in their service and remains faithful to them for just as
long as his own oath binds him, the representative of the
extreme side rather of the Scottish trooper.[1]   And when
Sir James Turner, to whom we owe several quaintly
interesting works on the art of war, writes: "I had
swallowed, without chewing, in Germanie, a very dangerous
maxime, which militarie men there too much follow, which
was, that soe we serve our master honestlie, it is no
matter what master we serve";[2] we perceive at once
that these lax principles were not inbred, but reluctantly
adopted.   Men could not help breathing the tainted moral
atmosphere that surrounded them.

In the principal source for this period of blood and
war on the continent, the contemporary chronicle of the
deeds of Mackay's Regiment by Colonel Robert Munro,[3]
we find instead of lax morals a firm trust in God's providence and remarks on the virtues and duties of a soldier,
the duties of mercy towards the wounded for instance,
which bear testimony to the humane and noble character
of its author.   Two other books, chiefly founded upon
these memoirs, give us a very interesting account of those
terrible times of religious warfare and the part played in it
by the Scots: the *Memoirs and Adventures of Sir J.
Hepburn*, and the *Story of the Highlanders under Mackay,
Lord Reay*.[4]

Guided by these authors and by such material as we
have been able to gather from German sources, we will
now proceed to sketch the history of the Scotch Brigades
in Germany during the Thirty Years' War.

Colonel Hepburn, General and Maréchal of France in
later years, was a young, well educated man, descended
from a noble, Catholic family.   Already before entering

[1] John Hill Burton, *Scot Abroad*, ii. 316.
[2] *Memoirs of his own Life and Times*, p. 14.
[3] The book has a very long title; it is usually cited as *Munro's Expedition*.
[4] Jas. Grant, *Memoirs and Adventures of Sir J. Hepburn*.

the service of the King of Sweden, he had fought against
Stanislas of Poland for the new elected King of Bohemia,
Frederic, whose wife was, as we have seen, a Stuart
Princess. Patriotic feelings had overcome his religious
scruples. Many of his like-minded countrymen under
the leadership of Sir Andrew Grey had gone with him
and everywhere earned the greatest praise for their
bravery. Whenever an enterprise of a particularly daring
character was to be undertaken, it was mostly Hepburn,
who was chosen for it; and thanks to his eminent gifts
of strategy and his equally great courage, he generally
succeeded in bringing the matter to a victorious issue.

There was in his regiment a certain Colonel Edmond,
the son of a baker at Stirling. He once performed the
feat of swimming, his sword between his teeth, across the
Danube, stealthily passed the Imperial outposts and,
favoured by the darkness of the night, penetrated into
the Austrian camp, where by stratagem and his giant
strength he managed to bind one of the most famous
warriors of the day—the French Count and Imperial
general Bucquoi. Then he swam back with his prisoner,
and having arrived amongst his own, introduced him to
his General, the Prince of Orange. Others equally
daring were not wanting, notably three brothers Haig,
Robert, George and James. Their mother had been
nurse to the Queen of Bohemia. All three fell in the
war fighting bravely for their fair foster-sister.

In 1630, the Scots whom Colonel Lumsden had in the
meantime brought to Germany, the corps of Hargate and
Mackay's Highlanders, were united in one Brigade, bearing henceforward the name of the Green or Hepburn's
Scottish Brigade.[1] Mackay's Highlanders had taken part
in the unfortunate struggle of the King of Denmark, who
was fighting on the side of the Protestants against the
Imperialists. They had distinguished themselves in the
siege of Stralsund, so long and so obstinately attacked by

---

[1] It was the second of the thirteen Regiments of Scotch soldiers in the
army of Gustavus Adolfus. The name is not derived from the colour of
the standard, but of the tartans.

Wallenstein, by their energetic labours for the defence of the city, and had then by order of the King retired to Wolgast after the loss of five hundred men, leaving the defence of the great fortress in the hands of the Swedes and of their famous countryman, General Alexander Leslie. Finally, when a separate peace between the Emperor and the King of Denmark had been concluded, they were with 'abundant thanks and rich rewards' dismissed by the latter (1629). In the same year their leader Mackay was made Colonel by Gustavus Adolfus.[1] His newly levied Scottish regiment, however, suffered shipwreck off the coast of Rügen Island, on the way to the Swedish army, and Rügen was still held by the Imperialists. The soldiers had saved their lives and their muskets, but they possessed no ammunition. In this plight Colonel Munro succeeded in discovering an old castle, belonging to a Duke of Pommerania and a secret friend of the King of Sweden near the small town of Rügenwalde. For a present of powder and lead he promised him to clear the island of the enemy. A well prepared and executed midnight-attack put him in possession of the town. A panic spread among the Imperialists, who had never expected any danger in this direction, and it was not long before the whole island was in the hands of the Scots. They retained it for nine weeks, when Colonel Hepburn came to relieve them, who formed the lairds and peasants of the district into a small army and led it well-armed and well-drilled to the King of Sweden. In the meantime the Highlanders had marched to Schiefelbein, a small fortified place in Brandenburg, in order to obstruct the passage of the Austrians, who were advancing for the relief of Colberg. They were commanded to hold the town as long as possible and to defend the castle or fort to the last man. How well they fulfilled this task an eloquent Latin Ode

---

[1] Valuable documents of this time in possession of Lord Reay were thought lost for a century. They were discovered in 1885. Amongst them are original letters of the King of Denmark, Count Rantzau and Gustavus Adolfus. See Appendix.

tells us, printed in front of Munro's Memoirs and bearing the title: "Schiefelbeinum urbs et arx Marchiae Brandenburgicae a generoso Domino Roberto Munro bene defensae."[1]

The first exploit of the united Scottish Brigade was the taking of the two strong fortresses: Frankfurt-on-the-Oder and Landsberg. During the assault on the former, Hepburn himself was wounded in the leg. Gustavus Adolfus had inflamed the courage of his Scottish troops by reminding them of Tilly's pillage of New-Brandenburg, where so many of their countrymen, after a stubborn, nine-days' defence, had fallen victims to the enraged and cruel general.[2]

Hepburn then marched to Leipzig (1631). Sir James Ramsay was in command of the vanguard, and then it was on the 7th of September "after we had in the early morning, as the larke begunne to peep commended ourselbes and the event of the day to God," that the great battle commenced.[3] Whilst the Imperial cavalry scattered the Saxons on the left wing, the Scotch stood firm, firing for the first time in platoons. Hepburn formed a square and, when the Austrians had approached near enough, caused his victorious pikemen to advance. In the meantime Lord Reay's Highlanders were equally successful. With terror did the Imperialists see them, the 'right hand of the King' as they were called, and it was not long before they yielded to their impetuous onslaught. Soon the defeat became a rout. If it had not been for the dust favouring their flight, the loss of the enemy would have been much greater still. "We were not able," says Munro, "by the rising of the dust to see about us, much less discerning the way of our enemies or the rest of our brigades, whereupon, having a drummer

---

[1] The author is a certain M.D., also known as a Latin poet with the name of Narsius. Cp. *Allgem. Deutsche Biographie*, vol. 23.

[2] The records of New-Brandenburg (in Mecklenburg Strelitz) have unfortunately been destroyed by fire in the XVIIth Century. Boll in his *History of Mecklenburg* (ii. 99) mentions that Lieut.-Colonel Lintz (*i.e.* Lindsay), a Scottish Baron, held the post at the Gate of Treptow.

[3] Munro, *His Expedition*, ii. 63.

by me, I caused him to beat the Scotch march, which recollected our friends unto us."[1]

Gustavus thanked the Green Brigade publicly before the whole army for their splendid services. An enormous booty fell into his hands; but instead of making use of the opportunity of pursuing the wounded General Tilly, he victoriously marched on to Halle. Seeing Hepburn there at a great parade he dismounted and gave his officers a long address praising the courage and the discipline of the Scottish troops. The Swedish generals jumped from their horses and kissed the King's hand, whilst the soldiers amidst the deafening din of the drums and the lowering of the standards filled the air with shouts of "Vivat Gustavus."

It was on the 11th of September 1631 that Hepburn took possession of the town. On the evening of that day the King, accompanied by all his officers, went to the Ulric Church to thank God for the victory, and there "I heard," says Munro, "the sweetest melodious musicke that could be heard and I also did see the most beautiful women Dutchland could afford."[2]

On the following Monday the Elector of Saxony and other Protestant princes came on a visit. Hepburn was presented to them and received abundance of praise. To his friend Munro the King said jestingly, taking him by the hand: "Munro, I wish you could to-night be our field-marshal of the bottle and the glasses to entertain my guests, but you have not the head for it."

From Halle the army proceeded in two distinct columns across the Thuringian Forest[3] into Franconia, to clear the country of the enemy. At Würzburg the forces of Hep-

---

[1] This "March of the Scots" was the terror of the Spaniards in Holland and the Austrians in Germany. German and Swedish troops often used it to secure their positions from attacks. It was composed in 1527 for the old guard of King James V. See Munro, *Exped.*

[2] Munro, *His Expedition*, ii. 74.

[3] "On September 28th the King marched from Ilmenau even into the thickest of the Duringer Forest. And for the soldiers better seeing their way in the night time, were there wisps and cresset-lights made in pans and hung upon the trees, with other such like provision." *Swedish Intelligencer*, ii. 6.

burn and the King reunited. The town itself surrendered
without striking a blow; the keys having been presented
to the King in the name of the bishop and the terrified
citizens by another Scotsman named Ogilvie, who was a
priest in the Scotch Benedictine Monastery. A more
difficult task it proved to reduce the strongly fortified
Marienberg on the other side of the Main-River. Situated
on a rock, and one arch of the bridge over the river being
broken, it almost seemed impregnable. Moreover the guns
of the fortress swept every approach. But the rumour
of the great treasure heaped up in the town, and of the
famous cellars with the still more famous wines, excited
the soldiers to dare their utmost. Only a single plank
stretched from arch to arch some fifty feet above the
rapid stream, and yet the Scots, under Sir James Ramsay
and Sir John Hamilton, succeeded, partly in boats, partly
filing across the bridge in swift succession, to carry the
out-works, after which the success of the final attack by
the Swedes was assured. Thirty-four cannons, rich
treasure in money and in silver and gold vessels from
the treasure-house of the Prince and the Churches, many
wagon-loads of wine and stores great enough to feed
them for many a year, fell into the hands of the Swedes.
The nuns of the towns were brought back under military
protection. The library of the Jesuits was sent to the
Swedish University of Upsala, and rich rewards were
given to the chief commanders. Sir James Ramsay
received estates in Mecklenburg in acknowledgment of
his excellent services and was made Governor of Hanau.

In the meantime the King flushed with success knew
no rest. Scarcely had the Imperial troops at Frankfurt-
on-the-Maine surrendered and the Scots found out that
the wine in that neighbourhood was sweet "and ripe and
as abundant as water,"[1] when the Spaniards in the
Palatinate engaged his attention. The great difficulty

[1] Munro gives a very enthusiastic description of Frankfurt. "The
towne is so pleasant for ayre, situation, buildings, traffique, commerce
with all nations by water and by land that it is and may be thought the
garden of Germany." *Exped.* ii. 89.

was the crossing of the Rhine, especially as the enemy had destroyed and burned every craft they could lay hands on. Count Brahe, however, and Hepburn succeeded at last in finding some small boats, in which they crossed the river ; having entrenched themselves in all haste they drove away the Spanish Cuirassiers, who fled partly towards Mainz, partly towards Oppenheim, a strongly fortified place on the Rhine, well defended by a body of brave Italians and Burgundians, "such seasoned old blades as the King of Sweden had not met since the Battle of Leipzig."

Colonel Hepburn received the command to capture the "sconce" that was lying opposite the town on the other side of the river. On the afternoon of the 4th of December, a bitterly cold day, when the country was covered far and wide with a sheet of snow and ice, he was sitting with his friend Munro behind the earth-works enjoying the contents of a jug of country-wine. Suddenly the garrison of Oppenheim, being roused by the light of the watch-fires reflected by the snow, fired a thirty-two pounder across the river, which buried itself quite close to the two friends in Hepburn's old travelling coach. All night the firing continued. A sortie of two hundred Burgundians was repulsed by the Scots. On the following day the "sconce" surrendered on favourable terms.

Then the King on one side and Hepburn, who had crossed the river on 107 boats sent by Gustavus, on the other, commenced the assault of the castle. But how great was their astonishment, when they met fugitives leaping the walls, throwing away their arms and crying for quarter. There was heard also musketry-fire within. The mystery was soon explained. Colonel Ramsay in his impulsive eagerness had on secret paths penetrated into the castle with only two hundred Scots before the King, and when the latter saw the little band drawn up at the gate to salute him, he addressed them with : "My brave Scots, why have you been too quick for me?"[1]

[1] The *Swedish Intelligencer*, a contemporaneous newspaper of London, confirms these facts and adds, that two hundred Spaniards were cut

Encouraged by this victory the King at once marched against Mainz, one of the strongest fortresses in the whole seat of the war. Here also Hepburn was given the most dangerous place in the besieging army. He threw up his parallels not far from the so-called Galgenthor, *i.e.* gallows gate, and before daybreak he had sufficiently screened himself from the fire of the enemy by gabions earth-works, etc. Munro gives us a very graphic account of these days. One night the Swedish Colonel Axel Lily had come on a visit. Hepburn and Munro had chosen a spot where the snow had been cleared away and sitting before a large fire, enjoyed what their cooks had been roasting on old ramrods. Every moment there was a flash of light on the dark ramparts of the citadel and the canon balls whizzed over their heads and were lost in the night or fell into the deep Rhine. Then Lily said jestingly, stooping after one of those flashes, "What would they think of me, if anything happened to me here? I have no business here and am exposed to their cannons." Immediately after these words the enemy fired another shot, which, after piercing the defective entrenchment, tore away his leg. Hepburn's men carried him to a surgeon in a sheltered place and the King showed him every attention. Don Philipp, the commander of Mainz, surrendered unexpectedly on the following morning without waiting for the final assault. Gustavus entered the town in triumph. Eighty cannons and the rich library of the Elector were among his booty. He received moreover 200,000 florins as ransom and 180,000 from the Jews, who thereby purchased the safety of their Synagogue. Hepburn remained in Mainz until the month of March.[1] Later in the year he contributed

down in this action, and eight colours taken, the first the King ever took from Spain. *Sw. Intelligencer*, ii. 47. Jas. Grant, *Memoirs*, p. 144.

To this day the so-called Schwedensäule = Swede's column, indicates the place where Gustavus crossed the river at Oppenheim.

[1] About the same time Kreuznach, Bingen and Bacharach were taken by the Scots under Sir James Ramsay. Another Colonel Ramsay, Alexander, was made Governor of Kreuznach.

essentially to the success of the Swedish King before
Donauwörth, by occupying a strategically important point,
and entering the town by a circuitous route whilst the
King assailed it in front.   After the capture and when
some quiet had been restored, the King sent for the
colonel, who had to work his way through streets crowded
with fugitives, broken gun-carriages, dead horses and
soldiers, till he came to the beautiful house, where
Gustavus, Frederik, the King of Bohemia, and other
princes were regaling themselves after the labours of the
night.   The King thanked Hepburn for his faithful
services and ascribed the conquest of the town to his
advice to circumvent it.   After Donauwörth Augsburg
was occupied on the 8th of April; [1] Munich on the 7th of
May.   Hepburn was made governor of it, and it was to
his regiments that the King entrusted, much to the disgust
of the Swedes, the protection of his person.   Munro's
description of the palace is full of interest.   Round about
it there were beautiful gardens with fish ponds and
fountains.   One of them represented Perseus with the
head of Medusa.   In the large park "plentie of hares
could be seen"; there were also Tennis Courts in which
the kings sometimes "did recreat" themselves. [2]   In connection with the palace there were magnificent galleries
and a rare library with many precious books.   It was
here that the two friends Hepburn and Munro walked
together recalling to their memories the old University
days of Cambridge, or turning up the long neglected
Classics.   In the arsenal the King found an enormous
booty; the so-called "twelve apostles" and many other
cannons were found hidden under the floor.   In one of
them there were discovered 150,000 ducats sewed up in
cartridges.   Hepburn remained in Munich whilst Gustavus
Adolfus took up his quarters at Augsburg and General

---

[1] Munro is careful to give us the text of the sermon preached at the
thanksgiving service in the Church of St Anne before the King of
Sweden, the King of Bohemia, the Duke of Weimar and other poten-
tates.   It was contained in the fifth verse of the 12th Psalm.

[2] *Exped.* ii. 125.

Ruthven was pursuing the enemy as far as the Lake of Constanz.

In the beginning of June the whole Protestant army was drawn together at Nürnberg to oppose the progress of Wallenstein. With incredible exertions the town was fortified by the King. But where open violence did not succeed, famine and sickness did their work. After a close siege of fifty-eight days on the day of St Bartholomew (Aug. 24th) Gustavus Adolfus, who had tried in vain to drive the Imperial leader out of his strong position by sorties or to starve him by intercepting his provisions, ventured to attack his almost impregnable camp. The fight lasted for ten hours. "Finally when the night came on," Schiller writes in his *History of the Thirty Years' War*, "the King anxiously looked for an officer to order a few Swedish regiments which had penetrated too far, to retreat. His eye caught Colonel Hebron, a brave Scotsman, whom his innate courage only had driven out of the camp, to share the dangers of the day. Angry at the King, who not long ago in a perilous military enterprise had preferred a junior officer to him, he had made a rash vow never to draw sword for the King again. To him Gustavus now turned and having praised his heroic courage, he requests him to order the retreat of the regiments. 'Sire,' replied the brave officer, 'that is the only service I cannot refuse Your Majesty, for there is danger in it,' and he immediately galloped off to deliver his message."

Not long after this meeting the King withdrew in good order to Neustadt, and here Hepburn and Hamilton took their leave of him. The reason adduced by Schiller has not been the only one, that caused the proud Scot to take a step which must have been distasteful to an officer of his merit, but it contributed perhaps to make the cup of discontent flow over. As we have seen above, he could not brook the King's jest about his religion. He was proudly conscious to have drawn his sword for the Queen of Bohemia, a princess of his own native country. Added hereto was the opinion then common amongst the Scottish officers, that neither the Marquis of Hamilton nor Lieut.-

Colonel Douglas had been treated by the King with due respect.[1] Be this as it may, a rupture ensued, and Hepburn and the Marquis, together with two other Scottish officers, left the Swedish service. Their remaining countrymen accompanied them about a mile from Neustadt, and when the moment came for these noble heroes to "bid a long good-night to all their loving comrades, the separation was like that which death makes betwixt friends and the soule of man, being sorry that those who had lived so long together in amitie and friendship, also in mutuall dangers should part; fearing we should never meet againe, the splendour of our former mirth was overshadowed with a cloud of grief and sorrow, which dissolved in mutuall tears."[1]

As to Hepburn this fear should not be realised. He was to meet his old companions in arms again, if only for a short time.

In the meantime the Scottish Brigade had been weakened by the terrible losses, especially before Nürnberg, to such an extent, that the King resolved not to take it on his march to Saxony, but to leave it in quarters in Suabia to recruit their strength. Thus he took leave of his faithful Scots at Donauwörth before the whole army. "The King in particular expressed his affection to me," says Munro, "showing he was so grieved to leave us behinde, yet in respect of the long march to Saxony and considering the weakness of both our regiments that were weakened by the toill of warre, and in consideration of that former good service he had ordered musterplaces for us, the best in Schwabland, against his returne, and then calling on Palsgraf Christian, to whom he had given command over us recommending us particularly unto him and desired him to give us contentment of the monies that were then resting unto us, the first money was to be received at Augsburg."[2]

---

[1] The Marquis after his first little army had been decimated, expected to have another army to command, but the King "amused him with delay." As to Douglas he had by some breach of etiquette incurred the King's displeasure. [2] Munro, *His Expedtion*, ii. 159.

"As soone as His Majesty had dined," continues Munro, "with the Queene, going to his coach I took leave of His Majesty in presence of General Baner, Palsgraf Christian and Sir Patrick Ruthven; being the most dolefull parting I ever suffered having been both I and the Regiment with His Majesty on all services of importance since His Majesty's upbreaking from Stettin till his parting at Donauwörth on the 11th of October 1632.[1]

Hepburn paid a short visit to his native country, using the opportunity of levying another 2000 men for the King. Shortly afterwards he offered his services to the King of France at that time an ally of the Swedes. No sooner had he arrived in Paris than he was made a 'maréchal de camp'[2] and attached to the army of Turenne, who was waging war against the Imperial troops in Alsace. After he had distinguished himself in the siege of La Mothe, he crossed the Rhine in mid-winter and hastened towards Heidelberg in order to succour the small, hard pressed Swedish garrison there. The mountains were covered with snow. The castle, surrounded by wall and moat, had a special interest for him, as Princess Elizabeth Stuart, the wife of the sovereign of the land, had built there in imitation of her old palace at Linlithgow the so-called English Buildings. Scarcely had he reached the town, when he placed himself at the head of his troops and fighting bravely broke the encircling lines of the besiegers, drove them out of the Neckar-valley and made himself master of the famous castle.

Not long afterwards Duke Bernhard of Weimar, then one of the first leaders of the Swedish army, effected a junction with the troops of Louis XIII, having himself about 4000 horsemen and about 2000 Scottish soldiers, all that had been left of the thirteen regiments in the service of the King of Sweden. With beating of drums,

---

[1] Munro, *His Expedition*, ii. 160 f.
[2] In the Scottish Guard of France, so intimately connected with the most glorious days of the French army and commanded by the Marquis of Huntly Gordon, he found many old companions of arms.

music and loud cries did these Scots salute their old commander, and the last remaining piper of Mackay's
Highlanders played a long, shrill note of welcome on his
warlike instrument. Having been incorporated with the
Franco-Scottish Guard they now formed the "Régiment
d'Hébron,"[1] as it was called, one of the best equipped as
well as the bravest regiments of the whole of the French
army.

It is well known that the campaign of the French
troops against the Imperial general Gallas and the Duke
of Lorraine finally ended in disaster (1635). The army
of La Valette, Bernhard of Weimar and Hepburn cover-
ing the rear had to beat a retreat from the Rhine through
the hills of Lorraine, closely pressed by the enemy.

During this terrible time Hepburn proved the nobility of
his character. He comforted and encouraged those whose
energy was about to flag; whilst he at the same time
sternly opposed the mutinous. Many wounded soldiers
had to be left behind on this terrible flight, falling a
prey to the wolves and to the "hyenas of the battlefield."

The end of Hepburn's career we can only touch upon
shortly. It lies outside the scope of our immediate
subject and may be read in full elsewhere.[2]

The King of France, Louis XIII, resolved in the spring
of 1636, nothing daunted by the terrible legacy of 1635,
to carry on the war with renewed vigour. He appointed
La Valette again Commander-in-Chief and made Hepburn
'Maréchal de France.' But the days of the latter were
numbered. The siege of Savernes or Zabern in Alsace
was his last exploit. The guns of Duke Bernhard had
at last succeeded in making a breach in the walls, and the
French and Scottish troops advanced to the final assault.
With flying colours over heaps of ruins and exposed to
a murderous fire they reached the hilltop. But here
the commander of the little fortress, Colonel Mülheim,
confronted them with his heavily armed Germans. A

---

[1] This is the way the name of Hepburn is spelled in French, "le nom
d'Hepburn étant difficile à prononcer."

[2] Cp. J. Grant, *Memoirs of Hepburn.*

last, frightful struggle ensued, during which the plumes of Turenne and Hepburn were seen waving in the thickest melee. Then—after a carnage of three hours—the French had to retreat. Two other attempts to take the place were made, both equally fruitless. At last the three commanders resolved to redouble their efforts and make a last attempt. For this purpose Hepburn was inspecting a breech under the fire of the hostile batteries. His glittering armour gave the enemy a welcome aim; a bullet hit him in the neck, on a spot that his mail did not protect. He fell from his charger and his faithful Scots carried him away. With the thunder of the canons in his ear, his sword by his side and surrounded by his faithful comrades, his face turned towards the setting sun, the gallant warrior breathed his last at the early age of thirty-seven years and before the Marshall's staff, sent by King Louis, had reached him. His last words expressed a regret, that he was to be buried so far from the lonely church of his native place.[1] His death was the signal for the fourth assault, which led to victory. The dead body, helmet and sword were brought to Toul and deposited in the southern aisle of the magnificent cathedral. Louis XIV erected a monument in honour of the departed, bearing the terse incription: "To the best soldier in Christendom."

In the meantime those Scottish soldiers that had been levied in 1631, consisting of five battalions under Lieutenant-Colonel Robert Stuart, Sir Arthur Forbes, Sir Frederick Hamilton, Col. Munro of Obstell and Col. Robt. Leslie, had been doing good work in the

[1] When Cardinal Richelieu heard the sad news, he wrote to La Valette: "I cannot tell you, how deeply I am moved by the death of poor Hepburn, not only on account of the great esteem I personally have felt for him always, but because of the fidelity and zeal with which he always served His Majesty the King. I am, indeed, quite inconsolable and no doubt you will say the same of yourself. He was just the man needed in our position then as well as now. I have ordered that all honour should be shown to his memory, prayers said, etc. Savernes has been paid for dearly, but we must bear in submission what God has sent."— *Richelieu to La Valette, July 20, 1636.*

North of Germany under the leadership of the Swedish general Todt. They helped to clear all Mecklenburg of the enemy and to storm many fortresses. But none of their own officers obtained the fame of Hepburn or Munro or Alexander Leslie.

During the second half of the Thirty Years' War we do not hear so much of Scottish soldiers and their deeds as before. The death of Gustavus Adolfus had robbed it of its military lustre : none of the present leaders on the Protestant side could vie with him as to fame and generalship. Moreover, the Battle of Nördlingen, in which the Protestants were defeated (1634), had decimated, nay, well nigh annihilated the Scots, and their native land was not able continually to replace the lost forces. Finally, the political situation in Scotland most urgently required the presence of officers and soldiers at home where the thundercloud of civil war was threatening and at last broke forth in storm and lightning.

Now and then, however, the report of new levies reaches us. Thus in 1637, when the Captains John Skene, John Kerr, John Finlayson and Lumsden raised several regiments for service in Germany. They were to be transported by sea to Wolgast, a small town and harbour in Pomerania on the Baltic. But fate was against them. From Leith, where part of the troops had taken shipping on board a Lübeck barque called " Falcon," —Captain Cockburn,—they sailed to Aberdeen there to take in provisions. On the fifth night, however, there arose such a tempest accompanied by a tremendous tidal wave, that the ship was torn from its anchorage, driven into the open sea, and thrown a complete wreck[1] on the neighbouring shore. Many recruits were drowned ; others, " that in the danger of death thought themselves released from their oath," deserted. The Magistrates of Aberdeen confirm the sad fact in a long letter to the Queen of Sweden and to the senate of Lübeck.[2]

---

[1] " Fracta in minutissimas partes."

[2] Letter dated October 10th, 1637, in the Propinquity Books of Aberdeen.

We get a glimpse in this report of the growing dis-
organisation of these troops.   In time the material became
worse and the misery caused by these long-continued
forced levies greater.   Already ten years earlier the
King of Scotland and his Council, in order to meet the
demand for Scottish mercenaries on the part of the
King of Denmark, Count Mansfeldt and Lord Reay, had
to have recourse to extreme measures.   The order was
given to seize upon all vagabonds of the high road, all
incorrigible bankrupts and all vagrants of whatever description.   Moreover, the attention of the chiefs of the
Highland Clans was drawn by a letter written by the
King's own hand to the fact, that there were many
young idlers on their vast estates, who could not do
better than to don the uniform.   In this remarkable
way in the year 1626-27 alone, ten to twelve thousand
Scotsmen were sent abroad, in other words, about the
twentieth part of the whole male population.[1]

The question what became of all these men is not
hard to answer: the majority of them rest unheeded and
without stone or cross on the blood-drenched battlefields
of Germany; some were fortunate enough to see their
native country again and perhaps relate their adventures
in foreign countries to a crowd of eager listeners, or
possibly to again take up arms for Leslie on the side
of the Covenanters or for Montrose and the King.   No
doubt those of them fared best—speaking relatively—
who at once entered the service of Gustavus Adolfus.
There they had at any rate a noble pattern, and discipline
and regular pay were, if not always accomplished, at least
aspired to.

It now remains to us shortly to indicate the fate of
some other Scottish officers during the Thirty Years' War.

Donald Mackay, or Lord Reay as he is usually called,

---

[1] See Masson in the Introduction to the *Register of Privy Council of
Scotland*, 2nd series, vol. i., Edinb. 1900.   The levies had first been
set afoot by a pressing letter of Gustavus Adolfus, dated Sept. 23rd,
1623.   In the same year Sir James Spence levied 1200 men for the war
in Poland.

the leader of the Highlanders, returned to Scotland as early as 1632. The premature death of his patron, the King of Sweden, was a terrible blow for him. Of the large sums of money he had spent to pay his recruits, he received nothing back; being thus compelled to sell part of his estates for the payment of his debts. During the Civil Wars, fighting on the side of the King, he was made prisoner. His liberation, as being a Danish officer, was vainly demanded by the King of Denmark. Set free at last by Montrose he retired to Copenhagen and the court of his first sovereign. In Denmark he died, highly honoured, of grief for the execution of Charles I, in 1649. A Danish frigate brought his body in state to Scotland.

Baron Foulis or Fowlis, Colonel Robt. Munro, one of the forty or fifty officers of that name in the army of Gustavus Adolfus, had been wounded in his right foot at the crossing of the Danube in 1632 and carried to Ulm, where Sir Patrick Ruthven was Governor. Here he lived in the house of a barber and surgeon called Michael Rietmüller and died towards the end of April of the same year. By permission of the magistrates he was buried in the Franciscan or " Barfüsserkirche," where also his standard, armour and spurs were hung up. Magister Balthasar Kerner delivered his funeral sermon on the 29th of April.[1]

One of the most interesting men among the Scottish officers of the Thirty Years' War, a man who reminds one of Wallenstein in his tragical fate, is doubtlessly the above-mentioned General Sir James Ramsay. German poetry and prose have taken hold of him as of a great central figure in the fierce struggle, and the research of the German historian has left us a portrait of him more accurately sketched than that of other Scottish officers.[2] Even the great German Biographical Dictionary has given

[1] See Appendix.
[2] In the famous seventeenth century novel *Simplicissimus* by Grimmelshausen Ramsay is introduced as the hero's uncle and it is said of him, that he was " a brave and heroic soldier " (i., chapters 19-34, ii., 1-13).

him a place among its German heroes, and whilst it relates
his valorous deeds and sad end in words of praise and
pity on the authority of historical documents, legend and
tradition have been busy weaving a string of wonderful
stories around his unknown grave.

Born of noble race about the year 1589 Ramsay
received a good education and university training in
Scotland. He seems to have developed early a warlike
as well as a poetical spirit.[1] When James VI became
King, he accompanied him to England and for some time
held some office at the court. In 1630 he entered the
army of the King of Sweden under the Duke of Hamilton,
known henceforth as the " black " Ramsay to distinguish
him from a second Sir James Ramsay called the "fair."
In the battle of Breitenfeld he commanded part of the
reserve of the first line-of-battle, and during the attack
on the Marienberg, the strong citadel of Würzburg, he
received, as we have seen, a shot in his left arm, which
disabled him from taking part in the campaign of the
following year. After the disastrous battle at Nördlingen
in 1634 annihilating, as it did, with one fell stroke all
previous advantages gained by the Evangelical armies,
he was chosen by Bernhard, the Duke of Weimar then
in chief-command, as Governor of the important fortress
of Hanau situated on the Main River, a short distance
from Frankfurt; and this appointment had been confirmed
by Count Philip Moritz of Hanau-Münzenberg, who
owned the town and the surrounding district.[2] On the

His picture appeared first in the *Theatrum Europaeum*, iii. 910, with the
following legend: Illustris Generosus Dominus Dominus Jacobus Ramsay,
Scotus, Eques auratus, Gen. Mag. sc. Anno Aetatis 47, 1636. In
English literature nothing is known of him but the meagre sketch of his
life by Lord Hailes (Dalrymple). The chief German source is Colonel
R. Wille's book: *Hanau in the Thirty Years' War, Hanau im Dreissig-
iährigen Kriege*, Hanau 1886, a most fascinating and painstaking work.

[1] The German-Latin poet John Cressius says of him : " Scotia quem
genuit, quem lactavere Camoenae." (Dalrymple, *Life of Ramsay*.)

[2] He was one of the many weak princes attached to the Protestant
side. When misfortune overtook the Swedes, he fled before the
approaching storm to the Hague in Holland; leaving the defence of his
own capital and country to Ramsay.

second of October 1634 he entered the fortress, the
garrison of which, inclusive of the militia, amounted to
about 3000 men.   Immediately he set to work to prepare
everything that was requisite for a successful and probably long-continued defence of the place.   But besides
this according to the approved maxim that the greatest
strength of the defence consists in the garrison taking the
offensive as often as possible, he made a series of skilfully
conducted and successful sallies.[1] By these means he not
only encouraged the spirit of his troops but solved the
problem of bringing in supplies often from a great distance.

In spite of these temporary encouragements the distress
in the beleaguered town rose to a terrible height.
Together with the scarcity of money and bread the
plague or the " Black Death," as it is called in German,
appeared and increased during the hot summer months,
rendered still more violent by the crowding together of
so many fugitives in a narrow space and by the pestiferous
exhalations of the stagnant waters in the fosses.

But neither Ramsay nor the citizens who shared his
patriotic adherence to the evangelical cause, ever thought
of surrender, although the trenches of the Imperial
general Lamboy, who was conducting the siege, now
completely surrounded the town in a wide circle.   On
the other hand the Governor, " an astute and excellent
schemer," discontinuing his sallies on account of the small
number of his troops, commenced a series of sham-negotia-
tions with the enemy.[2]   At one time he proposed sending
a messenger to the Swedish Chancellor Oxenstierna or to
the Duke Bernhard in order to obtain their consent to
the surrender of the fortress, a consent which at that time,
as he knew well, was not to be thought of; at another
time he advanced the still more extraordinary proposition
to hand over the town provisionally to the protection

---

[1] Especially brilliant was the retaking of the small town of Gelnhausen,
then occupied by the Imperialists.   The careless enemy, surprised in his
sleep, lost many dead and prisoners, also twelve standards, the whole
baggage and all their provisions.

[2] Wille, *l.c.*, p. 236.

of a neutral prince, such as the King of England or the Prince of Orange, and when the parties had at last agreed to accept the Landgraf George of Hesse-Darmstadt and the Elector of Mayence as mediators, he managed to protract their deliberations from month to month till they were broken off as useless. After this period of rest the old sallies and punitive expeditions were again resorted to; and the Governor was so "joyful and of good courage" in consequence of the successful issue of the most of them,[1] that he presented General Lamboy, who had sent him the scornful gift of two fat pigs, with fifty pounds of carp, caught in the moats, in return; adding for the fun of it ("aus Kurtzweil") the mocking request to "send him some news, especially as to the rumour current in his part, of the town of Hanau being besieged."[2]

In the meantime Lamboy had received reinforcements so that his forces now numbered 4000 to 5000 men. His soldiers grew daily more insolent, his officers already divided the best quarters of the doomed town amongst themselves, whilst within the fortress the situation became daily more serious. Without the iron rule of Ramsay, combined with his skill and his strict justice, which was acknowledged by all;[3] without the equally great self-sacrifice of the magistrates, a further defence would no longer have been possible. As it was, the strictest measures were adopted and most conscientiously carried out, which appeared necessary. Against threatening mutiny the utmost severity was shown; orders against the waste of powder and shot were issued; the ammunition of the Scottish company, which formed an unshaken and always reliable body-guard of the Governor, was doubled. Ramsay further regulated with extraordinary care the supply of food-stuffs; all public-houses were

---

[1] Once he captured four ships loaded with provisions and ammunition on the Main River by night. Wille, *l.c.*, p. 249.

[2] Chemnitz, *Der Schwedisch-Deutsche Krieg* (*The Swedish-German War*), ii. 963.

[3] The Magistrates acknowledged Ramsay's great merits by presenting him with a costly gold chain on the 31st Dec. 1635. Wille, p. 262.

closed except one, where, under the supervision of the
military, twice a week a certain small quantity of wine was
being sold. In spite of all these measures, however, a
terrible time of misery commenced in the beleaguered
town in the spring of 1636. People ate horse and dogs'
flesh; and a contemporary chronicler relates that "cats
were esteemed venison." It was no rare occurrence that
the flesh of dead men and beasts was bought or stolen
from the executioner. Mortality had increased at a fear-
ful rate: the garrison being reduced to only 400 or 500
men. Only for a few weeks longer was resistance possible.
Hanau's deliverance is due to two causes; the inexplicable
delay of General Lamboy in proceeding to the assault; and
in the final resolution of Landgraf William V of Hesse-
Kassel not to consider himself bound any longer by the
existing truce, but to hasten to the assistance of the
distressed fortress. He was urged to adopt this course
by his wife, a high-minded and noble lady and a native
of Hanau. On the 22nd of June he joined his forces
with those of the Swedish Field-marshal Alexander Leslie.
Ramsay, who maintained an excellent service of scouts,
had received the welcome news of the approach of his
friends. Losing no time he gave fire-signals from the
top of the castle-tower and fired his guns at frequent
intervals. Early on the 23rd the attack on the strong
position of the Imperial general commenced, and it was
not long before the enemy was completely routed. Landgraf William and Leslie entered the town amid the
ringing of bells and the joyful shouts of the populace; six
hundred waggon loads of provisions and herds of cattle
for slaughtering accompanied them.[1] After a solemn
thanksgiving service the prince at once visited Ramsay,
the brave defender, in his quarters to consult about further
military measures.

The following time of rest the Governor, whose power
also extended over the fortified places of the surrounding

[1] In remembrance of the deliverance of the town the so-called
"Lamboy" festival is celebrated at Hanau to this day on the 13th of
June.

district, employed in the most effectual manner. First
of all he increased his garrison, and having succeeded in
doing this he again undertook frequent and far extending punitive incursions to the terror of his enemies.
Travellers who showed themselves in the territory of
Hanau had to produce "Ramsay-passports"; this order
extended to the merchants from Cologne and Holland,
who desired to visit the great Fair of Frankfurt. In
short, the whole country was seized with a "Ramsay-
terror." [1]

But there was more work cut out for the restless
General. Cries of help had reached him from the
garrison of Hermanstein or Ehrenbreitstein on the Rhine,
as it is now called, which was then besieged by the
Imperialists. He therefore undertook the difficult and,
considering the straitened circumstances he himself was
placed in, splendidly generous task of revictualling the
fortress by way of the river. The bold enterprise
succeeded the first time, but on being repeated a second
time the ship fell into the hands of the more watchful
and suspicious enemy.

Ramsay seems even to have considered the plan of
reconquering the Palatinate for the unfortunate nephew
of Charles I. Already in 1634 he had received the
visit of Sir George Douglas, the English ambassador to
Poland,[2] and it is possible that already at that time he
offered his services. This offer he now, at a more
favourable juncture, repeated, if 6000 men were placed
at his disposal. But England hesitated, and the proper
moment was lost for ever.[3]

Moreover, the Imperial troops again commenced— in
the beginning of July—to attract his earnest attention.
After the final fall of Ehrenbreitstein the besieging forces
of General von Werth had become free and were marching

---

[1] The fair at Frankfurt in 1637 was postponed on account of the
frequent sallies of the garrison of Hanau.

[2] Douglas was formerly officer in the Swedish army and governor of
Kreuznach.

[3] *Wille*, p. 410 f.

in the direction of Hanau. Ramsay, who knew that a second siege, owing to the superior power of the enemy and the scarcity of food would be disastrous, communicated with the Elector of Mayence, the Landraf of Hesse-Darmstadt and the city of Frankfurt with a view to an honourable treaty. After a great many subterfuges on the part of the allies, this treaty was finally signed by all parties.[1] It contained as chief-paragraphs the complete pardon of Count Philip Moritz, a free pass for Ramsay to the Swedes, the payment to him of 150,000 marks, the cession of the Mecklenburg estates that had been given to him by Gustavus Adolfus or suitable compensation, and the placing of Imperial hostages in the hands of the Swedes till all the conditions were fulfilled. From the first, however, it became clear to the penetrating mind of Ramsay, that there were not only great omissions in the treaty, but that the allies could and would not fulfil their promises. In spite of this or, shall we say, just because of this, he appended his signature to the document and the Imperial ratification was not long in following. Philip Moritz, the fugitive, was asked speedily to return to his country and Ramsay requested to give up Hanau at once. This, however, he was not prepared to do, as long as the conditions of the treaty remained unfulfilled and no mention was made of money or estates or hostages. Then followed a long time of a wearisome war of the pen; a time of proposals and counter-proposals, of allegations, irony, craft and cunning. Ramsay himself wrote several times in terms, that did want neither clearness nor bitterness. The negotiations nevertheless were continued till February 1638. At that time the wily General succeeded in procuring the original of the Imperial ratification and in

---

[1] The first sketch contained nothing of Ramsay's remuneration, nothing of the fate of the garrison. The General therefore sent it back to Mayence with the words addressed to the messengers: " Go and tell your Elector that if he does not put in the proper conditions, I shall come with my army and devastate his whole country. What would you say if I kept you here ? "

establishing the astounding fact, that the text of the treaty, as concluded at Mayence on the 31st of Aug. 1637, and that of the document signed by the emperor on Sept. 14th *did not agree.* Immediately he had his secretary draw up a collateral copy of the documents in question and sent a calm and dignified letter to the allies, in which he pointed out the contradictions.[1] But before there could be an answer to this startling communication the doom of our hero had been sealed. Philip Moritz, who seemed to have no other thought now than to get rid of the troublesome Swedes and their general and to embrace the cause of the emperor without reserve, returned to his capital in spite of Ramsay's remonstrances and before the negotiations had been concluded. All his obligations towards Sweden, all his gratitude towards the man, who by his bravery and perseverance had saved his sovereignty, were forgotten. Openly and secretly he urged the removal of Ramsay.[2] The Hessian Regiment, which formed part of the garrison, was recalled. Ramsay replied by sending letters to his countryman, General King,[3] then commanding Swedish troops in the neighbourhood of the Weser, in which he asked for reinforcements. He also sent urgent messages into Franconia for the supply of provisions. But all these plans were rendered futile by Philip, who on his part despatched other forged letters countermanding the request of additional troops and supplies.

No wonder that the Governor saw himself compelled to adopt stringent measures. He ordered the castle, which is at the same time the citadel of Hanau, to be occupied by his soldiers and the intercourse of the Count with the outside world to be restricted. Not even the

[1] See Appendix.

[2] Mayence openly proposed after the occupation of the fortress to proceed against Ramsay and his Scots according to the usage of war. (*Wille, l.c.,* p. 455.)

[3] Born about 1589 in the county of Aberdeen. After having spent some sime in the service of King Charles I, he joined the Swedes, became General, and died at Stockholm about 1651. He was buried in the Riddarholms Church.

Countess was allowed to confer with her husband. And yet violence and treason succeeded in outwitting Ramsay. A certain Major Winter, jointly with the Imperial General Graf Ludwig Heinrich of Nassau-Dillenburg, offered to seize the fortress on condition that, being successful, he should receive the 150,000 marks deposited for Ramsay. Out of his own means he had levied about 200 men for this purpose, Mayence contributed another 200, the Count of Dillenburg 300. With the greatest secrecy everything was prepared by means of bribed messengers to and from Philip Moritz; false keys for the gates were manufactured and certain signals agreed upon. On the 22nd of February, at the dawn of morning, this force succeeded in occupying the Altstadt, old town of Hanau, of surprising Ramsay's weak garrison and of getting possession of the castle. On the following day the count sent a flag of truce to the Governor asking him to surrender, a demand which was at once indignantly refused.[1] Then the fire was opened upon the New-town, during which Ramsay, according to one report in the defence of his house, where he and seventy of his soldiers had barricaded themselves;[2] according to others whilst walking up and down in front of the "White Lion," his headquarters, and giving orders,[3] was struck by a bullet in his back penetrating as far as the hip. He now felt that the further shedding of blood was useless; a drummer was sent to the Count "to ask for quarters for the General and his soldiers, as he had been badly wounded," to which the request was added that the treaty of Mayence should be observed. Ramsay was then hastily dressed and brought to the Guard-Room. Later on, when his wound seemed to admit of his removal, he was carried to the Castle of Dillenburg.[4] Here his treatment was at first friendly and considerate. He was

---

[1] *Wille*, p. 471.

[2] Pufendorf, *Schwedisch-deutscher Krieg* (*Swedish-German War*), 1688, book x.

[3] *Wille*, p. 471.

[4] Major Winter was loaded with favours at the Imperial Court and ennobled as " Baron of Güldenborn."

given a cheerful room; he was allowed to have his
secretary Dr Henckel with him. The Count, who could
not but admire his brave conduct, invited him to his table
at dinner and supper-time. He was able to receive
visitors, amongst them the most learned men of the
neighbourhood and members of noble families. He
frequently went to the "Schlosskirche" (chapel), where
service was being held in the reformed persuasion, and
partook of the sacrament. In short he proved a sort of
imprisoned lion, but a lion, whom they had not ceased to
fear. Especially at Vienna great spite and great fear were
shown towards the prisoner. They tried by force and
favour to extort all manner of secrets from him, amongst
others, how he got in possession of the original treaty;
what did he mean by saying he had a spiritus familiaris;
what were the Swedish plans of war? To all these
questions the prisoner replied calmly and deliberately, that
he was not a common culprit and not subject to the Holy
Roman Empire, but a prisoner-of-war and subject to the
Crown of Sweden, which he had always served faithfully.
It was not his fault that the treaty had been broken;
the two texts of it had been revealed to his councillor
and secretary Dr Hasman by two Imperial Commissaries.
As to his spiritus familiaris, it consisted in this, that he
knew how to put ducats upon ducats and Rosenoble upon
Rosenoble so as to procure good scouts.[1] To the
insinuation of delivering up military papers he replied
curtly, "that it was against the rule of the service and
the fidelity of an officer, to give the enemy any information of his sovereign's military plans."

Disappointed in their attempts, the Court at Vienna
had recourse to violent measures. Ramsay's secretary
was seized, carried to the capital and there put to the
rack, under the tortures of which he "gave up his
ghost." The Count of Dillenburg, who was willing
to liberate the prisoner on receipt of a high ransom
offered by him, and thus to have at least "some
feathers of the bird before he let him escape," received

[1] *Wille*, p. 481 f.

stringent orders under no circumstances to set free one that had proved an inveterate enemy to the Empire.[1] Ramsay then tried to enlist the sympathy of the King of France, now an ally of the Evangelical party; of the Queen of Sweden and of England : but all in vain. The old faithful servant had been forgotten; only death could now deliver him. "Easy it would have been for him indeed," says Wille, "to gain his liberty at once at the expense of his honour; but Ramsay's fidelity and obedience to duty repudiated and scornfully with-stood the temptation and the suggestion to earn the vile reward of treachery."

To complete the tragic fate of the prisoner it so happened, that the good and friendly relations hitherto existing between him and the Count latterly became strained. There were scenes of violent reproaches and recriminations, rising from very slight causes and, no doubt, mainly attributable to the irritable and gloomy temper of the sufferer. The Count even allowed him-self to be carried away so far by his anger that he ordered the General to be cast in irons, placed a strong guard in his room and limited his food to bread and water. Only after the lapse of several days the chains were removed, chiefly owing to the merciful interfer-ence of Count Ernst of Wittgenstein. But the hardest blow for the prisoner was the communication, withheld some time, of the Imperial order forbidding his liberation. "Now all my hopes are buried for ever," cried the unfortunate man, and abandoned himself to gloom and despair. His condition became worse every day in spite of the good-natured administrations of the Countess, and the skill—such as it was in those days—of four doctors in attendance. On the 21st of April he drew up his will,[2] but only on the 29th of June 1639 did death put an end to his cruel sufferings.[3] The Swedish Commander-in-Chief and Lady Isabella Ramsay, the widow

---

[1] *Wille*, p. 482.   [2] See Appendix.
[3] *Wille*, p. 490. The tales of his having starved himself to death or of having died insane are entirely legendary.

of the deceased, then living at St Andrews, were at once informed of the sad event. But his body was finally buried on August 18, 1650, in the town church of Dillenburg,[1] the lady mentioned, "for want of means," not having taken any steps to have his remains brought to the land of his birth.

"Thus ended the life of James Ramsay, the immortal defender of Hanau, rich in friends and admirers when fortunate, in misfortune abandoned by all and rewarded with the most cruel ingratitude by the prince who, to him alone, owed the continuance of his sovereignty."

Unlike many of his former companions-in-arms, who from motives of selfishness or dissatisfied ambition deserted their colours, he had in sufferings and imprisonment, in danger and death, kept the oath of allegiance to his Queen unshaken and in spite of temptations. But his sad end between prison-walls was none the less honourable and worthy of a brave officer, than the natural death of a soldier amidst the roar of the battle, which he had listened to so often. Honour be to his memory![2]

We now turn to another Scottish General in the service of Sweden, already mentioned in connection with the relief of Hanau, Alexander Leslie.

Field-marshal Alexander Leslie, born about 1582, who, before entering the Swedish army, had already seen service in the Netherlands as a young man, was made a knight and a general by King Gustavus at the time when the latter received the Order of the Garter in the camp at Dirschau from the hands of the ambassadors of Charles I (Sept. 23, 1626).

In May 1628, at the head of five thousand Scots and Swedes, he cut himself a way into the town of Stralsund, which was then closely invested by Wallenstein. Having thus provisioned it, he took the command instead of Colonel Seatoun, who had hitherto acted as such with a Danish force, and conducted the defence so skilfully and vigorously that he contributed much

---

[1] Ramsay's tomb cannot now be discovered.   [2] *Wille*, p. 492.

to the final retreat of that famous general. The grateful town ordered rich presents to be given to him, amongst them a gold medal struck in commemoration of the siege.[1] Leslie remained commander of the Baltic cities until 1631, when he went to England to assist the Marquis of Hamilton in his levying of troops for the Swedish service.

In the following year he met him in Germany and was appointed joint-commander of the English-Scottish auxiliaries with him. After having assisted at the siege and the taking of Frankfurt on the Oder, he was made governor of the place. As such it fell to his task to see to the proper state of defence and the provisioning of Crossen and Guben, two towns in the neighbouring district, by which the King's rear was to be protected on his southward march. Towards the end of the year Gustavus had reached Mainz, where he was joined by Leslie. Later on he shared with his leader the glory, though not the fate, of the battle of Lützen, after having timely recovered from a wound in his foot. How deeply he felt the loss of the King, which quite overclouded this victory and endangered the future of Protestantism, is seen in a letter written to the Marquis of Hamilton from Stade, on the 26th of November 1632. In it, as Terry says,[2] he emerges from his habitual reticence and gives a touching expression to his genuine grief.

"I have thought it expedient," the letter runs, "to mak your Excellencie this sad narration of the lamentable death of our most valarouse and worthie chiftaine, who, in the sixt (16th) of November, did end the constant course of all his glorious victories with his happie lyffe,

---

[1] This medal, which is still preserved in the Leslie-Melville family, shows on the obverse the arms of Stralsund surrounded by a laurel-branch and the words: Deo Optim. max. Imperio Romano Foederi posterisque 1628; on the reverse the words: Memoriae Urbis Stralsundae Ao. MDCXXVIII. Die XII. Mai a Milite Caesariano Cinctae aliquoties oppugnatae Sed Dei Gratia et ope inclytor. Regum Septentrional. Die XXVII. Juli obsidione liberatae S.P.Q.S.F.F. (fabricari fecerunt). (Sir W. Fraser, *Family of Leslie-Melville.*)

[2] Terry, *Life and Campaigns of Alexander Leslie*, 1899, p. 29.

for his Majestie went to farre on with a regiment of
Smolandis horsemen, who did not second him so well
as they showld, at the which instant ther came so thick
and darke a mist, that his owin folkis did lose him, and
he being seperate from his owin amongst his foes,
his left arme was shote in two, after the which whill he
was lying, one asked him, whate he was, he answeared,
King of Sweddin, wherupon his enemies that did compasse
him thought to have carried him away; but in the
mean while, his own folkis comeing on, striveing in
great furie to vindicate his Majestie out of ther handis,
when they saw that they most quite him againe, he
that before asked what he was, shote him through
the heade; and so did put ane end to his dayes, the
fame of whose valoure and love to the good cause sal
nevir end.   When his corpes were inbalmed ther waes
found in them fyve shottes and nyne woundis, so ar
we to our unspeakable griefe deprived of the best and
most valorouse commander that evir any soldiours hade,
and the church of God with hir good cause of the best
instrument under God, we becaus we was not worthie
of him, and she for the sinnes of hir children, and
altho' our lose who did follow him sal be greate, yit
questionlesse the churche hir lose sal be much greatter
for how can it be when the heade which gave such
heavenly influence unto all the inferiore members, that
nevir any distemperature or weaknes was seene in them;
how can it be, since that heade is taken from the body,
bot the members thereof sall fall unto much fainting
and confusion.   But this I say not, that ather I doubt
of God's providence or of these whom he hes left as
actores behind him, for I am persuaded that God wil
not desert his owne cause, bot will yit stirre up the
heartis of some of his anoynted ones to prosecute the
defence of his cause, and to be emolouse of such
renowne as his Majestie hes left behind him for evir,
and I pray the Almightie that it would please his
Supreame Majestie now to stirre the King of Boheme
and to make choyce of him in this worke, which indead

is brought unto a great mesoure of perfectioun, neither doe I think that ther salbe any defect in these his valourous souldiours and followers, in whome ther is not the least suspicioun of jelousie; bot this al men knowis, that a bodie cannot long subsist without a head, which gives such lyffe and influence, ather good or bade, as it has radically in itselfe, when it is present; and when it is cutt away, cutts away with itselfe all lyffe and influence. . . .

Now it remaines that we turne our sorrow to revenge, and our hearts to God by earnest prayer that he would stirre up the heartis of such men, as may doe good to his cause, and now tak it in hand when it is in such a case.

I have no further wherof I can wreit to your Excellencie at this tyme . . .

your Excellencies faithfull servant till death

A. LESLIE.

During 1633 we hear nothing of the writer of this remarkable letter. What we know is, that, after the siege of Landsberg and the capture of Minden and Osnabrück (1636) he was made Field-marshal in the place of Kniphausen. In the meantime, the treaty of Prague had provided him with the opportunity of paying a visit to his native country, during which he received the freedom of Culross and judiciously invested some of his wealth in landed property. After his return he joined the Landgraf of Hesse, and marched South to the relief of the fortress of Hanau, then hard pressed, as we have seen, by the Imperialists. This and the victory at Wittstock in 1637 were his last successes. Soon afterwards the position of the Swedes became critical. Leslie had to retire to Stettin and describes his case in a letter as well-nigh desperate. "It were to be wished, that such as have a mind to helpe us would steppe in whiles it is tyme, before all bee lost, for then it may proove too late," he writes.

From Stettin Leslie embarked for Stockholm, to concert further measures with Oxenstierna, the Swedish chancellor.

He was sent back to his command in Pomerania, and finding the Swedes under Baner, who had in the meantime succeeded in repelling the Imperialists, about to march towards Bohemia, he very probably joined them. This last campaign, however, did not last long, for in summer 1638, after the outbreak of the civil troubles in Scotland, he obtained permission from the Queen of Sweden to retire from her service which was granted in terms of great gratitude. He was also presented with two guns and 2000 muskets, a fact which seems to prove Turner's statement, that the rebellion in Scotland was fomented by Sweden and France.[1] After a long and chequered career the old general of Gustavus died in 1661, having been made first Earl of Leven by Charles in 1642.

The honour of being solemnly knighted by the King of Sweden in his camp at Dirschau was shared with Leslie by Sir Patrick Ruthven. He was a man of great courage and a very trustworthy leader. But it was his chief renown to be able to drink deeper and longer than anybody else at the King's festive boards. If Gustavus Adolfus entertained foreign ministers or officers and wanted to get at their secrets " he used to appoint Ruthven Field-marshal of the bottles and glasses, for in spite of his immoderate drinking, he always kept a cool head."[2] After Ruthven had taken part in the march through the Forest of Thuringia to Würzburg and Mainz, he was made Governor of Ulm. As such he succeeded by his vigilance to suppress two conspiracies, and to reduce a number of Catholic towns of the neighbourhood, though his garrison only amounted to 1200 men. In recognition of his faithful services Gustavus Adolfus gave him the valuable estate of Kilchberg, formerly the property of the Fugger family.[3] In December 1631 he shared with Sparruyter the command of General Baner's troops until

---

[1] Turner, *Memoirs*, 13. Terry, *l.c.*

[2] Ruthven Correspondence in the Publications of the Roxburgh Club (xliii.).

[3] Originally the Fuggers were merchants at Augsburg. They soon became very rich and held the positions of Rothschilds. During the Thirty Years' War a Count Fugger fought on the Imperial side.

the recovery of the latter from his wound. Afterwards he took part in the skirmishes and battles in Mecklenburg with the army of the North, and after he had on various occasions visited England for the purpose of levying new recruits, he left the Swedish service, like Leslie in 1637, and returned to Scotland, where he joined the party of the King. He died at Dundee in 1651, being then Field-marshal and Earl of Forth. Powerfully built, almost unwieldy, covered with scars, and better able to wield the sword than the pen, he is the type of an honest, blunt, brave, old " Haudegen " of the time.[1]

The part played by the Marquis of Hamilton in the Thirty Years' War is a somewhat doubtful one. It was Lord Reay who first drew attention in Scotland to the largeness of his collected forces. Whilst, no doubt, the news of such powerful reinforcements from Scotland and England—above 6000 men—assisted the cause of Protestantism in Germany, people in his own country saw dark and ambitious designs in it as if the crown itself was in jeopardy. No doubt this is foolish enough, but the fact remains that the character of the Marquis—scheming, unscrupulous and deep as it was—lent itself to these accusations.

In the meantime his enterprise in favour of Gustavus Adolfus was not crowned with success. First of all, the 6000 men, which the King of Sweden had insisted upon, could only be got together by force. Only 1400 hailed from Scotland, the rest were English, made up for the most part of men of doubtful character and of small physical endurance.[2] Add to this as natural consequence

[1] Cp. Munro, *His Expedition*, p. 102 : "carrying the marks of his valour in his body." Ruthven's second wife was the daughter of a landed proprietor in Mecklenburg, named Berner (*Ruthven Papers*, xii.).

[2] " They ate too much of the German bread which is dark and heavier than at home ; they likewise suffered from eating of honey too greedily ; neither did the German Beer agree with them."—*Munro Expedition.* To meet the expense of these levies the King of England handed over to the Marquis his income from the duties on wines for six years, realising a sum of about £20,000 annually (*Hist. of the Illustrious Family of Gordon*, ii. 157).

that disease of every description raged amongst his soldiers from the very first day of their landing in Germany. Finally, Hamilton's own position near the King was not one based upon mutual confidence. The latter spoke bitterly of Charles I, resented his plans to interfere, with the help of a large army commanded over by the Marquis, in his politics concerning Bohemia; resented above all his claim to a voice in the matter of concluding peace. Thus it came to pass, that not only the English-Swedish Alliance, which Sir Henry Vane, the ambassador, was to press, failed, but the Marquis became a man who, on account of his being cousin to the King of England and surrounded by a princely entourage, was to be treated with all the forms of royal courtesy, whilst at the same time he was as firmly refused any position in which he might do more than merely assist the King as one of the many Scotch officers.[1] It was for this reason that he was refused the command of an army after his own mercenaries had been decimated. He was employed in guarding the fortresses on the Oder. But scarcely had he taken possession of Crossen and Guben, two small towns in the district of Frankfurt on the Oder, than he was recalled by Gustavus and attached to his staff, and though weary of being a volunteer, his applications for better employment were constantly set aside; he was 'amused by delays.' At last—in 1632—he returned, with all outward tokens of honour, to England.

A more interesting and a more creditable part is that played by the namesake, relation and successor to the Marquis in command of the Scottish troops: Sir Alexander Hamilton, called "Sandy." He had been of great service to Gustavus Adolfus as a captain and later on as skilful general of artillery. He was also invaluable by his ability to manufacture pieces of ordinance. For a time

---

[1] See Burnet, *Memoirs of Hamilton*, 1677, pp. 17, 19; J. Grant, *Adv. of Hepburn*, p. 205. "He followed the King as volunteer," says Burnet, "of which he was weary, but he found that the King was so jealous of him, that he was not to expect any trust near or in the Palatinate, where he desired most earnestlie to be employed" (p. 22).

he held the post of Governor of Hanau. After the King's death, he served the Duke William of Saxe-Weimar, for whom he established a small gun-foundry at a place called Suhl or Suhla in the Thuringian forest (1634-35). Three letters of the Duke to Hamilton have been preserved.[1] They are addressed to him in Suhl and refer to his employment there. The first is dated Erfurt, Jan. 24th, 1634, and runs: "We should be sorry if this your work, the manufacture of pieces of small ordnance, should be interrupted by all kinds of inconveniences" (want of money among other things!). But We cannot help it at present, and must put our decision off till the return of the Chancellor. In the meantime, though there should be some delay, We entreat you to remain patiently at Suhl. We also send you along with this a letter to the Magistrates there, so that you may at least get what is necessary for your livelihood. Nothing more this time. We remain graciously and well-inclined towards you &c."

The other two letters of the Duke have reference to an assault committed by one of Hamilton's lieutenants upon no less a person, than the "Ambts-Schulzen" or burgomaster. He orders a judicial inquiry and provisional imprisonment of the culprit.

In the following year (1635) Hamilton returned to England furnished by the Duke with very flattering letters of recommendation to King Charles. After an eventful and honourable career in Scotland Hamilton died in 1649.

Among the long list of prominent Scottish officers Sir James Turner, the author of *Military Essays* and an interesting memoir of his own life, deserves a few words. When a youth a restless desire for military renown filled him, and having joined the forces levied

---

[1] In Sir W. Fraser's *Memoirs of the Earls of Haddington*; where also several letters of Gustavus Adolfus and of Oxenstierna are found, the latter referring to the pay of the Scotch troops which had been in arrears for a long time, two years it was said. The town of Halberstadt was to furnish the sum.

by Sir J. Lumsden in 1632 when only eighteen years
of age, he landed at Rostock. But there a too greedy
consumption of fruit, for which that part of Germany
is famous, made him very seriously ill. He was
laid up at Bremen for six weeks and was only then
able to continue his military service under the Duke of
Lüneburg and General Kniphausen. Having taken a
prominent part in the victory of Hameln he afterwards
fought under the Scottish general King in Hessen and
Westphalen, and returned to Scotland, like so many of
his companions at arms, at the commencement of the
Civil Wars. In his Memoirs he shows a delightful
sense of humour and drollery, which in an atmosphere
of smoke, blood and incredible misery that fills the reports
of this dreadful war, does not fail to produce a bracing
and refreshing effect. Thus he relates of the year 1634:
" I was lodged at a widow's house in Oldendorf (Hesse),
whose daughter, a young widow, had been married to
a Rittmaster of the Emperor's. She was very handsome,
wittie and discreet : of her, though my former toyle
might have banished all love-thoughts out of my mind,
I became perfitlie enamourd. Heere we stayed six weeks,
in which time she taught me the High Dutch to reade
and write, which before I could not learne but rudelie
from sojors. Having then the countrey's language, I
learned also the fashion and customs of the Germane
officers ; and about this time was both regiments reduced
to two companies, two captains-lieutenants and two ensigns
(whereof I was one) only allowed to stand, all the rest
casheered and in great necessitie and povertie. The
two companies were bot badlie used, tossed to and
fro, in constant danger of the enemies and without pay.
But I had learned so much cunning and became so
vigilant to lay hold on opportunities that I wanted for
nothing, horses, clothes, meate or moneys, and made so
good use of what I had learnd, that the whole time I
served in Germanie I sufferd no such miserie as I had
done the first yeare and a halfe, that I came to it." [1]

[1] Sir James Turner, *Memoirs of my own time*, p. 7.

Not a few of the Scottish officers in the Continental armies were married to German ladies. One of them was Colonel Sir William Gunn, a Roman Catholic, whom we first meet in the ranks of the Swedes, later on in the service of the Austrian Emperor. A few interesting details concerning him have been unearthed at Ulm, the famous town and fortress in Würtemberg. In 1640 he hands a letter of recommendation from H. M. in Great Britain to the Magistrates and Council assembled, and receives the permission to reside in the city. On June 5th he invites the Town Councillors to his wedding, his bride being the young baroness Anna Margaretha von Freiberg, and the banquet taking place at the inn called the "White Ox." Two members of the Magistrates were deputed: the Burgomaster Marx Christoph Welser and the counsellor of war Johann Albrecht Stammler. They presented to him the gift of the town: a silver-gilt cup. Gunn remained at Ulm till 1649. After that time he mostly lived in Vienna. The last mention of him is in 1655, when he conferred with the town as Major-General.

As to the Field-marshal Sir Robert Douglas, he won great fame by a clever cavalry attack in the battle of Jankowitz. But owing to his being early recalled to Sweden his share in the achievements of the Thirty Years' War is not great.[1]

Much might be told still of the brave deeds of the Munroes, the Drummonds, the Lumsdens,[2] and others;

[1] In Sweden Douglas obtained the very highest distinctions. His funeral took place with almost royal ceremonies; the King and Queen of Sweden followed the hearse (1662). He was one of the last veterans of Gustavus Adolfus. His grandson Count William Douglas was Adjutant to Charles XII. Belonging to the Douglases of Whittinghame, he was the ancestor of the Counts Douglas now flourishing in the Grand Duchy of Baden in Germany. There was another Douglas, Sir G. Douglas, who played a prominent part in the War under Gustavus. He was imprisoned by the King for some breach of discipline but afterwards released. In later times he was ambassador of the English King to Poland (Turner, *Memoirs*, and p. 97).

[2] There were three brothers Lumsden with Gustavus. Sir James is the most famous one, and is often mentioned in conjunction with Hepburn.

but we must hasten to glance at the opposite camp in the Great War and recount the part played by the Scot there.

If Gustavus Adolfus by preference levied his foreign troops in Protestant Scotland, we find in the Imperial camps the Irish Catholic soldier prevailing. But there were also not a few Protestant Scottish officers, notably the two, Walter Leslie and John Gordon, well known not only from Schiller's *History of the Thirty Years' War* but also from his great tragedy of *Wallenstein*. In *Wallenstein's Death* the poet has fused for artistic reasons these two men into one: the old, good-natured, faithful Gordon. But besides the name there is nothing historical; this Gordon is merely a creature of the imagination. History knows nothing of the days of his boyhood being spent together with Wallenstein at Burgau,[1] neither is the Gordon of history the weak-minded old man such as Colonel Butler, the Irishman, describes him. It must be granted, however, that we know little enough of his life. He was Governor of the Fortress of Eger or Egra in Bohemia, the town where the murder of Wallenstein was perpetrated, in which he took a prominent part. Like Leslie he was richly rewarded by the Imperial Court at Vienna in the service of which he continued until the end of the war. In 1648 he was taken prisoner by the Swedes in Wismar (Mecklenburg). As Baron of the German Empire he died at Danzig, but was buried at Delft in Holland.[2]

We are better informed of Walter Leslie. He was the second son of the tenth Baron of Balquhain in Aberdeenshire. When quite a youth he went to Germany and, though a Protestant, entered the service of the Emperor.

He showed great bravery in the taking of Frankfurt on the Oder in 1631, fighting in the midst of his troops, where the fire was hottest. The remembrance of New Brandenburg had enraged the assailants and they caused a sad massacre in the town. Lumsden took 18 colours. He was Governor of Osnabrück in 1635.

[1] Schiller, *Wallenstein's Tod*, iv. 1-7.
[2] His will, written at Lükeck, was the cause of much legal wrangling. Cp. *Scottish Notes and Queries*, Oct. 1900.

A regiment of Scotch and Irish were under his and
Gordon's command.   In the skirmishes and battles around
Nürnberg, especially in the hilly surroundings of the
Altenberg, he showed great pluck and endurance.   The
Imperial General intended to cut off the retreat of the
Swedish Colonel Taupadel, who had undertaken a sortie
towards Freystadt (1632).   With the utmost courage,
seeking shelter behind the rocks, shrubs and trees the
regiment stood firm after the rest of the Imperial troops
had fallen back before a greatly enforced body of Swedes.
But when General Gonzaga also took flight, Major Sparr,
the commander of the regiment, had to surrender.   The
latter remained a prisoner in the hands of the Swedes, as
he had before broken his word of honour.   Gordon and
Leslie, however, were set free by Gustavus Adolfus who
knew how to acknowledge heroic conduct in an enemy.
During five weeks they stayed at Nürnberg and were
the guests of their countrymen, Hepburn and Munro.
In banqueting and feasting they celebrated their meeting and recalled the days of old.   Two years later
Leslie arrived at Eger with his Scots and Irish for
winter-quarters.   It was from this town that he
addressed a letter to the Imperial General Piccolomini,
as a "Protector of all foreign officers to intercede
in his favour with his colonel Trczka;" but we do not
know if there had been any misunderstanding between
these two.   At Eger also he heard for the first time, possibly
from Wallenstein himself, of the plans of the latter to
desert the cause of the Empire, and of the Emperor's order
to seize the prescribed General's person dead or alive.
Time was pressing.   Milder measures were overruled by
the necessity of immediate action.   The murder of
Wallenstein is decided upon.   Leslie gives the signal for
the massacre of the generals Kinsky, Illow and Neumann
during supper in the castle.   Then hastening into the
town, he makes the guards take the oath of allegiance,
and calls out a hundred dragoons for the maintenance of
order.   After the murder of Wallenstein himself, who
received his death-blow from the pike of the Irishman

Devereux, the body was brought in Leslie's carriage to the citadel. On the following day the sergeant-major—for up till then Leslie did not occupy a higher rank—started on his journey to Vienna, where he arrived on the sixth of March. Here he found the Emperor extremely gracious. Although on the one hand masses in the churches were ordered for the soul of the dead Wallenstein, and although the murder was repudiated as the rash act of anticipating officials : no wish of Leslie's, the chief actor in the tragedy, remained unfulfilled. He requested the command of a regiment and he received it ; he desired the title of Count, and the Emperor sent him the diploma with his own signature : "Annuit Maiestas S. Caes. motu proprio et libentissime, antequam quisquam Dominorum Consiliariorum consuleret, contestans id se facturum etiamsi nemo consuleret."[1] He advanced from Colonel to General, from General to Feld-zeugmeister[2] (1646) and finally to Field-marshal (1650). Moreover he received the golden key of a privy counsellor and the estate of Neustadt, formerly the property of Trczka.

His military career ended with the battle of Nördlingen in 1634, where he took a conspicuous part, and in the carefully executed revictualling and fortifying of Petrin in Albania, where his new dignity as Governor of the Turkish-Austrian boundary-district had called him. After this he was chiefly entrusted with diplomatic missions, in which he proved himself a skilful negotiator. He travelled to Italy and obtained a subsidy from the Pope for Austria, amounting to 20,000 crowns and from Naples even 100,000 crowns for the same purpose. No less successful was his journey to Constantinople, which he undertook, as an old man of sixty and infirm, at the express wish of the Emperor, who shortly before had decorated him with the Order of the Golden Fleece (1665). The reason of this embassy was the ratification of the treaty of Vasvar. Valuable presents had to be delivered ; a fleet of thirty-six gaily decked ships carried him down the Danube as

---

[1] Art. Leslie in the *Allg. Deutsche Biographie.*
[2] Master General of the Ordnance.

far as Belgrade.   Loaded with gifts from the Sultan, and
followed by sixty Christians delivered out of Turkish
imprisonment, but ill himself, he returned about Christmas
time to the Austrian Capital.   There he died on the third
of March 1667 and was buried, having previously
embraced Roman Catholicism, in the vault of the Church
of the Scottish Benedictines with great pomp and magni-
ficence.   His great riches he had used to render the family
estates in Scotland free of debt.

There is no doubt whatever that Leslie served his
imperial master with skill and fidelity.   The question of
guilt in his betraying Wallenstein stands and falls with
the much debated question of the guilt of Wallenstein himself.   At any rate there is no need of assuming that Leslie
was nothing but one of a band of low, hired assassins.[1]
It seems to be more just to say with the greatest of
German historians,[2] that he did the deed " forced to it
by the feeling of military obedience towards his sovereign
and by the duty of an oath which could not be broken
at will."

The nephew of Field-marshal Leslie, who had been
made the heir of his childless uncle, was carefully
educated and served with distinction under the Emperor
Leopold.   He commanded the Galizian Regiment, No. 24,
which was called Leslie's Regiment during 1665-1675.
At the siege of Vienna he proved himself a daring and
skilful leader.   Afterwards he was, like his uncle, much
used for diplomatic missions, never losing the favour of
the imperial court.   He held the title of Count, the
rank of a Privy Counsellor and of Major-General.   When
he was married to the Princess Maria Theresa of Lichten-
stein the Emperor as well as the Empress and the highest
nobles of Austria were present at the ceremony.

He left no children either, and another nephew, James
Ernest, became third Count Leslie.   Of him we know
little more than that he built a hospital for invalided
soldiers at Neustadt in Bohemia and left a legacy to tne

[1] See Hallwig, Artikal Leslie in the *Allg. Deutsche Biographie.*
[2] Cp. Ranke, *Leben Wallensteins.*

Scottish Monastery at Regensburg for the education of young Scottish gentlemen, especially those of the name of Leslie. He died in 1694.[1]

The brilliant career of so many brave Scottish officers, which we have hitherto traced, if alone taken into account, would indeed give us a wrong impression of the life of the Scottish mercenary. There is a sad, dark side of the picture as well. No sooner has the wardrum ceased to beat, than we meet with the familiar figure of the old Scottish soldier receiving alms from his countrymen in the seaport towns on the Baltic. Or we find him poor, ragged, ill, perhaps crippled for life in the company of idle Lanzknechte, gipsies, Jews, beggars and vagabonds, who, like a swarm of locusts, overran the country. In a few graphic lines a contemporaneous sketch of him has been preserved in the archives of the city of Breslau. Towards the end of the XVth Century a band of such vagabonds had been dragged to the Rathaus there on the charge of begging and using loaded dice. There were many Scots among them, mostly men, who had vowed a pilgrimage to Rome and were now returning home by way of Danzig; others had been soldiers. One of these is introduced as Thomas Woysheit (?) from Edenburgk, "die beste stat yn Schotten," *i.e.* the best town in Scotland. Of him the clerk notes down: 'He has not been in Scotland for XII. years, and is a nobleman and went after military service and served under the King of France and of the Romans, and in the wars, which he has gone through, he has lost his all, and has been at Rome and from one town to another begging, so that he might feed his wife and children." [2]

---

[1] The male line of the Counts Leslie became extinct in 1802. The estates passed into the hands of the heirs of Prince Dietrichstein, the first Count having married a princess of that house. They again became extinct in 1858. The Scottish heirs now came forward and their claims were recognised in 1861. But on some Austrian noblemen protesting a law-suit followed, which lasted till 1867, when a compromise was agreed upon to that effect that five-twelfths of the count's estates should go to the Scottish claimants.

[2] . . . 'ist yn XII. jorn yn Schutten nicht gewest und ist eyn edel-

Nothing could be more tragic than this concise statement. Other facts like these, unrecorded, perhaps, but none the less numerable, awaken the sounds of the old song again : ' O woe unto these cruel wars ! ' and they dim the glory which Scottish valour gained abroad. But we must follow still further the traces of the Scots as revealed by history.

The century between the Thirty Years' War and the Seven Years' War in Germany is chiefly filled by two Wars of Succession, in both of which Scottish troops and Scottish leaders have taken a not inglorious part. But now they were fighting no longer as mercenaries of a foreign power, but as trained soldiers of an allied king.[1]

In the Spanish War of Succession (1702-1713), in which the Austrians and the English opposed the French and the Bavarians, it was the Duke of Marlborough, who, with the heroic Prince Eugen of Savoy, obtained immortal fame, handed down to us in song and story. The following Scottish regiments accompanied the Duke :—

1. The Royal Scots Dragoons, commonly called Scots Greys.

2. One battalion of the Royal Scots Foot Guards.

3. The Royal Scots.

mann und hot dem dinste nach geczogen und hot gedint dem Konige czu (in) Frangreich und bey dem Romischen Konige und bey dem dinste ist her (he) komen yn den krigen von allem, das her gehat hot, und ist gewest czu Rome und von eyner stat czu der andern, und bettelt, uf das her seyn wayp und kynder mocht dernern (ernähren = feed)." Original in the Stadt-Archiv zu Breslau, undated, but probably belonging to the close of the XVth Century.

[1] In the intervening time Scottish officers at German Courts were not wanting. Thus William Ker, formerly English Consul at Amsterdam, in his " Remarks on the Government of several parts of Holland and Germany, 1688," relates that he met on his travels in Germany the following Scottish officers in Hanover :—Steelhand Gordon, who had already served at the Court of Poland, Grimes and Hamilton ; and in Lüneburg-Zell, Col. Graham, Coleman, Hamilton, Melvin and others. At about the same time (1687), Sir David Leslie, Earl of Leven, served as colonel under the Elector of Brandenburg at Berlin, after having been recommended by the Electress of Hanover. He was in high favour at the Court, busily engaged in the interests of the Prince of Orange. (Sir W. Fraser, *Melville and Leslie*, vol. i. 248 f.).

4. The Royal North British Fusiliers (21st Foot).

5. The Cameronians.

In the battle of Blenheim they had the first opportunity of distinguishing themselves. But in spite of their impetuous advance on the strongly entrenched village of Blenheim, an advance which brought them so close to the pallisades that their General, Rowe, is said to have stuck his sword into them before giving the order to fire, they did not succeed in driving the French out of their stronghold. Only after the fate of the battle had already been decided elsewhere did the brave defenders of the village surrender to the Earl of Orkney.

Besides the regular troops there were not wanting volunteer officers from Scotland in the Imperial army, whom the brilliant generalship of Prince Eugen of Savoy had attracted. Special mention deserves John, Earl of Crawford, who in 1735 went to Germany and was attached to the Prince's staff, taking part in the engagements near the Moselle river. He distinguished himself in the battle of Claussen (17th Oct., 1735), where his friend the Count of Nassau was killed at his side. Later he fought against the Turks under the Russian flag, but returned to Austria in 1738. Under General Wallis and the Prince of Waldeck he was present before Peterwardein and in the battle of Krotska. It was there that he discovered the Turkish outposts in a churchyard, and after having charged them drove them across the river. On the battle proceeding his horse was killed under him and he himself severely wounded in the left thigh. Half dead from the loss of blood, only hastily bandaged up, he remained lying by the road-side waiting for the sleeping-coach of General Waldeck, which had been promised to him. In vain he tried to persuade his faithful servant, a German named Köpp, to leave him to die, handing him at the same time his watch and his purse as a reward for his services. At last the vehicle appeared and the wounded man, who suffered the most intense agony, was safely conveyed to Belgrad only three days prior to the surrounding of the town by the Turks. Here he spent weeks, hovering between life and death, until his strong constitution gained the upper hand. On the 27th of October 1738 he succeeded in reaching Vienna on the Danube in a primitive boat. Thence he went to Baden to take the waters, but though greatly improved in health, he never altogether recovered. His wound kept discharging splinters ever and again and accelerated his death in 1749 after he had taken a prominent part under the Earl of Stair in the battle of Dettingen (June 16th, 1743).[1]

In the war of the Austrian Succession (1742-1748) in which, as is well known, the forces of France and Bavaria as enemies of Austria opposed those of England, Holland and Prussia, it was chiefly this battle of Dettingen, where the Scottish troops under the eyes of King George II. himself distinguished themselves. Prominent amongst them Colonel Sir Andrew Agnew, who commanded the Royal North British Fusiliers. The impetuous attack of the French Cuirassiers left them no time to form a square; all they could do was to draw up in a line and to receive the enemy with such hot musketry-fire from all sides that only a few of the gallant troopers escaped.[2]

It is no secret that the advice and the plan of the Earl of Stair,[3] "the only tolerably bright man in the army," to pursue the enemy, was not accepted, and that he himself, incensed at the growing Hanoverian influence in matters of military tactics, soon resigned his command.

Passing on to the age of Frederic the Great of Prussia, our attention is soon attracted to the scions of an old, famous, Scottish family, the Keiths. No less than six

[1] Many members of the Crawford family have excelled in foreign military service in Poland, Sweden, etc. As to Lord James Crawford in Augsburg, see Appendix.

[2] The story is told that the king after the battle rode up to Agnew and called out to him: "Well, Colonel, I saw the French Cuirassiers get into your lines to-day!" Agnew coolly replied: "Ou aye, your Majesty, but they didna get out again!" Cp. Carlyle, *Friedrich*, v. 292.

[3] Cp. Carlyle, *Friedrich*, v. 297. The Earl of Stair had been fighting gallantly under Marlborough; he had saved the life of Frederic of Hesse, afterwards husband of Ulrike Eleonore, Queen of Sweden, by shooting a Frenchman who was just aiming at him.

Scotsmen of this name have played a more or less important part in the life of the Prussian king.

Far away in the extreme north-east corner of the county of Aberdeen, struck by the storms of the North Sea, there stood, a few years ago, the lonely ruins of the Castle of Inverugie, the family seat of the Earl Marischals. There they lived lives of hardihood and energy, constantly engaged in and often directing the shifting fates of their native country. Here George Keith was born in 1693, his brother James in 1696, brothers throughout their long career deeply and affectionately attached to each other. They were the sons of the ninth Earl Marischal, and were educated by a Catholic mother and a Protestant father in the principles of unswerving fidelity to the Stuarts. Very soon these principles were put to the test. It was on the 20th of September 1715, that the two youthful brothers, together with other Highland nobles at the old Market Cross of Aberdeen, proclaimed Charles Edward King of Scotland as James VIII. But when the war-like enterprises in favour of the Stuart dynasty miscarried and the new-made king, after the defeat at Sheriffmuir, in which the elder Keith commanded two squadrons of cavalry, was compelled to seek safety in France, the two brothers, like so many others, were declared outlaws and their estates forfeited. George, nothing daunted, went first of all to Spain, and obtained the command of a small Spanish force, that was to land on the Isle of Lewis in the north-west of Scotland, take Inverness and again raise the standard of the Stuart. But this foolhardy expedition could not but end in disaster. Scarce had the handful of warriors reached the mainland, when they were attacked by General Whitman and scattered. The Highlanders dispersed to their mountains, the Spaniards, 274 in number, surrendered. Keith was wounded, but escaped to the islands and from there in disguise to Spain. Here he continued to live in the town of Valencia, still busily intriguing for his hero. Again in 1744 he was to command and lead an expeditionary force of the enemy into Scotland, but the plan was not carried out. In the following year Keith went to Vienna, and shortly afterwards, being invited by his brother, to Berlin. Here he gained very soon the complete confidence and enjoyed the close friendship of Frederic the Great, whose philosophical views of life he shared. He became a member of the Academy, and in 1751 ambassador of Prussia to the King of France. This post, however, he soon gave up, owing, no doubt, chiefly to the irritation of England at seeing a Jacobite outlaw appointed to one of the most responsible diplomatic positions. Frederic honoured him by bestowing upon him the Order of the Black Eagle and nominating him Governor of Neufchâtel in Switzerland, then part of the Prussian possessions.

His administration bore the stamp of Frederic's humane and tolerant philosophy; the use of the rack, and public penance done in the churches were abolished, not without bitter hostility on the part of the enemies of light and progress. Rousseau, the banished philosopher, was offered an asylum and friendly assistance. Keith procured for him many favours of his royal master, and so great was his esteem for this much abused man, that he offered him a house in Scotland or in Potsdam, where the two might continue their intercourse, and when Rousseau refused, he granted him a pension of 600 francs.[1]

The stay of the Earl Marischal at Neufchâtel extended over ten years, but it was often interrupted. In 1759, for instance, Keith was sent on a diplomatic errand to Madrid, where King Ferdinand of Spain had just died. But though this embassy did not procure any tangible benefit for Prussia, it proved of the greatest advantage to Keith himself. He gained the goodwill of Pitt by communicating to him the family-compact of the two houses of Bourbon, and thus, aided by the powerful intercession of his royal friend, he smoothed the way towards a final removal of all his Jacobite disabilities.

---

[1] Rousseau's description of his intimacy with Keith is very charming. "La grande âme de ce digne homme," he writes, "ne pouvait se plier que sous le joug de l'amitié, mais elle s'y pliait si parfaitement, qu'avec de maximes bien différentes, il ne vit plus que Frédéric du moment, qu'il lui fibt attaché" (*Confessions*, ii. 524 f.).

King George II issued a patent declaring the Marischal able to inherit, parliament assented and voted a considerable sum in lieu of his confiscated property, and Keith, now no longer under the ban of outlawry, at once entered on possession of the inheritance of the late Earl of Kintore, who had died without issue. He was presented to the King in 1760 on the 16th of August.

Three years later, he visited his old home at Aberdeen, where his kinsmen did all they could to persuade the Earl not only to settle among them, but to marry and give them welcome heirs of the loved name of Keith. However, King Frederic wrote an urgent letter, (Febr. 16, 1764), which was not to be resisted. "I do not wonder," he said, "that the Scots fight for your possession, and wish to have progeny of yours, and to preserve your bones. You have in your life-time the lot of Homer after death: cities arguing which is your birthplace. I myself would dispute it with Edinburgh to possess you. If I had ships I would make a descent on Scotland, to steal off my dear Mylord and to bring him hither. Alas! our Elbe-boats can't do it. But you give me hopes, which I seize with avidity. I was your late brother's friend, and had obligations to him; I am yours with heart and soul. These are my titles, these are my rights. You shan't be forced in the matter of progeny here, neither priest nor attorney shall meddle with you, you shall live in the bosom of friendship, liberty and philosophy."[1]

Keith gave in, removed in 1764 to Potsdam, where Frederic had built him a villa, and lived there, peacefully and hale in body and soul till his death in 1778.

King Frederic lost in him a true friend, who had proved useful to him in many ways, not only sharing his tastes and his philosophy, but showing an interest also in his plans of industrial and agricultural improvement. He even bought paintings for him and procured him his favourite tobacco from Spain. Moreover, he was a

[1] *Œuvres de Frédéric*, xx. 295.

strictly upright man, a cheerful, 'excellent, old soul, honest as the sunlight.' His king loved him, 'almost as one boy the other.' His conversation was that of the wise, not without some dry humour, some 'little vein of wit';[1] his manner of living was eccentric, a strange mixture of Aberdeenshire and Valencia.[2] Frederic's letters to him are all full of true friendliness. Thus he writes in 1758 after the death of the Field-marshal, his brother: " There is nothing left for us, mon cher Mylord, but to mingle and blend our weeping for the losses we have had. If my head were a fountain of tears, it would not suffice for the grief I feel.

" Our campaign is over, and there has nothing come of it, on one side or the other, but the loss of a great many worthy people, the misery of a great many poor soldiers crippled for ever, the ruin of Provinces, the ravage, pillage and conflagration of flourishing towns: exploits these which make humanity shudder; sad fruits of the wickedness and ambition of certain people in power, who sacrifice everything to their unbridled passions! I wish you, mon cher Mylord, nothing that has the least resemblance to my destiny and everything that is wanting to it. Your old friend till death."[3]

The brother, to whom this letter alludes, James Keith, is better known in history. His life was full of adventures, warlike deeds and escapes. He was a Scotsman, a Frenchman, a Spaniard, and a Russian till he ended his career on a Prussian battlefield.

After he had taken part in the Jacobite insurrection in Scotland, he also was compelled to take flight, and went first of all to Paris, where he was well received at court. Having for some time studied under Maupertuis, he travelled to Spain and took part in the siege

---

[1] Not even during his illness did he lose his good-tempered nature. He offered to the British Ambassador at Berlin to take any message to Pitt, who had died a fortnight previously.

[2] See *Memoirs of Sir R. M. Keith*, i. 129. " He, the Earl Marschal, is the most innocent of all creatures and has a conscience fit to guild the inside of a dungeon."

[3] *Œuvres de Frédéric*, xx. 273.

of Gibraltar. But as his Protestant faith barred the way of his promotion, he offered his services in 1728 to Russia. Here his career was brilliant and rapid. From General-Major and Colonel of the Body Guard of the Empress Anne he rose to be Army-Inspector on the Volga and the Don. In the Polish war of 1733-35, as well as in the war against the Turks in 1737, he proved his great military skill. After having been wounded during the siege and the storming of Otczakoff by a bullet in the knee, the Empress is said to have exclaimed: "I would rather lose ten thousand of my best soldiers than Keith." In 1740 he was made Governor of the Ukraine, where his just administration procured for him the love of the people. After the war against Sweden, in which he forced 17,000 of the enemy to surrender at Helsingfors, and conquered the Aland-isles, he was honoured with the post of Russian ambassador at Stockholm (1744). But then a gradual reversion of fortune took place. The favours so lavishly bestowed upon him by the Empress excited the jealousy and the envy of high officials and generals, especially of Bestucheff, the Vice-Chancellor. One command after the other was taken from him; his brother was not allowed to visit him at Riga and his position become daily more difficult and dangerous. Circumstances like these would in themselves have been sufficient to explain his sudden departure from Petersburg in 1747. But there seems to have been another very potent reason for this step, which has only lately come to light in the correspondence of the Field-marshal with Chevalier Drummond at Berlin. This was nothing more nor less than the growing affection of the Empress, which threatened to assume a form incompatible with his station and his security. In her letters she calls him the only man, " who can bring up a future heir of the throne in my mind and in the footsteps of Peter the Great," and he himself writes to Drummond as early as 1745: "The empress is resolved to raise me to a height, which would cause my ruin as well as her own." This being so—in other words, Siberia looming in the distance,—Keith's sudden departure is more than sufficiently accounted for. At Berlin he was received with open arms, the King nominating him Field-marshal and Governor of the capital. With his new sovereign he lived on terms of cordial friendship. He was of great service to him in times of war and of peace, taking an active interest in the importation of English woollen cloth, promoting the affairs of Scottish merchants, endeavouring to open up trade to the East Indies, translating the English parliamentary debates, and even drawing designs for bridges across the Spree River.

Unfortunately the King was not long to enjoy the services of his devoted friend. After the siege of Prague in 1757, which had to be raised in consequence of the disastrous battle of Kolin, we find the Field-marshal as victorious commander of the second army corps at Rossbach. Then followed the long and futile siege of Olmütz, stubbornly defended by the Imperial general Marshal, another Scotsman; the masterly retreat before the forces of Loudon, and finally the fatal day of Hochkirch (1758). In vain Keith had expostulated with the King on the weakness of his right wing, and when 'on that misty morning of October' the furious and sudden onslaught of the Austrians shook the ground, he was not able to withstand the shock nor to retake his former position. Forsaken by his very aides-de-camp the Field-marshal was thrice wounded, the last time mortally. Not even his body could be found. At last the Austrians discovered it, plundered by the Croats and naked, and carried it into the church, where General Lacy, who had fought under him in Russia, recognised it by a scar as that of the intimate friend of his father and had it buried with all military honours; 'twelve canons salvoing thrice, the whole corps of Colloredo with their muskets thrice. Lacy as chief-mourner, not without tears.'[1] Four months afterwards the body was brought to Berlin and there interred for a second time in a still more solemn manner.

[1] Carlyle, *Friedrich*, viii. 112. About the Irish Lacys in the service of Russia and Austria, see Jas. Grant.

"Keith now sleeps in the Garnisonkirche far from bonnie Inverugie; the hoarse sea winds and caverns of Dunottar singing vague requiem to his honourable line and him.[1]"

The epitaph erected in the little church at Hochkirch by Sir Robert Murray Keith, a kinsman, bears the inscription: "Dum in Praelio non procul hinc inclinatam suorum aciem mente, manu, voce et exemplo restituebat, pugnans ut heroas decet, occubuit. Die xiv Octobris MDCCLVIII." [2]

The King was deeply moved at the premature death of his favourite. His works bear witness how highly he esteemed the brilliant general and the true friend. The Earl Marischal lost in him, as Carlyle expresses himself, "more a father than a younger brother." The Field-marshal died poor.

Among the Scottish officers abroad, he was, without doubt, the foremost. He will also be remembered as the inventor of the "Kriegs-Spiel" or its precursor, the "Kriegs Schachspiel" (Game of War-Chess).[3]

Two other remarkable members of the family of Keith, known and esteemed by the Great Frederick, were the Murray-Keiths, father and son, ambassadors at Vienna. Of them we shall have to speak later on. Here we have to mention still two other brothers: Keiths, the pages, who did play a passing part in the life of young Prince Frederick. They were not related to the Earl Marischal's family, though also descended from Scottish forebears. They were born at Poberow in Pomerania. Peter Karl Christoph von Keith, the elder, was privy to the secret flight of the Crown Prince, and when the plans were discovered, he was warned by his master in a short letter

---

[1] See Carlyle, *Friedrich*, viii. 112.

[2] Two statues of Keith are at Berlin; a bronz-replica was presented to the town of Peterhead by King William in 1868. Prince Henry of Prussia also honoured his memory. On an obelisk erected at Rheinsberg, he inscribed: 'With the greatest uprightness he joined the most extensive knowledge.'

[3] S. Varnhagen v. Ense, *Life of Feldmarschall Jacob Keith*, pp. 109–113.

containing only the words, "Sauvez-vous; tout est dé-
couvert." He had time left to escape to Holland, and
with the assistance of Lord Chesterfield to England. His
image was hung on the gallows at Wesel. After a short
stay in Portugal, where he served as major, he returned
to Berlin, when the Crown Prince had succeeded his
father as King Frederick II. There he was made equerry,
Lieutenant-Colonel and Curate of the Academy of Sciences
with a good salary. But even then he complained and
thought himself but poorly rewarded. His character, so
different from the splendid and lofty unselfishness of the
Earl Marischal, soon forfeited the favour of the King.
He died in 1756. Of his younger brother almost nothing
is known except that he served in a regiment of infantry
at Wesel.

Besides the Keiths, there were many other Scottish
officers in the army of Frederic. A Major Grant of
Dunlugas, the same that brought the news of the victory
at Leuthen (Dec. 5, 1751) to England, distinguished
himself at Kolin. There the King had placed himself,
after desperate efforts of collecting his troops, at the
head of a small body "against a certain battery." But
in his rear, man after man fell away, till Grant ventured
to remark : "Your Majesty and I cannot take the battery
ourselves!" upon which Frederic turned round, and,
finding nobody, looked at the enemy through his glass
and rode away.[1]

Again we find the names of Lord John Drummond and
Lord John Macleod mentioned. Both were attracted by
the military genius of Frederick and entered his service as
volunteer officers. Drummond was adjutant or aide-de-
camp in 1747;[2] Macleod came from Sweden and published
later on a description of the first summer campaign of 1757.[3]

---

[1] Carlyle, *Friedrich*, viii. 227. Grant had formerly served in the
Russian army as the Adjutant of General Lascy. He was made
General and Governor by Frederick of the fortress of Neisse, where at
the age of 64 he died in 1764. See Supplement.

[2] Cp. *Red Book of Grantully*, i. 234, Drummond of Logiealmond.

[3] Macleod of Cromartie ; see W. Fraser, *The Earls of Cromartie*, i.
244; ii. 244.

Finally we must not forget the 10,000 to 12,000 English auxiliaries, who joined the army of the Duke of Brunswick at Soest on the 20th of August 1758, after public opinion in England had at last veered round in Prussia's favour. Amongst them were many Scots, but none distinguished themselves more than the Scots Greys and the 1000 or 1600 Highlanders. "Grand-looking fellows all of them," said the Germans. "And did you ever see such horses, such splendour of equipment, regardless of expense? Not to mention the "Bergschotten" with their bagpipes, sporrans, kilt, and exotic costume and ways. Out of all whom Ferdinand got a great deal of first-rate fighting."

The brigade of Maxwell particularly distinguished itself in the battle of Warburg (1760). They did some excellent practice with the bayonet, muskets, and cannon, "obstinate as bears."[1] But what pleased Prince Ferdinand most was the dashing bravery of the Highlanders under their colonel, Robert Murray Keith. He ordered even more regiments to be raised in Perth, Inverness, Ross, and Sutherland. In non-military circles of Germany, however, the notions entertained of the "Bergschotten" were still as singular as when the curious woodcut appeared at Stettin in 1627. Says the *Vienna Gazette* of 1762 : "The Highlanders are in dress, temper, and custom altogether different from the rest of the inhabitants of Great Britain. They are caught in the mountains when young, and they still run with incredible swiftness. The soldiers are of small stature and mostly either old or very young. They show an extraordinary love for their officers, who are all handsome and young. Their good endowments, proving the innocence of nature before being corrupted by example and prejudice, make us hope that their King's laudable though late endeavours to bring them up in the principles of Christianity will be crowned with success."[2]

On the side of Austria the following Scottish generals

---

[1] *Archenholtz*, i. 350. Carlyle, *Friedrich*, viii. 124 ; ix. 45.

[2] There is also mentioned an Austrian "Generalmajor Gibson" (1716). He was wounded before Belgrade and afterwards appointed Governor of Courtrai in Flanders (*Northern Notes and Queries*, iv. 81).

fought in the Septennial War: Ogilvie, St Paul, Wallis, and Loudon. Ogilvie has already been mentioned;[1] of St Paul little is known beyond his being created a count in 1786; Wallis was a scion of the Scottish Wallaces, though himself born in Ireland. Gideon Ernest, Baron Loudon or "Laudohn," descended from Sir Matthew Campbell of Loudon, in Ayrshire († 1574), must be placed in the foremost rank of military commanders. He alone could match the genius of Frederick; he was the one dreaded, resourceful leader of the enemy: a man who earned the high praise from the Prussian King, that he never committed a mistake, and that he was one he would rather see beside him than opposite him. The family of Loudon emigrated in the XVIth Century to Livonia and became possessors of two considerable estates, one registered under the old name of Loudon, the other of Tootzen. When Gideon was born in 1716 only Tootzen remained as property. His father had been Lieut.-Colonel in the Swedish army, but Livonia having been ceded to Russia in 1721, young Loudon, after a very defective education, entered the Russian army as cadet in 1731. He distinguished himself in the Polish War and against the Turks, and was promoted to the rank of Lieutenant. When the War of the Austrian Succession broke out, he was disappointed at Russia not taking part in it, resigned his commission and sought employment elsewhere. He seems to have contemplated taking service in Sweden or even offering his sword to England and the Dutch, who were then sending out a fleet to defend their possessions in the East Indies; but at last he resolved to go to Vienna and to call at Berlin on his way, where by the help of some Scottish friends he hoped to obtain an audience of the King, and, if possible, receive a commission. Frederick did not absolutely refuse his request, but kept him waiting fully six weeks, after which time he declared, in one of his fits of anger, that he indeed must needs have many squadrons at his disposal, if he was to give a command to every foreign officer. Nor

[1] See Supplement.

did a personal interview improve matters; the King declaring that the " physiognomy of that man did not please him." It is true, nature had not bestowed upon the future Field-Marshal an imposing stature or prepossessing features : heavy eyebrows overhung a pair of sad, grey eyes; his mouth was seldom known to smile; his stature was lean; his manners were modest and retiring. Baffled at Berlin, Loudon turned to Vienna, which he reached in 1744 in very straitened circumstances. At first he only obtained the command of a company under the famous Baron Trenck, whom he had known in Russia. This post he resigned in 1748, disgusted at the coarseness, cruelty, and insolence of his leader. Having been promoted to a captaincy in a regiment of Croats, he married a Miss von Haagen and removed to the Croatian frontier, where he lived a studious, happy, and retired life for the next eight or nine years. In 1750 he was made Major, and three years later Lieutenant-Colonel. On the outbreak of the Seven Years' War, the Austrian Chancellor Kaunitz, who had recognised in him " a man of iron nerve, of great precision of thought, of marvellous memory and great observing powers, a man fit not only to conceive bold plans, but to carry them out," entrusted him with the command of a battalion of Croats under Field-Marshal Brown, an Irish-Austrian. Here he soon gained by experience that striking characteristic of a great military leader : swiftly to detect the weak point of an enemy's position and to fall furiously upon it. After the battle of Kollin he received the command of four companies of Grenadiers, two thousand Croats, and six hundred Hussars, with which he formed the vanguard of the army. His boldness and dashing spirit displayed itself everywhere, in striking contrast to the hesitancy and caution of his Commander-in-Chief, Daun, who often deprived himself of the fruits of his dearly-bought victories. How Loudon distinguished himself at Olmütz, where he cut off the supplies of the enemy; at the battles of Hochkirch and Kunersdorf, where his urgent request to pursue the shattered armies of the Prussians was rejected; at the subsequent battle of Landshut, the taking of Glatz, the storming of the strong fortress of Schweidnitz, which enabled the Austrians for the first time to winter in Silesia: all this is a matter of history.

Nor were the rewards for such splendid services wanting. His grateful sovereign, the Empress, decorated him with many high orders, presented him with two houses in Vienna and the estate of Klein Beczwar in Bohemia. He was made Feldzeugmeister, and Field-Marshal and Generalissimo. After the conclusion of peace in 1763 Loudon went to Karlsbad to take the waters. Here he met the famous German poet Gellert, who gives a very characteristic account of him, calling him "his dearest acquaintance, an earnest, modest, religious, somewhat sad man, who never speaks of his own exploits." His quiet life at Beczwar was interrupted only by his regular visits to Vienna twice a year to pay his respects to his sovereign. In 1769 he accompanied the Emperor Joseph II on a visit to Frederick at Neisse, and in 1770, when the King of Prussia returned the visit at Neustadt in Moravia, he commanded one of the divisions in a great sham-fight with such skill that he earned the greatest praise from the royal guest. It was here at the banquet, when Loudon was about to take a seat low down on the side of the table opposite to his own, that the King called out: "Come here, Field-Marshal Loudon. I would rather see you at my side than opposite me!" On two subsequent occasions Loudon's services as commander were required, once in 1777, when the war of the Bavarian Succession broke out, Austria claiming certain parts of Bavaria after the death of the Elector, and in 1787, when Austria joined Russia in a war against the Turks. The former campaign ended ingloriously, as a battle against Prince Henry, the Prussian Commander, had to be avoided because of the strict order of the Empress; the latter was distinguished chiefly by the capture of Berber and Belgrade.

During the years of peace the now aged Field-Marshal lived at Hadersbach, near Vienna, a large estate, which contained a castle, some twenty farm-houses, and a mill.

Here he farmed his own land, spending his time amongst his people, building, gardening, planting, and improving, often visited by the Archdukes Leopold and Ferdinand, Chancellor Kaunitz, and other friends. Here also he died on the 14th of July 1790, in his seventy-fifth year, after having been the sword and the shield of the House of Habsburg for nearly half a century. Great as he was as general, he was no less great as a man; a true friend, a loving husband, a man all whose thoughts were lofty.[1]

His last words were words of comfort to his weeping nephew, who was kneeling by his bed-side. "Love your God," he said, "never injure your fellow-men; reverence your sovereign, and be a true defender of your country. Providence raised me from the dust to a greatness which I never sought. I have always only tried to do my duty. In that let me serve as your example."

Passing on to later times, a word or two must be said about Sir Charles Gordon, who served in the wars in Holland under the Duke of Brunswick in 1787, and about Lord Lynedoch, who accompanied the Austrian army to Italy in 1796, as Military Attaché of Great Britain. As such he distinguished himself during the siege of Mantua by the French. This strong fortress was held by a brave Austrian garrison; but famine threatened, and unless provisions could be sent from headquarters, the fate of the town was sealed. In this emergency Lynedoch volunteered to carry the message to the Austrian General commanding. He disguised himself as a peasant, left Mantua in the midst of winter during a terrible snow-storm, and reached his goal on the sixth day after many hair-breadth escapes during his march through morass and swamp.[2]

We have now come to the limit of our task. In the great struggle of Europe against Napoleon during the first fifteen years of the new century, Great Britain had her own glorious share. Once again, at Waterloo, the Germans by the side of the British against a

---

[1] Baron v. Janks, Leben Loudons. Mallison, Js. Grant.
[2] John Murray Graham, *Life of Thomas Graham, Baron Lynedoch.*

common foe, and spilling their blood, repaid for the many good services rendered by their brethren-of-arms during past centuries on German soil.   But of Scottish soldiers fighting for a German cause, we hear no more.[1]

Only the famous old Scottish names of the Hamiltons, Douglases, Leslies, Gordons, Campbells, Gaudis, Johnstons, Spaldings, and others, still occurring in German Army lists, remind us of days long past, when the drums of the recruiting officer awoke the echo of every glen of Scotland, and when the world-famed kings and heroes of battle in Germany attracted the scions of her nobility under their victorious banners; banners of all colours and emblems, but banners which they never disgraced.

[1] Excepting only a battalion of Highlanders serving in the army of General Walmoden in the North of Germany in 1813.

PART III.

THE CHURCH.

THE CHURCH.

It is a remarkable fact that in the history of the development of the human mind the great spiritual movements did not always proceed from the most famous and the most powerful nations or cities, the so-called centres of intelligence, but, similar to the mighty rivers of the world, had their sources in localities small, hidden and unknown. Eisleben and Haddington were joined to Nazareth, Marbach to Stratford, Ecclefechan to Königsberg.[1]

This being true, it need not excite our astonishment when we observe how the ecclesiastical and religious life of the Vth, VIth and VIIth Centuries in Europe, from Iceland to Italy, from Paris to the Alps, was fanned by an almost unknown country, filled by half-savages—Ireland. Not only was ecclesiastical art in the North of Ireland at a very early time in a remarkably flourishing condition, but the spirit of Christianity itself, combined with the fiery and venturesome spirit of the Celts, had produced a number of Christian men, who in zealous enthusiasm sailed across the sea, and with wallet and staff traversed France, Germany, Switzerland and Italy. Thus St Catald, the Patron Saint of Tarentum, left the seminary of Lismore; his brother Donat (Donncadh) becoming Bishop of Lupice in Naples. St Columbanus († 615) founded the monasteries of Luxeuil in France and Bobbio in the Appennines. The Irish monk Gallus gave his name not only to a town but to a whole canton of Switzerland, while St Kilian († ab. 689) is inseparably connected with Würzburg, Marianus with Ratisbon.

There can hardly be any doubt that the oldest of the

---

[1] Marbach, the birthplace of Schiller; Eisleben of Luther; Königsberg of Kant, the philosopher.

so-called Scottish Monasteries on the Continent owe their
origin to the Irish "Scoti." At the same time, we must
not forget the fact that these "Scoti" soon crossed the
narrow water that divided their country from what we
to-day call Scotland, but was then named Albania, and
settled in the Highlands and the county of Argyle, with
the far-famed Iona as their centre. In the course of
centuries they became amalgamated with the Picts and
formed the great nation which gave their name to the
country, while the Scoti of Ireland, a small remnant
excepted, soon succumbed. There may have been, therefore, Scotch as well as Irish among the "Scoti," who in
later years entered the Scotch Monasteries in Germany.
In tradition and popular history, however, these foundations were never separated from the inhabitants of Scotland
proper, and when quarrels arose among the new arrivals
and were referred to arbitration, the decision of the
superior courts was always given in favour of the Scottish.

During the XIVth and XVth Centuries, however, these
monasteries were entirely filled with Irishmen, and their
gradual decay is chiefly attributed to this cause. Obedient
and gentle at first, they became proud and overbearing,
enriching themselves with the property of others. Their
buildings and their morals showed an equal decline in spite
of the Councils of the Church at Basle and Constance. In
the Scottish Monastery of Nürnberg in 1418 they sold
wine; mitre and staff of the abbot were pawned; the
library contained only two volumes and no vestments. If
a husband was looking for his wife, the common reply was:
Go and find her "apud Scotos." Nor was the state of
matters better in Vienna. Here the buildings of the
monastery were in a ruinous condition, bells and chalices
in pawn. Both these foundations were therefore transferred to the German monks. Ratisbon alone and its
Monastery of St James of the Scottish Benedictines out-
lasted the storms of the Reformation and the mismanagement of Irish Abbots, and it was only in 1862 that the
Bavarian Government bought it from the Scottish for the
low price of £10,000, to convert the building into a

clerical seminary.   There had been only Scottish Abbots
at Ratisbon from the year 1515 onward.

After these general remarks we must now follow the
history of this monastery, the head and mother of so many
other religious houses, a little closer.

About 1067 Marianus Scotus,[1] along with some other
monks, came from Ireland to Bamberg in Bavaria, where
he became a Benedictine.   On his later pilgrimage to
Rome he passed through Ratisbon, where he was prevailed
upon by his countryman the monk and "inclusus"
Mercherdach [2] to make a short stay.   When he was about
to continue his journey with his companions, his friend
advised him first to seek a revelation from God by prayer
and fasting.   In the last night, the legend continues,
Marianus received the divine command to set out very
early on the next day, and to remain where he should
first see the light of the sun.   In obedience to this vision
he took up his staff long before daybreak, and walking
along he came to a very old church, built in honour of St
Peter.[3]   Here he entered to say his prayers.   Scarcely
had he risen to go on his way comforted when the first
rays of the sun shone across his path.   Marianus then
settled permanently in Ratisbon, to the great joy of the
city, in which the Benedictines were then in great favour,
on account of their strict obedience to religious duties
and their love of learning.   The pious Abbess of Obermünster handed over to him the church and a plot of
ground, and thus arose, aided by rich contributions in
money from other quarters, the first monastery of the
Scottish Benedictines in Germany, the so-called Priory of
Weih St Peter (1075).[4]   In the course of time the

[1] Not to be confounded with Marianus, the historian.   His proper name
was Muiredach trog mac robartaig, *i.e.*, Marianus miser filius Robertaci.

[2] v. Waldersdorff, St Mercherdach and St Marian in the *Verhand-
langen des Historischen Vereins zu Regensburg*, xxxiv. 207.

[3] The foundation of this Weih St Peter is lost in the remote darkness
of the reign of Charlemagne.

[4] *Beiträge zur Geschichte der Schottenabtei zu St Jacob* (Contributions to the Hist. of the Scottish Monastery of St James at Ratisbon),
by G. A. Renz, Stift Raigern, 1897.

settlement increased,[1] and already in 1090 the larger
Monastery of St James was founded and taken under
his special protection by the Emperor Henry V.
Another letter of protection, dated March 26, 1112,
endowed it with the estate of Monespach and freed
it from all imposts and services. Nor were the
popes behindhand. Calixtus (1120) and Eugen III
(1148) issued bulls in favour of the new establishment, according to which the monastery was immediately
subject to the Holy See only. In the year 1152
Abbot Christian set out for Scotland ('ad nostrum
regem') to King David I in order to collect further
sums for the building of a new church and the enlarge-
ment of the abbey, which was afterwards rebuilt
" lapidibus quadris ac politis." With rich presents and
accompanied by several monks he returned in 1153,[2] and
it was not long before the very beautiful church of St
James, one of the finest specimens of the Norman style of
architecture and of Celtic ornament in Germany,[3] was
built. Then there began a time of great prosperity. A
monk completed the " Vita Sti. Mariani," valuable as the
oldest source of information concerning the Scottish
foundations at Ratisbon; the abbots tried to preserve
discipline and the dignity of the monastery;[4] presents and
pious donations were received from many parts. But
above all the mother-house renewed itself in a number of
young foundations. As such are mentioned, the monasteries of the Virgin and St. Gregory at Vienna; the St.
James' monasteries at Erfurt and Würzburg; St. Giles at
Nürnberg; St. James again at Constance; St. Nicholas at
Memmingen; the monastery " Sanctæ Crucis " at Eichstadt,
and the priories of St. John at Kehlheim and Altenfurt

[1] The Benedictines of Ratisbon carried on extensive missions as far as
Poland (Wattenbach, *Die Congregation der Schottenklöster*, i. 28).
[2] Brockie, *Monasticon Scoticum*, Pedeponti, Stadt am Hof, Ratisbon,
1752, p. 112.
[3] Riehl, *Denkmale frühmittelalterlicher Baukunst in Bayern* (Archi-
tectural Monuments of the early Middle Ages in Bavaria), p. 85 f.
[4] Repeated resolutions are passed against the " vagrant " monks. Thus
in 1211 and 1329

near Nürnberg.   These eleven monasteries[1] were formed
into one body at the Lateran Council of 1215. Every
three years the combined Chapter assembled with the
Abbot of Ratisbon as president.   He also became the
Provincial of the Order and the " General Visitator "
(head inspector) ; the right to wear the Mitre and the
other Pontificalia was granted to him in 1286.[2]

Unfortunately this flourishing condition was not of
long duration.   Vienna was handed over to the German
Benedictines by order of the Council of Constance for
reasons already alluded to (1418) ; Constance ceased to
exist in 1530.   The half ruinous buildings were pulled
down by the Magistrate, the garden made into a burial-
ground.   The last abbot, John, signed an agreement in
1533 waiving all his claims for an annual payment of
40 gulden.   Nor did the priories fare better.   Weih
St Peter at Ratisbon was razed to the ground by the
troopers of Count Eberstein in the Schmalkaldian War
"for military reasons."   Only the bells and the altar were
saved.   In St James's prosperity had been succeeded by
a period of decay.   Two abbots, named Macrobius, are
mentioned towards the end of the XIIIth century as
"viri vere prodigi et bonorum monasterii dilapidatores,"
i.e. as great prodigals and squanderers of the property
of the monastery.   Then matters changed for the
better for some time; the monastery recovered under
the honest and energetic administration of one Henry
of Rotteneck.   The small estate of Einbach and some
houses in the city were acquired as donations.   But
then a series of Irish abbots followed and the mismanagement steadily increased up to the time of the
Reformation.   The first of them was called Nicolaus
(1326-1332).   Of him it is said : "Those Irish had
been received by the Scottish for some years past;
but latterly they had increased to such an extent, that

---

[1] Twelve, if we add Öls in Silesia (Cp. Wattenbach, *l.c.*).

[2] A letter of protection of Henry VII granted the Abbot and Prior to
bear in their arms the divided Eagle of the Empire (Reid), but the
genuineness of it is disputed.

they were able to elect their countryman Nicolaus abbot. He was deposed by the Bishop of Ratisbon as a prodigal and banished."[1] Of his successors, Nicolaus II, Eugenius and Matthaeus V, we are told that they assumed the title "prince," though neither emperor nor king had given permission.[2] Philippus II (1401-1418) and Mauritius II (1446) were again prodigals, and Benedictus (1442-1444), "multa mala fecit," did much evil. Thus the disgraceful catalogue continues to the last Irish abbot, Walterus or Gualterus (1499-1515), who was not only deposed on account of his misrule, but was kept a prisoner in the bishop's castle at Wörth. Add to this a destructive fire in 1433, and it does not surprise us, that at the beginning of the era of the Reformation the once wealthy monastery was nearly reduced to beggary. To stave off complete ruin the hand of an energetic and upright ruler was wanted. To accomplish this object Pope Leo X took the important step of giving back the monastery to the Scottish and of appointing a very able Scotsman, John Thomson, who had hitherto lived at Rome, to fill the vacancy as abbot; "being," as the Bull of Confirmation has it, "the true and legitimate owner of the Monastery, since he is Scottish by birth and not an Irishman." Serious dissensions arising out of Walterus's protests were quelled by the firmness of Leo and the Duke of Bavaria. Joannes called around him monks from Dunfermline, Inchcolm and Paisley, and thus gradually the condition of the Scottish Benedictine Abbey began to improve. Unfortunately the number of monks still remained small, falling as low as two during the rule of Abbot Thomas (Anderson). To remedy this help was forthcoming from Scotland, whence help was least expected. There the rapid spread of the Reformation had been followed by wholesale banishment and flight of the adherents of the old faith. A great number of monks were driven out of the country, and sought refuge on the Continent. Among them was one of the most zealous and gifted defenders of the Catholic Religion,

---

[1] Brockie, *l.c.*, 131.   [2] *Ibid.*, *l.c.*, 137.

a man blameless in life and famed for scholarship : Ninian Winzet, formerly schoolmaster of Linlithgow. He had been born in 1518 at Renfrew in the diocese of Glasgow, obtained his degree of Master of Arts, and was made priest in 1540. Eleven years later we find him again holding school in the old royal residence of Linlithgow, the birthplace of King James V, and then a centre of ecclesiastical activity. Expelled in 1566, he sought an asylum with Queen Mary at Edinburgh, who probably made him her chaplain and confessor also. It was here that he entered the arena against John Knox, and while the palace resounded with the blows, cuts and thrusts of theological disputants, Queen Mary was reading Livy every day after dinner with her teacher Buchanan. Here also he wrote his first book entitled, *Four Score and three Questions*, a work which, on account of its outspoken concessions on the one hand, and its unshaken firmness on the other, exercised no small influence on vacillating minds at that time.[1] The author of such a book could not long remain unmolested in Edinburgh. The magistrate endeavoured to seize him, and it was only with great difficulty that Ninian escaped to Flanders on board a ship. Thence he went to Louvain, the place of refuge for many Roman Catholics (1562). Later, he visited Paris, in order to finish his studies, and Douay, a university then newly founded, where he obtained the degree of licentiate of theology (1575). In the same year he accompanied Bishop Leslie, Mary's ambassador, to Rome, at the express desire of the Queen.

Two years afterwards, when the death of the abbot of Ratisbon, Thomas Anderson,[2] became known in the Vatican, both the Pope himself and the Bishop of Ross being convinced of the necessity of placing an energetic, and withal a prudent and moderate man at the head of the monastery, a man who might bring about a new season of prosperity, Ninian Winzet was elected

[1] At first this book was only read in manuscript copies; it was printed at Antwerp in 1563.
[2] Thomas had never been confirmed by the Pope.

abbot and duly confirmed (1577). Nor did he dis-
appoint his superiors in their expectations. For the
present, indeed, there were but few monks to welcome
him at St James's, and the condition of the buildings
was still deplorable. But the new abbot soon succeeded
in mending matters. A secular seminary was opened
where he not only supervised the teachers conscientiously,
but taught the higher branches of education himself.
In the year 1583, the estate of Hopfengarton was
acquired for the monastery, the purchase-money amounting
to 2000 guldens, and an agreement was concluded with
the Abbess of Obermünster concerning the revenues of
Weih St Peter. To all these efforts must be added
Winzet's unwearied exertions on behalf of those religious
houses in Germany, which had formerly belonged to
Scotland. In this he was supported by Queen Mary
herself, his friend and patron, Bishop Leslie, and many
crowned heads. It was Leslie's special mission to obtain from
the Emperor and the other Catholic Princes of Germany,
protection for the Scots who were exiled on account of
their faith, and at the same time to urge the restoration
of these monasteries. In a letter dated April 30th 1578, the
unfortunate Queen explained her wishes to the Emperor
Rudolph,[3] and the latter answered by sanctioning the
claims of the Scots with regard to Ratisbon, Würzburg
and Erfurt, they being the "original owners."[2] But he
refused the prayers of Abbot Ninian, which he had laid
before the Emperor in a pamphlet, entitled, "Eleven
reasons for the restitution of the Scottish Monastery at
Vienna."[3] Nor could Nürnberg or Constance be resumed.
In Nürnberg the magistracy held out promises to Leslie,
and revelled in polite words,—but nothing more. As
to Constance, new negotiations were entered upon in
1608, when Joannes VII was Abbot of Ratisbon. But the
magistracy answered, that there was not a stone left of
the old monastery, the former revenues had been
expended "ad pias causas." The only result was a sum
of 1500 guldens which was paid to the Monastery of

[1] See Appendix. [2] See Appendix. [3] Ninian Winzeti.

Ratisbon as compensation, and that the duty entered upon
by the city of Constance of maintaining regular divine
worship in the " Friedhofskapelle " (Mortuary Chapel).[1]

Winzet displayed a like energy in the affairs of the
Scottish monastery at Erfurt. He restored the buildings
and gave it an excellent abbot in the person of John
Hamilton.[2] In the meantime the Pope had interceded
on his behalf with the German Emperor, the Dukes of
Bavaria, and the Bishop of Ratisbon,[3] whilst Queen Mary
wrote again recommending him to the Archbishop of
Mainz, Duke Albert of Bavaria and his consort, a princess
of Lorraine. All these high dignitaries of Church and
State replied in terms of friendship and commiseration,
and promised their protection to the new abbot.[4]

With all his labours in Ratisbon and elsewhere, Ninian
did not neglect his literary work. In 1581 he published
at Ingolstadt his commentaries on the Epistles of St Paul,
and in 1582 his polemical "Flagellum sectarium," the
Sectarians' scourge, which he dedicated to the Duke of
Bavaria. Besides this he wrote epigrams and occasional
verses in his leisure hours and translated the large Catechism of Canisius, the Jesuit, into the Scottish vernacular.
With his friend Professor Robert Turner of Ingolstadt,
a Scotsman by extraction, if not by birth, he frequently
exchanged letters until death put an end to his active life
in 1592. In him the Catholics lost a candid friend, the
Protestants an honest foe, and the world of letters an
independent thinker; an advocate of practical reform,
though a faithful adherent of the old Church.[5]

Winzet's successor was Joannes VII, whose family name

[1] G. A. Renz, l.c., p. 16 f.   [2] Ibid. p. 15.
[3] Letter to the Emperor 17th of July 1577; to Duke Albert on the same
date. Cp. King Hewison, l.c., ii. 16.
[4] The Duke of Bavaria wrote on the 6th of Sept. 1578 that he would
take the abbot or any other Roman Catholic Scotsman under his
protection, and his duchess promised the same in a touching French
letter, dated Münich, Sept. 12 1578. Cp. King Hewison, l.c.
Append. W.
[5] Cp. Bellesheim, Hist. of the Cath. Church in Scotland, ii. 35. See
also Appendix.

was White or Wight.   He discharged his office till 1623, when he retired.   The chroniclers call him "a scholarly man and one well versed in polemics."   It was during his rule that those negotiations with Constance took place of which we have spoken.   Renewed appeals to the Emperor for the purpose of regaining the Scottish establishment at Vienna were again fruitless; in spite of the assistance of Cardinal Berberini and the Bull of Pope Urban VIII of April 27th, 1624, in which the Emperor was called upon to restore the monastery to its owners, German Benedictines retained possession of it.   Würzburg, however, which since the year 1497 had been occupied by the Germans, was returned to the Scots by Bishop Julius, whose statue adorns the place in front of the Hospital, and peopled with six monks from Ratisbon.

Then there came the Thirty Years' War with its frightful train of plague and plunder, of war contributions and impoverishment.   Ratisbon was occupied by the Swedes under Duke Bernhard of Weimar in 1633 and great damage was done to the town and the Monastery. Of the 75,000 florins exacted from the clergy, the Scottish abbey of St James had to pay 1000 gulden. The buildings decayed, a great number of monks died, the revenues were reduced to 1200 gulden a year or a little more, scarcely sufficient for the maintenance of four "patres."   During ten years, from 1630-1640, there were no abbots but only managers ('administratores').

It was not till 1646 that an attempt was made to improve this sad state of matters.   In that year the energetic and learned Alex. Bayllaeus (Baillie), who had formerly been Abbot of Erfurt,[1] was chosen for the same dignity at Ratisbon.   He took pains first of all to redeem such of the monastery's property as had been pawned, to restore the buildings and to buy new Church vessels. Then he turned his attention to the political interests of

---

[1] Since 1636. He was succeeded at Erfurt by Macarius Camerarius. The abbot of the Scottish Monastery there had been appointed "Conservator et judex" of the University by Pope Martin V in 1427 (Feb. 11th).

the Monastery. Owing to his skill the attempts of Ferdinand III and IV to hand it over to the Carmelites (1641), or even to the Irish (1653), failed, and Pope Urban VIII as well as Innocent X expressed themselves again in favour of the Scottish Benedictines.[1] With the University of Salzburg, excellently conducted by the Benedictines, an agreement was concluded by which the Abbot of St James's at Ratisbon was to take the place of the Abbot of St Peter's, Salzburg, at the time of the election of a new Rector.[2]

After Baillie the most eminent abbot was Placidus Fleming (Flaminius), under whose long and beneficent rule the monastery greatly recovered its former flourishing condition. He was born at Kirkoswald in Ayrshire, and was related to the Earls of Wigton. In his youth he is said to have been a naval officer and to have been once captured by pirates in the Mediterranean Sea. As Abbot of St James's he showed uncommon energy, learning and zeal in matters of education. The library owed, if not its existence, its rich book-treasures to him. He founded a professorship of Philosophy at Erfurt, always to be held by a Scotsman. He built a Seminary for young Scottish boys of better families, first at a small place called Griesstätten (1713) and later in Ratisbon (1719); [3] and finally he formed the three remaining Scottish Religious Houses of Ratisbon, Erfurt and Würzburg into a closer union, in which the abbot of the first-named should always take the highest rank on account of the "great age of the Monastery and its many privileges granted by Popes and Emperors."

It was during Fleming's rule that the Monastery of St

---

[1] Wattenbach, *l.c.*, p. 58.

[2] Renz, *l.c.*, p. 18. Already in 1618 Abbot Benedict of Ratisbon had signed the agreement of the united Benedictine abbots for the maintenance and the appointment of professors and officers at the University of Salzburg, then about to be founded. (P. M. Sattler, *Blätter zur Geschichte der ehemaligen Benedictiner Universität Salzburg*, Kempten 1889.)

[3] Scottish monks were also active in the service of education at Waldsassen and Munich.

James's began to be used as an asylum for members of the old Scottish aristocracy, who, like George Gordon, the brother of the Earl of Aboyne, desired to spend their last years in peaceful retirement, or who used their utmost efforts secretly to restore the Stuart dynasty. Between Paris, Ratisbon and Rome an unceasing communication took place ; but all the Stuart letters were lost, when Strahlheim, one of the estates of the monastery, where these documents had been deposited, was consumed by fire.

Fleming's successor was the learned Maurus Stuart. During sixteen years he had been a professor at Erfurt. He died before his consecration and was succeeded by Bernard Baillie. Well versed in history and philosophy he had likewise filled a professor's chair at Erfurt, but had been recalled by Fleming to superintend some improvements and additions to the buildings of the monastery at Ratisbon. He took a great interest in the library and gained the affection of his monks. After his death in 1742 Bernard Stuart, a nephew of the above-named Maurus, was raised to the dignity of abbot. He was a man of great natural gifts, but of a character little noble or loveable. Excelling in provinces of learning far removed from the requirements of his office, he very frequently absented himself from Ratisbon. Born in Scotland in 1706, he early showed great aptitude for mathematics. He was educated at St James's seminary, and became priest in 1726. Some years after he obtained the chaplaincy of the Nonnberg near Salzburg, which enabled him to prosecute his studies in that University with a view mainly to perfect himself in Canon law. During 1733-1741 he himself taught as professor of mathematics, filling at the same time a number of other important offices. Thus the Prince-Archbishop appointed him his clerical adviser and inspector of buildings ('rei ædilis director'). As such he successfully drained a large bog near Salzburg after a labour of three years, and drew the plan of the Archbishop's castle Leopoldskron. In 1742 he visited at St Petersburg his brother, who was a general in the Russian service. After his return the city of Augsburg nominated him her "director aedilitiae" with a salary attached of 1800 florins. A theatre or public-hall for the pupils of the Jesuit seminary is his work ; more useful was a strong embankment which he built on the river Lech, and which can be seen to this day. For this the grateful city presented him with a gold cup. The Imperial Court of Vienna likewise employed him as Inspector of Fortresses in Swabia. In 1743 he was chosen Abbot of St James's at Ratisbon. During his term of office the above-mentioned estate of Strahlfeld was acquired for the monastery after a long law-suit, and the Jacobite intrigues culminated in 1745, when a messenger from the monastery to the "King" at Rome, Father Macdonnell, actually proposed the raising of a regiment of Bavarians to assert the rights of the Royal Stuart. The "King" was prudent enough to thank the messenger for his good intentions, but to decline the proposal. Another priest of St James's accompanied the Pretender on his invasion of England as confessor, and was wounded at Culloden. Only with great difficulty and after many adventures he succeeded finally in escaping to the Continent disguised as the servant of the Bavarian ambassador's secretary. This was Gallus Leith. Born in 1709 he had early entered the Ratisbon seminary. After having professed he studied divinity and Canon law at Salzburg, and was then sent to Rome on business (1736). In 1756 he was chosen abbot and proved himself a capable ruler, only "too narrow-minded with regard to himself and others," as the chronicler puts it.[1]

In brilliant gifts, aristocratic bearing and a lofty and amiable disposition however, he is far surpassed by Benedict Arbuthnot, the last abbot, a true prince of the Church. The long period (1775-1820) during which he held office was very eventful for Ratisbon. For no sooner had the Diet meeting within its walls roused deeper interest in science, literature and art, promoting at the

[1] Brockie, *l.c.*

same time a refined social intercourse,[1] than the troublous
events in the world of politics made the country resound
with the tumult and rumours of war, and brought the
French within the very gates of the city.   We possess a
graphic account of the life in Ratisbon then from the pen
of Thomas Campbell, the poet, who was, at the beginning
of the century, the guest of the monastery; and the
skirmish, which he witnessed under the walls of the
building, gave rise to one of the most famous lyrical
poems of the language.[2]

Particularly interesting is Campbell's description of
Arbuthnot himself as we find it in his letters.   After
praising his unusually tolerant views he adds: " Dr.
Arbuthnot is one of the handsomest and strongest men I
have ever seen." . . . " Not to love him was impossible."
. . . " The whole of Bavaria," they told me, " lamented
his death.   When I knew him, he was the most commanding human figure I ever beheld.   His head was then
quite white, but his complexion was fresh and his features
were regular and handsome.   In manners he had a per-
petual suavity and benevolence.   I think I see him still
in the cathedral with the golden cross on his fine chest,
and hear him chanting the service with his full, deep
voice." [3]

Our sketch of the abbot would be incomplete, however, without having mentioned his scientific achievements.   He was especially learned in mathematics and
chemistry.   His lectures on these subjects were well
attended, and several of his essays were printed in the
Publications of the Royal Bavarian Academy of Sciences,[4]
of which he was a member.   Well stricken in years, he

[1] The worthy abbot was a conspicuous figure in the aristocratic circles
of the day.   The British Ambassador often made use of his services as
an interpreter.
[2] The well-known "Hohenlinden."
[3] Beattie, *Life and Letters of Th. Campbell*, vol. ii. 575.
[4] In 1775 he obtained a prize for a chemical essay.   See *Publ. of the
R. Bav. Ac. of Sc.* ix. 410, 436.   See also vols. vii. and viii.   A good
portrait of Arbuthnot is to be seen in the library of the Benedictine
Abbey at Fort Augustus, Scotland.

died in 1820, after having ruled the monastery for forty-four years.[1]

Two other remarkable men, who lived at St James's during his government, were P. Archibald M'Ivor and Romana Robertson. M'Ivor was a teacher of the Crown Prince of Bavaria and later Dean of Ratisbon Cathedral; Robertson served his monastery and England on several occasions in matters of political import. It is said of him that, when Napoleon decreed the secularisation of monasteries in 1803, Robertson wrote a petition, which he personally presented to Napoleon at Paris, and thus gained a postponement of the measure for the benefit of his Order. But according to tradition of a more trustworthy kind, it was Marshal Macdonald, Duke of Taranto, one of Napoleon's most famous generals, that successfully interceded for the monastery of his countrymen.

The second affair in which Robertson was implicated is as well attested as it is strange. There was at that time a Spanish general, called the Marquis of Romaña,[2] a fearless man, whose intense love of liberty had lost him the favour of Napoleon, then about to conquer Spain. In order to get rid of the patriot and his troops, he sent him to the Danish island of Fünen, in the far north of Europe, ostensibly with the purpose of co-operating with Bernadotte. Here the proud Marquis wasted away his days in hateful inactivity. To rescue him from this ignominious position, England accepted the services of Robertson, whose fitness for a mission of daring and secrecy had strongly impressed itself on the Duke of Richmond, then on a visit to the Scottish monastery at Ratisbon. He had proposed the name of the humble prior to the Duke of Wellington, and after an interview in London, when Robertson's reward was fixed and also the promise given to provide for his mother and two sisters in Scotland in case of failure, the bold messenger started on his journey (1808). His message to the general was that English ships were ready to carry him

[1] See the inscription on his monument in Appendix.
[2] Hence Robertson's name, " Romana Robertson."

and his troops to any port he wished, and that, if an insurrection against the usurper should take place in Spain, England would be ready to throw in her lot with that country. After many adventures Robertson left Heligoland, then English, and landed in Germany on board a smuggling vessel. A revenue cutter, the captain of which had been bribed, next brought him to Bremen, a city then in the hands of the French. Here he succeeded in procuring a passport under the name of an acquaintance of his, a German, who had died lately. On he went on his journey, heeding no warnings, by way of Lübeck to Kiel. Having laid in a stock of cigars and chocolate, he resolved to continue his expedition as a commercial traveller. At last Fünen was reached. But now the difficulty was to approach the Marquis so as not to rouse suspicion. After some futile attempts he in the end succeeded in obtaining an audience for the purpose of effecting a sale of his wares. Having given an account of himself by producing his papers, he was told by the Marquis, after some hesitation, that he accepted the English proposals. Robertson's mission was effected, and Romaña, making use of the opportunity of a grand parade of troops, which had been ordered by Bernadotte, and at which he himself intended to be present, collected as many soldiers as possible at Nyborg, his headquarters; and when the Commander-in-Chief arrived there, already some 10,000 men had embarked on English ships, which had been lying ready opposite the little town. They sailed first to England, thence to Spain, where Romaña's assistance was highly welcome.[1] As to Robertson, he reached the coast of Germany and London after many escapes and on all sorts of round-about ways cleverly

[1] General Romaña died in 1811. The Duke of Wellington, on the 23rd of January of that year, issued the following eloquent tribute to his memory: "His talents, his virtues and his patriotism were well known to H. M. Government, and I myself shall always gratefully acknowledge the assistance I received from him either in the field of action or in council. In him the Spanish army has lost its greatest ornament, his native land its most upright patriot, and the world the most active and zealous defender of a cause which still claims our attention."

contrived. He had been closely but ineffectually pursued by the French.[1]

Arbuthnot was the last abbot of the Scottish Monastery of Ratisbon. After him there were only priors, the number of monks gradually decreased, and, although a few Scotch boys were still taught at the seminary,[2] the final extinction could no longer be staved off. All appeals to the fact that the monastery for centuries had done good work in secular education also, were of no avail. Primate Dalberg prohibited the further reception of novices or pupils. This prohibition was withdrawn by King Ludwig I of Bavaria in 1827, but when the Bishop of Ratisbon declared that he wanted the buildings of the monastery for the extension of the clerical seminary, the Scottish Episcopacy acquiesced, an agreement was at last arrived at between Bavaria and the Vatican, and the Monastery was dissolved by a Breve of Pope Pius IX on the 2nd of September 1862 for the sum mentioned above. The old, time-honoured foundation of Marianus passed into German hands.

With regard to the "Schottenkloster" at Erfurt, the foundation of which is likewise lost in the obscurity of the XIth Century, we have to add that its existence, much chequered by the reverses of fortune, never produced any deep and lasting impression on its surroundings except in its connection with the University. In 1198 it was granted a privilege, afterwards confirmed by the Emperor Rudolf of Habsburg, according to which every damage done to its present or future property was punished by a fine of 100 talents "of pure gold." Towards the end of the XVth Century it was, as one of the chroniclers relates, "almost entirely ruinous," so that nobody trusted himself to live in it. About the same time Irish monks seem to have been received. There was a series of Irish abbots from the end of the XIVth Century. In the year 1450, Thaddæus II, the last of them, presented

---

[1] See Robertson, *Story of a Secret Mission to the Danish Isles*, 1863.

[2] From 1713-1855 one hundred and forty-one Scottish youths received their training at the school of the monastry. See Appendix.

a pamphlet to all the teachers of the University, in which he defended himself against a certain Magister Heynemann, and others, who had publicly maintained that the monastery did as much belong to them as to him, *he being Irish.* Abbot Matthæus commenced the building of a new monastery; but this edifice was burned down to the ground, together with the church, at the time " when the fatal conflagration took place " at Erfurt in 1472. Then, indeed, misery and distress reached their height. "The abbot, however, did not become discouraged," the old chronicler continues; "he collected contributions from his countrymen in Germany and received a 'considerable' writing, with seals attached to it, from the abbots of Ratisbon, Würzburg and Constance and other prelates, who all of them spoke in moving terms of the pitiable condition of the Scottish Monastery at Erfurt, exhorting pious Christians to contribute their donations. The sum collected, however, was not sufficient to repair the damage in any way. The abbot therefore saw himself obliged to pawn fields, vineyards, houses and other property of the Monastery, in order to make the most urgent repairs and to have a roof over his head again." [1]

At the beginning of the next century Abbot Benedictus was in a similar plight. He also was anxious to rebuild the ruined edifice (1510), but not having the means, and the " great Lords rather putting him off with letters of recommendation than affording him any real assistance, he likewise resorted to the sale of monastic property, by which means he was able to restore the church in the way it remained until the year 1724." [2]

In 1514 the altar dedicated to St Ninian and given and endowed by two citizens of Erfurt, Scotsmen by birth, named Balthasar Barding (?) and Jacob Flamingk (Fleming), was erected.[3]

During the period of the Reformation there was

[1] Falkenstein, *Thür. Chronik,* 1738, iii. 1065.
[2] *Ibid.,* p. 1066.
[3] Tettau, *Bau- und Kunstdenkmäler* (Monuments of Architecture and Art), at Erfurt, 1890, p. 180.

temporarily only *one* monk in the monastery. But he continued regularly to say mass. Matters became still worse after the occupation of Erfurt by the Swedes in 1632. The monastery of the Scots was then made a present to the community and afterwards sold by the magistrates. It had, however, to be given back to the Order after the Peace of Prague [1] in 1635.

Finally, the use of the church of the monastery was granted to the congregation of St Nicholaus in 1744; the definite property of which it became in 1820, when the secularisation took place. Joseph Hamilton was the last prior, a man whose great benevolence is repeatedly mentioned. Every morning between nine and ten o'clock he gave free advice to the sick, and tried to cure them with the help of electricity. He also willingly paid visits to poor patients in their houses, carrying with him his electric machine. [2]

The former monastery served for some time as military store-house; afterwards the military academy was built on its site (1858).

We are better informed of the history of the Scottish monastery at Würzburg (Herbipolis) in Bavaria. To the north of the Marienberg, afterwards strongly fortified, on the western banks of the Main River, rises the hill of Girsberg or Geiersberg. At the time of the foundation of the monastery in the XIIth century there was no human dwelling on it; a bare and bleak mountain, waiting for its cultivation from the industrious hands of the monks. Here then Bishop Embricho, in answer to the prayer of an Irish-Scottish monk, named Christian, granted the foreign pilgrims a home for the sake of St Kilian, the apostle and martyr of Franconia. Thus the primary destination of the building appears to have been a resting place (hospitium) for the Irish pilgrims to Rome and for the missionaries. As coat-of-arms the young foundation showed a shield with a scallop-shell and two

[1] Tettau, *Bau- und Kunstdenkmäler*, p. 136.
[2] Hartung, *Häuser Chronik des Stadt Erfurt* (Chronicle of houses in the town of Erfurt), 1878, ii. 180.

crossed pilgrim-staves. Pope Coelestin in 1195, Clement
IV in 1348, and the Emperor Charles IV in 1355, confirmed all its privileges, liberties and possessions.[1]

And these were already large. Embricho had given
his estate of Wolfsthal, with all its "meadows, forests
and waters," to the monastery, and endowed the chapel
with a "meadow along the Main," and with the river
itself, "as wide as the meadow" (1142). Other pious
men and women left other estates, houses and vineyards.
Sums of money also were forthcoming, nay, even serfs
and their services were handed over to the monastery as
legacy.[2]

The political events of the times, however, did not
allow this flourishing condition to continue long. Already
the year 1400 proved disastrous to the free development
of the new foundation, in consequence of a war waged
by the citizens of Würzburg against their Bishop Gerhard.
How severe these losses must have been appears from a
convention arrived at by Bishop Johann and the citizens
of Würzburg in 1402, when the latter agreed to pay the
sum of 40,000 pounds' weight of pence for damage done
to various religious houses.[3] On other occasions also
rapacious hands tried to possess themselves of monastic
property. It required a bull of Pope Martin V in 1418
to stem this course of spoliation.

An important resolution was arrived at by the Abbots
of Würzburg and Erfurt, and the Prior and Monks of St
James's at Ratisbon, after the death of their Abbot John
in 1479 (October 22nd); according to which the Abbot
of Würzburg had the right to nominate a candidate for

[1] *Reg. Bav.* i. 365. *Royal Archives* (Würzburg) *Copeibuch,* fol. 28
and 28b. Cp. M. Wieland, *Das Schottenkloster zu St Jakob zu
Würzburg* (The Scottish Monastery of St James at Würzburg) in the
*Archiv des Historischen Vereins (Society) von Unterfranken und Aschaffen-
burg,* xvi. 2, p. 1-182 (1863).

[2] Wieland, *l.c.,* p. 168.

[3] The monastery also received as the emoluments of a canonry, bread and
wine in daily rations, corn at certain seasons, meat at Martinmas, and
two pounds of mustard (!). In the division of certain tithes, payable to
the cathedral, it received a share like every canon. Wieland, p. 80.

the abbacies of Constance and Memmingen with the consent of the other Scottish abbots. If he had no other suitable individual, the monastery of Ratisbon was to furnish one. Other paragraphs aimed at the restriction of the power of the Abbot of Ratisbon, who, it would appear, had exercised it somewhat arbitrarily and too severely. It was further agreed, that no prelate should be allowed to sell any property of the house, except with the consent of the other prelates; that no benefice of the Scottish nation should be given to a German, and that all the elections for vacant offices had to take place at Ratisbon.[1]

In spite of all these efforts the tide of decay that set in towards the end of the XVth Century, could not be stemmed. At the death of Abbot Philip (1497), there was not a single monk left; there was no grain nor wine in barn or cellar, and the walls of the building threatened to come down. The reason of this seems to have been partly the mismanagement of the abbots, partly the unruly times, partly the ignorance of the foreign monks of German law in their frequent legal difficulties arising out of property, tithes, and other questions.[2]

Be this as it may, Pope Alexander VI, taking charge of the deserted monastery, tried to mend matters by introducing German monks. But his hopes were doomed to disappointment. The Peasants' War had plundered and destroyed the sacred buildings, and the Germans in 1547 arrived at the same end, after an administration of only about fifty years, as the Scots after three hundred.

It was then that a new helper arose in the person of the excellent Bishop Julius. When attending the Diet of Ratisbon in 1594, he took up his quarters in the Monastery of St James, and was received and entertained with princely honours by its abbot John James White (Albus), a scholarly and generous man, who did not lose the opportunity of pressing the claims of the Scots to the foundation of Würzburg, with his noble visitor.

[1] Wieland, *l.c.*, p. 172 f.   [2] *Ibid., l.c.*, p. 13.

This reason would have been quite sufficient to explain the Bishop's later actions with reference to the Scottish monastery. But the people's mind in those days required more than cold logic; it loved to trace back every great event, every ancient foundation of Church or Cloister to a miracle, a direct interference of Providence. It was a dream that once led the old Irish monk to build his narrow cell at Ratisbon; it was an illness unto death that made Bishop Julius vow to restore the monastery at Würzburg to its rightful owners, and thus become its second founder in the case of his recovery. The violent fever left him, he returned to Würzburg, restored the monastery, paid its debts, and requested the Abbot of Ratisbon to send some learned Scottish[1] monks. These were most solemnly, in the presence of the most noble men of Franconia, reintroduced into their own. After this time the existence of the monastery was no longer disturbed, although it continued to suffer much from the war. Many good abbots directed their attention to missionary and educational work; the library[2] was increased; a guest-house built, the other buildings were enlarged and improved. At the same time the fortifications of Würzburg gradually encroached upon the Girberg. One large vineyard after another was lost, besides many houses and properties, which paid their rents to the monastery. The owners, of course, were compensated,[3] but the fact of being now placed within the rayon of fortifications led to many hardships. At various periods the precincts of the monastery were requisitioned by the military for their stores. Latterly

[1] Wieland p. 17.

[2] *Ibid.* p. 67. It contained about 8000 volumes at the time of its secularisation. In 1715, 745 guests used the hospitality of the monks.

[3] In 1645, the compensation awarded by Prince Bishop Johann Philip, amounted to 733 gulden in money, 46 quarters of corn, 4½ of wheat, 3 of oats, 1 quarter of peas, 1 waggon-load of wine, 1 ox, and 1 hundredweight of carp. In 1664 were added: several rents; wine; 200 fl. ready money; 2 cwt. of carp; 1 cwt. of cod; 50 lb. of butter; a quarter of a tun of herrings, salt, etc. All this annually. See Wieland p. 18.

the difficulty of obtaining monks and novices from Scotland was experienced as in Ratisbon, so here also. In 1803 the old foundation was secularised; the books were incorporated with the Royal University Library; the archives now formed a part of the Royal Archives; the wonder-working relics of St Macarius, the first abbot, were transferred to St Mary's Chapel on the Market Square, and the whole buildings were converted into a military hospital.[1]

To this short sketch of the history of the "Schotten-kloster" at Würzburg, we now add some biographical notices of its monks and abbots.[2] The first abbot was Makarius; he was early reverenced as a saint, and died in 1153. His burial place was for a long time unknown, until it was miraculously rediscovered in 1614 by a monk Gabriel. Abbot Philippus was made chaplain to Charles IV (1355), and showed great diplomatic skill. Franciscus Hamilton, one of his successors, obtained his degree of divinity at the University of Würzburg, and was elected Abbot in 1602. As such he worked hard to pay off the debt of the monastery. In 1609 he re-signed and went to Munich in the service of William and Maximilian of Bavaria. He was followed by Guilelmus Ogilbaeus (Ogilvie), who increased the number of monks and decorated the buildings. It was during his tenure of office that the town was besieged by Gustavus Adolfus, and after a last desperate resistance surrendered. Ogilvie

[1] What became of the many pictures, among others of an original portrait of Queen Mary and of that of General Alex. Hamilton, the gun-maker, painted by Van Dyck, we do not know.

[2] For a list of abbots see Appendix. The income of an abbot at Würzburg in the XVIth Century amounted to about 200 gulden. He received as honorary gifts: a glass of wine from the Chief-Magistrate on the third day after Whitsunday at the close of the "Vespers"; a wreath of flowers on Corpus-Christi-day from the parishioners of Burkard, when they proceeded to the Scottish Church early in the morning at four o'clock, and a large candle at Candlemas from the Cathedral after High Mass. (Wieland, p. 87.) Besides this he was lord of the manor of Gerchsheim, over which he had the jurisdiction. (Wieland, p. 88.) A solemn court of justice was held there annually between Christmas and Ash Wednesday, and the abbot had the privilege of bringing with him 12 horses, 12 mounted men, 1 servant, 3 dogs and 1 hawk.

met the conqueror with the keys of the city in his hands,
and by his pleading succeeded in assuaging the anger of
the King (1631).

A man of equally high character and untiring energy
was Abbot John Audomarus Asloan. A friend of the
Bishop he ruled wisely and well, always mindful to have
the account-books and the tithe-rolls of the house in
good order. So well known were his excellent business
qualities, that the monks at Ratisbon desired him for
their abbot, when in 1639 Algacus had left their
monastery in a deplorable condition. For a time he
seems to have gone and assisted there as temporary
"administrator."[1]   He died in 1661.

Ambrosius Cook, who ruled the monastery from 1689-
1703, was a man of a very different type. He showed
a weak, vacillating, worldly character; now rigorous, now
lax; often abroad, preferring the intercourse with boon
companions to the solitary life of a religious house. In
1697, when one of the Patres, Macarius Brown, had
died in Scotland and left a legacy to Würzburg, he
set out himself for that country, to receive it. But
instead of four weeks he stayed a year, without writing a single line either to his monks or to the Bishop.
When summoned (Feb. 18, 1699) to appear in person
before his superiors, he replied from Paris, that he
intended to enter the religious fraternity at La Trappe,
asking at the same time that his post might be kept
open for him during his novitiate. But the severity of
the Trappist rules appears to have been too great for
him. He returned to Würzburg and for a time seems
to have lived soberly and honestly. But he relapsed
again; his way of living became so offensive, that after
having been shut up in the fortress for his misdeeds, he
was deposed in 1703. Towards the end of his life he
travelled much and finally retired to the Cistercian
Monastery of Düsselthal, in the diocese of Cologne,
where, piously obedient to the strictest rules, he at last
found peace.   He died in 1727.

[1] Cp. Part iv.

There were no abbots from 1703-1713 nor from 1753-1756. The last two filled their office worthily. Augustine Duff from Fochabers in Scotland is called the type "of a good shepherd."[1] He was an excellent scholar and a patron of the library. His death in 1753 prevented him from finishing the reconstruction of the chapel of St Makarius. Placidus Hamilton, finally, the last abbot, was of noble descent and united great prudence with scholarly attainments and a large experience of men and manners, which he had gathered on extensive travels. But as a ruler he was scarcely successful. Having retired to London in 1763 with a pension of 200 gulden from the Prince-Bishop, he died there in 1786.[2]

From this time to the dissolution of the monastery there were only priors at the head of it.

Among the monks, a list of whom is given in the Appendix, Gabriel Wallace deserves a special notice. He is described as a man of great humility and excelling in the mortification of the body. He slept only three or four hours and was girt with a heavy, stout iron-chain.[3] Like many other ascetic monks he was given to visions and dreams. During one of his prayerful nights he heard, as the story goes, repeatedly and long continued "music of angels' voices" issuing from a certain place of the church, where it was said, but now forgotten, that St Makarius slept his last sleep. Having reported the matter to his superior he received permission to make a search, and when he had raised the floor he came upon a stone with the inscription: "Hic jacet Macarius, primus Abbas hujus ecclesiæ, per quem Deus vinum in aquam convertit." He also found other written documents testifying the same thing (1614). Bishop Julius then had the relics with great solemnity transferred to the main church and deposited in a stone coffin (1615).

---

[1] Wieland, *l.c.*, p. 133. [2] For a complete list of abbots see Appendix.

[3] " Vir humilitate et corporis sui castigatione insignis, quatuor tantum horas dormiens, catena ferrea lumbos cingens ponderosa satis et crassa." Wieland, *l.c.*, p. 106.

Of monks and priors, who excelled in literature, we shall have to speak elsewhere.[1] It only remains to mention the sad fate of Marianus Gordon of Banff, who, a descendant of the Marquis of Huntly and the Dukes of Gordon, entered the monastery in the 14th year of his age as a pupil. He showed great aptitude for learning, and having obtained a degree in arts as well as in theology, he went to St Gall for the study of Oriental languages, and remained there about a year and a half. After his return to Würzburg he was made a priest. It appears that Marianus had for some time past corresponded with Protestants, and not only read Protestant books, but taken steps to escape from the monastery and embrace the Lutheran doctrine. Some of his letters to Protestant authors were intercepted; Protestant books were discovered in his cell together with writings of his own, which were sufficient to convict him of heresy. He was sentenced to imprisonment for three years (1732). At first he was detained in St James's Monastery, but, when new letters of his to his Protestant friends were discovered, his prison was changed to the so-called " Pfaffen-thurm " (Priest's-tower) in the fortress of Marienberg. Here the unfortunate young man, against whose moral conduct not a voice was raised, died by his own hand on the 12th of November 1734.[2]

At the time of the secularisation of the monastery in 1803 there were still eight patres in it, viz.: Placidus Geddes from Edinburgh, prior; Kilian Pepper from Crieff, for some time missionary in England; Columban Macgowen from Balquhain, an excellent disciplinarian and a zealous monk, who was prior twice; Gallus Carmichael from Perth, who died as octogenarian at Würzburg in 1824; Andreas Geddes from Cairnfield; Maurus Macdonald from the Hebrides, a good botanist; Joannes Bapt. Anderson, who during an eventful life had been a slave in Africa, and who died at Würzburg in 1828,

---

[1] See Part iv. : Statesmen and Scholars.

[2] This story has been published with all the documents in the *Journal for Franconia* (i. 114-361, ii. 558).

reverenced and loved for his piety; and lastly, Benedictus Ingram, who removed to Frankfort-on-the-Main.[1]

The last prior, and also the last Scottish monk in Würzburg, was Placidus Geddes, who died at Würzburg at the ripe age of 82, in 1839.

Once again at the time of the Reformation an intimate intercourse in matters of religion, a mutual giving and taking, took place between Scotland and Germany. In the early centuries of the Middle Ages the question was one of working out a monastic ideal to the glory of Rome; now scores of Scottish pilgrims went to Wittenberg to enrich their armoury and to sharpen their swords in defence of a new doctrine.

Already in 1525 (July 17th) the Scottish Parliament had passed an Act prohibiting the introduction and the reading of "Luthyr's" books.[2] In August of the same year the King issued an order to the Magistrates of Aberdeen (the University of which town was then upholding the Erasmian teaching), mentioning not only strangers in possession of Luther's, the heretic's, books, as did the Act of Parliament, but others as well. The law is to be rigorously enforced. All those that favour the new doctrine are to be deprived of their goods. To this the Lords of Council, disquieted at the rapid spreading of the reformer's opinions, added two riders in 1527, explaining that all subjects of the King being "assisters" to the heresy should likewise be punishable, and that the permission formerly granted of "disputing and rehersing" those "opunyeouns" should be restricted to "clerkis of the sculis alanerlie."

But no restriction could quench the new spirit.

One of the first that felt its influence and was to seal it with his blood was that noble Patrick Hamilton, the precursor of Knox and the protomartyr of the Scottish Church. The year of his birth cannot now exactly be fixed; generally 1504 is adopted as such. During 1524-25 Hamilton studied at St Andrews where he incurred

[1] See Part iv.: Statesmen and Scholars.
[2] *Acts of Parliament (Scot.)*, ii. 295.

the suspicion and the hatred of Cardinal Beaton. He had formerly, probably during his stay at Paris, become acquainted with Luther's writings, but not till 1525 did he publicly express his adherence or at least his sympathy with the prescribed doctrines. To study these at their source and to avoid further proceedings on the part of the Cardinal, he left Scotland in 1526, accompanied by John Hamilton, Gilbert Winram, and a servant. In Wittenberg he made the acquaintance of Luther and Melanchthon. As, however, his name as "cives academicus" does not occur in the album of that University,[1] but appears as the thirty-fourth among the names of the one hundred and four students who signed the roll at the opening of the newly-founded University of Marburg,[2] the hypothesis " that he left Wittenberg on account of the plague which raged in the city and necessitated even a temporary removal of the University," seems to be deserving of some credit. Hamilton stayed at Marburg for six months only; a time too short, one would think, to commence the study of theology, but long enough for him to receive powerful impressions and to purify and strengthen his faith. He was particularly influenced by the venerable Lambert of Avignon, then Professor of Theology, and by Hermann von dem Busche, one of the leading humanists of the day. It was Lambert that persuaded him to write the only little treatise we possess from his pen, his so-called "loci" or "theses," in which he explains Luther's doctrine of justification by faith in the words of the New Testament. He had much intercourse besides with Tyndale and Frith, his friend, who having left Worms had sought the protection of the Hessian prince. It is a remarkable fact that the small town, so picturesquely perched on a hill above the Lahn River, should thus have harboured at the same time three future martyrs of the New Faith within its walls. Tyndale died at the stake at Vilvoerde on the 6th of August 1536; Frith suffered martyrdom three years earlier.

In the meantime there arose in Hamilton, after he had strengthened his views in personal contact and friendly

[1] See Appendix.   [2] See Appendix.

communion with the greatest reformers of Germany, the ardent wish to speak and to proclaim this faith to his countrymen. His time of flight and of preservation of life was followed now by the time of fight and self-sacrifice. He left Marburg, in spite of the urgent advice of his remaining Scottish friends, in the autumn of 1527. His fate is known. On the 28th of February 1528 he gave up the ghost after long-continued terrible sufferings at the stake. Lambert says of him: "His learning was for one so young uncommonly great, and his judgments in matters of divine truth extremely clear and well founded. His intention in coming to Marburg was to become still more rooted in the truth, and I can honestly say that I seldom met anyone that could talk of the Word of God with greater depth of insight and with a firmer conviction. We often conversed about these subjects."[1]

In close connection with Hamilton the history of the Scottish Reformation mentions Alexander Alesius, whose proper name was Alane. He was born on the 23rd of April 1500 at Edinburgh, and was in his youth a canon of the St Augustinian Monastery at St Andrews, and a zealous opponent of Luther. He even undertook to convert the imprisoned Hamilton. But the contrary happened; he himself, profoundly moved by the firmness of the martyr, began to be doubtful about the truth of the Roman doctrines. More and more convinced of his own errors, he attacked the luxurious life of the priests, especially that of his prior Hepburn, who, having been educated in France, had grown up a proud and prodigal prelate. As a consequence he was several times cast into prison by his enraged superior, from which finally not even the intercession of the King could save him. With the help of his fellow-canons he succeeded, however, to escape and to gain the shores of the Firth under the protection of night. Neither did his hope of meeting a vessel[2] there deceive him. Before daybreak he was on

---

[1] Cp. Lorimer, *Life of Patrick Hamilton.*
[2] The owner of the vessel is called by Alesius a "homo germanus," not necessarily implying that the ship was a German ship.

board, and when the troopers of his enemy appeared on the scene he was already on his way to Dieppe. A violent storm, however, carried the ship away to the north, as far as the Sound and the town of Malmoe in Sweden. Here Alesius encountered, to his astonishment, a community of Scottish merchants who, as they commonly did in foreign lands, kept their own preacher and had accepted the new teaching two years ago. At last the ship reached Antwerp and Bruges, from which latter place our exile went to Cologne (1532). But in spite of the friendly reception of Hermann von Wied[1] he did not stay long. He was drawn towards Wittenberg. There in the enjoyment of most familiar intercourse with the great reformers, especially with Melanchthon, who confessed to a predilection for the Scots,[2] he declared his adhesion to the Articles of the Augsburg Confession, or, in other words to the Lutheran Church, although, as he expressed himself, " in some things he missed moderation and a certain sense of justice," remaining an advocate of conciliation to the end. During this his first stay at the University he chiefly studied Greek and Hebrew and composed his treatise against the prohibition of the Scottish bishops to read the Bible in the mother tongue. It was this pamphlet that prepared the victory of the Reformation in Scotland, although the right which Alesius claimed was only granted to the people of Scotland ten years later, in 1543. It was this pamphlet also which drew upon him the censure of the famous controversialist on the Catholic side, Dobeneck or Cochlæus,[3] against whom he frequently entered the lists with his pen or his spoken word. In 1535 he went to England as the bearer of Melanchthon's letters to King Henry VIII and Archbishop Cranmer. He was

---

[1] An archbishop favouring the Protestant cause (1477-1552).

[2] In a letter to the University of Wittenberg Melanchthon writes: " We owe something to the Scottish nation, for although disciples of the apostles established churches in Germany, they were afterwards destroyed by the Honeti and Huns, and the Scots with great labour restored them " (Feb. 1, 1542). *Corpus Reform.* iv. 770.

[3] Born 1479, died 1552.

well received, the Court at that time being anxious for a union with the Protestant princes of Germany. The post of public lecturer at Cambridge was given to him, and he taught Hebrew and Greek in the same college where Erasmus had been lecturing before him. Soon, however, on his friendship with Melanchthon becoming known, he was subjected to all kinds of indignities. A leader of the Roman Catholic party, who had challenged him to a public debate, but had failed to appear on the appointed day, now secretly agitated against him. Riots among the students followed, and Alesius' life was in danger. Thus compelled, he returned to London, where for about three years he gained a scanty livelihood by the practice of medicine, to the study of which he had already given some attention. But when the King tried to enforce the doctrine of transubstantiation and the celibacy of the priests, he resigned his office as public teacher, sold whatever he possessed, and, being timely warned by the Archbishop, fled to the house of a German sailor, who conveyed him in the disguise of a sailor on board a vessel bound for Holland. Two friends, John Macalpine and John Fyffe or Fidelis, accompanied him. Having safely reached Wittenberg, he accompanied Melanchthon soon afterwards to Worms.[1] But the greatest service that his friend rendered him was that of procuring for him the appointment as Professor of Divinity at Frankfurt on the Oder. *Thus Alesius became the first academical teacher of the new doctrine in Brandenburg.* In his inaugural dissertation, " De restituendis scholis," he energetically advocated the necessity of a University training for clergymen. After a stay of two years the "perfervidum ingenium" attributed to Scotsmen led him into what seems to have been an unseemly quarrel with the magistrates of the city on the subject of the suppression of prostitution. Being thwarted, he resigned his office suddenly, much to the

---

[1] Cruciger in a letter to Luther, dated Nov. 6, 1540, announces the arrival of Alesius. See Burckhardt, *Luther's Briefwechsel* (Correspondence).

disgust of his friend Melanchthon,[1] and went to Leipzig, where he was honourably received and made Professor of Theology in 1544. Now at last the " wanderer "[2] was at rest. The remaining twenty-one years of his life he spent at this famous University. Twice, in 1555 and 1561, he was chosen Rector. Here he published most of his exegetical and apologetical writings, one of the most important of which was his *Cohortatio ad concordiam pietatis* ("Exhortation to unity in love "), dedicated to the Scottish nation, its barons and prelates. In it he eloquently pleads for brotherly union, a cause which Knox took up after him with much energy. The whole tendency of his mind in religious matters was, indeed, one of conciliation, like that of his great German teacher and friend. The extreme views of the Lutheran party he disliked. Accordingly, when at the Diet of Ratisbon in 1541 a mutual approach of the two hostile parties among the Evangelicals appeared possible, we find him heading a deputation, which was sent to Luther at the instigation of the two brothers Georg and Joachim of Brandenburg, to try and make this man of iron yield.

Honoured by his colleagues and his Prince, loved by Melanchthon; courageous, where courage was needed, and yet showing a moderation rare among the reformers of his adopted country, Alesius died in 1565, on the 17th of March. His only son had at a tender age preceded him. Probably the father rests in the same grave in the church of St Paul, though there is no stone to mark his last resting-place.[3] Beza says of him: " He was dear to all scholars and beloved by them, and would have been an ornament to Scotland if the light of the

[1] See Letter of Malanchthon to J. Camerarius : " Alesius the Scot has left Frankfurt, and although he has done so against my advice, some seat is to be sought for him." *Corp. Reform.* iv. 760.

[2] Alesius was the name given to Alan by Melanchthon. Its meaning is " Wanderer."

[3] Alesius invites Melanchthon in a friendly Latin letter to the wedding of his youngest daughter in 1557. Cp. Mitchell, *Scottish Reformation*, p. 300 f.

Gospel had been granted earlier to that country. Rejected by Scotland and England, he was warmly welcomed by the Evangelical Church of Saxony, and highly esteemed to the end of his life."

As to the above-mentioned friends of Alesius, they also obtained high positions among the scholars of the age. Macalpine, or Maccabaeus, as Melanchthon had christened him, became Doctor of Divinity at Wittenberg,[1] Luther himself presiding at the ceremony, and afterwards accepted a call from King Christian III to his University of Kopenhagen, having been recommended by the two German reformers. There he laboured as Professor of Divinity till his death in 1557. He was a very learned, pious and moderate theologian. Denmark owes to him and some of his friends the Bible translated into Danish.

Joannes Fidelis, alias Faithus or Fyffe, was for a time evangelical preacher at Liegnitz in Silesia, after having obtained a thorough mastery of the German tongue. Afterwards he was called to Frankfurt-on-the-Oder as the successor of Alesius.

Thus we see that the precursors of Knox during the first period of the Scottish Reformation, *when the foremost question was the separation from Rome, turned to Wittenberg and Luther*, whilst in the second period, *when the new ideas were to be embodied into a sharply defined doctrine and system of Church government, the Scottish theologians flocked to Geneva and Calvin*. Wishart was the first of these. He was followed by John Knox.

The connection of the latter with Germany is, though slight, not without interest or importance. It was in the year 1554 that the call reached him at Geneva to be one of the preachers of the English-Scottish Congregation of refugees at Frankfurt-on-the-Main. Driven out of England

---

[1] In Denmark also the Scots have played a part. The son of Maccabaeus was a clergyman of high rank ('Prälat') and a gifted Latin poet (†1598). A Scot, P. Davidson, formerly a teacher at Cologne, was called to Kopenhagen as Professor of Theology, when this University was founded in 1479.

during the persecution of Bloody Mary, they had settled in
this city and obtained permission to worship in the same
church with the exiled Walloons and French, provided
a common form of divine service could be arrived at.
After a good deal of bickering, the English Prayer-Book
in a modified form had obtained the sanction of Knox and
Calvin. The new order of worship was provisionally
adopted for one year; differences of opinion during that
time were to be decided by Calvin and Bullinger. All
went well, until the year 1555, when a certain Dr Cox,
afterwards Bishop of Ely, arrived at Frankfurt. He at
once commenced a quarrel about the liturgy; grave
breaches of decorum occurred during service, and Knox
saw himself obliged to rebuke his adversary sharply.
Apparently he gained his purpose; the conditional permission to use the church may have prevented the opposite
party from open rupture. But in secret they agitated
and continued to agitate against the new preacher. Cox
even went so far as to inform the Magistrates that in
Knox's *Admonition to the true Professors of the Gospel*,
there occurred a passage in which the German Emperor
was compared with Nero.[1] Thereupon the senate, being
afraid the Emperor, who was then at Augsburg, might
issue an order to surrender Knox, banished him from the
city. It was on the 26th of March 1555, that the
Scottish reformer, accompanied for some miles by a number
of friends, proceeded on his return journey to Geneva.
On the previous night, before an audience of some fifty
people, he had preached a powerful sermon in his own
lodgings on the death and the resurrection of Christ and
the blessed reward of believers after the tribulations and
persecutions of this world. In the whole affair he had acted
with rare moderation, and Calvin in a letter to Cox complains of the rough and arbitrary treatment of his friend.[2]

[1] Knox apostrophises England and foretells utter ruin for her if she
insists upon returning to Egypt, that is, to conclude alliances, marriages
and treaties with princes, who maintain idolatry such as the Emperor
(" who is no less an enemy of Jesus Christ than Nero ever has been ").
[2] Letter dated May 31, 1555 : "This one thing I cannot keep secret,

Before we complete our account of the Scottish Reformers in Germany by giving a short sketch of the brothers Wedderburn, who by their spiritual songs and psalms contributed so much to the popularising of the new doctrine, a word or two must be said about John Willock, a friend and companion of Knox. He had fled from London to Emden in Friesland in 1553, the disastrous year of the English Mary's accession. Here he practised the art of medicine, in which he was an adept, and having recommended himself to Anna, the energetic ruler of the duchy by his skill and discretion, he was sent twice to Scotland by her on diplomatic business, to congratulate the queen on her accession and to promote better commercial facilities between the two countries. After 1558 he supplied the place of Knox in Edinburgh, became moderator of the General Assembly in 1563, and died in 1585.

John Wedderburn was descended from an old family of merchants at Dundee, where he was born in 1500. Early already he showed an inclination towards the new teaching, which was still further strengthened by the influence of John Major at St Andrews, and by the cruel death of Hamilton. He evaded persecution by timely flight in 1539 or 1540, and turned his feet, like so many of his friends, towards Wittenberg, "the city of the prophets." The name of "Joannes Scotus," entered in the University album between those of Alesius and Maccabaeus, is very probably his own. During a stay of two years' duration in this place, he doubtless acquired that fixedness and depth of principles and that clear insight into the fundamental requirements of the Protestant theology, which shows itself so distinctly and repeatedly in his book of songs. Being, like his brothers, poetically gifted, he was especially influenced by the German sacred poetry, and Luther, in his masterly. terse and homely employment of

that Master Knox was in my judgment neither godly nor brotherly dealt with." See *Brief Discourse of the troubles begun at Frankfurt*, p. 51. See also *Original Letters relat. to the English Reformation*, ii., letters ccclvii. and following. (Parker Soc.)

the German language, became his prototype.   After the
model of the German " Geistliche Gesänge, Psalmen und
Lieder " (Spiritual songs, psalms and hymns), especially
those that had appeared in the hymn books of Magdeburg
and Strassburg, he resolved to publish a collection of
songs in the Scottish vernacular.   In doing so, he proceeded in the same manner that the development of
German hymnology had taught him : he started from the
secular poem, the love-song, the hunting-song, and so
forth, and filled these songs with a new spiritual meaning,
whilst very frequently retaining the tune of the old
popular song also.   To this he added a large number of
translations from the German.   It is to this wise, if to
modern readers sometimes startling, adaptation of that
which was already living in the people's hearts, and was
affectionately cherished by them, that his collection owed
its enormous and until recently not sufficiently acknowledged success and influence on the newly awakening
religious life of the nation ; a nation to which the divine
arts had meted out their gifts more sparsely, indeed, than
to other nations favoured by a milder sky and softer surroundings, but a nation that had in this great struggle not a
mind only to be convinced, but a heart also to be cheered
and warmed and filled with the soft glow of enthusiasm.

The book of the brothers Wedderburn,[1] the first hymn
book of the Scottish Church, was published in 1567,
under the title, " Ane compendious Booke of Godlie and
Spirituall Songs," or shortly called the " Dundee Psalms." [2]

It contains first a calendar; then follows the catechism; the
ten commandments, the Apostolic creed and Lord's Prayer,
baptism, etc., being translated from the text of Luther.
These six items are succeeded by five hymns on faith,
baptism and the Lord's Supper, the originals of which are
also to be found with Luther.   A number of graces

[1] The younger brother of John, Robert, had a share in the compilation
of the book, though it is no longer possible to say which songs are his.

[2] Some of the songs appeared first printed on broad-sheets, exactly as
in Germany, where the two first hymns of Luther were thus published
in 1523.

before and after meat, such as appear in many of the old German hymn books, conclude the first part. The spiritual songs begin with two on the confession of sins; they contain, besides songs on the war of the flesh against the spirit and on the cross, a metrical paraphrase of the parables of the prodigal son and of Lazarus; and finally, a hymn on the passion of our Lord. Then follow the acknowledged translations from the German, twenty-two psalms, and several hymns.

In the third part we are introduced to the spiritually remodelled popular songs. It is now no longer the girl that calls out: " Quho is at my window? quho? quho?" but God. In the hunting-song : "With huntis up," the Pope is the fox, the hounds are Peter and Paul. It is only natural that here we should find much that sounds to our ears intolerable in its rudeness. As to the tunes, Wedderburn took them where he could find them, in Scottish popular songs and in German hymns.

As we mentioned above, the circulation of these songs was at once rapid and wide, and this in spite of a prohibition in 1549, which ordered a search for them to be made, and " the books of rhymes and songs containing such abominable defamations of the priests and heresies of all kinds," to be confiscated and burned, and in spite of the Act of Parliament of the year 1551, against the unauthorised printing of books of "Ballatis, sangis, blasphematiounis, rhymes, etc." [1]

Of John Wedderburn we have to add, that he was at Dundee in 1546, but was obliged to flee again. He died in England in banishment (1546).[2]

The Reformation in Scotland has been spared the humiliation of having reared in its bosom brothers destined to be each other's bitterest foes. It is true, that in Scotland the episcopal form of worship was not finally abolished until 1688, after severe and obstinate struggles; but then this form never was the popular one,

[1] *Acts Parl. Scot.* ii. 488 f.
[2] Some examples of Wedderburn's songs and their German originals, see in the appendix.

the one advocated by the reformers of the nation, but only something foreign, something obtruded from without. In Germany, on the contrary, the war was raging between Calvinists and Lutherans, amongst the people, the teachers, and the rulers. It infected and poisoned social intercourse, it was a matter affecting the hearth, the pulpit and the throne. For about three hundred years, two Protestant Churches, both having gained their independence from Rome after cruel struggles only, could and would not take the step towards a friendly union, nay, not even towards mutual forbearance; and when at last it was accomplished by royal command, it was considered an act of Cæsar and Pope combined, a violent measure, that could not be conducive to any peace.

This Calvino-Lutheran feud with all its cruel bitterness forms indeed one of the saddest and most disgraceful chapters of German history. No Calvinist was admitted a godfather, whilst a Roman Catholic was. The question was seriously and obstinately argued whether children of a mixed marriage, that is of a Calvinistic father and a Lutheran mother, or *vice versa*, should be buried with Christian ceremonies, it being a heretic's child. ("Ketzerkind"). In the church of St Nicholas at Berlin, the condemnation of the Catholics and Calvinists was shortly condensed into the words: "he who is not Lutheran, is cursed."

We admit that this condition of things was deeply felt and mourned over by the nobler natures in the nation, especially by laymen. Not a few well-intentioned rulers, even tried to cut it short by edicts against the Lutheran wranglers, but with small effect. The idea of a union of the evangelical confessions would have remained a monstrosity, or at best, only the dim, timidly expressed hope of some gentle scholar, but for the persistent, unselfish, almost fanatical labours of John Durie or Duraeus, the Scot. What the liberation of Jerusalem was to the crusader, this peaceful union was to him: it filled his whole soul; it became the watchword of his life; the fountain in which his drooping courage was rejuvenated, and an ideal, which he never surrendered, though famishing by the roadside, weary of war and surrounded by enemies.

Let us now communicate to the reader what the most recent research has brought to light about the stirring life of this international Scotsman.[1]

The father of John Durie was Robert Durie, an Edinburgh clergyman of the strict Presbyterian type. He was known for his efforts in the cause of the evangelisation of the Orkney and Shetland Islands. When King James VI insisted upon introducing Anglican bishops into Scotland, he was banished with many others in the year 1606, and betook himself to Leyden in Holland, where he preached to a congregation of Scottish exiles. In this town, his son John, born in Edinburgh in 1595 or 1596, received his education. After having finished his course of divinity in Holland and at Sedan, he became tutor to the son of one Mr Panhusen, who was then pursuing his studies in France. This office he filled until the year 1624, when he was called to Elbing in the East of Prussia, as minister of a small congregation of Scottish and English Presbyterians. We cannot, however, exactly state the date of his arrival there. At all events in this small, out-of-the-way town Durie arrived at the turning-point of his life, which gave a peculiar direction to his whole future career. The King of Sweden, Gustavus Adolfus, of whom we have spoken so much in the second part of this book, had established at Elbing, then occupied by Swedish troops, a High Court of Justice, of which a certain lawyer and Doctor of Laws, Godemann, was the president. This learned man, being deeply interested in religious matters as well, became Durie's friend and sent him on one occasion a pamphlet, written by himself,

---

[1] F. Brandes, Joh. Duraeus in Germany. *Catholic Presbyterian Review*, 1882. July and August. Klähr Joh. Duraeus in the Monthly Review of the *Comenius Gesellschaft*. 1897. Tollin, Joh. Duraeus in the *Geschichtsblätter für Stadt und Land Magdeburg* (Historical Review for the town and district of Magdeburg), 1897, ii., 1898, i.

on the union of the Calvinists and the Lutherans in the
doctrine of the Lord's Supper (1628).   In this Durie
saw the hand of God, and his work in the interest
of this union he henceforth considered a divine call,
('vocatio interna').   With unwearied courage, and an
optimism which left him only towards the close of his
long life, he dedicated himself entirely to this task,
convinced to the last of its practicability with a blindness
almost tragic.

No doubt his chances appeared favourable in the commencement.   Godemann perceived that the precarious
position of the Protestants after the battle near the White
Mountain, after the successes of the great Wallenstein and
his consequent endowment with the Duchy of Mecklenburg
in 1629, rendered a close harmony between the Protestants
absolutely necessary.   And when Sir Thomas Roe, the
English Ambassador, who was to mediate between Poland
and Sweden, embraced the cause of the union likewise,
gaining over to his side the powerful Swedish Chancellor
Oxenstierna, success did not seem altogether impossible,
especially when calculating upon the expected energetic
assistance of the King.   To secure this success with a
still greater probability it seemed of first-rate importance
to the Swedish statesmen, that the work should be undertaken by a State which had remained neutral during the
internal strife of Germany.   Such a State they conceived
England to be; and, after having persuaded Durie to
resign his position in Elbing, they sent him to London,
well furnished with letters of introduction from Roe
(1630).   Here Durie succeeded in gaining the assent of
Archbishop Abbot and three other bishops; only about
twenty scholars and clergymen of the English and Scottish
Church gave in their adhesion to his plans of unification.
But it never occured to him, that Abbot was no longer a
man of commanding influence,[1] and that, the number of
English friends won over to his cause being infinitely
small, his mission had proved, if not altogether a failure,
yet only a very partial success.   He took with him the

---

[1] He had been superseded in power and jurisdiction in 1628.

letters of commendation and assent of these clerical dignitaries, and, calling himself a delegate of the English Church, he returned to Germany. There matters seemed to have improved in the meantime. At the Church Conference held at Leipzig in 1631 the Court Preacher of Brandenburg, a Calvinist, had declared himself in favour of peace, and the Lutheran champion, Hoe of Hoenegg, Court Chaplain at Dresden, lamenting the interconfessional quarrel, had advocated an amicable settlement. Durie himself, if he was present at the conference, does not appear to have taken a prominent part in it. It is certain, however, that in the same year he went to Gustavus Adolfus, then at Würzburg, to deliver a letter from his friend Roe. The King received him kindly and conversed with him for several hours. He also perceived the great advantage that would accrue to the Protestant Church, if the hostile parties could be reconciled. Yet he committed himself to no more than promising Durie a letter of recommendation to the Protestant princes of Germany, and commissioning a Lutheran clergyman to confer with the Lutherans, whilst Durie himself undertook to do the same with the Calvinists.[1] Unfortunately the promised letter, written by Sadler, the private secretary of the King, never reached its address. Durie thought he would first come to an understanding with the theologians before applying for it, but when in the following year King Gustavus had been killed at the battle of Lützen, neither his nor Oxenstierna's signature could be had any more. Durie's correspondence with the Calvinistic preachers and academies in Germany and elsewhere was of an amazing bulk; his efforts on journeys here and there to convince his friends of the nobility of his aim by word of mouth were no less surprising. But his hopes were still concentrated on the King of England as the chief promoter of his scheme, especially since, after the death of the Swedish Royal Champion, his expectations in the direction of Sweden had been considerably brought down, if they had not entirely collapsed. On a second journey to England

---

[1] Tollin, *l.c.*, p. 235.

in 1633 he found everything sadly changed. The
gentle Abbot had died. In his place there ruled
Laud as Archbishop of Canterbury, who refused to have
anything to do with Durie, a Presbyterian; so that the
latter had no other course open to him than to embrace
the Anglican creed, unless he wanted to relinquish his
cherished plans of a union of the Protestant Churches
with the help of England. He did not do so without
misgivings; he even thought it necessary to defend the
step he took with the excuse, that the confession of the
two Churches, the Presbyterian and the Anglican, was
really the same, and that mere outward forms and ceremonies had to give way before higher purposes. The
immediate effect of his ordination as clergyman of the
Church of England was his appointment to a living in
Lincolnshire, the income of which seems to have been
very acceptable to him just then. As to the rest, we
may well doubt if Durie's changed attitude in Church
matters really procured him the wished for advantages.
In the meantime he only received a letter of commendation,
written in general terms by Archbishop Laud and endorsed
by the learned Ussher, Archbishop of Armagh in Ireland.
On the other hand his Presbyterian friends called him
a Proteus, whilst his Anglican fellow-clergymen looked
upon him very much as upon a Presbyterian spy.

In the retinue of Roe he returned to Germany in 1634
and went to Frankfurt where a great meeting of Evangelical States was being held, called together by the
Landgrave William of Hesse, who at the same time had
invited the Prince of Orange and the States General of
Holland to this "work of peace." Here he presented his
"Judicia Theologorum Anglorum et aliorum de Pace Pro-
testantium sacra," and being supported by Oxenstierna
procured at least the resolution of the eight delegates that
"the efforts for peace were laudable and necessary, and
that both parties were to use moderation until the views
of their respective sovereigns could be ascertained and full
powers be received." Then came the terrible news of
the Swedish defeat at Nördlingen; the meeting was dis-

persed, and Durie saw very clearly that at the present
moment Germany offered a very unfavourable basis for
his peaceful experiments. He therefore went to the
Netherlands, where, at the Synod of Utrecht in April
1636, his efforts on behalf of "the good and sacred"
union between the Church of the Augsburg Confession
and the Calvinists met with the warmest and most genial
approbation. Moreover, Durie enjoyed the renewed
friendly intercourse with the famous Hugo Grotius,[1] who
suggested to him the idea of an English-Swedish Confession of Faith as the counterpart of the political alliance to
be concluded in the near future between the two countries.
He also made the acquaintance of Petrus Figulus Jablonski,
a Bohemian, known as the son-in-law of Comenius.[2] This
faithful friend accompanied him henceforward for seven
long years on all his journeys as secretary. But his visit
to Holland did not practically bring him nearer the realisation of his plans. Still less successful was his journey to
Sweden in 1636. Notwithstanding the friendship of the
Chancellor and the favour of the Queen during the first
months of his sojourn, he could neither overcome the intolerance of the Synod nor the enmity of Bishop Rudbeck
who hated "the stranger confessing the cursed heresy of
Calvinism."[2] Moreover, he had drawn upon him the disapproval of many by his inordinate love of publishing
matters not ripe for publication as well as by his attempts
to pose as a Lutheran. Oxenstierna was at last obliged to
discard the former favourite, and Christina, the Queen,
published a decree on the 7th of February 1638 to the
effect that the English clergyman, John Duraeus, having
given much offence to the Swedish clergy during his stay
in the country, was ordered to leave the kingdom without
delay.[3] A severe illness, however, brought about by
over-exertion and excitement, compelled Durie to post-
pone his departure until the month of August. He had
consecrated himself anew to his sacred task, and his

[1] Hugo Grotius, the famous Dutch scholar and statesman, was born in
1583 and died in 1645.
[2] Brandes, *l.c.*   [3] Tollin, p. 246.

undaunted enthusiasm served him well, for in Lübeck also and in Hamburg, whither he went after having left Sweden, he was unable to win the clergy over to his plans. The same spirit of harsh intolerance, which caused the poor English fugitives under John a Lasco, the pious reformer of Poland, to be driven out of these cities in mid-winter 1554, was still ruling.[1]

It was with the German princes that Durie found the readiest approval and support. The dukes Frederick Ulrich (†1635) and August, the founder of the famous library at Wolfenbüttel, in the arranging of which he lent a helping hand, showed a warm interest in his work, as did the princes of Anhalt, of Zweibrücken, the Landgrave of Hesse-Cassel, the counts of Isenburg and Solms, and above all the Elector of Brandenburg. In the meantime, however, he had been called to London to assist in the work of the Synod of Westminster. So studiously and unnoticed by the world did he apply himself to the labours of this assembly, that many of his friends on the Continent believed him dead. Politically he had done his utmost to save the unfortunate King Charles I by preparing a set of documents for him which were to prove his innocence.

After Cromwell had taken up the reins of government Durie yielded to pressure and for the sake of his one great object turned Puritan. He was appointed librarian of St James's, and received not only friendly letters from the Protector, but also a yearly stipend, which was to enable him to continue his journeys in the interest of religious peace. But it soon became clear that these recommendations, far from being a furtherance of his objects, became, in part at least, a danger and a snare. Many of the princes, as well as the Lutheran divines, turned from him as from a murderer of the King. Only in Switzerland his reception was enthusiastic. At the General Church Assembly of Aarau in 1654 he was celebrated as the "famous ambassador of the Protector." At Zürich a considerable sum was handed to him as a

[1] Dalton, *Johannes a Lasco*, Gotha, 1881, p. 433 f. 437 f.

national gift of honour towards his travelling expenses.
From almost all the reformed cantons he received com-
mendatory letters, and his cause was spoken of as one
worthy to be promoted by every Christian believer. The
above-named Calvinistic princes also received him warmly,
only the Elector of Brandenburg, influenced, no doubt, by
the attitude of Bergius, his Court Chaplain, who dis-
countenanced Durie's fickleness in joining a party of
murderers, preferred to treat with Cromwell direct about
the Evangelical Union through his ambassador in England.[1]
The senate of Frankfurt presented him in 1655 with
bread and wine ; that of Bremen promised him support.
In the Netherlands also he found ready consent. Thus he
returned loaded with documents and full of hope—a hope
which was, however, raised only by the Calvinistic parties
—in the following year to England. In London there
was satisfaction with the results of his efforts, and steps
were taken to make use of the new connections formed
by him as a basis for further international and inter-pro-
testant deliberations, when Cromwell died. After the
short rule of his son Richard, Charles II entered London
in triumph. It was a cruel dissappointment for Durie.
Neither the Archbishop of Canterbury nor the Bishop of
London nor the King himself noticed his letters. He,
as a friend of Cromwell, had no longer any chance in
England. Accordingly he left London in 1661. Henceforward he could no longer count on the support of this
country. But not even then did his courage fail him.
Though ageing fast he took up the work of reconciling
Lutherans and Calvinists in Germany with renewed
zeal. On the one hand the time chosen did not seem to
be inopportune. In the religious assembly at Cassel in
1661 the divines of Rinteln and Marburg had adopted the
" Tolerantia ecclesiastica," and the University of Rinteln
had been handed over to the Reformed or Calvinistic
Party. Frederick William, the Elector of Brandenburg,
had not only forbidden his subjects to study at Wittenberg,
in consequence of the most violent and scurrilous polemic

[1] Tollin, *l.c.*, p. 261.

of the learned Lutheran, Doctor Abraham Calovius, a professor at the said seat of learning (1662), but had also strongly commended peaceableness and moderation in their pulpit utterances to his clergymen,[1] and a more "amicable" attitude towards Calvinists. All uncharitable references to the latter as "heretics," "syncretists," were to cease, and instead of them, the sermons were to contain exhortations towards true Christian piety. In the opinion of this wise prince the "dissension" of the Evangelicals was "not fundamental."

On the other hand Durie had not sufficiently taken into account the growing enmity of the orthodox Lutheran clergy. This was the barrier which the most strenuous labour of a man, even in conjunction with powerful rulers, could not break.

A colloquy at Berlin, for the purposes of a union, took place under the presidency of Otto von Schwerin, a distinguished statesman and Durie's friend. But already during the discussion of the first question Reinhardt, a Lutheran clergyman and member of the consistory, declared, that "he could not recognise the Calvinists as brethren," whilst Paul Gerhardt, the famous author of some of the finest German hymns, added: "nor as Christians either."[2]

The assembled representatives of the two persuasions wrangled and debated until May 29th, 1663. Finally, the Elector, getting tired of all this, issued his so-called "Toleranz-Edict" in 1664, which punished with instant deprivation such recalcitrant clergymen as continued to decry their evangelical brethren. The solution of the question by a mere arbitrary "Le roi le veult" was, however, not what Durie insisted upon. He wanted *a union based upon conviction, and a conviction based upon brotherly love.* He made a last attempt. Aided and supported by the Landgravine Hedwig Sophia, the pious sister of the Great Elector, he commenced new negotiations in the City Chambers of Berlin on the 21st of August 1668; but

[1] Landwehr, *Kirchenpolitik des Grossen Kurfürsten*, p. 205.
[2] Tollin, *l.c.*, p. 274.

these also remained without result, partly, it must be owned, through the vagueness of Durie's own proposals. His unselfish zeal was praised; the hope was expressed that his good intentions would yet be rewarded; he was even presented with a gift of 100 thaler; but that was all. He received not even a written communication, owing to his old well-known weakness of rushing into print, and the Elector indirectly sent him this message:[1] "It has been represented to His Electoral Highness, how Joannes Duraeus, an English clergyman and a member of the reformed church, has been endeavouring to promote peace among the evangelical persuasions in his quality as a private individual, and has been devoting all his life to this end. In this his Christian zeal deserves duly to be praised, whilst H. H. confidently hopes that his efforts will in no way be prejudicial to the Church. We therefore wish him the blessing of God Almighty, and remain always his gracious sovereign."

This was satisfactory as far as it went; but it did not go far, did not even go any distance.

Nor was Durie's reception in Heidelberg in 1667 by the otherwise broad-minded Elector Karl Ludwig more promising. The probable reason assigned for this is that the wife of the Elector, separated from him by all sorts of scandalous facts, was at present living at Kassel, the same town where Durie had his home and enjoyed the favour of the Hessian Court.

The last years of this apostle of peace were embittered not only by the growing enmity of the Lutherans, of which we have spoken, but by the desertion of some of his Calvinistic friends. The former called him "Apostolastrum," "an interpreter of peace fallen from the sky," "a bird without wings," "a weather-cock," "a new Thomas Munzer,"[2] "a regicide." The latter had taken it amiss that he accepted the Lutheran doctrine of free grace, as opposed to the predestination of the sister Church; they were incensed at his later dream of ad-

[1] Tollin, *l.c.*, p. 277. Landwehr, *l.c.*, p. 334 f.
[2] The well-known head of the Anabaptists.

mitting even Roman Catholics into his universal union, and at the hearty reception he had given to William Penn, the Quaker, when he visited Kassel in 1677.

In these circumstances it was fortunate for Durie that the Landgravine Hedwig Sophie had offered him a permanent resting-place at her Calvinistic court, granting him a free house and board, and even paying the large expenses incurred by his incredibly extensive correspondence.

His courage, however, and his hitherto unconquerable optimism, after having supported him during sixty years of a laborious life, left him in the end. "Le fruit principal qui m'est revenu de mon travail," he writes in 1674, in the dedication of his commentary on the Book of Revelation to his sovereign-lady, "est ceci, qu'au dehors je vois la misère des Chrétiens, qu'elle est beaucoup plus grande, que celle des payens et des autres nations ; je vois la cause de cette misère, je vois le défaut du remède, et je vois la cause de ce défaut, et en dedans je n'ai d'autre profit, que le témoignage de ma conscience." And in a Latin letter[1] to the senators of the Swedish Kingdom he adds : "I have done what I could to advance the union of saints. Henceforth I shall solicit the help of no one, because I have asked them all. Neither do I see any Patron in Germany, whom God would point out to me as fit for the work."

John Durie died in his eighty-fifth year on the 28th of September 1680 at Kassel, where he is also buried. It is sad but intelligible, that, at a time when intolerance was considered strength, tolerance weakness ; when people thought they could confine absolute truth in the long-necked, narrow bottles of confessions of their own manufacture, Durie's attempts to restore unity and peace must end in failure. Many of his proposals, too, lacked definiteness and clearness. And yet his unwearied testimony has not remained without fruit. To him as to the champion of freedom of conscience

---

[1] Durie corresponded in five or six different languages.

and of the political equality of religious creeds, the great achievement of our times, under the protection of which the adherents of the various confessions, united not by the same form of certain articles, but by the conviction that they are brethren in love and charity and branches of the one Catholic Church, live and have their being: to him and to his memory, in Scotland as well as in Germany, honour is due for his self-denying labours.[1]

It is curious and reads like a belated recognition of Durie's work by the voice of history, that it was another Scotsman, who more than one hundred and thirty years afterwards played an active part in the realisation of the Union between the Protestant parties in Prussia by the King's command.

Descendants of the old Scottish family of the Earls of Ross had settled in the Netherlands and on the Lower Rhine as far back as the XVIIth Century. One of these, William John Gottfried Ross, was born on the 7th of July 1772 at Isselburg. He was the son of a clergyman, studied at Duisburg, then a Calvinistic University, and, having been ordained, worked with the greatest acceptance as pastor of the small parish of Budberg [2] for thirty-three years. He was so active in promoting the education of the people and the welfare of his whole district, that he not only won the love and esteem of all classes and all creeds, but also attracted the attention of the King of Prussia, Frederick William III, who summoned him to Berlin, to consult with him about the condition of the Evangelical Churches in Westphalia and the Rhine Provinces, and after some pressure even persuaded him in the following year to leave Budberg and to settle in the capital. Here Ross devoted himself with untiring energy to the cause of the Evangelical Union. The King made him first Bishop of the new Church and General Superintendent of Westphalia and the Rhinelands. Ross was also greatly interested in the cause of education

---

[1] See the remarkable letter of the famous Grotius to his friend Bernegger in Strassburg in the Appendix.

[2] Near Rheinberg, Lower Rhine.

and of the orphanage, persuading his cousin, Count Ross,[1] an eccentric, rich, old man then living at Berlin, to leave a considerable legacy to the latter.   The title of Count was offered to him also by the King, but he always refused it as being incompatible with his calling.   In 1843 he received a congratulatory address from the University of Bonn thanking him for his long-continued efforts and his conciliatory attitude in Church matters.   In appearance he was imposing ; goodness and benevolence were seen in his eyes.   His influence on Frederick William was very marked.   Finding, however, that his advice was neglected under King William IV, he resigned his offices and retired into private life.   He died on the 27th of October in 1854 and was buried in the Protestant cemetery at Budberg.[2]

Turning now to the religious organisation of the Scots, who had settled in such great numbers in Poland and Germany during the XVIth and XVIIth Centuries, as we have seen in the first part of our book, we have reluctantly to confess that not very much is known about it.   The old records in Germany have been partly lost during the turmoil of endless wars, partly buried beyond the hope of speedy recovery under cart-loads of official paper rubbish. In Scotland we have to content ourselves with an occasional reference.   What we have been able to glean under such discouraging circumstances will be put before the reader in what follows.

The General Assembly of the Church of Scotland has sometimes taken notice of its scattered countrymen on the Continent.   One of the most interesting references is that

[1] This Count Johann Ross (1787-1848) saved the life of the King of Prussia at the Congress of Vienna when threatened by a would-be assassin.   There have been several officers in the German Army, who belonged to this family.   A Count Ross died in 1883 at Bonn, in consequence of injuries received at the explosion of the powder magazine when the Germans entered Laon in 1870.   Two brothers Ross, an archæologist and a painter, both born in Holstein, are also descended from the old Scottish stock.

[2] The lines on his tombstone are taken from 2 Cor. i. 24 : "Not for that we have dominion over your faith, but are helpers of your joy."

of the year 1587, when Andrew Melville, who was then Moderator, was ordered "to pen a favourable writing to the ministrie in *Danskine* (Danzig) congratulating their embracing the treuth in the matter of the Sacrament."[1] From this notice it appears that already in that year there existed at Danzig a Scottish-Evangelical Church. But more than that, it did not only exist but prove its inner life and its keen religious interest by rejecting the Lutheran doctrine of consubstantiation; for this is the meaning of the last clause.

About sixty years later, on the 31st of August 1647, the Assembly writes the following interesting letter to the Scots in Poland and Germany:—"Unto the Scotch merchants and others our countrie people scattered in Poleland. . . . and among other things of this nature we have here particularly taken into account the sad and lamentable condition of many thousands of our country-men, who are scattered abroad, as sheepe having no shepherd, and are, through the want of the meanes of knowledge, grace and salvation, exposed to the greatest spirituall dangers. . . . We have therefore thought it incumbent to us to put you in mind of the one thing necessary, while you are so carefull and troubled about the things of the world; and although we do not disallow your going abroad to follow any lawfull calling or way of livelihood, yet seeing it cannot profit a man, although he should gain the whole world and lose his own soul, and seeing you have travelled so farre and taken so much pain to get uncertain riches, which cannot deliver in the day of the wrath of the Lord . . . we doe . . . most earnestlie beseech and warn you to cry after knowledge and lift up your voyce for understanding, seeking her as silver and searching for her as for hid treasures, and so play the wise merchants, in purchasing the pearl of price and in laying up a sure foundation. . . . We shall hope . . . you will rather bestirre yourselves timely to pray that God would give you Pastors according to His heart . . . to consult also with consent of your superiors . . . for

[1] *Buik of the Universal Kirk*, f. 148, 6.

setting up the worship of God and ecclesiasticall discipline according to the form established and received in this your Mother Kirk . . . and in the mean time we exhort you that ye neglect not the worship in secret and in your families and that ye continue stedfast in the profession of that faith, in which ye were baptised, and by a godly, righteous and sober conversation adorn the Gospel; and with all, that distance of place make you not the less sensible of your countrey's sufferings. . . .

"This letter we have thought fit to be printed and published, that it may be with greater ease . . . conveyed to the many severall places of your habitation or traffique. . . .

"ROBT. DOUGLASSE, Moderator."[1]

Finally, we find in the year 1698 a recommendation to those Presbyteries and Parishes "that have not yet sent in their collection for helping to build a church of the Reformed Religion at Königsberg" to send the same to John Blair at Edinburgh, Agent of the Kirk; and in 1699 the receipt of a letter is duly registered from the consistory "of those of the Reformed Religion at Königsberg," expressing thanks for "the Charity of this Church and Nation to help them build their church."

In German sources we find, as to Danzig, that already in 1577, when the town levied a force of 700 Scottish mercenaries, permission was given them, as being of the reformed faith, to bring with them a preacher of their own persuasion.[2] Now it is very probable that the reformed congregation of Danzig formed itself gradually around this nucleus, till it attained to that independent position, in which we find it ten years later, when the above "friendly letter" was written by the Moderator of the General Assembly. Everything fostered such a formation. The number of Scottish settlers was already great, greater numbers were continually pouring in, and many of the merchants had by this time acquired wealth and position. The privilege of freely enjoying their own

---

[1] Acts of the General Assembly.   [2] See above.

religious services was possibly extended, and thus we find in 1587 a body of men with a settled "ministrie," fearlessly discussing the crucial points of evangelical theology. At first, no doubt, the meetings of the members of the Reformed Church met in private houses or in a hall. We hear of a preacher named Jacob Brown, who alternately preached at Danzig and at Königsberg in the time of Charles I.[1] Soon after him Alexander Burnet came to Danzig (1689) and remained there till his death in 1712. He was born in 1654, studied at Aberdeen, and had been minister of Crichton near Edinburgh. During his time of office the amalgamation of the so-called English and Scottish "nations"[2] took place at Danzig, consequently upon the Union of England and Scotland at home. Through the efforts of Robinson, the British Consul, the Churches also were united. The Poor-Box of the Scots, which had been in existence since the beginning of the XVIIth Century, became the property of the new "Nation of Great Britain" ("Groszbrittannische Nation"). Five elders were appointed, of which three were always to be Scotchmen. As to the form of divine worship, a happy medium between the Scottish and the English was peacefully adopted. It was arranged that the clergymen should alternately be called out of Scotland and England, and that they should conform to the usages of the Church at Danzig. A new building, called the "British Chapel," was erected in 1706, the Scots throughout Prussia and Poland having most liberally contributed towards it.[3]

Since then the number of members of the "British Nation" gradually diminished, owing to the very rapid absorption of the Scottish into the German element, and to the almost entire cessation of immigration. During the time of the French oppression for sixteen years there was no

---

[1] See below.

[2] The Scottish nation was by far the more numerous one.

[3] Twenty-seven names of Scotsmen in Danzig alone are mentioned among the contributors. Thos. Leslie gave 1000 gulden; S. Ramsay 1200.

English clergyman at Danzig.   Previous to it the worthy
Dr Jamieson, a Scot, had gained the reverence and the
affection of the inhabitants, as we are told in the charming *Memorials of my Youth,* by Johanna Schopenhauer
(1768-1790).   Now there is hardly work enough for
an English Seamen's Missionary.   The descendants of
the old Scottish congregation have joined the Reformed
Church.

We are better informed with regard to Königsberg,
the second largest town on the Baltic, although here also
the very first beginnings of a Scotch Divine Worship are
lost in obscurity.   When the "Reformed Congregation"
was founded in 1646, out of seven elders three were
English, or rather Scotch, two Dutch, and two Germans.

Very soon the want of a preacher became apparent,
but whether the above-named Brown ever preached in
English at Königsberg, as he did at Danzig, must remain
uncertain.   We only know that he, during his stay in the
city in 1658 or 1659, in "matters concerning the public
worship and the rules of the Church," was found wanting
and in the wrong.   "His errors smacked[1] of the Quakers";
they were chiefly manifest in his disapproval of the praying of children, "who knew nothing about it"; in his
rejection of set prayers, of saints'-days and holidays, and
of organ music in churches.[2]

In spite of this the Great Elector had appointed Jacob
Brown minister of the newly formed Scottish-English
congregation, after he, at the urgent request of some
Scottish families at Königsberg, had given them permission to have divine service in their own tongue,
embracing its "complete 'exercitium' with all its actibus
catechisationis, visitationis of the sick, administrationis of
the Lord's Supper, Baptism, and other spiritual exercises,
appertaining there unto."

This royal rescript was dated the 4th of December
1685; it granted at the same time the use of the "large

---

[1] " Übel riechend."

[2] Sembritzki, " Die Schotten und Engländer in Ost-Preussen," in the
Altpreuss. Monatsschrift, vol. xxix. pp. 3, 4.

Hall in the Castle" for these services. In these circumstances the congregation could do nothing else but acquiesce in the appointment of Brown, who, in the meantime, had declared his willingness to abide by the rules and forms of worship as adopted in Königsberg. Strangely enough we know nothing of his future career there, except that his stay only extended to the year 1689, when he preached at the Scots' Church at Rotterdam.[1]

In Königsberg, as elsewhere, the Scots took the most prominent and active share in the promotion of the welfare of the congregation. Without them and their generosity the building of its new church would hardly have been completed. Three men are especially mentioned in connection with this great enterprise: Thomas Hervie, Francis Hay and Charles Ramsay.[2] The first of these, born in 1621 at Aberdeen, had settled in Königsberg in 1656 as a merchant. When he died in 1710 it was said "that without his zeal this our temple would scarcely have been built."

He also promoted the establishment of a "home for widows" by advancing considerable sums of money. The two other men were the originators of the collection throughout Scotland for the building of the church, amounting to over 4000 thaler, or nearly £700.

After the completion of the church, to show their gratitude towards the Scottish brethren, the fourteen front seats were handed over to them and their successors by the members, for their free use. They were distinguished by the letters S. B. = "Schottische Bänke" (Scottish seats) and by the Scottish Lion rampant. The latter coat-of-arms, however, disappeared after the French had occupied the church as a hospital.

A school and a poor-fund existed in connection with the church since the XVIIth Century. After the union of the two kingdoms in 1707, here, as in Danzig, the "Scottish and English Nation" formed a "Brotherhood

---

[1] Sembritzki, *l.c.*
[2] Cp. *Scottish Hist. Soc. Miscellany*, i. p. 326 *n.* Brown died in 1713.

of Great Britain" ("Groszbrittannische Brüderschaft").
Two elders (Älterleute) watched over the welfare of
Scottish and English residents or travellers. The poor-
fund, which was made up of the interest of an old
capital, the amount of annual collections and the pew-
rents, served also to support shipwrecked or otherwise
disabled sailors, and to provide for the maintenance of
Scottish or English poverty-stricken invalids in two separate rooms of the Royal Hospital. The two Scottish
burying vaults in the churchyard now became common
property likewise.

The same reasons for the rapid decline of the "Brüderschaft" which we adduced when speaking of Danzig were
at work in Königsberg. In 1819 there were no longer
any British subjects using the pews.[1] Only six, mostly
very old persons, four of them Scottish, received a
monthly dole out of the Poor's Box. The British coat-
of-arms disappeared from the English pew and went the
way of the Scottish lion, and with the 1st of January
1820 pews as well as church funds were taken over by
the officers of the German Reformed Church.

As in the two largest Baltic ports, so in many of the
smaller towns of Eastern and Western Prussia, we can
trace the formation of Calvinistic or "Reformed" congregations back to the Scots.

In Memel, for instance, we hear of a Reformed congregation, consisting mainly of Scottish and Dutch people,
since 1640.[2] Three or four families, among them Bar-
clays, Ogilvies, and Fentons, had engaged a sort of
domestic chaplain and teacher in the person of one
Wendelin de Rodem, a native of the Palatinate. But
he was obliged to leave the town in 1641 owing to the

---

[1] Sembritzki, *l.c.* p. 245.

[2] The first preaching according to the rites of the Calvinists took
place much earlier in connection with the Scottish-Swedish garrison.
In the Church Registers of Memel we find the following entry: "1631,
on the 4th of Febr. there were married in the house of Littlejohn:
Johannes Deglarius (?), natione Scotus, the concionator (preacher) of
the Governor" (Francis Ruthven). Cp. Sembritzki, *History of Memel,*
p. 150 ff.

complaints of the Lutheran party of the Duchy. It was not till twenty years afterwards that Wendelin obtained the permission of the Elector to come to Memel once in every quarter for the purposes of ministration. By degrees a separate house was acquired for divine worship; and finally a preacher was procured, after the receipt of a "Privilegium" from the prince. The person chosen was one Petrus Figulus, the son-in-law of the famous founder of our modern system of education, Amos Comenius.[1] He knew the English language well, and discharged his duties up to the year of his death in 1670. His successor was Paul Andreas Jurski, a native of Lithuania, who had married a Scotchwoman. During his ministry the house in which the Calvinists hitherto held their meetings was burned to the ground (1678). But a new church was completed in 1681. The members of the congregation were mostly Scottish;[2] there were, however, a few Dutch and French and English. The Germans constituted the minority, though, in later years, only German was used in preaching. Here also there existed a "Poor-Fund of the Scottish Nation," but it became amalgamated with that of the German "Reformed Church."

The Scots in Memel never ceased to show their attachment to the Reformed Church, even long after every trace of Scottish nationality had disappeared. A rich merchant, Ludwig Simpson, presented to it in 1802 the large sum of 8000 gulden, the interest of which was to be set aside for the raising of the schoolmaster's stipend; and John Simpson, a cousin of Ludwig, gave a large donation in 1760, when the rebuilding of the church had become an urgent necessity after the damage done to it by the Russians.

The formation of the Reformed congregation at Tilsit proceeded much on the same lines. It was composed first of all of the Scottish; but we are not informed as to the exact year in which this union of the Calvinistic

[1] 1592-1670.
[2] Sembritzki enumerates thirty Scottish names, some of them in existence still. *Hist. of Memel*, p. 152.

settlers from Scotland took place. It must, however, have been some time before 1667, as a Scottish Poor Fund is mentioned in that year.[1]   The treasurer was one Alexander Krichton, but the general supervision lay with the whole " Brotherhood."   The fund then amounted to 230 gulden, lent out to three members: Albrecht Ritsch (Ritchie), Peter Kerligkeit (?) and William Schamer (Chalmers).   There were other voluntary contributions besides, as well as the proceeds of a collection from house to house undertaken by two prominent men annually about the time of " Michaelmas-fair."   Divine service must have been held before 1669, for in that year a small hall in the Elector's castle is set aside for this purpose.   As in other towns, the congregation during the XVIIth Century increased rapidly and drew the Scottish settlers of the district to it, so that the appointment of a special clergyman soon became necessary.   We are told that a rich Scottish merchant, a member of the congregation, William Ritsch, went to Berlin in order to obtain the requisite permission from the Elector.   Falling on his knees before the sovereign, he obtained by his eloquent pleading a royal edict (16th of March 1679), which not only granted the Tilsiters their own preacher, but allowed a stipend of 200 thaler out of the Electoral purse as well. The first call was given to Alexander Dennis, born at Königsberg, but of Scottish descent.   He had been trained in Dutch universities and got ordained at Danzig. From the day of his induction by the Court Preacher Blaspiel on the 11th of October 1679, the Reformed congregation at Tilsit reckons its existence.   Eleven days later the first communion was held.   Among the 27 communicants there were only two Germans and two French. The number, however, soon increased, there being 160 communicants in 1680 and 206 in 1681.   The firm adherence to their own faith, so earnestly inculcated by their General Assembly at home, clearly showed itself on

---

[1] We find Scottish settlers in Tilsit already in the XVIth Century. Cp. Bartsch, *Skizzen zu einer Geschichte Tilsits* (Outlines of a History of Tilsit), p. 31, where in 1592 trial of two Scotsmen is mentioned.

these occasions, when people came from Insterburg, a distance of between thirty and forty English miles, or did not shun the long journey of ninety miles from Lyck. Many did this more than once in the year. In 1682 Dennis had a service at Lyck, in which about 36 Scottish settlers in Masuren took part. From 1687 onward he visited this place as well as Insterburg annually at regular intervals, until at the beginning of the XVIIIth Century both these congregations obtained their own clergymen. About this time (1711) the church at Tilsit received a legacy of 42,000 gulden from the Scottish member, John Irving.[1]

Whilst we thus meet the Scottish as the founders of the Reformed congregations in Eastern and Western Prussia, they also appear as the supporters and upholders of Protestantism in general. It is clear from this that their lives, opposed as they were in a two-fold way to the religious feelings of the people of their adopted country, must often have been troubled with irksome restraints and threatened with persecution and danger. As they were confounded with the Jews on account of their trading and money-lending, they were thrown together with the heretics on account of their faith.[2]

As an illustration of this we shall quote a case of religious persecution of the year 1620.

On the 9th of June of that year there appeared in the Court House at Putzig, not far from Danzig, the 'Instigator' (Public Prosecutor) of the Royal (Polish)

---

[1] Pastor Roquette at Tilsit some years ago delivered a lecture on "the English-Scottish Colony and the Reformed Congregations of Lithuania" before the Lithuanian Literary Society. A copy of it was very kindly placed at my disposal and I have largely availed myself of its contents. He gives a long list of members, about 84 in all, of which only about half a dozen are not Scottish. Added to it must be many Scottish settlers at Insterburg, Stallupönen, Lyck, Goldap, etc., about 60 souls at the time of Dennis. See also Part i. and Sembritzki, *l.c.*, 233. During the year of the plague (1710-1711) many Scottish settlers died, among them Gerdes, Dunkan and Karr from Heidekrug, Larzell (Dalziel) from Ragnit, and three Muttrays.

[2] Let it be remembered always that the orthodox Lutherans were opponents quite as bitter as the Roman Catholics.

House, David Schwarte, contra Jacob Dziaksen (Jackson), a Scot, who declared that His Grace the Woywode had distinctly forbidden Dziaksen to allow any religious meetings in his house, to preach sermons or to have them preached, an order in which Dziaksen at that time acquiesced. " But now he had, contrary to his pledge, made bold to have a sermon read in his house on the Sunday of Whitsuntide last, for which disobedience their book, out of which they had been reading, was confiscated by command of His Grace. On this account the ' Instigator ' had received strict orders, inasmuch as Jacob Dziaksen had disobeyed the royal command and broken his own engagement, to accuse him before the magistrates and to demand his punishment.

To this Jacob Dziaksen, present, replies that he acknowledges the prohibition of meetings and reading of the sermons. He also admits that in his presence the Krämers (pedlars) had read their books, but they had been his guests and had never been told not to do so. If the order was to apply to everybody the magistrates would have to send to every house, search it, and take the books away from everybody. He therefore does not think himself punishable."

The following is the finding of the magistrates : " After having heard Jacob Dziaksen's admission that he had allowed the Scots to read their books in his house, in consequence of which their books had been taken from them ; confessing thereby to have acted contrary to the express command of the authorities ; *and as it is to be feared that through such meetings and sermons more heresy might become prevalent in the town*, which must be prevented in due time, the Court decrees, that Jacob Dziaksen, on account of his disobedience . . . be sentenced to pay to the church at Putzig . . . the sum of 20 florins. He *as well as other citizens* of this town are also strictly commanded not to hold any meetings in their houses or have sermons read, but altogether to abstain from such under pain of heavy fines."

Jacob Dziaksen, considering himself unjustly dealt with, appeals to the higher court.

Examples like these could be adduced in great numbers. Enough has been said to show that the Scottish emigrant was not afraid of his religious opinions. The second generation, indeed, was more German than Scottish. Language and even the names changed. But, notwithstanding this, the old attachment to Scotland remained with very many of them, like an old legend, that outlasts centuries.

Looking back upon the long period of religious development, from the foundation of the "Schottenklöster" to the union of the evangelical confessions in Prussia, here also we have to admit, that on the Catholic as well as on the Protestant side, Scotsmen have not been wanting, who have left memorable traces in Germany, without for one moment underrating the enormous and paramount influence of German thought on the world of letters of the Middle Ages.

PART IV.

STATESMAN AND SCHOLAR.

STATESMAN AND SCHOLAR.

NOBODY will expect, in a book like the present, a complete history of the foreign policy of Scotland. Our purpose is the less pretentious one of showing in some characteristic examples that Scotland did not want eminent representatives among her statesmen in Germany. In a second division we will then, from among the great number of Scottish scholars in German universities and high schools, select those that seem to be most deserving of a lasting recognition.

And first among the statesmen mention must be made of Alexander Erskine, who, during the time of the Thirty Years' War, as Minister of War, deserved well of his master Gustavus Adolfus, the King of Sweden, and his Protestant allies in Germany.

His parents, Walter Erskine and Anne Forest, had settled in Pomerania towards the end of the XVIth Century, and here, in the small town of Greifswald, Alexander was born in 1598, October 31st. He first entered the service of Queen Sophia of Denmark, but soon exchanged it for that of the Swedish Government. As Kriegsrath, counsellor of war, no less than in a diplomatic capacity, as Swedish Plenipotentiary during the conferences which ended in the treaty of Münster (1648), and, later on, as President of the Court of Appeal in the then Swedish duchies of Pomerania, Bremen and Verden, he served with such distinction, that he was created Baron by King Charles Gustavus in 1655. During the last ten years of his life he accompanied the Swedish King on his invasion of Poland, having been placed at the head of the military jurisdiction, a position similar to our modern minister of war.

When the Swedish garrison was besieged in Warsaw,

and afterward forced to capitulate, he was among the prisoners of war, and the Poles removed him to Zamosz. Shortly afterwards he died of enteric fever, on the 24th of August 1656. His body was removed to Bremen, and deposited in the cathedral on the 6th of May 1658. But when in 1812 a general panic seized the inhabitants at the approach of the French, his tin-coffin was melted down, lest it should fall into the hands of the conqueror, and his remains were reinterred in the "Klosterhof." The vault in the church shared the fate of the coffin, it was ruthlessly taken down, and all its parts removed.[1]

Whilst the Thirty Years' War was raging in Germany, inviting into the land countless Scotsmen, who followed the fortunes of "Bellona," the struggle against absolute monarchy in England had gradually assumed a very threatening aspect. To strengthen his throne Charles I of England had made every effort to gain allies on the Continent. One of his and his successor's most versatile ambassadors was a certain Sir John Cochrane or Cockeran. He had been recommended to the English King by Elisabeth, Queen of Bohemia, and his knowledge of foreign languages as well as his familiarity with foreign Courts apparently rendered him a proper person to act as diplomatic agent. In the years 1642 and 1644 he was sent by Charles to his nephew, the King of Denmark, to procure his assistance. But the war between Sweden and Denmark, during which Jutland was overrun by the enemy, did not allow King Christian to heed the pressing request. In the following year we find him again as ambassador to Duke James of Curland, who on account of his colonial enterprises desired the friendship of England, and actually furnished three men-of-war, over twenty cannons, and much corn and ammunition for the use of the English King.[2] At the same time Cochrane was sent on a like errand to Hamburg and to the Scots settled in Danzig. In the former place his offensive and overbearing manners on the one hand, and the firm resolve of the magistrates on the other, to observe a strict

[1] See Appendix. [2] Cp. *Scottish Hist. Soc. Miscellany*, i. 146 f.

neutrality during the civil imbroglio in England, added to
the outspoken republican feelings of most of the members
of the English Trading Company settled there, produced
a series of unpleasant and ruffianly actions, which culminated in the attempt, carried out on the instigation of
Cochrane,[1] to seize the English preacher, a certain Dr
Elburrow, on his way to the chapel. This intention
was only frustrated by the citizens of Hamburg coming
to his rescue.

Nor was the other attempt of the enraged ambassador,
to secure the persons of the republican ringleaders of the
English Company by enticing them on the neighbouring
Danish territory, more successful, and he had, much to
the relief of the magistrates, to leave the city without
having effected his purpose.[2]

In December 1649 Cochrane was at Danzig. He
found the town "extrêmement affectionée aux affaires
de mon Roy," as he expresses himself in his wonted
exaggerating style in a letter to Duke James, and what
was more, he met with Scottish merchants willing to
furnish him with 1000 "tonneaux de seigle" (wheat).[3]
Early in the following year, however, his activity suddenly
terminates. The suspicion of his dishonesty became
almost a certainty,[4] the Duke of Curland withheld his
aid, and King Charles II declared, in a letter to the Scots
in Poland, that he at no time had given any orders to his
ambassador to "extort large sums of money" from them,
or to obtain the King of Poland's authority for it. "As to
Cochrane's successor Croffts," continues the curious document, "that at his demand you are again pressed with a
requisition of the third part of your goods and merchandise

---

[1] See Dr Hans Fernow, *Hamburg und England im ersten Jahr der
Republik*, p. 10. This writer is not convinced of Cochrane's dishonesty.

[2] Cp. *Scottish Hist. Soc. Misc.* i. 175 f., where Cochrane's report is
fully printed from the Original in the Advocates' Library, Edinburgh.
See also Fernow, *l.c.*

[3] One of them was a certain Albrecht Law or Low; possibly a
relation of one Thomas Law of Anstruther, a lace-maker, who obtained
civic rights in 1634.

[4] See also Part i. and *Deeds of Montrose*, p. 246. Cp. Fernow, *l.c.*

for our use, we do admit that he was despatched by us from
Holland to the King of Poland, our royal and esteemed
brother, but in nowise empowered with any open authority
to extort anything from our subjects trading in that
Realm." The moral indignation with which he—a
Stuart—in conclusion rejects the idea of being capable
of ever levying taxes without the consent of Parliament
cannot fail to provoke a smile.[1]

After Cochrane, Lord Crofts was sent on a similar
mission. He was accompanied by Denham, the Poet
Laureate, to whom we owe a valuable description of
Poland. Crofts was succeeded again by Lieut.-General
Middleton in 1656. The instructions issued for the latter
are of a very urgent character. "We doe more especially
recommend and intrust you to our well affected Subjects
of the Scots Nation who now live under the dominion of
the King of Poland or the Marquis of Brandenburg,"
they say, "the former of which have already given
Us ample testimony of their affection (!),[2] (for which
you shall returne Our Princely thankes to them), and
we doubt not but they will, since We are in the same
straits and necessitys We were then in, *if not greater*,
renew their expressions of affection and kindnesse to Us
. . . and We doe hereby authorize you to receive all
such Summes of Monney as they or any of them shallbe
willing to lend to Us and your acquittance shall oblige Us
to the repayment of the same as soone as God shall
enable Us."

The King further instructs Middleton to obtain
assistance in ships, ammunition, men, and arms from
the senate of Danzig, and the ambassador found the
town well-inclined towards his royal master. He even
succeeded in levying a few men for service in England,
but had to disband them again for want of means. The
Scottish merchants were either unwilling or unable to
contribute the desired "Summes of Money." Nor is

---

[1] See Appendix, and compare with it the authority given to Cochrane
to raise money on the King's behalf in Part i., App.

[2] That is to say, the most unwillingly paid tax of 1650. See Part i.

this much to be wondered at, since Cromwell also had a representative in the town, who of course did his utmost to render Charles' efforts ineffectual. After a short time Middleton himself got into pecuniary diffi-culties, and the King was compelled to ask the senate for a loan of 1000 Thaler.[1]

Thus the English embassies from the unfortunate Duke of Montrose (1648-9), who carried home little else[2] than his new dignity of Imperial Field-marschall— granted to him by the Emperor Ferdinand III, on account of his great renown, and his knowledge of the war— down to General Middleton, proved failures.

Much greater skill, joined to higher qualities of character and more auspicious times, was shown by two English-Scottish ambassadors at the Court of Frederick the Great : Lord Hyndford, and Sir Andrew Mitchell.

Hyndford had been sent on an extraordinary mission to Breslau in 1741, to try and smooth the way for a peace between the King of Prussia and Maria Theresa.   He was unwearied in his efforts, and proved himself a stubborn, somewhat heavy, astute Scotsman, who like a good British bull-dog watched every movement of his master. After many secret diplomatic moves, and countermoves, and the successful removal of many obstacles, the treaty of Breslau was brought about on the eleventh of June 1742.   How much of this great result was attributed to the co-operation of Hyndford by the two Courts of London and Berlin appears from the bestowal of the Order of the Thistle upon him on the part of the King of England, and from the very solemn investiture held by the King of Prussia himself.   All the generals and the high dignitaries of the State, two Queens, and all the members of the higher nobility were present at the ceremony. As his private gift to the ambassador Frederick added

---

[1] *Scottish Hist. Soc. : Scotland and the Protectorate*, 1899, pp. 337, 358 f.   See also Appendix.

[2] The Elector of Brandenburg had promised him " decem millia imperiales " as subsidy, but he excused his non-payment with the difficulty of raising a loan (July 27, 1649).   See *Deeds of Montrose*, p. 506 f.

a Silver Dinner-Service, and the right of carrying the Prussian eagle in his coat-of-arms.[1]

Very different again and quite unparalleled in history was the position occupied by Sir Andrew Mitchell, since 1756 British ambassador to the Court of Prussia. He was the only son of a clergyman at the church of St Giles, Edinburgh, and was born on the 15th of April 1708. The premature death of his young wife and his baby-daughter made him give up his reading for the Scottish Bar, and seek comfort and relaxation on long journeys through Holland and Belgium, France and Italy. After his return in 1742 he was made Under-Secretary of State for Scotland, member of parliament for the Elgin boroughs in 1754, and ambassador to Prussia in 1756. As King Frederick was then on the point of being engaged in the memorable Seven Years' War, this was a service of no small danger, hardship and difficulty. It was in Berlin that the thousand and one finely spun threads of European policy met. Only a man of uncommon intelligence and uncommon qualities of mind could hope in the intercourse with such a "fiery soul" as Frederick to extricate himself out of the maze of conflicting interests, to serve his country, and to save his soul alive. Mitchell succeeded by his sound common-sense, his manliness, his energy, his incorruptible and straightforward honesty, not to lose for one short moment the most complete confidence of his royal master and friend. He was an honour to his native country; hard-headed, sagacious, averse to all mere shows, but able to seize the fact, and stubbornly, if needs be, to hold to it; abundantly polite, watchful and discreet, full of common-sense and a certain rugged sincerity: in short, a man, whose true value Frederick immediately perceived and a resource, no doubt, to the King in his lonely roamings and vicissitudes in those dark years. Thus Carlyle describes him.

It was a matter of necessity that with a character thus

---

[1] Cp. Carlyle, *Life of Friedrich II*, vol. v. 197. Lord Hyndford's family-name was Carmichael. The present representative of the family is Sir Thomas Gibson Carmichael, Castle Craig, Scotland.

differently constituted from and at variance with the old
received pattern of a useful diplomatist, times of tension
and friction with the Cabinet at London were not in-
frequent and might have ended in Mitchell's recall, if it
had not been for the powerful veto of the Prussian King.
Once, when he had received a long letter from England
reproaching him for omitting to communicate numerous
and bitter sarcasms which, no doubt, escaped Frederick concerning the English, he replied that he considered himself
as entrusted with the care of maintaining and strengthen-
ing the ties that existed between his country and a valuable ally; that his desire had been to prove a minister of
peace and union; that if it were intended to make him a
minister of hatred, pitiful bickerings and despicable tale-
bearings, he wished nothing more than that the King
would immediately name his successor.[1] "It was his duty
to remind the Cabinet that to judge accurately of a man
so extraordinary, or even of his utterances, it was doing
little, indeed, to collect the mere words he spoke, if to
these were not added a knowledge of the time, in which
they were pronounced, under what circumstances and with
what views."[2] Finally he added: "I was born an enemy
to falsehood, deceit and double dealing, and have ever had
an equal contempt and abhorrence of those that practise
either." "Honour," he writes an other time to the
English Minister, "Honour, my lord, cannot be bought
with money."[3]

The same straightforwardness characterises his intercourse with Frederick. He was the only one who sometimes ventured a word of reproof, and the King, who was
possessed of a piercing insight into human nature, not
only forgave him but valued him all the more. The plain
man, who shortly after his arrival at Berlin created quite
an uncomfortable sensation by his inability to play at cards,
soon occupied the envied position as one of the King's
most intimate friends, who accompanied him on his cam-

[1] Bisset, *Memoirs aud Letters of Sir A. Mitchell*, i. 142.
[2] Thiebault, *Souvenirs de Frederic le Grand*, iii. 271; and Bisset.
[3] Bisset, *l.c.*, i. 269.

paigns, to whom he had recourse in times of joy and sorrow.   When in 1757 Sophia Dorothy, Frederick's mother, had died, and the disconsolate King for two days refused all intercourse with the outer world, it was Mitchell whom he sent for first, seeking and finding comfort in his conversation.   To him he poured out his grief, initiating him into the sad history of his youth.   " I must confess," Mitchell writes after this meeting, " that it cut me to the quick, how the King abandoned himself to his grief, pouring out expressions of the most affectionate filial love; recalling to his mind how much he owed to his departed mother; how much she had suffered, how nobly she had borne it all, and how good she had been to everybody.   His only comfort now was that he had tried to make her latter years more comfortable.   I was glad to prolong my visit as he seemed to be amused, and to forget for a time that load of sorrow with which he was overwhelmed."

It was Mitchell again to whom the King turned first in the joy of victory.   " You have shared the fatigues with me, I want you likewise to rejoice with me," he said to him after Rossbach.   In very many letters he expressed to him his unshaken confidence and love and, when he returned to Berlin after a visit to England in 1766, he made the Duke of Brunswick write to him: " Mon cher M. Mitchell.   Le roi attend sou bon M. Mitchell et non le ministre.   Selon ce charactère il vous recevra à Berlin."

Whilst the King thus honoured the ambassador with his intimacy, England was slow to recognise his merit; and whilst his successor, Sir James Harris, a much inferior man, was made an Earl, the other had to content himself with the Order of the Bath, remaining to the end of his life plain Sir Andrew Mitchell.   Plain also is his tomb: the inscription only telling the dates of his birth and death.

Let us now add some events in the life of the ambassador.   It was the wish of King George II, that he should accompany the Prussian King on all his campaigns, thus sharing the dangers of the battle and the privations of camp-life.   In his rare leisure-moments he loved to study German. When at Leipzig he took lessons from Gottsched, then a celebrated critic, and tried to convince him of the genius of Shakespeare in spite of his supreme neglect of the long adopted and cherished canons of dramatic composition. He also knew Gellert, the poet, and procured him an interview with the King.

His diaries give a very vivid sketch of the Seven Years' War with its victories and defeats; its diplomatic minings and counterminings. In the midst of all this Mitchell continued his straight course: to make Frederick's interests those of his own country. In this he succeeded in so far as the English subsidies continued to be paid during Pitt's administration, though a co-operation of the English fleet was found impossible. How deeply he felt the defection of England in 1762, when the pecuniary assistance was withdrawn, a letter of his reveals to his countryman Sir R. Murray Keith, the British ambassador at Vienna. "This goes by Walker," he writes on the ninth of June, "the messenger who has brought me an answer to my despatch of the 4th of May, and I will not detain him to give you a précis, because I imagine they will have sent you a copy of that most extraordinary piece. If they have not, let me know, and you shall, by the first sure opportunity, have a fair account of it. The news your own letters will give you, and I fancy it will be as unpalatable to you as it is to me. We must, however, obey and do our best; we are, indeed, the servi servorum, the beasts of burden, that must go as they are driven. Je suis las de mon s— métier; mais des considérations réfléchies m'empêchent de prendre encore aucune résolution subite. Aidez-moi, je vous prie, de vos conseils; la santé me manque et la situation des affaires m'accable de tristesse. . . .

"I have one solid comfort in the midst of my most distressful situation, which is, that I have done my duty fairly, honestly and freely, without consulting to please or acquire friends. I have sacrificed my ambition to the public weal. I have, in some measure, regained the confidence of the hero with whom I live, and he hears from me what, perhaps, he would not have patience to do from another.   This is, in truth, the reason, why I remain here.   I do not think it impossible that I may be recalled, though I have not asked it.   I shall retire with pleasure, for I am well able to justify everything I have done.   I heartily wish every man concerned in public business were in the same happy condition.

" I have profited of this opportunity to pour out my soul to you; it affords me consolation, and I have only to desire, that when you have read this letter, you will commit it to the flames.

" *P.S.*—When I think of our master, all the sentiments of tenderness, duty and affection rise up in my mind and I am afflicted beyond measure.

A. MITCHELL." [1]

There is no doubt that the writer's health was seriously shaken by the bad news from England; Carlyle even speaks of a paralytic stroke.[2]   To recruit his strength he obtained leave of the King and went to Spa (1764). Having returned to Berlin in 1766, after a visit to England, he remained there revered by all and loved by Frederick[3] in comparative retirement to the date of his death, the 28th of January 1771.

The following anecdotes proving his ready wit may complete the sketch of Mitchell.

" Do you never get the spleen, when the mail does not arrive ?' he was asked by the King.

" Never; but very often when it does arrive," was Mitchell's answer.

On another occasion Frederik had contemptuously spoken of the affair at Port Mahon and Mitchell replied : " England must do better another time.   She must put her confidence in God."

---

[1] *Memoirs of Sir R. Murray Keith.*   [2] *Friedrich,* ix. 332.

[3] In that eventful year 1762 Frederik wrote to Mitchell : " Quant à vous, Monsieur, je ne saurais assez vous exprimer combien je suis sensible à toutes les marques d'affection et d'attachement éternel et reconnaissant. . . .   Sur ce je prie Dieu qu'il vous ait en sa sainte et digne garde " ; and in his works he calls him the " Ministre vertueux."

"In God?" answered the King sarcastically. "I was not aware England had Him for an ally!"

"The only ally that costs us nothing," was the ready reply, slyly indicating the vast sums England had paid to her Prussian confederate.

It is a curious fact that, whilst England boasted of a representation so effective and creditable about the Court of Berlin in the person of a Scotsman, in Vienna also, the rival Court, towards the end of the XVIIIth Century the post of British ambassador was held by Scotsmen.

Already the name of Keith has been mentioned in these pages. It was from the same old, famous stock that the Murray Keiths, father and son, descended, who for thirty years represented Great Britain in the Austrian capital. They were the son and grandson of a Colonel Robert Keith of Craig in Kincardineshire. Robert Keith, the father, came to Vienna in 1747 and was a man of mild, conciliatory character. Maria Theresa entertained a peculiar regard for this Minister and testified it on every occasion during the nine years of his sojourn; and even on the day of his departure, which took place under the painful circumstances of a political rupture, she proved by valuable gifts,[1] that she knew well how to distinguish between the person of an ambassador and the political views of the Court that sent him. There is no doubt that Keith had deserved this confidence. To a stubborn honesty he joined a certain chivalry and delicacy of feeling, which, more than once, drew upon him the censure of the British Ministry, because he refused to deliver certain harsh and overbearing messages to the Empress in person, as he was desired to do.[2] Kaunitz, the Austrian Premier, wrote to him on his recall, that the Sovereign rendered all justice to the manner, in which he

---

[1] They consisted in a portrait, for which the Empress had given special sittings and in splendid dresses, embroidered under her own directions by the nuns of a convent she patronized, for his three daughters.

[2] Especially on one occasion, when he knew the Empress to be in interesting circumstances. Cp. *Memoirs of Sir R. Murray Keith*, i. 21.

had acquitted himself and that she would always recall the remembrance of it with pleasure.

His new appointment to the Court of St Petersburg did not please him. The stiff ceremonial there contrasted sharply with the familiar conversations with the Austrian Empress. Moreover, he was surrounded by intrigues, and rendered obnoxious to a certain clique on account of his not belonging to the highest nobility. In spite of all this he continued to try his best to promote a good understanding between Britain, Petersburg and Berlin. Filled like his friend Mitchell with admiration for the heroic qualities of Frederick he acutely felt the defection of England in 1762. At such a time the friendly letters of the " Great King" must have appeared especially valuable and comforting. On the 18th of February of that year the King writes from Breslau :

" Sir,—Feelingly alive as I am to all the proofs of affection and attachment which you have hitherto shown me, I have resolved no longer to delay expressing my gratitude. I beg you to be persuaded that I shall ever give you credit for them, and that I shall seize with pleasure all the opportunities which may present themselves to give you convincing proofs of my esteem. . . ."

A second letter, dated Breslau, March 24th, is written in a similar strain, and adds the wish that all the Ministers of Britain might be animated with the same zeal for the interests of the King.

The third letter, the most explicit of all, runs : "Sir —Your letter of the ninth gave me great pleasure, and I am the more obliged to you for the congratulations you address to me on the conclusion of my peace with the Emperor of Russia, that I can only attribute the success of this negotiation to the zeal with which you exerted yourself to make it succeed. It is a work due to your efforts alone, and I shall cherish for it a gratitude proportioned to the important service, which, on this occasion, you have rendered me."[1]

We can, however, not enter here upon Keith's political

[1] *Memoirs of Sir M. Keith,* i. 49.

career in Russia. Suffice it to say that he died suddenly near Edinburgh, where he had spent the last years of his life in rural retirement in the year 1774.

The love of peace, integrity and honour which distinguished his father were transmitted to his son Sir Robert Murray Keith. But added to it were a cheerful way of enjoying life, a humour that would not be chilled by any ceremonial, and a strong military bias which were wanting in his father. Born on September 20th, 1730, the future ambassador passed an ideally happy boyhood, rich in innocent fun and protected by the love of his devoted parents. When still young he entered the Dutch service, exchanging it later for that of Prince Ferdinand of Brunswick, in whose campaigns he took a distinguished part. During the year 1758 he stayed for some time at Münster, the garrison life of a dull little town being enlivened by his familiar intercourse with General Conway and his family. In the year following he was made major and commander of three newly-raised Highland regiments. At Eybach, Fellinghausen, and in other engagements, they performed "miracles of bravery," as the chief in command expressed himself. The time between the peace (1763) and his appointment as British ambassador to the Court of Saxony at Dresden (1768) Keith spent partly at home, partly at Paris. His letters from the gay Saxon capital are full of humour, and give us a most graphic and amusing description of his life among the high lords and ladies of the Court. "If we did not eat most unmercifully our town would be very agreeable," he writes on one occasion. Another time he tells his father that the Elector had expressed a wish to see him in his Highland uniform. "Send me," he continues, "a handsome bonnet, a pair or two of the finest knit hose, and a plaid of my colours sewed and plaited on a waist-belt. If to this you are so good as to add a handsome shoulder-belt and buckle, and the hilt of an Andrew Ferrara, I shall be enabled to show my nakedness to the best advantage." [1]

[1] *Memoirs*, i. 122.

Twice he visited his uncle, the old Earl Marischal Keith, at Berlin. When on his second visit King Frederick sent for him and conversed with him long and intimately. Keith gives an account of this interview to his father, and writes: "The King told me during our conversation more flatteries than would fill a quire of paper. His questions were so minute that it would have surprised you. He asked of you, ' Si vous étiez sur vos terres ? ' and I told him : ' Que pour des terres, vous n'en possédiez pas la grandeur de sa chambre, et que cependant il y avait trés peu de gens plus heureux que vous et votre famille.' "

He also expressed a wish that Keith should stay near him at Berlin; but being already on his way to Kopenhagen to fill the post of British ambassador there, this could not be accomplished.

The jovial companion and the favourite of the Dresden Court, who understood so well how to accept the brightest side of life, was now destined to witness the most romantic and tragic events in the modern Court history of Denmark ; events which called the other side of his character into activity : energy and unflinching courage. It was the time, so well known all over the world, of the Struensee conspiracy. We can only briefly indicate the part played in it by Sir Robert. When he heard that Queen Caroline, a sister of the King of England, had been arrested on the atrocious charge of having poisoned her husband, and that the judges were then sitting to decide her fate, he quickly took his resolution, made his way through an infuriated mob to the chamber where the meeting was being held, and declared with a firm voice that to touch only a hair of the Queen meant war with England. Then he returned to his house, sent a messenger to London and shut himself up in his apartments for four weeks, anxiously expecting the decision of the British Cabinet, the approval or the censure of his entirely unauthorized proceeding. At last the news arrived in the shape of a parcel. When he opened it, he perceived the insigna of the Order of the Bath !

Keith's later activity as the successor of his father in

Vienna, though much longer in duration than his Kopenhagen appointment, and extending to nearly twenty years,
was devoid of romantic and stirring incident. Instead
of it, his life was frequently embittered by frictions with
his superiors at home, who seemed to claim a right to
neglect the embassy in Austria. For many months Keith
received no answer to his dispatches and letters; his
representation, that his salary was not sufficient to satisfy
the demands made upon him by many hundreds of English
visitors, was not listened to. Moreover, it was foreign to
his nature to have to exercise an incessant petty vigilance
over the proceedings of others, not to speak of the
political inactivity, that was forced upon him. A very
outspoken letter of his led to his recall in 1788; but the
King refused to sanction it, and Keith returned under
improved conditions to his old post. He was welcomed
as a friend; for all the time his intercourse with the
imperial family, the members of the diplomatic body and
those of the aristocracy had been of the most friendly and
agreeable nature. The esteem which his father had
gained before him, was transferred to him in an even
greater measure.

In 1791 he represented England at the Treaty of
Sistovo, between Austria and Turkey, and his influence was
paramount. After this difficult and wearisome piece of
work, he felt the necessity of consulting his own health
and comfort. But he did not leave his post at the
beginning of a new reign (1792), without having given
a faithful and masterly summary of the state resources—
political, financial and military—of the empire.

Then only he retired to London, and the good wishes
he left behind him at Vienna could only be equalled by
the warm welcome of his friends at home.

Unchilled in heart and unsophisticated in character—
not a great man, but a good and loveable one—he died
suddenly at Hammersmith on the 7th of July 1795.[1]

---

[1] Shortly before leaving Vienna he had written the following characteristic letter: " I had the honour of receiving along with your
lordship's dispatch on Monday last His Majesty's additional instructions

There is a curious resemblance in the most characteristic features of these two Scottish statesmen : a simple
directness of speech and integrity of life, obstinate perseverance in the pursuance of their aims, and a sound
humour which we recognise in so many of the great men
of Scotland.

Frequently, indeed, the want of material prevents us
from making any attempt of examining into the character
of the Scots in Germany.   Sources like the Letters and
Memorials of Mitchell and Robert Murray Kieth are
rare.   In most cases we know little more than their names
or the titles of books written by them; now and then,
perhaps, some fulsome Latin distichs in remembrance of
them.

This is especially true with regard to the numerous
Scottish scholars, who learned and taught during the
past on German universities and high-schools.   The
number of these men is not as large as in France, where
from the XVth Century onward, almost every university
boasted of one Scottish professor or more from Paris,
to the comparatively new-founded universities of Sedan
and Pont-à-Mousson.[1]   Still Germany can point to not
a small number of Scotsmen who proved an honour to
their native land, either in the chairs of professors or as
private teachers.

Of the first great Scottish philosopher, Duns Scotus,—
for the assumption of his being a native of Scotland
proper does not now seem unjustified,—the great
defender of the immaculate conception, the " Doctor

on the subject of Foreign Secret Service Money, and I shall not fail to
pay the strictest obedience to them on any occasion that may hereafter
arise.   In the meantime I have the satisfaction to assure your lordship
that in the 23 years, during which I had the honour of serving H.M. in
various foreign missions, I never charged a single shilling for Secret
Service Money to the account of Government."

[1] No less than thirty times did Scottish scholars attain to the dignity of
Rectors of Paris.   There were besides Sedan four other Protestant
colleges in France : Saumur, Montauban, Montpellier and Nismes.
The last two were united in 1617.   Pont-à-Mousson was founded by
Charles II, Duke of Lorraine.

subtilis," whose system has not ceased to attract the attention of recent philosophers, it is known that he spent the last years of his life at Cologne, not, indeed, as a founder of the University there, for it was only called into life in 1388, but as a teacher in one of the schools of the great Monastic Orders. He died in 1308. A monument erected in his memory in 1513 in the Church of the Minorites, bears the inscription : "Scotia me genuit, Anglia me suscepit Colonia me tenet" ("Scotland bore me, England received me, Cologne holds me ").

The connection with Germany of his namesake Michael Scot,[1] whose scholarly attainments were soon overgrown with the superstitious belief by the people in his magic powers, is still slighter. We do not even know for certain whether he ever was in Germany. Still he deserves a word or two because of his having been the teacher of the Roman and German Emperor Frederick the Second at Palermo. As such he dedicated to his pupil on the occasion of his marriage with Constance, the daughter of the King of Aragon, following a then universal custom, his *Physionomia*, and later on, after he had gone to Spain for the study of Arabian Philosophy, his translation of Aristotle's *De Animalibus*, a book which was sure to please a friend of Natural History like the Emperor. Another proof of his connection with Frederick is to be found in a note at the end of his *Astronomia*: "Here ends the Book of Michael Scot, the Astrologer of the Roman Emperor Frederick, 'semper Augustus,' which he wrote in a simple style at the request of the Emperor."[2]

We are moving on firmer ground when we review the monastic erudition of the Scots. The Benedictines especially cultivated education and learning, and thus the Scottish monasteries in Germany, which followed, as we have seen, the rules of St Benedict, produced quite a series of eminent scholars. We have already spoken

---

[1] Born between 1175 and 1180 in the valley of the Tweed (?).
[2] In the copy at Oxford. Cp. Wood Brown, *An Inquiry into the Life and Legend of Michael Scot*, 1896, p. 22.

of *Ratisbon* and its famous abbots: Winzet, Stuart and
Arbuthnot, as well as of the Benedictine University of
Salzburg.   At *Erfurt* the position of the Scottish abbots
with regard to the University there was a very peculiar
one.   Since the year 1427 they bore the title of
"Universitatis Studii Erfurtensis Protectores, Privilegiorum Conservatores, Matriculae Custodes." [1]
Several instances are on record where these privileges
have been exercised.   Thus the abbots Dermicius in 1442,
and Edmundus forty-eight years later, settle a quarrel that
had arisen between the professors and the students of
the University as: "Judices competentes per sententiam
definitivam."   In a similar manner abbot Cornelius
relegated two "magistros," who refused to submit to
the decrees of the Council of Basel (1485); and Jacobus
exercised the same judicial office in 1532. [2]
There were, moreover, attached to the monastery at
Erfurt four Philosophical chairs,[3] the Scottish occupants of
which chiefly taught Mathematics, Algebra, Logic, Meta-
physics, and Natural Philosophy.   Very well known
amongst them in his time, on account of his experiments in
electricity, was P. Andreas Gordon, a scion of the old ducal
house of Gordon.   He was a member of the "Académie des
sciences" at Paris and of the "Royal Academy of Science"
at Munich.   Having been educated at Kehlheim, and at
the Scottish Seminary of Ratisbon, he started on a two
years' journey through Austria, Italy and France.   On
his return in 1732 he became a priest, and afterwards
Professor of Philosophy at Erfurt (about 1737).[4]   In his
inaugural address he spoke of the "Dignity and the Use
of Philosophy."   The hostility which his writings display

[1] Falkenstein, *Thüringische Chronik*, p. 1064.   The bull in question
was issued by Pope Martin V " anno pontificatus sui decimo, die 13 Feb."
[2] Falkenstein, *l.c.*, p. 1065 f.
[3] The Scottish Monastery originally only contained four monks.
[4] He wrote *Phaenomena electricitatis exposita*, Erfurt, 1744, and
*Philosophia utilis et jucunda tribus tomis comprehensa in usum studiosae
juventutis*, Pedeponti prope Ratisb. 1745; the 1st vol. of which com-
prises Logic, Ethics, etc.; the 2nd, Mathematics; the 3rd. Natural
Philosophy.   *Varia Philosophiae mutationem spectantia*, Erf. 1749.

against the Scholastic Philosophy involved him in long controversies with the clerical scholars of the day. Other monastic scholars famous for their learning were *Marianus Brockie*, the author of a History of the Scottish Monasteries,[1] *Bernhard Grant*,[2] *Hieronymus Panton*, Superior of the Monastery and Doctor of Divinity (1711); *Maurus Stuart*, abbot (1720), and *Boniface Leslie*, about 1730. Panton was elected Rector of the University in 1712 and died 1719; the others were Professors of Philosophy also.

Among the Scottish monks of *Würzburg* mention must be made of the Abbot *Johannus Audomarus Aslon*, who is said to have been Rector of the University there in 1646. About twenty years earlier *Alexander Baillie*, who later on became Abbot of Erfurt, was Prior of the Monastery (1622). He wrote a book against the heretics.[3] In the knowledge of the history of their Order excelled Silvanus Maine, and Boniface Strachan from Montrose, who compiled a very valuable work on the "Propagation of Christianity in Germany by monks of the Scottish Nation," the plan of which had been suggested to him by Maine.[4] To these must be added: Thomas Duffus (Duft), who died in 1636 and is called a "poeta celeberrimus," a very famous poet; and Marianus Irvin, a public teacher of theology.

Besides theology, medicine and natural philosophy have always proved a very attractive study for the Scots, even so long ago as the XVIth Century. Among the Scots in

[1] *Monasticum Scoticum*, Pedeponti, 1752.
[2] He was a well-known Mathematician. Born in 1725 he taught in various Benedictine Monasteries until he was appointed Professor at Erfurt. He died as Prior of Ratisbon in 1785. His mathematical works and those on Natural Philosophy were clearly written and introduced as text-books in many schools. *Lessons in Mathematics*, Erf. 1756. *Elementa Philosophiae*, Erf. 1762. *Lessons in Nat. Phil. and History*, Göttingen, 1779.
[3] He is called: "Zelo fidei catholicae et libro in haereticos conscripto conspicuus" by Wieland, *l.c.*, p. 106.
[4] "Germania Christiana sive de plantata et propagata christ. religione in Germania per Sanctos et Monachos Scoticae nationis. T. iii. M. ch. 9. 53, in the Royal University Library, Würzburg.

Germany we find three very eminent men in this province
of learning : *Duncan Liddel, John Craig* and *John Johnston.*
The first of these was born at Aberdeen in 1561.   When
about eighteen he emigrated like so many of his countrymen in those times to the "land of promise," Poland.   He
went first to Danzig, and from there to Frankfort-on-the
Oder, where John Craig, the Professor of Logic, became
his friend.   Under him he studied philosophy and mathematics for two years.   When Craig returned to Scotland,
Liddel went, furnished with letters of introduction, to
Breslau, where he derived much benefit from the intercourse with the learned Hungarian convert Andreas
Duditius and from the lectures of Paul Wittich, who
initiated him into the secrets of the Kopernican system of
astronomy.   In the following year we find him again at
Frankfort, but this time not as a student but as a teacher.
Here he remained till 1585 when the plague scattered his
pupils in all directions and compelled him to leave the
town.   He first betook himself to Rostock where he was
immatriculated in the month of October.   His residence
there seems to have been rendered very pleasant through
the kindness of Brucaeus,[1] a famous physician and philosopher, and of the learned Professor Caselius.   At first
he taught privately, but after having received his degree
as " Magister philosophiae" in 1587, when Nicolaus
Goniaeus was Dean of the Faculty, he read publicly on
the motions of the heavenly bodies according to the
various systems of Ptolemy, Kopernikus and Tycho Brahe
the great Danish astronomer.   With the latter he had
become acquainted on a visit to the island of Hveen where
the Dane's famous observatory had been built.   Against
the accusation of having claimed the honour of Tycho's
discoveries for himself, he defended himself most energetically, and maintained to have independently arrived
at the same results.   He owned, however, to have
received his first suggestions from Tycho.[2]   In the year

[1] A Dutch scholar with the name of van der Brook from Alost in Flanders.
[2] Kepleri, *Opera ommia,* i. pp. 227 f.   Cp. J. L. E. Dreyer, *Tycho Brahe, a Picture of Scientific Life and Work in the 16th century.*   Edinb. 1890.

1590 he went with his friend Caselius to the newly-founded University of Helmstädt where the latter had just been made Professor of Philosophy. He himself occupied the chair of mathematics and afterwards of geography and astromony. His mind, however, was chiefly inclined towards medicine. In 1596 he obtained his medical degree, having written a dissertation on "Melancholy." During his term of office he was several times elected Dean of the Philosophical and Medical Faculty. He was, moreover, physician to the Court of Brunswick and to many of the great country families. From the year 1604 onward, when he was elected Pro-rector, he limited himself to his medical lectures and to his medical practice. But the fame and the wealth thus acquired could not quench his desire to return to Scotland, especially since the political outlook in his adopted country seemed to become gloomier every year. Moved by these considerations he left Helmstädt in 1607 and went to Aberdeen, where he continued to reside until 1613, the year of his death. In his will he left a considerable sum for the endowment of a chair of mathematics, whilst he placed the rent of some of his lands in the neighbourhood of the town at the disposal of the University authorities for the maintenance of six poor students. He lies buried in the Church of St Nicholaus at Aberdeen, where a handsome brass of Dutch workmanship, beautifully en-graved, shows him surrounded by his books and instru-ments. Of his writings the most important are:

1. Disputationum medicinalium Duncani Liddelii Scoti, Phil. et Med. Doctoris in Academia Julia, Pars Prima. Helmstädt, 1605.

2. Ars medica. Hamburg, 1608, 1728.

3. De febribus libri tres. 1610.

After his death appeared his much talked of essay, "De dente aureo" ("Of the golden tooth") Its origin is the following. A certain doctor and professor at Helmstädt, with the name of Jacob Horst, had published an account of a boy born with a tooth of gold, explaining this curious fact by saying that the sun in conjunction with the planet

Saturn in the constellation of Aries had produced such enormous heat, that one of the teeth of the boy had been melted into gold at his birth.   Several other doctors supported this view, whilst Liddel opposed it asserting not without some slight humour, that the tooth in question, to examine which the parents of the child would not allow, was probably only gilded.[1]

Liddel's *Artis conservandi sanitatem libri duo* (" two books on the art of preserving the health ") also appeared after his death.   It was published by one of his pupils at Helmstädt, a Scotsman named Dun,[2] in 1651.

A little earlier than Liddel, *John Craig* was Professor of Mathematics at Frankfurt a/O. He had taken his medical degree at Basel and became in time, after having resigned his professorship in 1561, Physician to King James. He is chiefly known on account of his controversy with Tycho Brahe, whose book on the comet of 1577 he very probably received through Liddel.   Tycho had published a lengthy defence of his books against the attacks of Craig (1589) and had sent a copy of it to the Scot, who some three years afterwards undertook a refutation of the Dane denouncing " nec tam scotice quam sceptice " all those that dared to deny Aristotle's teaching about the comets. The friendship between the two scholars, however, does not seem to have suffered much, at least not until the year 1588; for in that year Tycho sends a mathematical book to Craig with the Latin dedication: "To Doctor J. Craig of Edinburgh, the most renowned and most learned Professor of Medicine, the very distinguished Mathematician, etc., Tycho Brahe sends this gift."   Three letters, which he wrote to the Danish scholar, are likewise couched in the most friendly terms   It is just possible that he accompanied King James VI on his visit to the isle of Hveen and its celebrated observatory.

In conjunction with Liddel and Craig must be mentioned *John Johnston*, called " *Polyhistor*," a man of less ambition,

---

[1] Cp. E. H. B. Hill, *Aberdeen Doctors*, 1893, p. 7.
[2] Patrick Dun was afterwards Rector of Marischal College, Aberdeen (1621-1649).

but vaster and more profound learning. He was the son of a certain Simon Johnston, who about the end of the XVIth Century, emigrated from Annandale to Samter in Poland, together with his two brothers Francis and Gilbert. A birth-brief issued at Lanark in 1596, of which copies exist at Vienna and Breslau, testifies the legitimate birth of the brothers and their descent from the old race of the lairds of Craigieburn, and recommending them at the same time to the sovereigns of Holland and Poland. The mother of John Johnston was Anna Becker, a German lady, known by the beautiful designation of "Mother of Alms." At the school of the Moravian Brethren in Ostrorog, and later at the High School of Beuthen-on-the-Oder, and at Thorn, the future scholar received his education. In 1622 he went to Danzig, and thence by way of Denmark to Scotland, the home of his father. Here he continued his studies in the College of St Leonard's at St Andrews University, devoting himself especially to the study of Scholastic Philosophy, "not to his great profit," as he himself confesses. Moreover he learned Hebrew well, and attended the lectures on Church History by the then Rector Glaidstone. At different times on the occasion of academic ceremonies, he delivered orations "de Passione Dei"; "de Spiritu Sancto," and "de Philosophiae cum Theologia consensu." It was of great use to him during his stay at St Andrews that the Archbishop John Spottiswood received him among the twelve royal alumni, for by one of their rules, three professors had to share their meals in the morning and in the evening, and to enliven them by Latin discourses on various subjects.[1] In this way Johnston became intimately acquainted with Hovaeus, Wedderburn, afterwards Bishop of Dunblane, and Melville, the Professor of Hebrew. He also enjoyed the protection of the Earl of Mar, the Marquis of Argyll, and Lord Erskine, as well as the friendship of John Arnold, the future Chancellor of the Archbishopric, and his brothers James, William, and George. During

[1] Elias Thomä, *Life of Doctor John Johnston*, Brieg, 1675.

his stay at the University, he proved an indefatigable reader and mentions as a special favour, that the librarian allowed him to take books to his own house, and that he had the free use of Professor Glaidstone's library. After his return from Scotland in 1625, he stayed for some time at Lissa in Poland, where he superintended the studies of the two barons of Kurzbach and Zawada, continuing at the same time his medical researches. Here also his zeal for reforming the educational methods of his time brought him into contact with that famous philosopher and pedagogue Johann Amos Comenius. His first work, the *Enchiridion Historiae Naturalis* (Handbook of Natural History) was very probably published at Lissa. Then commenced a long time of travels. Johnston visited the towns of Frankfurt, Leipzig, Wittenberg, Magdeburg, Zerbst and Berlin, not so much with the purpose of seeing their sights, but of conversing with their celebrated men. In 1629 he went to Hamburg and thence to the University of Franeker in Holland; in the following year to Leyden and England. In London he held friendly intercourse with John Wilson, Bishop of Lincoln, Dr Primrose, and John Pym, the famous leader of the Commons. In Cambridge also he was received by all the scholars "with great politeness." Indeed so great had his fame become by that time, that efforts were made in various quarters to secure his services. Primrose wanted to send him to Ireland in an official capacity, Vedelius offered him a chair in the University of Deventer, and the Woywode Belczky a professorship in Poland. Johnston accepted the latter call and embarked for Germany in 1631 in company with General Leslie. By way of Wolgast and Stettin, he arrived safely at Lissa and at Warsaw, where he remained till the following year, engaged in his professional duties. But the longest journey of four years' duration he undertook in 1632, as the companion and mentor of two Polish noblemen : the Baron of Leszno, who afterwards became Chancellor of the Exchequer of Poland, and a son of the Marschal of Lithuania, Wladislaw Dorostoyski.

The travellers visited the Netherlands, England, France and Italy. After having thus satisfied to the full his roving instincts, a desire for rest and rural seclusion took hold of Johnston which never left him. At first he settled in Lissa, where he married the daughter of the celebrated Polish Court-physician Matthaeus Vechnerus. But the restless and turbulent condition of the country, rendering the peaceful enjoyment of a country-life almost impossible, soon compelled him to exchange Poland for Silesia, where in 1652 he acquired the estate of Ziebendorf in the principality of Liegnitz. Here he spent his time in constant correspondence with the most learned men of Europe,[1] diligently reading and writing the last twenty-three years of his life. He died in 1675 aged seventy years, honoured by many friends and lamented in numerous elegies. Sinapius[2] says of him: " He was a man of sincere piety, old-fashioned honesty, without pride and frivolity, indefatigable in his industry, and in his conversation always lively and pleasing."

In connection with the above we must mention another doctor of medicine, the Königsberg physician *George Motherby*, who gained great fame by first advocating vaccination in his city (about 1770). A namesake and doubtlessly a relation of this George was *William Motherby*, who studied medicine at Königsberg and took his degree at Edinburgh in 1797. He practically introduced vaccination by means of cow lymph, which he brought from Edinburgh.[3] In defence of his method he published two pamphlets in 1801.

The passion for education, which forms such a prominent

---

[1] Jonston understood twelve languages. He declined a call as professor to Heidelberg, Frankfort-on-the-Oder and to Leyden.

[2] In a volume of the town-library at Breslau, containing a life of Jonston, there are printed no less than twenty-five Latin elegies by friends in Leipzig and Breslau, and by the teachers of the High School at Lissa. Sinapius is the author of *Schlesische Curiositäten* (Curiosities of Silesia). See Append x.

[3] J. Sembritzki, *l.c.*, p. 238 f. W. Motherby died in 1847. An oration in his memory is contained in the *Neue Preuss. Provinzial Blätter*, pp. 131-141.

P

feature in the character of the Scots and earned for them the title of "the Germans of Great Britain," was carried with them to the land of their adoption. We have seen how eager the Scottish emigrants of the XVIth and XVIIth Centuries were to obtain their own places of divine worship. With the same eagerness we find them endeavouring to procure the best education for their children born in a strange land. In their church-records the school is continually and prominently mentioned. Or they send their children to schools already existing. At Tilsit Rector Dewitz in 1644 entered three Scottish boys as pupils of his "Provincial School": Thomas Sumerwel (Somerville), Nicolaus Beili (Bailie) and Johannes Medlen.[1]

In 1699 the Scots in Königsberg—at the instigation, perhaps, of their countrymen and co-religionists in Polish Lithuania—complain that the Reformed, *i.e.* Presbyterian, school, which in former times had boasted of such a reputation as to attract even children out of Poland, now seemed to be on the decline. Even the towns-people took their children away and put them elsewhere. What was needed, they maintained, was a staff of new efficient teachers, and above all a rector well versed in the Polish language.[2]

The matriculation-rolls of the German Universities at that time likewise show a considerable number of students, who were either born of Scottish parents or descended from Scottish families.[3]

Not a few of these chose the study of divinity. Thus George Anderson, after having been rector, became pastor at Rastenburg (1699).[4] Also one *G. Douglas*, a native of the small town of Schippenbeil near Königsberg, was Presbyterian clergyman of Jerichow, in the district of Magdeburg, from 1758-1772. *John William Thomson*,

[1] Cp. Programme of the Royal High School at Tilsit (1873): H. Pöhlmann, *Beiträge zur Geschichte des Gymnasiums*, II. Stück (Contributions to the Hist. of the High School, II. Part), p. 27.

[2] Sembritzki, *l.c.*, p. 240 f.

[3] *Cf.* Appendix.

[4] D. W. Schröder, *Geschichte der Stadt Goldap*, 1818 (History of the Town of Goldap).

born at Königsberg in 1704, as the son of the rector of
the Presbyterian school, became Court-preacher in 1732,
and died on the 21st of December 1761; *David Hervie*,
probably a grandson of the generous elder of the Scottish
church at Königsberg, of whom we have spoken previously,[1]
was Presbyterian clergyman at Pillau from 1738-1775;
D. Wilhelm Crichton, the nephew of another Court-
preacher, a native of Insterburg, studied divinity at Frankfurt-on-the-Oder and at Königsberg, and in due time
became a chaplain himself.

Nor does the Lutheran Church in that district want
Scottish names amongst her clergymen. It was but
natural that the Scots in those places, where a Presbyterian service could not be had, should attach themselves
to the Lutherans. We are told of one *George Anderson*,
the son of a brewer at Angerburg of that name (1648),
who afterwards became the Lutheran pastor of Rosen-
garten, near his native town. *Andreas Murray*, from
Memel, in the first half of the XVIth Century was given
the charge of first pastor of the German congregation
at Stockholm; *David Stirling*, the son of a Scotsman at
Osterode in Eastern Prussia, was ordained Lutheran clergyman in Königsberg in 1740.[2]

The above list could without doubt be enlarged; but
enough has been said to prove that in the department of
divinity also the Scottish have proved worthy of their
traditions.[3]

Of other scholars among those of Scottish birth and
extraction in Germany mention must be made of the two
librarians of Ulrich or Huldrich Fugger in Augsburg,
whose wealth in those days favourably compared with
the Rothschilds and Carnegies of our times, *Henryson*
and *Scrimgeour*. The first named was a Doctor of
Laws and Professor at Bourges in France. He came
to Fugger about the year 1550, dedicated several of
his books to him, notably a translation of Plutarch,
and received for his faithful services an annuity from

[1] Cp. Part iii.: The Church. [2] Sembritzki, *l.c.*, p. 242
[3] Cp. Part iii.

his patron.[1] Henry Scrimgeour was born in 1506 and went, after he had studied at Paris and Bourges, to Italy as the secretary of the Bishop of Rennes. On his return he received and accepted a call as Professor of Philosophy to Geneva. Here he had the misfortune of losing all he had, including his books, in a conflagration. Under these circumstances he was only too glad to accept Fugger's offer of a librarianship. After a stay of several years in Augsburg he returned to Geneva in 1563, where he was elected *first Professor of Civil Law.* He was one of the most learned Scotsmen of his day. His name is mentioned as one of the witnesses of the last will and testament of Calvin. He died in 1572.

In connection with these two great masters of the law, we may mention a third, who, though not a Scotsman by birth, was yet descended from an old Scottish immigrant and settler at Elbing in Prussia. Among the earliest Scottish names in that town we find, as we have seen above, that of Thomas Auchinvale or Achinwall, as it was afterwards germanised, who died in 1653. His great-great-grandson, *Gottfried Achinwall,* was born at Elbing in the year 1719. After having studied the law in the universities of Jena, Halle and Leipzig, he became public lecturer on International Law, History and Statistics at Marburg, and since 1748 at Göttingen, where he soon obtained the proud position of one of the most celebrated professors of the University. He attracted a great number of hearers, chiefly on account of his lectures on Political Economy, a science which owes its existence and scientific treatment to him. Almost the only remarkable incident in an otherwise tranquil though honoured life seems to have been a long journey, undertaken with royal subsidies, to Switzerland, France, Holland and England. He died in 1772. His books on Political Economy were widely read and went through many editions. In all of them British

---

[1] He also published a *Commentary on Tit. X. Libri. sec. Instit. Justin.* in 1555.

candour and German thoroughness are most judiciously blended.[1] The year of Achinwall's birth was the death-year of another famous scholar of the law, Jacobus Lamb de Aberton, who was born at Elbing in 1665. He afterwards became Member of the Faculty of Law at Padua and Pro-rector. In 1701 he was made Doctor of Philosophy and Knight of St Mark, in 1702 Imperial Pfalzgraf. He died when on his home-journey in 1719 at Berlin.[2]

In the province of philosophy and kindred branches, *Thomas Reid*, the secretary of King James II, deserves a niche to himself. He received his college education at Aberdeen, where he also qualified for his degree in about 1600. Having taught as Regent in the University for four years, he went to Germany for the completion of his studies. In 1608 he was admitted public teacher at Rostock and three years later appointed Professor of the Latin Language at the same University, with a salary attached of 80 gulden and a free house. Like other scholars of his time he excelled in debate, and many were the so-called public disputations, especially with Arnisaeus, a Professor of Medicine at Frankfurt, that made the halls resound. Some time later he immatriculated at Leipzig, whence he returned to England. The last six years of his life were spent as Latin Secretary of the King. More than through his philosophical writings he will be gratefully remembered as the founder of the first public library in Scotland, for by his will he not only left his books to the city of Aberdeen, but the sum of six thousand merks besides to cover the expenses of a librarian, who was to keep the door "of the library patent and open on four dayes of the week the whole year."[3]

[1] *Constitutional History of the European States*, 1752 ; *Political Science*, 1763 ; *Elementa juris naturae*, Gött. 1750 ; *Autobiography*, 2 vols.

[2] Seyler, *Elbinga litterata* (1742), p. 87.

[3] *Scottish Notes and Queries*, vol. ix. Many of Reid's philosophical works were published in Rostock, for instance : *De accidente proprio theoremata philosophica* (1609) ; *Pervigilium Martis de ente* (1610) ; *Pervigilium Jovis de veritate et bonitate entis* (1610), and others.

Besides Reid we find other Scotsmen as teachers of languages in Germany. There is *Benedictus Ingram*, of whom we have already spoken, one of the eight last Scottish monks at Würzburg, who, after 1803 became lecturer of English at the University of the town, and published an English grammar; and a little later *Robert Motherby*, a brother of William, the physician, who lived at Königsberg as a teacher of languages. He is the translator of Shakespeare's *Merry Wives of Windsor* (1828) and issued a *Dictionary of the Scottish Idiom*.[1]

Above all, mention must be made of *Arthur Jonston*, not in his quality as physician to King James and Charles I, but as one of the most excellent Latin poets Scotland ever produced. He was the son of George Jonston of Caskieben, near Keithall, in Aberdeenshire. Here, under the shadow of mighty "Big Benachie," in the invigorating atmosphere of the Highlands, he passed his youthful days. He was taught Latin at Kintore. When his father died in 1593, however, he, being a younger son, had to shift for himself. Like so many of his countrymen he turned his eyes towards the Continent, but we do not know the place he first emigrated to. Certain it is, that he and one Walterus Donaltsonus, both being then styled "Magistri," were immatriculated at Heidelberg on the 11th of September 1599; and that two years later he had obtained the dignity of regens or professor. As such we find him presiding at a public "disputation" in the philosophical lecture-rooms of the University[2] (1601). But his stay at Heidelberg was not of long duration. He accepted a call of the Duc of Bouillon as professor at Sedan. And yet, the time spent at the beautiful Neckartown, the adopted home of a Scottish princess, had deeply impressed his mind. To the reader of his poem, or rather

---

[1] Sembritzki, *l.c.*, p. 239. The title of the book runs: "Pocket Dictionary of the Scottish Idiom, the signification of the words in English and German, chiefly calculated to promote the understanding of the works of Scott, Robert Burns, Allan Ramsay, etc., with an Appendix containing notes explicative of Scottish customs, manners, traditions, etc." Königsberg, Bornträger. Two editions.

[2] Cp. Appendix.

his cycle of poems, entitled *Querelae Saravictonis et Biomeae*, *i.e.* "The struggle between Austria and Bohemia," published at Heidelberg in 1620, this becomes at once apparent.   He passionately calls upon England and the whole of Europe to assist the Elector-King, and great is his anxiety for the fate of the Palatinate and its fair capital.   As a Protestant Manifesto of the times the poem, even apart from its poetical beauties, is interesting and well deserving a perusal.

Jonston returned to Scotland in 1622, became Rector of Aberdeen (1637), and died in 1641 when on a visit to Oxford.[1]

At this point of our survey we must not forget the grandfather of the great philosopher Emanuel Kant, who was born of Scottish parents.   In the draft of an answer to a letter of the Swedish Bishop Lindblom, in which the Swedish descent of Kant's father had been started, the philosopher says: "It is very well known to me, that my grandfather, who was a citizen of the Prusso-Lithuanian town of Tilsit, came originally from Scotland."

Now this notice gave rise to various doubts.   First of all, Kant's grandfather, Hans Kant, did not live at Tilsit, but at Memel, where he carried on the trade of a harness- and belt maker.   It had to be assumed, therefore, either that Kant wrote by mistake Tilsit instead of Memel, or that he confused grandfather and great-grandfather. For the latter view spoke the occurrence of one Balthasar or Balzer Kant, in a list of Presbyterian church members of Tilsit, a very aged Scotsman, who received relief out of the "Poor Box," in the year 1682.

Thus matters stood, when by the discovery of two

---

[1] Cp. *Musa Latina Abredonensis*, by Geddes, *New Spalding Club Publications*, vol. ii. p. 17.   Two other Latin poets of Scottish extraction in Germany were A. Aidy at Danzig, who published his *Pastoralia* in that city in 1610, and Andrew Leech, from Melrose, who lived for some time at Krakau, and whose name occurs polonised as Lechowicz or latinised Loechius.   He wrote: *Epithalamium* (1595); *Anagrammat. encomiastici,* Danzig and Krakau (1609); *Jani malifera strena,* Edinburgh (1617); *Musæ Priores* (1620); a Latin Grammar, etc.

manuscript-contracts, found at Königsberg amongst the so-called " house-books " of the district of Memel, a new light was shed on the question.   According to these documents, Richard Kandt, the great-grandfather, a publican at Werdden near Heidekrug, then, in 1667, an old man, gives over to his daughter Sophia, and to her second husband, Hans Karr, in consideration of the latter's claims against him, the whole of his well-furnished house, together with three hides of land, on condition, that the sum of 100 thaler be paid to his son Hans Kandt, then a journeyman harness-maker " in foreign lands," together with " six shirts of home-spun linen, six collars and twelve handkerchiefs," and that he himself was to receive board and lodging to the end of his life, whilst all his debts were to be paid by the said son-in-law.

Soon afterwards old Richard died, and his son Hans, returning from his travels, and feeling himself somewhat aggrieved by the settlement above, entered on June the 4th, 1670, " for the maintenance of peace and brotherly friendship," into a second agreement with his brother-in-law, which was drawn up at Memel.   The 100 thaler were increased to 150, the six shirts and twelve handkerchiefs changed into ten yards of linen, at five shillings a yard, and for this magnificent prospect, Hans Kandt gave up all his claims to the public-house and its " pertinentia " " sine dolo " for himself and all his descendants.[1]

Further discoveries in Memel confirmed the supposition of Hans Kandt's residence in that city.   He married there in 1694, had a house and workshop on the so-called " castle liberties," and by his wife another house situated in the old town, together with some fields on the common. He must have lived, therefore, in tolerably well-to-do, if humble, circumstances.   It was in Memel also, that the father of the philosopher Johann Georg was born and christened in 1682.

The year of Hans Kandt's death cannot now be ascertained correctly.   It is just possible that he

[1] See Appendix.

succumbed to the plague during $170\frac{9}{10}$, when the entries of deaths in the church books were very incomplete.

We therefore arrive at the final conclusion, that the supposition of *Balzer* Kant having been Kant's great-grandfather can no longer be maintained, but that the philosopher erroneously wrote Tilsit instead of Memel. This error becomes all the more probable and excusable, as Hans Kandt or Kant had to go to Tilsit for the purpose of obtaining his certificate of master of his craft, which could not be got at Memel, because at that time no leather-cutters or harness-makers existed there.[1] This certificate, issued at Tilsit, and, no doubt, preserved in the family, Emanuel Kant had in his mind when he wrote his answer to the Swedish bishop's inquiries.

Among the Scottish scholars in Germany, Carl Aloysius Ramsay occupies a prominent position. He was the pioneer of shorthand and was till recently believed to be the son of a certain Charles Ramsay, town-councillor at Elbing in Prussia. But this seems to be erroneous as the historians of this city are silent about him, though mentioning many members of this old and widespread family.[2] Certain it is that he lived the greater part of his life in Germany. He was in Leipzig and Frankfurt in 1677 and 1679, which is proved by the preface to his Latin translation of Kunkel's *German Treatises on Chemistry.* His most important work was his *Tacheography or the Art of writing the German tongue as quickly as it is spoken.* It appeared first in the form of articles written for a Frankfurt newspaper which were collected afterwards and published in book-form in 1678.

By this and his other books on shorthand in foreign languages, Ramsay became the most interesting of all early writers on the subject.[3]

---

[1] Down to the XVIIIth Century, the journeymen of Memel were obliged to go to Tilsit for purposes of the like nature. Cp. Sembritzki, *Neue Nachrichten über Kant's Grossvater,* 1899. See Supplement.

[2] There is a noble family of Ramsay in Austria, the predecessors of which are probably to be found among the Scottish officers of the Thirty Years' War.

[3] Cp. Junge, *Vorgeschichte der Stenographie,* p. 64 f.

The last name in our gallery of eminent Scotsmen is that of Johann von Lamont, the famous astronomer at Munich.   He was born at Braemar in 1805, as the son of an excise-officer, and spent part of his boyhood amidst the invigorating surroundings of his native scenery.   But when his father died early, the boy, who showed good intellectual gifts, was sent by a kind priest to the Bene-dictine Seminary at Ratisbon in Germany, where he received an education well fitting for his future career. His strong bent for scientific research found ample scope and, what is more, enlightened encouragement.   Prior Deasson recommended the young scholar to the Bavarian astronomer at Bogenhausen, not far from the capital, whose assistant he became.   In 1852 the assistant was elected Professor of Astronomy at Munich, and soon his writings and discoveries brought him ample recognition at home and abroad.   He was a member of many learned societies in Belgium, Sweden, Austria, Germany, England and Scotland.   His *Star Catalogue* and his book on the *Magnetism of the Earth* (1849) are standard works. Full of years and honours he died in 1879.

We have now followed the traces of the Scots in Germany to the end.   Many of them succumbed to the crushing revolutions of the wheel of time; many again have left their records in the dusty old parchments of German and Polish archives; many of them have handed down their names corrupted but uncorrupted deeds to a grateful posterity, that recognises in them much that was good and noble in Politics and Learning, in Peace and War.

The eastern and western parts of Prussia still retain their Simpsons, and Gibsons, and Macleans, and Murrays and Mitchells; the German Army list still embodies Douglases, Campbells, Hamiltons, Johnstons, Scotts, Spald-ings and Ramsays, while the German nobility mix and mingle many a proud Scottish coat of arms with theirs.

The rock of history is not a simple structure, but a growth.   It has its testimony as well.   Here also are embedded trilobites that delight the eye of the intelligent reader and puzzle the ignorant. No nation ever stood on its own merits alone. There has been during long centuries a continual fructification, a continual giving and taking of what is best in a nation, a continual fusion in peaceful rivalry. The more accurate our knowledge of history and its bye-ways becomes, the more enlightened and just our judgments upon other nations will be and the readier our hands to burn our war-hatchet for ever and to resort for glory to the quiet study, the busy office, the bright studio, rather than to the reek of the slaughter-house.

APPENDIX TO PART I

I. (Page 3).

Andr. de Moravia et Willelmus Wallensis duces exercitus regni Scotie et communitas ejusdem regni providis viris et discretis et amicis dilectis maioribus· et communibus de Lubek et de Hamburg salutem et sincere dilectionis semper incrementum. Nobis per fide dignos mercatores dicti regni Scotie est intimatum, quod vos vestri gratia in omnibus causis et negociis nos et ipsos mercatores tangentibus consulentes, auxiliantes et favora biles estis, licet nostra non precesserunt merita. Et ideo magis vobis tenemur ad grates cum digna remuneracione atque vobis volumus obligari ; rogantes vos, quatinus preconizari facere velitis inter mercatores vestros, quod securum accessum in omnes portus regni Scocie possunt habere cum mercandiis suis, quia regnum Scocie Deo regnaciato ab Anglorum potestate bello est recuperatum. Valete. Datum apud Hadsington in Scocia undecimo die Octobris Anno gracie millesimo ducentesimo nonagesimo septimo. Rogamus vos insuper ut negocia Johannis Burnet et Johannis Frere mercatorum nostrorum promovere dignemini prout nos negocia mercatorum vestrorum promovere velitis. Valete. Dat : ut supra.

II. (Page 7). See *Lüb. Urk. Buch*, iii. 66.

Robertus Dei gracia rex Scottorum consulibus et burgimastris civitatis Lubicensis, amicis nostris karissimis, salutem. Ad nostram noticiam jam pervenit quod mercatores civitatis vestre et mercatores civitatum Almannie aliunde cum mercimoniis suis regnum nostrum cupiunt frequentare, dummodo per nos et incolas regni nostri pacifice et curialiter admittantur. Quocirca tam vobis quam aliarum mercatoribus civitatum Almannie tenore presentium volumus esse notum, quod omnibus et singulis mercatoribus supradictis regnum nostrum frequentare volentibus per nos et nostros exhiberi volumus graciam et favorem et omnes consuetudines ac libertates quibus mercatores Almannie usi sunt temporibus predecessorum nostrorum, regnum Scocie, gratanter eis volumus observare. Datum apud Berevicium super Twedam, xxii die Aprilis anno regni nostri sexto-decimo.

IIIa. (Page 7).

Dilectis amicis nostris consulibus civitatis de Danczik salutem et amorem, amici karissimi, literas vestras nobis ultimo directas bene intelleximus tangentem deliberacionem Johannis Lange qui prout scitis deliberatur. Quare vobis specialiter supplicamus, quatenus Ricardum de Camera faciatis ibidem quod juris est et racionis, quod prout nobis videtur inutile est ambabus patrie vestre et nostre quod non exercetis patriam nostram prout solebatis, necnon si placuerit aliquibus patrie vestre nobis cum mercimoniis venire nos ipsos conservabimus indempnos pro aliquo fato. Valete; Scriptum apud Castrum nostrum de Dunbar. xxvi die augusti. Comes Marchie.

IIIb. Names of Scottish debtors to the Teutonic Order and its Head Business Manager at Königsberg.[1]

(1396-1417).

The "Grave" (Earl) von Duglos tenetur (owes)		216	Pounds Scottish.	
Item William Tuers	,,	82	,,	,,
Item Alan Balun (?)	,,	20	,,	12 sh.
Item Ian Cragge (Craig?)	,,	1	,,	19 ,,
Item Ion Lyberthun	,,	3	,,	12 ,,
Item Andris Gutswan (?)	,,	0	,,	17 ,,
Item Ion Haliwel	,,	2	,,	0 ,,
Item Allexander Carnys (Cairns)	,,	1	,,	4 ,,
Item Ion Czerneyer (Turner?)	,, }	0	,,	32 ,,
Item Gryndelaw		5	,,	5 ,,
Item Hutczlam (?)		4	,,	7 ,,
Item Kastumers (customers) von Eydenburg		20	,,	0 ,,
Item Watczamer (Watson)		2	,,	2 ,,
Item Ion Leth (Leith)		0	,,	33 ,,
Item Oswald Makely (Maclean?)		1	,,	0 ,,
Item Laubalim (or Lau Balun?) (Bailie?)		0	,,	38 ,,
Item William Hinrichczon (Henryson) tenetur		0	,,	32 ,,
Item Iors (George) Apristun (?)		0	,,	36 ,,
Item Norman Goppolt		40	,,	0 ,,
Item William Porbas (Forbes?)		20	,,	0 ,,
Item Tom Forman		0	,,	36 ,,
Item Ionas Spens		1	,,	0 ,,
Item Wathalige Bortun, der herre von Drelton = the Laird of Drelton		16	,,	16 ,,
Item Allexander Hueme		10	,,	0 ,,
Item Robyn Craffort		3	,,	2 ,,
Item Sir John Sethym (Seaton?)		4	,,	0 ,,
Item Allexander Setthym		3	,,	12 ,,

[1] Cp. Sattler, *Handelsrechnungen des Deutschen Ordens* (Trade Accounts of the Teutonic Order), Leipzig, 1887, p. 75 ff.

Item Sir Aczebald Stuert	8	Pounds	5 sh.
Item Sir Ion Daliel	3	,,	0 ,,
Item "die burger von Lettekow" (Glasgow)	17	,,	2 ,,
Item der grave (earl) von Agues (Angus?)	20	,,	0 ,,
Item Carithun (Carrington?) and Dusschun (?)	13	,,	13 ,,
Item Ion Lam "tenetur 2 saldir weisse"[1]	7	,,	4 ,,
Item "der Herre von Delkeit (Dalkeith)" ½ zaldir weisse[1]	0	,,	36 ,,
Item Modirbil (Motherwell) tenetur 2 bollyn (?)	0	,,	9 ,,
Item 'des losters weip von Aberdyn'[2] tenetur 2 bollyn	0	,,	9 ,,
Item Ion Abil tenetur 2 bollyn	0	,,	9 ,,
Item Lyon tenetur quarter[3]	0	,,	18 ,,
Item Sir Ion Setthun tenetur 1 quarter	0	,,	18 ,,
Item "ein weyp" tenetur 1 bollyn	0	,,	9 ,,
Item Tom Tormuel (Turnbull?) ½ zaldir	0	,,	18 ,,

IV. (See Page 7).

Jacobus Dei gratia rex Scotorum universis et singulis ligiis et subditis nostris ad quorum noticiam presentes litere pervenerint salutem. Sciatis quod suscepimus ac presencium tenore suscipimus dilectos mercatores nostros, cives et inhabitantes civitatem de Bremen eorunque servitores, intromissores et factores ac ipsorum naves, mercancias, victualia, res et bona quecunque infra regnum nostrum veniencia seu applicancia, sub nostra salvagardia, manutencia, tuicione, defensione et protectione speciali. . . . Insuper nostros confederatos benevolos et amicos attente requirimus . . . quatenus . . . ipsos et eorum quemlibet nostri contemplacione et amore favorabiliter et amicabiliter pertractare velitis. Datum apud Edinburgh, Febr. 3, 1453. (*Hans. Urk. Buck*, viii. 167.)

V. LETTER OF DANZIG TO ADMIRAL NAPARE (Page 6).

Magnifico et strenuo domino Alexandro Napare de Merchinstone (Merchiston) militi, deputato illustris principis et domini domini Alexandri ducis Albaniae, comitis Marchiae, domini vallis Annandie (Annandale) et Mannie admirallo regni Scocie, domino et amico nostro sincere dilecto, preconsul et consules civitatis Danzik in Prusia promptissimam ad quevis beneplacita voluntatem. Magnifice et strenue domine et amice noster dilecte. Constitutus coram nobis consulatui presidentibus providus vir Johannes Kilekanne, nauta et conburgensis noster

[1] Two bushels and ½ bushel of wheat.
[2] The litster's (dyer's) wife at Aberdeen. Bolyn probably bales of cloth.
[3] A measure for grain.

dilectus sua nobis insinuacione exposuit evidenter quod, cum
ipse de anno provime preterito cum sua navi certis bonis et
mercibus pressa et omusta regnum Scocie et precipue burgum
de Edinburing frequentare disposuisset et frequentasset, et
quendam Wilhelmum Holeson, nautam de Amstelredamm ex
Hollandia, tamquam nostrum et nostre civitatis prefate inimicum
et emulum cum sua navi ac bonis et rebus in eadem existentibus
mera justicia et racionis dictamine suadente manu atroci
invasisset et adjuvante altissimo, devicisset, cepisset secumque
in burgum Edinburgh prenominatum adduxisset, per dictum
Wilhelmum Holeson coram vestra dominacione magnifica
tractus fuit in causam ibidemque per eundem Wilhelmum, aut
saltem suum procuratorem assertum super capcione hujus tamquam violentia et spolio multipliciter accusatur, vexatus et
inquietatus temere et de facto cum de jure nullatenus id fieri
potuisset, ita ut demum post diversas hincinde partium prefatarum
habitas altricaciones juriumque suorum allegationem, eadem
vestra dominacio navi et bonis taliter ut premittitur captis in
manibus legis sequestratis et observatis partibus hincinde
predictis, ad suas vereficandas allegaciones coram vobis seu
vestris ad hec deputatis in pretorio burgi de Edinburg prescripti
terminum, videlicet secundum diem mensis septembris anni
presentis statuendi duxit et prefigendi, statuitque pariter et
prefixit, quemadmodum hec ex vestrae dominacionis literis
desuper emissis nobisque per dictum Johannem Kilekanne
porrectis et oblatis sane suscepimus significata. Quamobrem
vestram magnificenciam presentibus volumus non latere, qualiter
occasione differenciarum quarundam inter burgenses et inhabit-
tatores de Amstelredamme ab una et nostram civitatem ab altera
partibus dudum exortarum, prefati de Amstelredamme cives,
nautas et mercatores nostros in mari et ubicunque id facere potuer-
ant, tanquam nostri ac nostre civitatis emuli et inimici invaserunt,
spoliarunt eisque naves, merces et bona ceperunt, retinuerunt
atque inter se distribuerunt pluries et plerumque, prout
adhuc invadere, spoliare, capere, retinere atque distribuere non
desistunt neque verentur in hodiernum, quare et nos necessitate
compulsi dictis de Amstelredamme eadem mensura remecientes
pro talibus similia hactenus reddere non negleximus, prout
favente Domino neque negligemus in futuris, donec et
quousque inter ipsos et nos de contrario desuper fuerit ap-
punctuatum, dispositum et placitum Eapropter strenuam et
magnificam vestram dominacionem nobis plerumque com-
mendabilem cum omni qua possumus affectione rogamus,
quatenus justice et nostre contemplacionis intuitu supranominato
Johanni Kilekanne aut procuratori suo legitimo in causis

predictis vestre promotionis suffragia pariter et auxilia dignemini favorosius impartiri, causarumque predictarum meritis maturitate debita recensitis ut navem et bona predicta aut saltem eorum valorem ac congruum justicie complementum omnibus molestia et impedimento cessantibus consequi valeat cum effectu. Id ipsum erga vestram dominacionem et vestrates reciproca vicissitudine remerebimur requisiti. In quorum testimonium sepedicte nostre civitatis secretum presentibus dorsaliter est appressum sexta decima mensis Marcii die anno Domini 1462.

VI. Confessions of the Scots.

Scottish Pilgrims at Breslau (ca. 1470).

Among the documents marked "Criminal Akten" in the Town-Library of Breslau, there is a folio-sheet, apparently dating from the end of the XVth Century, which contains the confessions of various Scotsmen in a trial that they had to undergo on the charge of unlawful vagabondage, etc. The writer, a rather illiterate clerk it would seem, says *inter alia*:

"Item *Lorentz Gren* (Green) from Scotland, from Edenburgh thirty miles off Dondy (Dundee) has come from Rome and has had no shoes, and has been ill for three quarters of a year. Now he has found countrymen here and a [friend] at Brünn has advised him to move to this place and to buy pepper, worm-seed, white ginger for to take it in brandy with a spoon. He left Scotland 111 days before Michaelmas and has vowed a pilgrimage to Rome when at sea in distress, and his father's brother has written to from him Dantzke, that he should come to him."

"Item *Thomas Sneider* (?),[1] also a Scot from Dondy one mile out of a village called Boyschry (?) has left his country on All-Souls'-Day and has long been ill and vowed a pilgrimage to Rome and has been to Rome on Palm Sunday and has come here on the evening before Whitsuntide. . . . He wishes to go to Dantzke and thence towards Scotland."

"Item *Thomas Gybiscihen* (Gibson) from Dondy, the town, a sailor, and has vowed a pilgrimage to St James (di Compostella) and fell ill on the journey, and has been begging and came here on account of strife . . . hence to Dantzke that he might return to Scotland."

"Item *Valterius of Dessen* (Dess in Aberdeen), and has not been to Scotland for three years, has been at Dantzke, at Rome, at Meissen and had been a pedlar and wants to go thence to Dantzke."

[1] Possibly a "tailor" by trade, since very few Scots abroad were then known by their surnames.

Q

"Item *Reichart* (*Richard*) *of Wicke, Kathnes* (Caithness) in Scotland, has been serving a gentleman called the Dyspan and afterwards four years in the service of the Queen of Hungary."

"Item *Hans Robartez* (*Roberts*) from a village called Stewen (?) and left Scotland about Michaelmas and has vowed a pilgrimage to Rome during an illness and has now been at Rome and has been begging on the way and has been at Meininge, hence to Dantzke, from Dantzke to Scotland."

"Item *Andrea Heynersson* (*Henderson*) from Edenburgh, is a tailor and left Scotland eleven years ago and was at Rome during Lent, went there for the sake of adventure and his trade, and has been begging his bread and when he got a penny, he stuck to it."[1]

"Item *Simon of Dessart* (*Dysart*) is a linen-weaver and has been working at Swebissen (Schwiebus) with one Peter Wolf and comes from Leipzig and has been working in the sea-ports at Lupke (Lübeck), Hamburgk, and has also been begging for a crust of bread ; if he got a penny, he stuck to it."

The same is reported of *Alexander Kar* from Haringthun (Haddington). At the close mention is made of :

Bartholomes Deyse (?) from Lyth (Leith) in Scotland, has been at Rome and at St James and has been begging and did vow a pilgrimage during an illness, a fever."

VII. FROM A LETTER OF JAMES IV OF SCOTLAND TO THE EMPEROR MAXIMILIAN OF GERMANY (1510).

. . . Superbe nimis et imperiose Lubecus omnia turbat et nuper interminatus mare nostris interdixisse visus est, quibus ut armatos debellasse gloriosum sic mercatoriam navim invasisse inglorium nec impune futurum credimus. Saevitum in nostros agunt mercatores, alios cruce, alios ense aut aquis Lubeca classis perdidit. (*Epist. Reg. Sc.* i. 112 f.)

VIII. FROM A LETTER OF THE MAGISTRATE OF BREMEN TO QUEEN MARY (1567).

. . . Non dubitamus quin Regia Majestas Vestra ob justitiae et æquitatis multis praedicatam gentibus laudem vehementer et extreme hujusmodi detestetur Harpyas. (*Reg. of Pr. Council. of Scot.* xiv. 270 f.)

IX. LETTER OF JAMES VI (Febr. 22, 1625).

James R. Right trustie and right well beloved Councillour, right trustie and right well beloved cosins and connsillouris.

[1] German : "hot er yn (ihn) auch mit genomen."

We greete you well. Whereas the grite number of young
boyes uncapable of service and destitute of meanis of liveing
yearlie transported out of that our kingdome to the East seas
and speciallie to the town of Dantzik and there manie tymes
miserablie in grite numbers dyeing in the streets have given
quite scandall to the people of those countreyis and laid one
foull imputation on that our kingdome, to the grite hinderance and
detriment of those our subjects of the better, who traffique in
the saidis countreyis: it is our pleasoure that by oppin proclamatioun yee cause prohibite all maisters of shippis to transport
anie youthes of either sex to the said easterne countreyis bot
such as either salbe sent for by thair friendis dwelling there
or then sall carrie with thame sufficient meanis of meantenance
at least for ane yeare under the payne of fyfe hundreth markis
monie of that our kingdome toties quoties they sall offend
in that kind.

NEWMARKET, 22nd day of Feb. 1625.

X. COLLECTION OF BIRTH-BRIEVES FROM THE PROPINQUITY
BOOKS OF ABERDEEN.[1]

1637.

John Cheyne,	Citizen in Zakrozin, Poland.
Capt. Gairdyne,	,, Germanie.
Will. Watson,	,, Breslau.
Jas. Ross,	,, Danskin.
Dav. Barclay,	,, Queenisbrig.
Molleson,	,, Wisigrad, Poland.
,,	,, Poland.
Sibbald,	,, Spruce.
J. Mitchell,	,, Pomerania.
Allardyce,	,, Poland.
Dav. Ruirack (?),	,, Zakrozin.
A. Malone,	,, Queenisbrig.

1638.

Robt. Meldrum,	,, Tarnowa, Poland.
Al. Davidson,	,, Danskin.
Th. Cargill,	,, ,,
Jas. Rockemie (?),	,, ,,
Jas. Ranon,	,, ,,

[1] An incomplete list of names has been published in the *Miscell. of the
Spalding Club*, vol. v. The year in the list above always refers to the
date of issuing the Birth-brief. The names contained in it are only
those of natives of Aberdeen.

1641.

Auchindale,	in Krakau.
Davidson,	,, Poland.
Al. Ritchie,	,, Prussia.

1642.

Robt. Farquhar,	,, Posen.
W. Gordon,	,, Poland.
G. Williamson,	,, Danskin.
J. Nauchtie,	,, Poland.

1643.

A. Morrison,	in Monrovia, Poland.
W. Sillon,	,, Poland.
T. Smith,	,, ,,
T. Gunter,	Jeweller ,, Warsaw.
Ths. Gordon,	,, Spruce.
David (?)	† at Queenisbrig.
G. Auchinlek,	Sugarbaker at ,,
J. Davidson,	in Danskin.
Gilbert, ⎱ ? Andrew, ⎰	at Queenisbrig.

1644.

Alex. Welsh,	in Poland.
J. Burnett,	,, ,,
Alex. Forbes,	went to Poland sixteen years old and was killed on the journey.

1645.

John Simmer,	Citizen at Belgard, Pomerania.
D. Trough,	,, in Spruce.
A. Adam,	,, ,, Poland (place illegible).
W. Forbes,	,, ,, Krakau.
W. Ogilvie,	,, ,, Pomerania.
W. Rolland,	,, ,, Danskin.

1646.

John Cheyne,	Citizen at Peterco(Petrocow),Poland.
Patr. Gordon,	,, in Poland.
Jas. Coutts,	Merchant in Krosno, later Danskin.
Al. Innes,	Citizen in Poland.

1647-1648.

W. Blackhall,	at the University of "Bromyberie," Spruce (Bromberg ?)

B. Chalmers,   Merchant in Poland.
,, Innes,   ,,   ,, Lisna, Poland.
Robt. Meldrum,   ,,   ,, Poland.
Alex.   (?), ,,   ,, Spruce.
Alex. Greig,   ,, Poland.
W. Abercrombie,   went 16 years old to Poland.

1649.

Robt. Gordon, Merchant in Danskin.
Al. Nicholl,   ,,   ,, Poland.
Rob. Tullindaff,   ,,   ,, Danskin.
Alex. Johnston,   ,, Poland.

1652.

Jas. Burnet,   Citizen in Danskin.
Jas. Ross,   in Poland.
Jas. Ramsay,   † in Poland (1653).
A. Jaffrey,   in Poland (1654).[1]

1658.

Alex. Kemp,   in Danskin (left Aberdeen, 1648).
W. Clerk,   in Danskin (left Aberdeen, 1644).
J. Robertson,   in Zamoski.

1660.

John Molleson,   in Danzig (left Aberdeen, 1640)
Robt. Ross,   in Poland.
J. Meldrum,   in Spruce.
R. Gern,   in Poland.
Th. Nairn,   † in Posen (left Aberdeen, 1638).
J. Forbes,   † in Lublin.

1662-63.

W. Munro,   † in Poland (left Aberdeen, 1642).
P. Gordon,   in Wilsko (?), Poland.
Al. Fraser,   in Poland.

1664.

A. Alexander,   in Poland.
P. Livingstone,   in Warsaw.
A. Ritchie,   in Queenisbrig.
   Reid,   in Vangroba.
G. Kentie,   in Zamoski.
W. Forbes,   in Poland (left Aberdeen, 1661,
                      when 15 years old).

[1] In 1655-56 five Gordons are mentioned in Vangroba and elsewhere in Poland.

1666.

G. Cruikshank,	† in Danzig and left a fortune.
A. Hog,	near Danskin.

1667.

W. Milne,	† " betwixt the realms of Poland."

1669.

Patrick Forbes,	in Poland (left Aberdeen, 1650).
Robt. Dugat,	,, ,, (,, ,, 1639).

1670.

Alex. Aidy,	in Danskin (left Aberdeen, 1637).
Al. Chalmers,	in Warsaw.
,, Maitland,	in Poland.
W. Gordon,	,, ,,
W. Chesson (?),	,, ,,

1671.

Sir J. Chalmers,	in Silesia.
Robt. Chalmers,	in Danskin (left Aberdeen, 1630).
Alex. Alsyth,	,, ,, (,, ,, 1652).
P. Baillie,	,, Poland.
W. Clerk,	Merchant in Danskin.

1672-73

John Seton,	† at Lublin.
John Keith,	in Danskin (left Aberdeen, 1658).
A. Rait,	in Lissa, Poland (,, ,, 1655).

1677.

G. Buchan,	in Lublin (left Aberdeen, 1647).
A. Robertson,	† in Poland.
G. Smith,	in Kulm.
G. Gordon,	in Lublin (left Aberdeen, 1647).

1679-81.

Ths. Mortimer,	† in Westrod (?), Poland.
Rob. Ross,	† in Poland.
W. Irvine,	in Danskin (left Aberdeen, 1664).
John Maitland,	in Jaroslaw, Poland.
J. Smith,	in Culm (left Aberdeen, 1674).

1605-88.

W. Innes,	in Wratislaw, Poland (left A., 1647).
W. Maxwell,	in Spruce.

A. Farquhar,	in Lublin (left Aberdeen, 1693).
W. Farquhar,	„ Lissa („ „ 1640).
John Innes,	„ Posen.
A. Clerk,	† in Lublin, *ca.* 1690.

1695-97.

Gilbt. Moir,	in Poland.
G. Smith	„ Danskin (left Aberdeen, 1687).
Ch. Gordon,	first at Danskin, then Warsaw (1697).
W. Forbes,	in Culm.

1698-1705.

A. Clerk,	in Krakau.
A. Black,	in Posen (1698).
Two Gordons,	in Prisnitz and Culm (1703), for merly Dantzig.
J. Stuart,	in Poland (1705).

In the *Reg. Magni Sig. Scot.* Captain Jacob Henryson and Jas. Soutar ("a patre generoso"), both in Poland, obtain their birth-brieves. To the above list we may also add from the extract from the *Rec. of the Bor. of Edinburgh* (iv. p. 543), the names of John Knox, Jas. Hunter, Jas. Macmyllan, Patr. Carwood, P. Gilchrist, Nath. Moir, who sail to Queenisbrig in a ship from Dysart (1589), as well as three Johnstones from Craigieburn (Annandale), who went to Samter in Poland about 1596.[1]

XI. BIRTH-BRIEFS ORDERED BY THE TOWN-COUNCIL OF DUNDEE 1606-1638.

16th June 1606.—Alexander Abercrombie in Falkinburgh[2] in the duchy of Brandenburg, lawful son of Thomas Abercrombie of Gourdie and Grisel Sibbet, his wife.

26th June 1606.—Robert Duncan, traveller in Pomare, lawful son of David Duncan in Fowlis and Katharine Lecky, his spouse.

26th June 1606.—Robert Donaldson, traveller in Germany, lawful son of John Donaldson, Burgess of Dundee, and Bessie Ireland, his spouse.

July 1606.—Robert Scot, traveller in Bern[3] in Polen, lawful son of John Scot, Mill of Mains, and Eliz. Neish, his spouse.

---

[1] Their birth-brief, dated Lanark, May 15th, 1596, recommends them as being of noble birth to the Kings of Holland and Poland. (M. von Johnston Rathen, *Geschichte der Familie von Johnston,* 1891.)

[2] Falkenburg in Pommern.

[3] Probably Berent, a district and town not far from Danzig.

13th July 1607.—John Duncan, traveller in Prussia besyde Danskyn, lawful issue of John Duncan, mariner, and Bessie Vauss, his spouse.

22nd August 1607.—*Robt. Chrystie*, traveller in Louenburgh in Pomer,[1] son of James Chrystie in Adamstown and Anges Scugell, his spouse.

2nd April 1608.—*Robt. Andro*, Webster in Colpenahevine,[2] Denmark, son of Robt. Andro in Myreton of Brichty and Eupham Makie, his spouse.

11th April 1608.—*James Scott* in Bern besyde Danskyn, son of Thos. Scott in Dichty and Helen Jago, his spouse.

15th April 1608.—*George Belly* (Baillie), trafficquer in Skowne[3] under the dominion of Pole, son of G. Belly at Mill of Melgund and Janet Sinclair, his spouse.

20th April 1608.—*John Gelletlie*, traveller in Malsack[4] in Pruss, within the dominion of Pole, son of Walter Gelletlie and Janet Smart, his spouse.

11th March 1609.—*William Sowter*, traveller in Germany and Danskyn, son of David Sowter and Elisabeth Lyndsay, his spouse.

16th April 1609.—*Patrick Yeaman* (?), traveller in Pole, son of Will. Yeaman in Rattray, and Katherine Rodger, his spouse.

5th April 1610.—*James Fyiff*, traveller in Tarnova in Pole, son of Gilbert Fyiff in Forgound, and —— Gray, his wife.

21st May 1610.—*John Donaldson*, traveller in Pruss, son of Archibald Donaldson and Christina Ferraire, his spouse.

10th February 1611.—*Robt. Lovell*, Burgess of Rathoune[5] in Pole, son of John Lovell of Brunsie and Margaret Murdoch, his spouse.

May 1612.—*Stephen Bruce*, traveller in Pruss, son of Jas. Bruce and Gilles Will, his spouse.

May 1612.—*Andro Thayne* in Danskyn, son of Thos. Thayne in Gourdie and Katherine Barbour, his spouse.

17th August 1612.—*William Burgh*, now resident at Queenisbrig,[6] son of William Burgh of Craigy and Janet Gelletlie, his spouse.

27th June 1614.—*William Thomson*, skynner, inhabitant of Danskyn, son of Thomas Thomson and Christian Wichton, his spouse.

28th April 1615.—*Thomas Gelletlie* in Danskyn, son of George Gelletlie and Kath. Man, his spouse.

[1] Lauenburg in Pommern.   [2] Kopenhagen.   [3] Perhaps Scotscho?
[4] Mehlsack, a town in the district of Königsberg.
[5] Radaune?   [6] Königsberg.

20th May 1615.—*John Butchart*, merchant in Queenisbrig, son of Thos. Butchart, Grange of Cossyns, and Janet Watt, his spouse.

20th May 1615.—*James Wricht*, traveller in Pole, son of John Wricht in Bryddeston and Margaret Turnbull, his spouse.

16th March 1616.—*John Parker*, merchant in Polone, son of Pat. Parker in Bandene and Beatrix Kinmond, his spouse.

16th March 1616.—*Patrick Parker*, traveller in Polone, son of William Parker of Ballindean and Elizab. Anderson, his spouse.

13th July 1616.—*Andro Fraser*, traveller in the town of Lutzo,[1] son of Alaster Fraser of Glenshe and Elspeth Spalding, his spouse.

22nd August 1616.—*David Lawson*, traveller in Naumsburg[2] in Prussia, son of John Lawson, merchant in Dundee.

9th September 1616.—*Will. Durward*, traveller in Bitzo[3] in the Duchy of Mecklenburg, son of Charles Durward in Balnevis and Margaret Gray, his spouse.

27th March 1617.—*John Heriot*, traveller in Milhousin,[4] Pruss, son of Andro Heriot in Pheshemylne (?) and Helen Gray, his spouse.

7th August 1618.—*John Gardyne*, † at Samoche,[5] Polone 1618.

13th August 1633.—Alexander Brechine, traveller in Lumberg,[6] Duchy of Pomer, son of David Brechine in Monyfeith and Elizabeth Duncan, his spouse.

16th July 1636.—*William Watson*, merchant traveller in Poland, son of Math. Watson, merchant, and Janet Bomer, his spouse.

16th July 1636.—*James Watson*, merchant traveller in Poland, son of William Watson and Elizabeth Walles, his spouse.

19th September 1638.—*James Strathauchin*, merchant Scottisman in forane nations, son of James Strathauchin and Janet Robert, his spouse.

John Gardiner, a Glasgow citizen, travels to Danzig in 1595, and the son of Baillie Cunnyngham in 1654 receives a free passage to the same place in memory of his father. (*Extr. from the Rec. of Glasgow*, 312.)

---

[1] Bützow in Mecklenburg.

[2] There are many Naumburgs in Prussia ; here probably Naumburg-on-the-Queis or on the Bober, both in Silesia.

[3] Bützow, see above.   [4] Mühlhausen, in the district of Königsberg.

[5] Samostye in Poland.   [6] Probably Lauenburg, see above.

There are several other names of Scotch merchants in Denmark (Elsinore, etc.), Norway and Sweden given, which I have omitted here.

XII. Letters from Scotch Settlers at Danzig and Elsewhere.

Gabriel Maxwell, Daniskin, to Sir John Maxwell of Pollock.
31st August 1635.

Richt honoriabile, after my very humill dewtie remembrit, pleas now witt that I am in good helth, presit bie God, wising daylie from my hert the lyk of yow, and all youris. Plis your worship, wit that I hef receivit my bor brief, quherin I thaink your honour most humilie for the good fafour and painis ye heff takine concerning my bor briff; plis your hounor, caus on of your servandis resew fre the birar, Johne Alcoirne, one haime in takin off lowe. I prey your hounor to hold mie excusit off the wirth of it, for off a trouth at this occatione I can heff nothing that I can ofir in one takine off lowe to your hounor, becauis off the wiris (wars); and now, presit bie God, wie heff this wiek pice for sertantie : it is proclamit hir in the toune off Danniskeine and the King being in the toune in the myne tyme. Not troubling your honour fairder, bot commiting yow and all your afairis to the protectione of the Almychtie God, I rest,

your most humillie cussing to be commandit,

G. M.[1]

2.

Francis Craw to his family.

Loving dear Brother

After wishing the love and peace of God the Almighty to be with you and all my dear friends, I heartily salute you accounting it a great mercy that I have the occasion to show that I am in good health, wishing the like with you and all friends. Dear Brother I took shipping at Aberdeen the 29th of June and landed safely here at Dansick the 11th day of August. We had exceeding good weather. I was not sick at all, bot the first day I did vomit a little after which I had my stomach better than ever I had at land and so remaining still here at Dansigk. Few or none of the men stood in need of prentices, bot I engagded with one William Abernethy from Aberdeen in Gordoven within 20 or 30 miles of Queensbrige (Königsberg). He came not here himself bot a friend of his ane Gilbert Ramsay coming here from Queenbrig he desired him to find him a boy ; so William Bissat to whom I was recommended by Mr Andrew's friends at Aberdeen told him that I could not serve six or seven yeares as a boy bot if he would take me for four yeares I should accept. So Mr Ramsay told he had commission for five yeares and being a very honest man and a friend of Mr Bissat I have referred the writing of

[1] Fraser, W., *Memoirs of Maxwells of Pollock.*

mine indentor till he and my maister meet, he promised to me
to do as much upon my favour as upon his, so I cannot give you
an exact account of it bot the longest will be five yeares and
with the next occasion I shall give you a full account. But I
expect a letter from you with the first occasion from Leith
which I hope you will not be forgettfull to doe. You shall
direct it to my servitor Will. Abernethy in Gordonen to be
left at William Frippold in Dansigk; you may show William
Quhite that his brother is ded. I have not yet heard of Mrs
Wilkinson's brother, I take very well with this countrey and
have my health as well as ever I had, blessed be God. So
presenting my love and respect to you my dear mother, brothers
and sisters and to all my dear friends in Scotland
your loving and dear brother
Francis Craw.

Dansigk, 12th Aug. 1671—according to the Scotch Almonaks
  here in Dansigk they reckon ten dayes before us so that
  this day is the 22nd with them.
My cosin Patrick Lauder got a maister in Poiland in a town
called Warso with one Hog (?) whose brother came with us
from Aberdeen with whom I sent up my aunt's letter to my
cosine, he is bound bot for three yeares at the people where
he quartered. John Cormack went to Polland, you may show
Mrs Fleming her nephew has got a maister. I gave her letter
to William Frizell with whom he quartered. Remember me
kindly to all friends at Aberdeen and to all Mr Cockburns family,
to my dear friends at Gordon and to all friends in general.
(Addr.) For Mr Patrick Craw
of Broughhead [Ruch head]
  to be left at Mr Andrew Burns of Waristoun who lives
  in Aberdeen a little above Mr Wrights house on
  the south side of the gate.

2.

I have received ane letter from you with ane from my dear
unkle the 23d Sept. 74 being the first I received from you,
partly glad to hear of your welfare with the rest of all my
dear friends, likewise grieved to hear of my dear mothers sickness;
I pray God he would preserve her, you and all friends from all
evill inconveniences both of body and soul; likewise being
grieved to hear of my dear aunts death, bot inwardly rejoycing
whereas I hope she is enjoying the everlasting joy and happiness
in heaven, to which I pray God would accept of me, and you
all whensoever he may be pleased to call any of us out of this

world. Dear brother I likewise received another letter from you 2d of June 1675 being the fourth that you had written to me, wherein you refer all affaires to the bearer my old sworn brother Alex. Home.   It grieves me that I have not yet heard neither more or less of him   .   .   .   .
in this country, to the which I should never have advised him. It is a great wrong parents doeth to their childring to keep them beside them till they come almost to mans yeares so that then they are ashamed to serve for boys especially in this countrey, where all must learn two or three severall languages which it is hard for any come to age to attain to, likewise to serve five or six yeares, the recompense being bot about 20 or 30 dollars with ane suit of new clothes, the trading degenerating, the contreys daily impoverishing by reason of the long continued wars in every place, likewise you show me that you with my friends have thought fitt to send over my brother David this summer, wherefor now I pray God would bless him with all spirituall blessings and mercies, wishing he may be more fortunate than I have been.   Dear brother, my advice should rather have been to have put him to any tradesman, having once attained to the knowledge of any trade can be always able anywhere to earn his bread, as for to serve here, nowadays few there are that comes to any fortune, the proof of which I have already given.   Many before my coming here having served ten or twelve yeares remains in ane poor condition, severalls beccomming souldiers, so that for my own part although I have now served out I know not what hand to turn me to, having no stock to begin withall. To come home and visitt you being in as poor a condition as I came from thence would be a shame, for throughout this whole countrey of Sprussia there is bot slight service to be had except it be in Dansigk or Queensbrig where I was not fortunate to get service and for to have passed to Polland being disswaded by many (although the farr richer countrey) because of their great travellings and alwayes being in hazard of their lives, being almost savage people for the most part papistes, so for the present contenting myselfe with a little rather than have been in continuall jeopardy, so hopping you will accept of these imperfect lines in good part, written in haste with this bearer Mr Chiesley (?) who came over here one harvest with ane Hamilton as I suppose out of the west countrey who has here ane unkle serving in the wars under the Duke of Brandenburg, he is come to great preferment being the last 2 yeares in the wars against the Frenches (?); his lady lives not far from this toun a Dutch woman (*i.e.* German) and Lutherian, his nephew remains with her till his unkles home comming.   I never had

the occasion to come into discourse with Mr Chieslie till a little before his departure, who did tell me he was acquainted with Mr Burnett and had been severall times at his house in Waristoun, so hopping you will not be forgettfull to write to me with all occasions, recommending my love and best respects to you my dear mother, brothers and sisters and to all good friends wishing the love and peace of God Allmightie to be with you all I remain your loving brother

FRANCIS CRAW.

To be left at Robt. Hamiltons, merchant in Edinburgh at the head of the lukkin booths.

MEMEL, *June* 23, 1675.

3.

LOVING DEAR BROTHER

I received a letter from you the bypast year which was written 22nd August 76. I wrott to you severall times the last yeare bot as yet I have not gotten a line from you, which grieves me not a little. I have gotten three letters from my brother David, one the last yeare in which he showed me he was in good health bot there was a great pest thereabouts in the countrey. I have written to him severall times, he would gladly hear from you. I hope you doe write to me and also to him with every occasion, although they seldom come to our hands. My brother David is not with Mr Inglis in Warso as he informed me, bot with a Nicolay Gordon, dwelling in Vingroba not far from Warso of which I informed you last yeare. So if you doe write to him, direct it to him serving to the aforesaid man. He is bound to serve him six yeares. I am sorry that he is at such a distance from me and also that ever he should have come over to these countreyes, for he could have learned any honest trade perfectly in six yeares time, which had been far better than to serve here five or six years in which time they get little knowledge of merchandizing. Prentises for the most part in all these countreyes are honestly entertained in meat and cloaths bot when their times run out they must serve for a very little fie (!) with which they can scarcely uphold themselves in decent cloths and other necessaries. I have the by bypast week ingadged with my maister, again to serve him till this time 12 months for the value of 100 pound Scotch. I would have gladly visited you, my dear mother and all other good friends this year, bot seeing I have ingagded for another year I hope God willing to visit you next year, for ought I know if I remain in life and health; dear

brother, let me know of your condition and if my dear mother
be in life and health with my loving sisters and how all other
good friends are, the certaintie of which would be exceeding
comfortable and refreshing to me to know.   I have as yet
heard nothing of my dear comrade Allex Home which grieves
me exceedingly.   I have got no letter from my unkle bot that
which I got with yours four yeares ago as he was in Scotland.
I have got no letter from you that was dated the last or this
year.   Let me know with the first occasion how the[e] amber
beads are bought in Scotland whither they be bought by the
pound weight or by string wayes and whither great or small be
in greatest esteem, and whither yellow or reddish be bought.   If
you find no acquaintance to write to me this year, I entreat you
forget not to write to me the next spring when you write home (?).
I entreat you to try and if you can find a sure occasion to send
your letter to the town of Johnstone to one James Barclay whose
son lives a long time in Queensbridge and with whom I was
acquainted, or you can send your letter to the town of Dundee
to one John Fairweather, a skipper, who comes every year to
Queensbridge.   He is for the present here and has brought
letters to all the Scotsmen hereabouts who are for the most
part from there or thereabout.   I send this to you with him,
inclosed in my comrades letter, one Robt Rollo who serves
here in this town, who writes to the aforesaid Barclay desiring
him to send the same to you which I hope he will doe if it come
safely to his hand.   I entreat you again to send your letter for
me to him who would assuredly send them to me with the
Dundee ships, for they are the first Scotch ships that comes
every year to this countrey.   Let me know if you have heard
of my brother William since he past for Holland and if he
be alive and in what town of Holland he is in.   Here comes
several Holland ships to this town every year so I could have
written to him, if I knew where he was.   Let me know what
my cousin Lauder trades with.   Show me also if you or
Reston (?) knows where Allex. Home may be, and also how it
is with all our good friends, the presbyterians, for I have heard
they have been exceedingly persecuted.   Now I wish the good
God to bless you, my dear mother and sisters with all spirituall
and temporall blessings.   Thus recommending my love and affection to you, my dear and loving mother and sisters and all other
good friends.   Longing exceedingly to hear of all your welfare.
                    I rest your loving brother
                                        FRANCIS CRAW.

MEMELL, 20th July 1678.

4.

LOVING BROTHER

Having the occasion of this bearer, Mr Skeen, I lett you know that I am in good health wishing the like to you and all yours. He told me some years ago, being in this countrey that he did see you as he came through Aitoun (?) and that ye was very kind to him, and have written to you also with another friend more particularly and showed you that I did receive your letter with one from my sister Margaret, which was very acceptable to me, especially to hear that the Lord has blest you both with the bonds of matrimony. I wish you both again much joy and happiness. Dear brother, I showed you also that I would gladly have visited you this summer bot I was ingagded again with my maister for one year before I gott your letter, bot God willing the next year I intend to visit you if it please the Lord to preserve me in life and health. I would have written to you also with our next neighbour one Peter Morisone bot I was not at home as he past. I was in Memell at the Markitt. I would have written often to you this year for there hath been many Scotch ships here this year, bot I have travelled this whole summer, by reason my maister has been very sicke. I am also to pass for Tilsit within two weeks where we will keep markitt the matter of three weekes. Brother, my desire to you is, if it be in your power, to help me with a little stock, the matter of 100 dollars of money or moneys worth which you could send over with Alexander Home if he come over the next year to this countrey or with some other sure occasion, if ye cannot advance it, labour to get so much or more from some good friends upon interest. I could bring with me some little partie of lintt or other commodities that sells best in Scotland, whereof I hope you will inform me, so that if I arrive safely, I should restore the same, so that I might bot winn my expenses. Thus recommending you to the protection of almighty God I rest presenting my love and service to your help and bedfellow though unacquainted, to all my sisters and there beloved, to Alex. Home and his beloved and to all other friends.

I remain your loving brother
FRANCIS CRAW.

QUEENSBRIDGE, 4th Sept. 1681.[1]

XIII. PATRICK GORDON AND STERCOVIUS THE POLE.

Patrick Gordon, the Scottish "factor" at Danzig during the reign of James VI, prosecuted at the instigation of the King a certain Stercovius, a Pole, who after a visit to Scotland had

---

[1] Originals in the Advocates' Library, Edinburgh.

published a libel against the Scottish nation, ostensibly because
the inhabitants of some Scotch towns had laughed at the
Polish national costume in which he paraded the streets. He
was put to death, incredible as it may appear, in 1611. Under
this date we read in the Chronicle of Rastenburg, a small town
in Poland : " John Stercovius circulates a libel against the whole
Scottish nation; on account of which he was executed by the
sword after a public recantation." [1] King James was not satisfied
with this. We read in the same chronicle, under the date 15th
of February 1612, that, at the request of His Majesty the King
of Great Britain, an order was issued, to send all copies of the
libel still extant to the magistrates, well wrapped up and
sealed, and punishment was threatened in case of disobedience.[2]

There was a long epilogue to this sad story in settling the
question, who was to pay for the expense incurred by Gordon
in this prosecution. The Scotch inhabitants of Danzig were
first thought of, but finally the costs were divided between the
chief boroughs of Scotland.[3]

Gordon himself was accused afterwards for neglecting his
duties as consul. [4]

XIV. List of Scottish Settlers in Krakow and Warsaw. XVIth and XVIIth Centuries.

Krakow.

J. Alanth (Alland), 1573.
G. Amand (Almond?), 1603.
A. Blackal, 1651.
* K. Buchan, 1603.
A. Burnet, 1607.
Arch. Burnet, 1603.
Gilbt. Burnet, 1603.
Jas. Chambarz (Chambers), 1651.
W. Chrones (?), 1602.
J. Clarg (Clerk), 1623.
† Al. Czamer (Chalmers), 1676.
J. Czamer, 1651.

Robt. Czamer, 1620.
Jas. Drummond (Sir Jas. Drummond of Borland), 1600.
A. Dixon, 1607.
Al. Dixon, 1603.
Al. Dixon (son), 1651.
Bonav. Dixon, 1609.
Thos. Dixon, 1651.
Al. Duff, 1608.
Ths. Dumfries, 1577.
D. Dundas, 1576.
Al. Duncan, 1607.
Al. Driowski (Drew), from Edinburgh, 1577.

G. Emzle (Emslie ?), 1621.
*K. Henderson, 1606.
*W. Henderson, 1603.
P. Englis (Inglis), 1651.
T. Forbes, 1603.
*W. Forbes, 1687.
And. Fraser, 1551.
Abraham Freude (Froude?), 1651.
J. Fryer.
Jas. Geltens (Galt?), 1614.

---

[1] Beckherrn, *Schäfer's Chronik von Rastenburg*, p. 10. See also *Scot. Notes and Queries.*

[2] See Beckherrn, *l.c.*

[3] Dundee, for instance, had to pay £600.

[4] *Reg. of Privy Council of Scotland,* xi. Pref. cxli. ff.

Jas. Grick (Greig?), 1651.
W. Grim (Graeme?), 1626.
G. Gurk (?), 1651.
W. Hojson (Hewison), 1625.
R. Horne, 1603.
K. Hunter, 1651.
A. Young, 1603.
J. Karmichael, 1625.
*G. Kin (King), 1603.
*K. Kin, 1603, †1635.
G. Kin, 1583, 1607.
J. Korblet (?), 1651.
G. Kruksang (Cruikshank), 1651.

J. Larmche (Carmichael), 1651.
J. Legent (?) 1607.
Jas. Lindsay de Edzell, 16—?
J. Minkhaus (?), 1607.
J. Mora (Moir), 1610.
S. Mosman, 1603.
A. Oszerth (?), 1651.
A. Pniszel (Frizell?), 1614.
H. Rents de Erbroth (?), 1579.
J. Reth (Reid), 1651.
Th. Robertson, 1612.
A. Rusek (Ross?), Scotorum Factor, 1603.

J. Rynt (Owner of Sulphur Mines), 1607-52.
L. Smert (Smart), 1609.
W. Tory, 1626.
J. Tomson, 1603.
P. Vood (Wood), 1625.
G. Wanton, 1603, "thirteen years in Poland."
J. Whyt (White), 1620.
W. Wier (Weir), 1626.
P. Zutter (Soutar), 1577.

Warsaw.

†Al. Alon (Allan), 1697.
†An. Auchinleck, 1669.
†Al. Brun (Brown), 1669.
†W. Cowe, 1697.
†P. Ennisz (Innes), 1669.
†A. Frazer, 1613 (in Krakow, 1625).
†Al. Gern (?), 1697.
†P. Gern, 1676.
And. Goltz (Gault?), 1688.
Albr. Gordon, 1688.

†W. Gorski (Gore?), 1613.
†Th. Hog, 1669.
†Al. Innes, 1697.
An. Innes, 1617.
P. Innes, 1671.
†A. Janthon (?), 1613.
†J. Johnston, 1676.
†P. Jonston, 1669.
†P. Makalienski (Macallan), 1613.
†G. Mancos (Monkhouse), 1613.
†J. Orem, 1613.
†*P. Orem, 1613, at Krakau from 1600-1625.

†St Orem, 1613.
†Th. Orem, 1613, at Krakau 1603, and 1621.
†Al. Ross, 1697.
†W. Ross, 1697.
†Al.Ryd(Reid),1697.
†G. Rytt (Wright), 1669.
†W. Schmidt (Smith), 1676.
†A. Tamson, 1669.
†W. Tamson, 1669.
A. Vithman (Wightman?), 1576, and in Krakow.
W. Wan, †1618.

Of other places in Poland mention is made of Thomas Dunkison (Duncanson) in Lublin, "thirteen years in Poland," Robert Gilbert Porteous in Krosna, John and William Ramsay and Richard Tamson (Tomson), in Posen.

Those marked * were elders.

Those marked † Royal or Privileged Merchants.

XV. List of Scotch Settlers in the Town of Posen. a.d. 1605.

George Beem (Bain?).
John Benna (Bennie?).
Bernh. Bellendin (Ballantyne).
David Burn.
Robt. Brun (Brown).
Dav. Dunker (Duncan).
Forbes.

Jas. Frobell. Goltsmith.
Jas. Kaliel (Carlyle?).
„ Karkut (Cargood?).
Alex. Nielson.
Jas. Paterson.
John Ondron (?).

Robt. Ramza (Ramsay).
John Robertson.
David Skin (Skene).
Andr. Sterling.
„ Struders (Struthers).
John Thosse (Tawse).
„ Veneth (?).

The number of Scotch handicraftsmen at the same period being about equally large.

In 1651, the year when the money for the subsidy of King Charles II was forcibly collected, there were only eleven trading Scotch families left in Posen, Edward Hebron (Hepburn), James Heyt (Hyatt), William Huyson (Hewison), James Farquhar, James Lindsay, Daniel Mackalroy, Jacob and Andrew Watson, and Albert Schmart (Smart); curiously enough not one of those mentioned in 1605. This proves again the fluctuating character of the Scotch settlements.[1]

XVI. List of Scotch " Cramers " in the Duchy of Prussia. a.d. 1615.[2]

Jas. Aberkrummie.
Al. Agnitz (Agnews).
W. Agnuss.
W. Agnitz.
John Albrecht (?).
Ch. Agnuss.
H. Ahrnett (Arnott).
J. Altt (Auld).
Matth. Alt.
W. Alt.
Al. Andersson.
Dan. Andersson.
David Anderson.
Everett Anderson.
Jos. Anderson.
Dav. Annan.
Conr. Bachoun (Balquhon?).
B. Bailjer (Bilger?).
G. Bain.
Js. Baldt.
Al. Balfour.
M. Balfour.

Nich. Balfour.
Jas. Ballentine.
Jas. Ballwarth (Polwarth).
D. Balwaird (Balvaird).
D. Bartram (Bertrom).
Henry Bartelltt (Bartlet).
P. Beel (Biel).
John Bedderman.
J. Beinston.
W. Bennett (Benet).
J. Bertrom.
Henry Bethon (Beaton).
St. Binston.
W. Black.
Hillebrant Blackhall.
Jas. Blackhall.
M. Blackhall.
W. Bleer (Blair).
H. Blair.
Al. Bonnertt.

D. Bontrom (Bonthron).
D. Brant.
Ch. Breede (Braid).
S. Brinthon.
D. Brinthon.
Al. Bruin (Brown).
A. Bruin.
W. Bruin.
Th. Brunn.
H. Bruisz (Bruce).
P. Bruchte.
W. Bruch (Brough).
G. Bunckel.
D. Butcher.
H. Butcher.
H. Bussitt (Bissett).
Js. Bysirtt.
Ths. Bysirtt.
Albr. Curtte.
Al. Dahn (Dawn).
Al. Davidson.
Ths. Davidson.

[1] Cp. Lukaszewicz, *Hist. Statist. Bild der Stadt Posen*, i. p. 79.
[2] From the Royal Archives, Königsberg.

Andr. Deuffer (?).
Jas. Dennister (Demster ?).
J. Dick.
H. Doglasz (Douglas).
Alex. Donaldson.
Dan. Donaldson.
Dav. Donaldson.
H. Donaldson.
J. Drum.
J. Drummondt.
Laur. Droun.
Ab. Dunckan.
Al. Duncker.
Albr. Dunker.
J. Duncken.
Ths. Duncken.
Will. Duncken.
Dan. Dunckson (Duncanson).
Albr. Dustun.
J. Dusten.
Jas. Eicken (Aikin).
M. Ertzbald (Archibald).
Ths. Engels (Inglis).
W. Erdthur (Arthur).
Al. Erichtumb (?).
J. Fehnricht (Wainright).
Al. Ferfoul (Fairfoul).
Jas. Ferfoul.
Al. Ferbrus (Forbes).
J. Forbess.
Js. Ferbuss ⎱ (Forbes).
Js. Ferbus ⎰
J. Forgesse (Ferguson).
Al. Forgesam.
Jas. Forgrusson.
P. Fergusson.
H. Ferley.
H. Fermer.
G. Fleck.
Th. Foster.
Jas. From.
Mich. From.
Jost Fromme.

Ths. Frank.
And. Friesel.
Mich. Frisill.
W. Fyrley (Farley).
Geo. Gall.
P. Gall.
J. Gallfey.
Jas. Gern.
Al. Gieldt.
W. Gelletlie.
M. Gipson.
W. Gipson.
H. Gleg.
Js. Gloch (Gloag).
Al. Glennie.
2 Alb. Glenn.
Al. Glennie.
John Glenn.
John Glennie.
Erdtman Gordon.
John Gordon.
Alester Goleszy.
G. Grax (?).
John Grein (Green).
W Greiff. (?).
Al. Grey.
Andr. Grey.
Martin Grey.
2 Will. Grey.
Matth. Grey.
P. Grieg (Greig).
N. Grim.
G. Gyll.
L. Guthriek.
Alex. Hail.
J. Hammilthon.
Albr. Hamilton.
W. Hamilthon.
Junker Hasz or Haesz (?) Hays.[1]
J. Heindrich (Henry).
Jas. Heres.
Ths. Hering.
J. Hey.
J. Heyn.
Fr. Hey.
W. Hilston.

Albr. Hinderson.
Al. Hindrichson.
G. Hoigston (?).
Al. Horn.
D. Huntter.
W. Hunter.
Hillebrant Idell.
And. Ingelss.
J. Ingelss (Inglis).
And. Jairdon (Jardine).
E. and J. Jairdon.
H. (J.) Janson.
H. (J.) Jordon.
Al. Jung (Young).
And. Jung.
John Jung.
Stentzel Jung.
Will. Jung.
Albr. Kader (Calder).
Dan. Kair (Keir).
Ths. Kairnegie (Carnegie).
Gabr. Kamer.
Ch. Kamer.
Albr. Kastor.
Balth. Karmichael.
J. Karmichael.
Sam. Karmichael.
Al. Kastell.
J. Kaubrun (Cockburn).
Reinhold Kaubrun (Cockburn).
Ch. Kennitt.
W. Kimmitt.
Geo. Kinkeith (Kincaid).
Peter Kinkeith.
W. Kleils (?).
A. Kleyn (Clyne).
W. Klein (Clyne).
Albr. Kock.
Al. Kock.
Jas. Kock.
Will. Kock.
2 Albr. Kollier.
Albr. Köning (Cumming).

---

[1] Junker denotes "young squire" or "young laird."

J. Köning (Cumming).
A. Krimbser (Scrimgeour).
Ulrich Kuhnheyn (Colqohoun ?).
W. Krege (Craig).
J. Lahn (Lawn).
Js. Laing.
P. Lamm (Lamb).
Ths. Lamm.
Andr. Lason (Lawson).
Al. Leitsch (Leitch).
Al. and Jas. Lenge.
Jas. Litsch.
Dav. Linsay.
Geo. Linsey.
J. Lindtsack.
Jas. Linsey.
Jas. Linser.
Js. Logan.
Al. Lorne.
W. Lockardt.
Laur. Lumsdaill.
J. Lunden.
Andr. Lundie.
Paul Lundi.
Albr. Lundi.
John Macri (Macrie).
Geo. Macri.
Geo. Magall (M'Call).
B. Makgreger.
H. Magkreger (M'Gregor).
J. Mackertten (M'——)
M. Mackertten.
S. Macke (M'Kay).
M. Mackor.
G. Mair.
Ch. Malcolm.

Bartellt Maxwell.
Hercules Maxwell.
John Malise.[1]
2 Ths. Malise.
J. Malison.
Albr. Mersell.
J. Meder (Mather).
Dav. Meffen.
W. Melvin.
Ths. Meldrom.
2 Andr. Meson.
John Merten.
Chs. Mettwen (Methuen).
Ths. Meyne.
Ths. Meynich (Menzies).
J. Milson.
Js. Middleton.
Dav. Mill.
Abr. Moneypenning.
Ala. Morr (Muir).
Jas. Morton.
N. Moritz (Morris).
Al. Muer (Muir).
B. Murro.
John ,,
Jost ,,
B. Muir.
Bartellt Muer.
2 Gabr. Muffit.
Ths. Mundt.
A. Nickel.
Dan. Nickel.
Conrad Olipfandt.[2]
Erdtman Olipfandt.
J. Olipfandt.
W. Olipfandt.
Geo. Olipfandt.
Al. Pallmer.
2 Andr. Paterson.

Alex. Patoun.
Al. Peter.
Geo. Petri.
Jas. Petri.
Will. Platt.
J. Philipp.
W. Pibles (Peebles).
Balth. Pettekrug (Pettigrew).
Matth. Pettekrug.
Peter ,,
Albr. Porter.
W. Porter.
J. Portruss (Porteous).
Ernest Ramsack.
Jas. ,,
2 Henry Ramsay.
John ,,
Charles Ramse.
Thos. Ramse.
Dav. Rankielor.
W. Ranoldson.
W. Rattrech (Rattray).
Everett Ridt (Reid).
Albr. Reehe (Riach).
Bart. Reyn.
Hillebrant Roich.
Al. Ross.
Henry Ross.
W. Ross.
W. Ronaldt.
Albr. Rothero.
Ths. Rothero.
Reinholt Rubbertson (Robertson).
Thos. Rubbertson).
Ptr. Rust.
Js. Rust.
Al. Schmal (Small).
Ch. Schmal.
2 Jas Schmitt (Smith).

[1] The family name of the Earls of Strathearn.

[2] A certain Colyn Oliphant in Custorben, Poland, writes a renunciation of rent against the payment of £100 by Sir W. Oliphant. He dates his letter Qweinsbrig (Königsberg) Jan. 28, 1628, and the following four Scottish merchants at this place are his witnesses :—Jas. Reid, Andrew Inglis, W. Learmonth and Gilbert Blair (*The Oliphants in Scotland*, p. 217).

Ths. Schmitt.
W. Schmitt.
J. Schmertt (Smart).
Al Schort (Short).
Dav. „
Albr. Schotte (Scott).
Ernest „
J. Schringe (?).
Al. Schultz (?).
W. Simpson.
Adam Simson.
W. Stael.
D. and W. Steenson.
Ths. and J. Steffen.
Al. Stirk.
Baltzer Strethon.
Al.Stree-ehren(Strath-
earn).
Js. Strachin.
J. Stuertt ⎱ (Stuart).
Albr. Stuirt ⎰
Albr. Stubbertson (?).
A. Tamson (Thom-
son).

J. Tamson.
J. Tellfort (Telford).
Albr. Thery.
Jas. Torge.
Jas. Truip.
J. Trummel (Turn-
bull).
Laur. Turner.
W. Turner.[1]
D. Wadt (Watt).
D. Venthon.
Gill. Wallis (Wal-
lace).
Ch. Watson.
Dan. Wadtson.
Laur. Watson.
Reinhard Watson.
Ths. Watson.
Jas. Watson.
J. Watt.
P. Weille (?) (Wylie).
W. Weylandt.
Andr. Wilson.
2 J. Wilson.

D. Willson.
G. Willson.
Cl. Willke.
Chas. Willke.
Conrad Willke.
Dav. Willie.
Jas. Willkis
Geo. Wette and Peter
Wette.
Jas. Wobster.
B. Wischrodt (Wish-
art ?)
Erdtman Wischrodt.
Al. Woodt.
Jas. Wricht.
A. Wrichtt.
Henry Wrichtt.
W. Wroudt (Froude).
Al. Wuschrodt.
Alb. „
Andr. Wultson.
Albr. Wundrum.
Ths. Wundrum.

XVII. LIST OF SCOTTISH SETTLERS IN KÖNIGSBERG (QUEENISBRIG),
MEMEL AND TILSIT.

I. Königsberg (1700-1740).

Allen, George.
Anderson, Fred.
Barclay, Will.
Barnett, John.
Birell, Lorenz.
Couper, Gilb.
Cramond, Dav.
Craw, Francis.
Crayge (Craig), Gilbt.
Douglas, J. and Daniel.
Dunckam (Duncan), Will.
Ferwahter (Fairweather), Carl.
Forbus (Forbes).
Geren, Alex.
Gordon, George, Will, Peter.
Gray, Will, George, Alex.
Hunker, H.
Innes, Peter.

Irwing, Joh. Albrecht.
Karkettel, Alex.
Karr, John.
Kieyth (Keith), John.
Kiuck (?), James and two sons.
Lamb.
Lessly (Leslie), George.
Leyel (Lyall), John.
Liwingstone, Robt.
Maclair, Robt.
Mill, John, David, Andr.
Mitzchell (Mitchell), Dan.
Mitschelhill, Jacob.
Oufries (?).
Ouchterlono (Auchterlonie), Her-
cules.
Panton, H.
Ramadye (Ramadge), Ths.

[1] In the original named " Turner's knecht," *i.e.* Turner's servant.

Renny (Rennie), Jacob.
Ross, Joh.
Stronach, Robt.
Stuart, Th.
Thaw, Joh.

Tewendeil, Wilh. (Tweeddale?).
Trotter, John.
Turner, Carl.
Watt, Will.
Walt, Alex.

II. Memel. (XVIIth and XVIIIth Centuries.) [1]

Hans Littlesohn (Littlejohn), 1616.
„ Pesaller, 1616.
George Wölssel ⎫
(Welsh?), ⎬ from Aberdeen.
Alex. Smith, ⎭
Jacob Mechschin (MacCheyne),
from Edinburgh.
Arrot.
Barclay.
Crichton.
Durham.
Farquhar.
Grieg.
Irwing.

Maclean.
Marschal.
Mitchell.
Murray.
Muttray (Will. †1734. Martin
†1740, eighty years old).
Ogelbey (Ogilvie).
Palmer.
Ramsay.
Ritchie.
Scrumsour (Scrimgeour).
Simson (Andr. 1682, William
1684); later "Simpson."

III. Tilsit and District.

Allen, Andr. (1679) and four other
Allens (1679-82).
Arnot, Albrecht, Robt. and
Christoph. (1679-82).
Barclay, David (1673).
Bennet, Will. (1678).
Berryl, Laur. (1680), Anna,
Christina and John.
Berward (Bereward?) Peter, a
journeyman coppersmith.
Blair, Peter (1681).
Cant, Balzer (1682).
Coloidi, Herm. (?) (1679-82).
Chalmer, Wil. (1667).
Dennis, Alex., clergyman.
Drommel, Alb. (Trumbull)
(1679).
Duncam (Duncan, 1688).
Durham (1699).
Fraser, Andr., soldier.
Gordon, G. (1692).
Gray, Peter and James (1683).
Hamilton, Robt., sergeant (1681).
Harper, Jas., soldier (1697).

Henderson, Alex., old journeyman
from Edinburgh (1679).
Irwing, John (1677).
Karr, Richard (1688).
Kimmond, Will. (1679), and
John (1681).
Krighton, Alex. (1673), also
Thomas, Friedrich, Elisabeth.
Maclelen, J., soldier (1680).
Marschall, J. (1680).
Maxwell, J. (1680).

In *Angerburg* (East-Prussia, S.E.
of Königsberg):
Watson, David (1682).

In *Johannisburg* (on the Russian
frontier S. of Königsberg):
Gilbert, Hercules (1682).
Durison, Peter (1682).
Mitchelhill, Christof (1681).
Sander, Jacob (1682).

In *Schippenbeil* (Eastern Prussia,
S. of Königsberg):
Douglas, Will. (1695).

[1] See J. Sembritzki, *Geschichte von Memel*, 1900.

In *Neukirch* :
Allen, John (see above under Tilsit).

In *Wischwill* :
Hurt, Miss (1695).

In *Heydekrug* (North of Tilsit) :
Dunkam, J. (before 1695).
Ker, Jacob (1699).

In *Welunen* (*Willuhnen*) :
Bercelay, Albrecht, (Barclay) (1694).

In *Lyck* (Eastern Prussia, on the Russian frontier) :
Cant, David, Trooper (1682).
Lindsay, G. (1688), and wife.
Ramage, J. (1688), later on the spelling is Rametz.
Joung (Young) Erdmann (1682), and family.
Jung (Young), Dav. (1680).
Keith, Robert or Albrecht (1685).
Kemper (?), Arendt. (1680).
Kimmond, Andr. (1680), and daughter.
Knox, Andr., soldier (1687).
Magyll (Magill), Dav. (1687).
Marshall, Johann, jun. (1681), and wife. Also his son Robert and wife.
Ogyl (1680) and wife.
Ogylbie (Ogilvie), Fourier (1687).
Olifant, W. (1687).
Royer (Roger), Johann (1680).
Speed, J. (1687).
Spottswood (1687).
Turner, J. (1683).
Wright, Will. (1681), soldier.

In *Goldap* : [1]
Henning, Peter (1680).
Fletcher, Jacob (1687), brewer.

In *Oletzko* :
Watson, Johann (1682), journeyman.

Drommond, Thomas (1682), alderman.
Birrel, Joh. (1682).
Nisbett, Jost. (1682).
Murray, Jas. (1678).
Maclear, Em. (1687), joiner.
Nisbett, Alex. (1683).
Ogelbie, John, soldier (1680). Also Ths. and Anna.
Olifant, David (1674).
Palmer, Jacob (1682).
Pearson, „ (1680).
Pelfor, Jacob and Samuel, abt. 1680.
Rash, Nicol, journeyman-jeweller (1679).
Rennie, Alex., and wife, abt. (1679).
Ritsch, Albrecht (between 1667 and '71); also Wilhelm and Johann.
Robertson, Armer (1676).
Skoumser (Scrimseour?), J. (1686).
Stephen, Andr. (1683).
Thau (Thaw), Joh. (1681).
Wale, Andr., soldier (1681).

In *Stallupönen*. [2]
Walker, Alex. and Andr. (1680).

In *Insterburg* :
Arrot, Patrick (1682).
Crichton, John (1679); two other Crichtons (1687).
Canair (Kinnair), Dav., apprentice boy with Ogyl.
Goham (Graham) (1687).
Hultman (1680), tailor.
Jackson, Peter (1681), and wife.
Thornton, David (1688).
Wolson (?), Johann (1681), and his wife Sophia (1688).
Gordon, Robt. (1682).
Fergusson (1691), trooper.
Anwell (?) (1691).
Wessel, Mule (?) (1692).

---

[1] On the Russian frontier, east of Königsberg; Oletzko, south of it.

[2] Stallupönen and Insterburg, east of Königsberg.

Add to these names those occurring in *Jastrow* in Western Prussia :—
Barry or Bary, Schwan (Swan), Forbes, Sym or Sem, Hilliday (also
called Heiligentag, Elias Dens, Jacob Krudde, Adam Darby, Johannes
Duncker, Georgius Smedt (Smith).—Beginning of the XVIIth Century.

XVIII. Privilegium Scotorum Bidgostiensium.[1]

" . . . Inprimis fraternitas mercatorum Bidgostiensium ipsa
quotannis aliarum fraternitatum more et tempore solito seniorem
alterum e medio sui legitime eligant, alterum vero a consulatu
suo eligi petant atque postulent, quia ita electis et pro fraternitatis suae senioribus constitutis ea omnia . . . quaecunque in eorum
praesentis privilegii contrarietatem et domesticum damnum tam ab
ipsis mercatoribus extraneis quibusvis, quam etiam dictis reven-
ditoribus vulgo Schotowie dictis pertinere videbuntur, per eosdem
seniores suos providere . . . volebunt atque tenebuntur, ea
quidem ratione, ut cum mercatores extranei omnes et singuli
revenditores ipsi Schotowie supranotati civitatem nostram
Bidgostiensem advenerint mercesque suas quasvis et cujusvis
generis libra et ulna tantummodo venum exponentes quibusvis
diebus singulis extra nundinarum tempus vendere vellent et
praetenderent, eos tales mercatores extraneos ac revenditores
. . . fraternitatis seniores talia facere nullatenus unquam
admittant, . . . imo adversantes huic nostro privilegio . . . ab-
latione earum rerum venum expositarum ipsi seniores privent et
omnio coërceant, exceptis solummodo illis mercatoribus extraneis
qui non libra aut ulna sive mensura vetita, verum integris
pecüs (pieces) veluti panni (cloth), telae ceterarumque rerum
sericearum (woven) et piperis, croci (saffron), ac similium in
lapidis pondere integro vendere vellent, talibus forum liberum
omni tempore diebus singulis reservatum esse volumus et
declaramus. Revenditores insuper etiam omnes et singulos,
vulgo Schoti suprascripti inhaerendo constitutionibus regni nostri
in eosdem publice sanctis constitutisque ne a modo et deinceps
in eadem ipsa civitate nostra Bidgostiensi fundi haereditatem
seu domos in usus et commoditates suos emere atque comparare
praesumant hisce literis prohibemus ac omnino tanta libertate
privamus, eos ipsos tantum circa suarum domorum possessionem
reservantes qui antehac ibidem possessionati sunt et veram ac
legitimam mansionem jure nacti et adepti sunt. . . .

"Datum Varschovie die decimo septima mensis Septembris
anno domini millesimo quingentesimo sexagesima octavo (1568)."

This statute was confirmed by King Stephen in 1581 with
the following addition :

" . . . Inprimis quod omnes et singuli mercatores cives et

---

[1] Bromberg = Bidgosc (Polish) : Bidgostia (Lat.).

incolae Bidgostienses qui ulna et libra ponderare sive mensurare merces . . . extra nundinarum tempus voluerint, ü omnes et singuli fraternitatem mercatorum Bidgostiensium suscipere tenebuntur. . . . Quod autem attinet ad quatuor extraneos mercatores videlicet Schotos, qui antehac possessionem fraternitatemque consecuti sumt, si unus eorum decesserit et alius in locum ejus successerit vel jure successionis uti voluerit, literas quod sit honestis parentibus ortus, ostendere tenebitur. Deinde juramentum civitati praestare, jus civile suscipere, viginti marcas polonicales in cistam hujus fraternitatis mercatorum reponere tenebitur et alia juxta consuetudinem fraternitatis huius observare . . . erit astrictus. Damus et concedimus eisdem mercatoribus liberam facultatem pilea (hats) vulgo virilia et muliebria nuncupata . . . venum exponere et vendere sine ulla contradictione. Datum Varschovie anno dom. millesimo quingentesimo octagesimo primo."

Other confirmations followed in 1622 by King Sigismund III and 1636 by Vladislav IV, the latter introducing the following alteration :

". . . ea conditione adiecta ne statim post obitum unius ex quatuor mercatoribus Schotis alter in locum demortui substituatur, sed prorogato unius anni et sex septimaniarum spacio viduae et successorum defuncti ratio habeatur. Quae vidua si intra hoc temporis spaciuno aut non nupserit aut alterius rationis homini matrimonialiter copulata fuerit, tum demum post elapsum suprascriptum tempus, licitum erit, contubernio huic, alium in locum demortui substituere. . . ."

DATUM GEDANI (DANZIG), 28th Jan. 1636.

XIX. "SUPPLICATIONS" OF THE SCOTS IN PRUSSIA.

The petition of the 9th of Nov. 1599 to the Duke of Prussia is signed by the following Scotsmen : *Elias Dunckel (Duncan), David Gallo (Galloway?), Andr. Mattmichel, (M'Michel), Will. Guttfallo (Goodfellow), *Hans Rehn (Ray), Hans Davidtsohn (Davidson), David Malkom (Malcolm), Jacob Meldrim (Meldrum), *Ths. Meldrim, Ths. Mene (Maine), Jacob Kock, Zander Lockert (Lockhart), Henerich Schwurdi (?), George Leise (Linsay), Hans Elter (Elder), *Zander Lohren (Laurin), *Hans Melsen (Malison), David Grinck (Grieg?), *Hilbrandt Blackhall, Zander Mattmichel, Balzer Rossel (Russell), *Hans Stüer (Stewart), Davidt Drom (Trumb?), Zander Wud (Wood).[1]

[1] Those marked with * occur again in the great census of Scottish Cramers made in 1615 by Kock. The Christian name Zander is Alexander (Sandy).

The next in time is the petition of January 30th, 1600, signed by the "elders of the Scots in the districts of Holland,[1] Riesenburg and Preussisch Mark": Kalin (Colin), Nieper (Napier), Alex. Milgrest (?), Jacob Zschopman (Chapman), Jacob Lange (Long). Its terms are almost the same as in the petition of 1599.

The following is dated October 21st of the year 1600, and as it states the complaints and proposed remedies in a summary form is here given in extenso:—

"Most serene and high-born Prince," etc., etc. Most Gracious Prince and Lord; Y.S.H. and counsellors will no doubt well remember the petition which we foreigners in these lands last year about this time did most humbly address to you at full length, so that we only need to repeat its contents in a few words. Because Y.S.H., moved by some envious persons, has caused to be published an order, though we did by no means provoke it, forbidding us, poor men, to traffique with our packs in the country, we have with all due submission prayed to Y.S.H. for God's sake not to forbid us such trade but graciously permit the free exercise of it, especially since we have never injured anybody nor do so now, but rather are of service and convenience to the country-man, who lives far from any town. Nobody has ever complained about us except the guild's people, who envy us our hard-earned bread. Neither are the majority of us new and inexperienced young men, but have been settled in this country for some years, knowing full well how to act and to behave, so that nobody, God prevent, should take any offence. And why should Y.S.H. not allow us our poor calling and our miserable bread, since all other nations, wherever they come from, are permitted to follow it unimpeded?

"Yet we have, be it said without boasting, never refused any taxes or absconded when they fell due, but have willingly contributed, and shall continue to do so, whatever is demanded of us according to our means. We have likewise at all times offered to serve Y.S.H. both with our bodies, and our blood and with our property as it becomes true and faithful citizens. For we acknowledge no other prince and master in the trustful hope and expectation that Y.S.H. will not oppress the poor handful of strangers, but take us like others under his gracious protection.

"And although in the above named Edict it is among other things contended, that now and then deception and reprehensible

[1] Of course Holland in Prussia, about 60 miles S.W. of Königsberg, is meant.

cheatery especially in grain has been practised by some of us, we do hope that this did not happen in our district and we have likewise all of us declared ourselves willing, if any amongst us should do this to expel them, which offer we do hereby repeat.

" And because we have not yet received any answer to our humble supplication, we are now, after waiting patiently and dutifully, very anxious to know our fate, especially as we in these hard times, have to sit still without being able to earn our living. We therefore pray Y.S.H. most earnestly to graciously attend to our request and gladden us with a favourable rescript. We also offer Y.S.H. the annual payment of the sum of two Thalers into Y.S.H.'s treasury, said payment to be made now, if only we receive a favourable answer and each a scrip of paper in his own name for receipt and proof.[1]

" The Allmighty God may reward Y.S.H. here in time and in all eternity with a happy reign and a long healthful life.

" This is the prayer of Y.S.H. faithful and obedient subjects :

"Will. Setton (Seaton), Hans Pigott, Peter Rettrew (?), Henry Löw (Law?), Jacob Weilsohn (Wilson), George Schmidt (Smith), Jac. Koch, Hans Groll, Peter Pell (?), Dav. M'Gall, Ths. Menie (Menzie) and the subscribers of the petition of 1599."

The petition of the Scots in the Rastenburg district (1628) is signed by: Albrecht Linse (Lindsay), Ths. Boyde, Alex. Pieper (?) Hans Schepman (Chapman), Wilm Kore (Gore), Geo. Möller (Miller), Thos. Hamiltan (Hamilton), Ths. Nickell (Nicol), Thos. Litt (Leith?), Alex. Elschimmer (?), Alex. Freser (Frazer), Albr. Freser, Davidt Philip, Ernest Shaw, Albr. Benett, Jac. Schmidt (Smith), Geo. Krege (Craigie), Thos. Hunter.[2]

The proposal of the " Schutz-zeddel " or official receipt, which secured the owner against violent measures on the part of over-zealous bailiffs, seems to have been adopted in Prussia, and to have worked well; for in 1648 we have a long list of sixty Scotsmen, who in the month of June, availed themselves of it.[3] Their names are :—

Ths. Watt.	Al. Hendrichson.	Js. Kreger (Craig).
Will. Ohley (?).	H. Carmichell.	Al. Braun.
Dav. Klarck.	D. Kiedt (Kid?).	Andr. Grey.
Andr. Glenn.	A. Krugschank.	Hans Mitchell.

[1] This receipt is described in the petition of January 30, 1600, "as a paper which will protect us in the case of need, so that we cannot be taken up in such a violent manner by the authorities, but may be secure against it."

[2] The Original in the Royal Archives of Königsberg.

[3] *Ibid.*

Hans Lecock.
Hans Moutrier.
And. Furth (Ford).
Hans Simson.
J. Edler (?).
B. Davidtsohn.
A. Krell.
And. Hueth (Hewit).
H. Hueth.
J. Döhs (Daws).
H. Linson (Lindsay).
Th. Tellyor (Taylor).
J. Brand.
C. Schmal.
G. Stöhl (?).
H. Alexander.
J. Mitchell.

H. Nilson.
H. Panduhn (?).
J. Davidsohn.
G. Grey.
W. Brock.
H. Brock.
H. Morais (Murray).
W. Duglass.
J. Flehman (?).
W. Kinkeith.
W. Ebernet (Aber-
nethy,
J. Melrosz.
A. Hammelthon.
A. Wattson.
Jost. Born.
J. Elleson.

W. Moray.
W. Moray.
D. Tomason.
H. Laury
H. Merschell.
D. Rabb (?).
J. Marten.
P. Marisson.
H. Bely (Bailie).
W. Wach (Waugh).
A. Bely.
A. Bely.
H. Mackmoran.
H. Dorndon (Thorn-
ton).
P Stiven.

XX. List of Contributors towards the Restoration-Fund Marischal College, Aberdeen.

Patrick Forbes in Danzig (1684), £280.
John Turner   „   (1685), £666, 13s.
Al. Aedie,   „   (1686), £535.
J. Walker, collected in Elbing and Queensbridge (1687), £97,
Robt. Davidson in Danzig, £28.
   „   Gordon   „   £112.
      Low (Postmaster) in Danzig, £290.
Thomas and Walter Leslie   „   £203.
W. Miller, collected in Königsberg (1701), £595.
J. Robertson   „   Poland (1701), £957.
Js.   „   „   Danzig (1702) £159.
Al. Ross in Danzig (1703), £26.

The names of the fifty-four contributors belonging to the Scottish Brotherhood or Nation at Queenisbrig were (1701) :—

Thomas Hervie.
William Hervie.
David Hervie.
Jas. Kuick.
Will. Gray.
Robt. Stronoch.
Al. Smith.
Al. Menie.
Js. Ritchie.
A. Fuller.
G. Gordon.
John Gordon.

Ch. Ramsay.
P. Murison.
John Murison.
D. Mill.
W. Mill.
Fr. Hay.
G. Allan.
W. Allan.
And. Ramadge.
John Rait.
Al. Watt.

W. Watt.
Js. Rainy.
G. Coupar.
G. Gray.
J. Trotter.
H. Panton.
W. Mercer.
Gilbt. Craigie.
Dav. Cramond.
   „   Miller.
Geo. Lessly.

Young Men and Servants.

Thos. Hervie.	J. Lyel.	G. Gross.
John Birrell.	Js. Mitchelhill.	Dan. Mitchel.
Laur. Birrell.	H. Hunter.	E. Winster.
Jas. Tam.	W. Tevendel.	D. Bailie.
Francis Craw.[1]	G. Gordon.	Ths. Hay.
John Johnstone.	W. Gordon.	W. Douglas.
Ths. Ramadge.	F. Filleman.	

Collected in Poland by Robt. Gordon in Warsaw.

P. Watt, gulden 100.	Ths. Mashall, gulden 100.
Al. Paip and son, Danzig, dollars 20.	G. Paip, „ 30.
A. Majoriebanks, dollars 30.	Rob. Lowe, Warsaw, dollars 100.
G. Buchan, „ 30.	„ Gordon, „ „ 60.
G. Moyre, gulden 100.	G. Gordon, „ „ 2.

XXI. KABRUN AND GIBSONES AT DANZIG.

The part of Jacob Kabrun's will referring to Danzig runs as follows :—

"I have sought from my youth up food for the mind not only in my main profession as a merchant but elsewhere also, and I have found it in the arts and sciences, to which I owe many a pure joy during my life. This being my opinion and having had the occasion of making purchases on my travels, a collection of paintings, drawings, prints and books has been formed, which cannot indeed, be pronounced unique, but is still not quite unimportant.

"Amongst many proposals, which I considered beneficial for my native city, I had once formed the project of endowing an educational establishment for those youths, who were to devote themselves to commerce and the sciences connected therewith. I was then counting on the patriotic assistance of my fellow-citizens. But I experienced again that he who expects the fulfilment of his well-meant proposals from others in undertakings aiming at the common good, and setting aside all private advantages, is mistaken. Thus in this case also, partly from the want of public spirit, partly by reason of the unfavourable political aspect of the times, these my proposals had to remain amongst the list of unfulfilled wishes. Nevertheless I shall not doubt that success will ultimately obtain, if only after my death. I rather do hope that later on men will be found with the same good intentions but more good fortune, who amongst a band of public-spirited contemporaries, will be able to realise those ideas

[1] This is the author of the four letters given in the Appendix ; though Craw can scarcely be called a young man then, his first letter being dated 1671.

which I have already thrown out and which I need not repeat here at length.

I therefore do bequeathe all my paintings, drawings and prints and my whole library (together with the book-cases), of which special catalogues will be found after my death, for the foundation of an educational establishment, which has been wanting in my native city for so long a time, and I leave the sum of 100,000 gulden Danzig money in City shares, as a fund, out of which all expenses necessary for the most profitable working of this institution shall be defrayed." [1]

The Gibsons or Gibsones were another family of rich merchants of Scottish extraction at Danzig. They derive their title of nobility from one William Gibsone, who was employed by King James V on various diplomatic missions, amongst others to the Pope at Rome. By him he was ennobled, and received as coat-of-arms the three keys and the motto: "Caelestes pandite portae." A descendant, named Alexander Gibsone, was living at Danzig during the reign of Frederick the Great. There he was considered a clever, honest, well-to-do, if somewhat eccentric merchant. Towards the end of the year 1776 he submitted to the President of the Province, von Domhardt, his plea to settle in the territory of the King of Prussia and to buy the estates known as the Neustädter or Przebendowski estates for the sum of 150,000 thaler (*ca.* £23,000) for the benefit of his two nephews the young Counts Keyserling. In this document, which was duly forwarded to the King, Gibsone sets forth that he wished to prove himself a faithful vassal and a useful citizen of the kingdom by erecting factories at Neustadt for the manufacture of woollen cloths, stockings and hats; by improving the breeding and rearing of sheep and by settling Scottish colonists on his estates. At the same time he begged of the King to grant him the title of "Freiherr" (Baronet), which would enable him to live amongst the Polish noblemen, his neighbours, as one of their rank.

By an order of the King, dated Potsdam, January 7th, 1777, the patent as Baron von Gibsone was duly forwarded not without an additional note of Frederick insisting on his keeping his promise and buying the estates. [2]

The purchase was not completed without considerable difficulties and delays, first of all on account of disagreement

[1] Volkel.

[2] It seems that the Patent never reached Gibsone, but remained in the Seal Office of Marienwerder. Gibsone had refused to pay the stamp-duty amounting to only £180.

amongst the heirs. Gibsone again applied to the King and the later replied:

"Wellborn, most dear. Your settlement in my lands is by no means restricted to the purchase of the Przebendowski Estates. There are others in plenty, and you can attain your ends by purchasing those. I do not doubt that the sooner the better you will cause me to call myself your sovereign and feudal lord. Your gracious King.

"FRD."

"POTSDAM, *April 2nd,* 1777."

It was only in the year 1782 that the above-named estates were in the market for the sum of 220,000 gulden. Gibsone was not only ready to buy but to expend a further considerable sum on the repairs. On the other hand, he expects several privileges to facilitate matters and these the King grants with the exception of a reduction of taxes. The royal decree says:

"His R.M. of Prussia, etc. Our gracious Sovereign is well pleased that Alexander Gibsone in Danzig intends to settle in his lands and permission has already been granted to him. All privileges granted by royal edicts to strangers, colonists, their workmen, furniture, etc., shall also be accorded to him and his at his request. Only the common taxes, which compared with English taxes are a trifle, can not be remitted, much less can the permission be given to establish factories on his estates against the clear tenor of the laws of the kingdom. Their proper place is in the towns. He may settle weavers if he likes, but otherwise the common law can not be changed for the sake of one man, but each subject, just as in England, must duly obey it. This His M. did not wish to conceal from the said Gibsone in reply to his letter of March 26th.

"FRD."

"POTSDAM, *April 3rd,* 1782."

Gibsone's importunities finally roused the anger of the King. "You trouble me too often with your affairs," he writes on May 28th, 1782. "A foreigner must absolutely obey the constitution and the laws of the kingdom."

At last the purchase was concluded. Gibsone swore the oath of allegiance at Marienwerder on the 12th of June of the same year. But far from trying to live at peace now, he entered into a series of conflicts and law-suits partly with his government, partly with the magistrates of Neustadt, where he assumed the right of appointing the members of that august body. These quarrels lasted till 1796; and even then new dissensions arose between Gibsone and the Count Otto Alexander Keyserling, to whom the estates had been transferred in that year. Keyserling refused to give up his own patrimonial estate and solely to farm the Neustadt property.

Embittered and disappointed the hard old man retired at last to his office at Danzig. Here he carefully drew up his will, leaving the bulk of his fortune, amounting to over £70,000, to a nephew from Scotland, whom he had taken into business, reserving the small sum of £3000 only for his recalcitrant nephew Keyserling.

No blessing seems to have rested on Gibsone's money. There was trouble and vexation in store even after his death in the year 1811. It was Napoleon, who under the pretext that the deceased was an English subject, caused his fortune to be seized and only released it after the representations of the Courts of Vienna, Berlin and Dresden. In the mean time, however, it had diminished considerably, because it had become mixed up with the unsettled debts of war of the former free-state of Danzig.[1]

It is not quite certain in what year Gibsone's nephew Alexander[2] arrived in Danzig. He was a man of many excellent qualities, and so efficient was his assistance in the defence of of his adopted City in 1807, that General Kalkreuth, the Commander, publicly thanked him and appointed him his aide-de-camp, that he might be included in the capitulation, which the French insisted on confining to the garrison for the express purpose of depriving Mr Gibsone of the benefit of it. His Majesty, the King of Prussia, afterwards wrote to Gibsone, thanking him in the strongest manner for his services and subsequently conferred upon him the Cross of the Order of the Red Eagle. During the dominion of the French, Gibsone was indefatigable in his endeavours to rouse the patriotism, and having become associated in these exertions with General Gneisenau, a warm friendship commenced, which only terminated with the death of that Commander. Gibsone was appointed British Consul at Danzig in 1814 and Consul General of Hanover some time later. His death was viewed by the whole community of Danzig as a general calamity. To the business-talent and the energy, which he shared with his uncle, he added a kindness of heart which gained him the love of everybody, and an ardent Prussian patriotism, which made the interference of the German courts on his behalf a natural expression of gratitude.

1 The direct descendants of Gibsone's nephew are still alive in Danzig and have again acquired great wealth. One Gibsone is President of the Steam Navigation Co., Weichsel.

2 He was a younger brother of Sir James Gibson-Craig of Riccarton; old Baron Gibsone belonged to a branch of the Durie family.

Gibsone's connection with Stein, Gruter and the other principal actors of the Prussian rising against the "Corsican Tyrant" is mentioned in many memoirs of the time.   His co-operation seemed especially valuable on account of his being a native of Great Britain : the idea of British auxiliaries in German pay, who were to land in Prussia, just then engaging the attention of the Prussian patriots.

Of his friendship with Gneisenau the following letter of the famous Prussian general gives an interesting account.   It is dated Berlin, Nov. 21st, 1819, and runs :—

" My dear and honoured Friend,

"It is only now, that my son-in-law has sent me the cup of Bonaparte, taken from his carriage during the night of the 18th of June 1815 and which I left with him at Coblenz.   I now fulfill my promise of presenting it to you, that were never tired of the struggle against the victorious general even when the greater part of Europe bowed before him without hope of redemption.   If all the ministers and all the generals had opposed him with the like zeal, we should certainly never have been conquered by him.

" I was very sorry to hear that your brother John died so unexpectedly and prematurely.   When I saw him last he never appeared to have enjoyed better health of body and greater peace of mind.   His death held out to me the hope of your visit, but you have not been able to come.

" Like so many others you will have been puzzled at the intentions of our government published in the papers, but he who is tolerably well acquainted with the history of all this, is not amazed.   It is only the natural development of certain premises.   Once the incident terminated and all the documents being published, people will perhaps perceive among the motives of the procedure of government a certain fear needlessly increased by the circumstances ; but at the same time they will be convinced, that serious measures against unseemly acts, punishable plans and, in part at least, detestable principles had to be taken by the crown.

" I can only say this much, knowing only the smallest part of the progress of the investigation, all the rest and the latest being as yet concealed from me.

" Baron Schön will be satisfied with the steps taken for the restoration of our Northern Alhambra—as Prince Hardenberg calls the ruins of the Marienburg.[1]   Schinkel [2] is delighted with the plans.

[1] The ancient seat of the Teutonic Knights.   [2] A famous architect.

"What you say about the pleasures of a life in the country finds an echo in my heart. It seems quite incomprehensible to me, how I could exchange the slavery of town-life for the country. But I thought it right to sacrifice my wishes to duty. Since you can do as you like and have tasted its pleasures you ought surely to give it the preference. If I could get you in our valley an estate with good shooting, I should like you to buy it. But such a thing is not to be had here. Another plan would be for you to buy the lands over which your present shooting extends, and for me to acquire an estate in your neighbourhood. As it is I am parcelling out part of my Magdeburg property. May God keep you, and may you remain my friend as I shall always remain

"Yours most affectionately,
"G."

Gibsone sent this letter together with one of his own, in which he modestly deprecates the praises given to him by Gneisenau, to his sister, who was at that time living at Leith. The cup also went to her as a contribution "towards her museum."[1]

XXII. Frederick II and Anderson.

Frederick the Great everywhere promoted the commercial enterprise of the Scots in his countries. In the year 1748 he concluded an agreement with George Anderson, who had proposed to erect large tanning-works at Berlin with a capital of £6000. Anderson, however, made the condition, that not only should the travelling expenses of himself and six workmen be paid, but also that the latter and every other workman of his should be exempt from military service. The King granted these requests, and offered moreover to erect the buildings for preliminary trials with certain kinds of skins. The document concludes with these words: "Toutes ces conditions ont été accordées à Mr Anderson."

[1] Cup and letters are now in possession of Sir Thomas Gibson Carmichael, Castle Craig, Dolphinton, N.B. Much of the above is taken from communications kindly sent to me by Professor Schulz at Culm.

APPENDIX TO PART II.

A.—THE DEATH OF DOUGLAS.

I. SCOTTISH SOURCES.

1. *Forduni Scottichronicon* (ed. Goodall), ii. 416.

Isto anno proditionaliter interfectus est ab Anglis nobilis Wilelmus de Nithisdale super pontem de Danskin in Spruza, qui tunc amirallus electus fuit ducentarum et quadraginta navium ad oppugnandum paganos, qui eo tunc, præ caeteris ad mensam honoris magistri de Spruza ab herellis praeconizatus est Dominus de Clifford Anglicus, invidens probitati ejus, mercede conduxit Anglicos ad delendum memoriam ejus de terra : ob hoc, quod propter simultates inter eos, nescio qua occasione exortas, Clifford appellavit ipsum dominum Wilelmum de duello, et die de se defendendo constituto, interim dictus dominus Wilelmus transtulit se ad Franciam, ad securiora arma sibi componenda.   Quo audito Clifford credidit dictum dominum Wilelmum subterfugere ut at terminum belli constitutum in loco non auderet comparere ; et propterea improbe Clifford ipsum scandalizavit.   Quod comperiens Douglas conductum petüt et obtinuit et ad locum et terminum statutos comparuit.   Sed et Clifford, excusationibus chlamydatus, ob ingentem fortitudinem Douglas comparere recusavit ; et abhinc recessit in Spruzam dictus dominus Wilelmus et ibidem ab Anglis circumseptus in multitudine extinctus est. Ob cujus mortem, illud sanctum passagium interceptum est.

2. *Boethii, Scotorum Historia.*   Edinb. 1526, fol. 347.

Eodem anno (1390) Wilelmus Douglas, vir nobilis virtuteque apud exteras etiam nationes clarus a Prutiae magnatibus dux ducentarum quadraginta navium ad oppugnandos fidei hostes electus, quum ad Dansicam pervenisset, per fraudem ab Anglo quodam nobili Clifford, a quo ad singulare certamen provocatus erat, in ponte Dansicensi confossus est.   Ita magni optimique principum conatus fortunae invidia frustra fuere.

3. *Georgii Buchanan, Scoticorum Historia.*   Edinb. 1582, fol. 102.

Eodem anno (1390) Gulielmus Duglassius Nithiae regulus (quem diximus virtutis ergo generum a rege ascitum), Dantisci ad Vistulam occisus fuit percussoribus a Cliffordo Anglo in eum submissis. Duglassius enim rebus domi tranquillis, ne in ocio languesceret, in Borussiam ad bellum sacrum profectus, tale specimen virtutis detit, ut universae classi, quae maxima et ornatissima erat, praeficeretur. Orta vero altercatione cum Anglo ex antiqua æmulatione eum honorem moleste ferente ad certamen singulare ab eo fuit provocatus. Provocator, secum cogitans, in quam ancipitem Martis aleam se demissurus esset, hominem per sicarios tollendum curat.

4. *Metrical translation of Boethius.*[1]

William of Douglas in that samin yeir
Into Danskine throw tressoun of ane freir
Efter in weir greit worschip that he wan,
With Inglismen that same tyme wes slane than.

. . . .

Syne on the morne as he wes wont to pas
Onto ane kirk into the town that was,
With twa servandis he passit and no mo,
On to that kirk as he was wont till go,
Than Inglismen into his way did lig
As he come hame at the end of ane brig,
In his passage quhair that he suld over pas
Ther Inglismen, into his gait that was,
Accusit him and shairplie he than did speir
Quhat wes the caus that he troublit their freir?

After an altercation the English suddenly fall upon him. Douglas himself unarmed snatched the sword of one of his servants and wielded it mightily against his assailants.

Quhill baith his servandis slane war in that tyde
Him self also buir deidlie woundis wyde
And weill he wist the woundis he had tone
Wald be his deid, thairfoir lyke ane lyoun
To keip his corse that tyme he tuke na cuir
Amang his fais with sic force he fuir
That fyve he slew. . . .

The wounded Douglas then drags himself to his house, sends for a priest of his nation, and having confessed receives absolution. Then he dies forgiving his enemies. The poet concludes the episode with the following lines:

" In Danskene sen as that citie stude
Wes never none, shortlie to concude
Better lovìt baith with wyfe and man
And more menit no wes the Douglas than."

Here we plainly perceive the instincts of the poet; the friar

[1] Added for the sake of completeness, not for its historical importance.

is introduced; the number of ships is raised to two hundred and fifty; Clifford himself is present at Danzig and escapes from there after Douglas had challenged him before the assembled Lords, etc.

5. *Book of Pluscarden* (*Hist. of Scotland*, vii. 325).

William Douglas, being very high spirited, served in repeated campaigns with the chivalry of Prussia on the borders of the heathen enemies of Christ. At length, one day, he was by chance found by the English taking a walk on the bridge of Dansekyn and killed. (Transl. from the original Latin.)

6. In the edition of Fairbairn of *John Major's History* (1521), it is said that Douglas was slain: "super pontem de Dansken in Sprusa, 1390."

This seems to have been an unsurmountable difficulty to the English editor, who translated the work for the Scottish Hist. Society. In a note, he welcomes the extraordinary emendation of the above into: "Dunglas over the Pease (!)."

II. GERMAN SOURCES.

(a) *The Chronicle of Wigand of Marburg.*

1391. Interimque fit dissensio ex parte Anglicorum et Schotorum. Nam dominus Wilhelmus de Duclos Schotus interfectus fuit in ponte juxta summum,[1] qui cum uno pede ad foramen corruerat et viriliter se defendit ut eciam unus de familia sua cum eo occideretur. Hirsch, *Scriptores Rerum Prussicarum*, vol. ii. 644.)

(b) *The Chronicle of J. von Posilge.*

Auch wart eyn Herre von Schottlant, der von Duglas,
Also there was a Lord of Scotland, he of Douglas,
czu Köngsberg von den Engelschen geslagen, das czwetracht
at Königsberg by the English slain, so that discord
wart undir den von Frankrich und Engelschen, das der
arose among those of France and the English, so that the
eryntisch czu Köngsberg nicht gehalden wart; und also
table of honour at Königsberg not kept was; and thus
irhub sich der Meister[2] mit den gesten und czog in reysze.
arose the Master with the guests and went for crusade.

(*Ibid. Scriptores Rerum Prussicarum*, vol. iii. 172.)

III. FRENCH SOURCES.

Le livre des Faicts du Mareschal de Boucicaut. *Comment Messire Boucicaut alla la troisième fois en Prusse et comment il voulut venger la mort de Messire Guillaume de Douglas.*

Et ainsi comme il s'en retournait et ja estait à Königsberg,

---

[1] Hirsch supplies: "altare."

[2] Hochmeister, the head of the Teutonic Order.

advint telle advanture que comme plusieurs estrangers fussent arrivez en la dicte ville de Königsberg, lesquels alloient pour estre à la susdicte guerre, un vaillant chevalier d'Escosse appelé messire Guillaume de Duglas, fut là occis en trahison de certains Anglois. Quand ceste mauvaistié sceie, qui desplaire debvoit à tout bon homme, messire Boucicaut, nonobstant que à celuy messire Guillaume de Duglas n'est nulle acquointance ; mais tout par la vaillance de son noble courage, pour ce que le faict luy sembla si laid qu'il ne deust estre souffert ne dissimulé sans vengeance, et pour ce que il ne fut là nul chevalier ni escuyer qui la querelle en voulust prendre nonobstant qu'il y eust grand foison de gentilshommes du pays d'Ecosse, ains s'en taisoient tous, il fist à scavoir et dire à tous les Anglois qui là estoient, que s'il y avoit nul d'eulx qui voulust dire que le dict chevalier n'eust esté par eulx tué faulsement et traistreusement, que il disoit et vouloit soustenir par son corps que si avoit et estoit prest de soustenir la querelle du chevalier occis. A ceste chose ne voulurent les Anglois rien respondre, ains dirent que si les Escossois qui là estoient leur vouloient de ce aulcune chose dire que ils leur en respondroient : mais à luy ne vouldroient rien avoir à faire. Et ainsi demeura la chose et Boucicaut s'en partit et fut tout à point en Prusse à la guerre qui fut la plus grande et la plus honorable que de longtemps y eust eu. (Michaud et Poujoulat, *Collection des Mémoires*, 1ère Série, Tome ii. p. 232.)

IV. Obligatory Note of James Douglas[1] (1390 ?).

"Noverint universi presentia visuri seu audituri quod ego Jacobus de Douglas miles agnosco publice per presentes, me unacum meis heredibus teneri et obligari famoso militi Roberto Stewart[2] et suis heredibus decem . . . . Prutenicalis monete, quas decem—— promitto sibi solvere hic in Dantzic super festum Paschae nunc proxime affuturum, quod si non fecero ex tuto promitto in bona fide et honore nulla arma militis induere nisi cum illud fuerit cum suo.

"In huius rei testimonium sigillum meum presentibus est appensum.

"Datum Dantisci anno millesimo tercentesimo."[3]

B.—The Craffters (Crawfords) in Augsburg.

James Crawford, the youngest son of David, the third Earl, accompanied the Scottish Princess Eleanor Stuart to Germany in

---

[1] Of Dalkeith. [2] Sir Robt. Stewart of Durisdeer.

[3] Only this copy of the document has been preserved. The year 1300 is a mistake of the copyist instead of 1389 or 1390. See *Report of the Royal MSS. Comm.*, vol. ix.

1449, where she was married to Archduke Sigmund of Austria. On the journey he remained at Augsburg in Bavaria, where he himself marrying a rich heiress became the founder of a prominent and very wealthy family, the Craffters, as they were called. Raphael Custos,[1] a writer of the XVIIth Century, has the following rhymes referring to the Scottish descent of the family :

" Als eine Königin aus Schottland kam	When a queen came from Scotland
Herauss, Ertzhertzog Sigmund nam,	Forth, Archduke Sigmund to take,
Kam mit ihr aus dem Königreich	There came with her out of the kingdom
Auch einer von Crawfurdt zugleich,	Also one of the Crawfords,
Adelichen Stammes aldort,	Of noble family there,
Diser blieb in Deutschland hinfort,	He remained in Germany henceforth,
Auch desselben Posteritet	Also his posterity
Sich hernachen gen Augsburg tet,	Afterwards went to Augsburg,
Da, als mit den Geschlechten von Herren	There, when with the race of patricians
Sie sich verpflicht zu heurat's ehren	They had bound themselves to the honour of marriage,
Seins nach altem gebrauch und gewohn	They according to old custom
Der ehrbarn Gesellschafft zugethon."	Were added to the honourable guild.

The four great-grandsons of this Crawford were ennobled by the Emperor Charles V in 1547, and admitted amongst the patricians of the city as so-called " Mehrer der Gesellschaft " = patrons of the Society. One of these brothers, Hieronymus, is mentioned in an epitaph formerly in the church of St Anna.[2]

CONDVNTVR . HEIC.

HIERONYMVS . CRAFTER.

AVGVSTANVS.

HIERONymi Filius LAVRENTii Nepos

JACOBI . DE . CRAFORDIA . NOBilis SCOTI . Pronepos

NEC . NON.

LECTISSIMA . FOEMINA . HELENA.

IOANnis HENRICI . HOERWARTI . Filia.

IOAN . N . HENRICI . P.

CONIVGES . CONCORDISS.

EORVMQ . FILIOLVS . HIERON . MINOR.

TRIDVO . A . PATRIS . MORTE . DENATVS.

CVMQ . EO . VNA . HVMATVS.

PIE . OMNES . BEATEQ . DE . F.

HELENA . CRAFTERINA . F.

IOAN. MATTHAEI . HEINZELII . VX.

SIBI . ET . PARENTIBVS . DVLCISS.

HONOR . AMOR . DOLOR.

M . P.

[1] Patriciarum stirpium . . . in Augusta . . insignia (1613).
[2] Daniel Prasch, *Epitaphia Augustana, Aug. Vind.* 1624, i. 176. Hieronymus (the first named) seems to have first accumulated riches.

C.—Letters from Gustavus Adolfus to Donald Mackay.

We, Gustavus Adolfus, by the Grace of God, King of the Suedes, &c., &c.

Be it known to all by these presents, that we have appointed the noble and highly beloved Donald, Lord of Reay, to be our Colonel over a Regiment of foreign soldiers which he is to raise and equip, conduct and command for our service, which Regiment, the officers as well as the soldiers, shall at all times fulfil this letter of agreement, and, participating in our advantages, shall not turn away from us in times of misfortunes, and, as becometh such honourable and brave cavaliers and soldiers, they shall always be ready cheerfully and indefatigably to venture body and life, whether in presence of or away from the enemy, in battles, in skirmishes, and on watches, in attacks, in sieges, and in garrisons; and on all occasions, whether with the whole army, or on any special service to which they may be ordered by us or our generals, they shall, by day or night, by water or by land, fulfil our articles of War, and thereby attain to honour and renown; also, the soldiers, wherever they may be, on the march or in quarters, shall do everything that is necessary in approaches, sieges, trenches, or strongholds of the enemy; shall throw up earth-works, and when attacked, defend same; and shall also repair and build any necessary field-works with all despatch wherever they may be needed.   In fulfilling this engagement, we hereby agree to give to the Colonel and the Regimental Staff, the following allowance or monthly pay, reckoning the month at thirty-one days.

The Colonel,	300 Rex-dollars, Swedish.	
Lieut.-Colonel,	130	,, ,,
Quarter-master,	50	,, ,,
2 Chaplains at,	30	,, ,,
4 Surgeons and 4 Provosts,	20	,, ,,
1 Regim. Clerk,	50	,, ,,
1 Court Martial Clerk,	30	,, ,,
1 Regim. Judge,	50	,, ,,
Court Martial Beadle,	30	,, ,,
2 Orderlies, each	6	,, ,,
The Executioner,	12	,, ,,

And to each company there shall be given monthly each :—

Captain,	100 Rex-dollars.	
Lieutenant,	50	,,
Ensign,	50	,,

Towards the end of XVIIth Century the family disappears from Augsburg.

2 Sergeants,	16	Rex-dollars.
1 Quarterm. Serg., ⎫		
1 Armourer, ⎬	12	,,
1 Muster Clerk, ⎭		
Drummers, Pipers,	8	,,
6 Corporals,	11	,,
15 heads of sections,	9	,,
21 Under-Sergeants,	7	,,
90 Pikemen and Musket.,	6	,,
4 Scouts,	5	,,
40 Reserve Men,	5	,,

Then follows a list of further considerable remunerations amounting to almost half of the regular pay. After this the King
continues :—

" And we undertake and expressly agree always to provide a
sufficient monthly allowance, and to make a settlement twice in
the year, and to pay at that time whatever balance may be then
found due for the preceding six months ; also that we shall not
reduce the soldiers' pay ; but if any of the men shall have care-
lessly damaged or broken their accoutrements, the cost of same
shall be deducted from their pay, and they must at all times
undertake to keep and deliver them to us again in good order.
. . . Also, that the Regiment shall without demur be bound to
muster in whole or in part at any time or place we may be
pleased to appoint ; and further, that no officer shall venture to
draw the balance due to any dead, disabled or absent soldier, for
the balances due to all such shall in every case revert to us and
our kingdom of Sweden. . . . If any officers or soldiers should
be taken prisoners by the enemy, while in our service, we shall
ransom them at our own cost ; and if any officers or soldiers
. . . shall be bruised or in any way disabled, so that they are
incapable of taking part in warlike operations, we shall provide
a temporary home for them in our own dominions ; but should
they prefer going beyond our kingdom, a month's pay shall be
given to each. In testimony whereof we have subscribed this
with our own hand and attested the same with our Royal Seal.
Done in the Camp of Marienburg, June 17th, 1629."

" GUSTAVUS ADOLFUS."

Of the two Latin letters of the King to Mackay the first 15th
March 1631, refers to the sack of New Brandenburg by Tilly,
and expresses a regret that nearly the whole of the soldiers had
been massacred. The King hopes that the three regiments may
be filled up by levies from Scotland. The second Latin letter

dated 4th July, 1631, from the Camp at Werben is addressed:
"Illustri Tribuno nostro, nobis sincere dilecto ac fideli Domino
Donald Macquei, Domino de Reay et Streinever." In answer
to a letter from Mackay, who was then in England, endeavouring
to procure new recruits for His Majesty, the King says:—

"It is very agreeable to us to learn that the levies of the
Marquis of Hamilton are favoured both by the King himself and
the English States; and as we have undertaken the burden of
this war not only to be avenged for injury done and for our own
security, but also for the relief of our oppressed friends in the
afflicted Evangelical Religion, so we wish his Serene Majesty,
the English King, our brother and friend, to be quite convinced,
that if he will help us we shall not be unmindful of the King of
Bohemia and the oppressed House of the Palatine; but we shall
vindicate his dignity and former state as the Divine favour shall
help us. For this purpose there is now the most favourable
opportunity, seeing that the enemy has been expelled from the
whole of Pomerania and nearly all the Electorate of Brandenburg.
. . . It is pleasing to us that the Marquis of Hamilton raises his
levies with so much ardour; and although it has been reported
to us that the munitions of war which we were sending him
have been intercepted near Dunkirk, we do not doubt that our
agent, Eric Larson, has provided for the promised amount."

The King then urges the Marquis of Hamilton to hurry and
bring his troops into Germany without delay, and explains that
he has given orders to Larson to pay Mackay the sum of 9600
Imperial dollars for the expense of enlisting. He concludes
with promised proofs of his favour and recommends him to God.[1]

D.—LIST OF THE PRINCIPAL SCOTTISH OFFICERS EMPLOYED BY
GUSTAVUS ADOLFUS IN GERMANY.[2]

Three Field-Marshalls :—
  Sir Alex. Leslie, Governor of
    the Baltic Provinces.
  Sir Patrick Ruthven, Governor
    of Ulm.
  Sir Robt. Douglas, commanded
    the left wing of Torstensohn's
    Army at Iankowitz.
Four Generals :—
  James, Marquis of Hamilton.
  Sir James Spence.

George, Earl of Crawford-
    Lindsay.
  Andr. Rutherford, afterwards
    Earl of Teviot.
Lieutenant-General :—
  Alex. Forbes, tenth Lord Forbes.
Majors-General :—
  Sir James King, Governor of
    Vlotho.
  Sir D. Drummond, Governor of
    Stettin.

---

[1] J. Mackay, *An Old Scots Brigade,* p. 234 f.
[2] From various sources.

Sir James Ramsay, Governor of
Hanau.
Alex. Ramsay, Governor of
Kreuznach.
John Rentoun.
W. Legge, Governor of Bremen.
John Leslie.
Th. Ker, † at Leipzig.
Sir G. Douglas.
Colonels :—
Sir J. Hepburn.
Robt. Munroe, Lord of Foulis †
at Ulm.
Sir Donald Mackay, Lord Reay.
G. Lindsay, † at Neu-Branden-
burg.
Lord Forbes, † at Hamburg.
Sir Hector Munroe † at Bux-
tehude.
Lord St Colme.
Lud. Leslie.
Will. Baillie.
W. Bonar of Rossy, in Fife.[1]
A. Ramsay.
Sir J. Ruthven.
Sir Jas. Lumsden, Governor of
Osnabrück.
Sir J. Hamilton.
Sir J. Innes.
W. Ballantine.
Henry Lindsay, † at Hamburg.
Alex. Lindsay.
Jas. Macdougall (called Dew-
battle. He stormed Lands-
berg, defended Schweinfurt
and beat the Imperial troops
at Liegnitz).

Henry Fleming.
W. Bruntsfield, † at Bux-
tehude.
William Stewart, brother of the
Earl of Traquair.
Seven other Leslies, amongst
them George Leslie, Gover-
nor of Vechta in Oldenburg.[2]
Six Hamiltons.
Two Lumsdens.
John Sinclair, son of the Earl of
Caithness, † at Neumark in the
Palatinate.
Robt. Munroe, † at Witten-
berg.
Fr. Sinclair.
J. Lindsay, † at Neumark.
Captains :—
— Annan.
— Armin, wounded at Stralsund.
— Beatoun, wounded at Stral-
sund.
A. Gordon.
W. Gunn, afterwards Colonel
and Imperial General.
John Gunn, afterwards Colonel.[3]
G. Heatley.
Rob. Hume.
John Innes, † at Stralsund.
P. Innes, † at Nürnberg.
G. Learmouth, † at Boitzenburg.
W. Mackay, † at Lutzen.
Three other Mackays.
Moncrieff, † at Brandenburg.
Three Stewarts.
Alex. Tulloch.
And many others.[4]

E.—Colonel Robert Munro and his Death at Ulm.

In the minute-books of the Town Council of Ulm in Würtemberg we read (Feb. 20. 1633):—

[1] He settled in the Duchy of Bremen, where he bought the Castle
of Gnadenfeld. He died in 1674. One of his sons became a Danish
General. See Gauhen, *Adels Lexicon*, i. 141.
[2] He died in 1638. See Pufendorf, *Schwed. Kriegsgeschichte*, ix. § 42.
[3] Buried at Ohlau in Silesia. He had married a Miss von Arnim,
† 1649. See Supplement.
[4] J. Mackay, *An old Scots Brigade*, Appendix.

"Michael Rietmuller, the surgeon, has permission to have Colonel Munroth (!) in his house, until the time of his recovery.

May 2nd 1633.

"Received by me Paul Held, secretary to the Board of Works of the Church from the Brother of the late Robert Monroth a Scottish Baronet and Colonel to H. M. the King of Sweden the sum of 100 Reichs Thaler, which had gratefully been left to the said Board ad pias causas, because the Magistrates had the above named Robert interred in the Franciscan Church and his standard, armour and spurs hung up there; for which the Swedish Mayor again thanked the Board and begged to express his gratitude to the Council.

Contin. fol. 159.

"According to a decree of the Council, dated Friday, May 3, of the 100 Reichs Thaler left by the late Swedish Colonel Robert Monro, because of the permission to be buried in the Franciscan Church, one half, namely 75 Gulden or 25 Ducats at 3 fl. shall be given to the Hospital, and in future, when such donations shall occur again, it shall be held likewise."

In the Register of Deaths of the Church mentioned above we find the following entry :—

"I, Magister Balthasar Kerner have done my 96th Funeral Sermon for Robert Monraw, Baron of Failis (!), late Colonel of H.M. the King of Sweden of two regiments of foot and horse, on the 29th of April hor. 3. He lies buried in the said Church."

The Latin Poet Joannes Narssius, who lived at Hamburg in the beginning of the XVIIth Century and wrote a long Latin Poem on the Thirty Years' War, which he called " Gustavis," dedicates the following epithaphium to the memory of Munro :—

Ingenti clarus Robertus robore Munro
  Qui Baro de Foullis, Munroidumque caput:
Bina cui legio peditumque equitumque ministra
  Quam sociat Patriae ac Religionis amor.
Lipsiacis postquam certavit gnaviter oris,
  Et passim Austriacis Martia damna dedit,
Hostili tandem prostratus vulnere multo,
  Ulmiaco liquit membra caduca solo.
Spiritus exsuperans ingenti robore mortem
  Heroum in superis praemia digna capit.
Discite, Germani, grataque evolvite mente,
  Pro vobis, fortes quot cecidere viri!
Pro vestra Heroes quot libertate necantur,
Gente Caledonia Munroidumque sati! (1633).[1]

[1] Munro, *His Expedition.*

Another Munro, whose Christian name was John, was killed at Bacharach on the Rhine and lies buried in the Church of St Peter. But there is neither stone nor inscription to indicate the spot.

F.—I. LETTER OF GENERAL JAMES RAMSAY RELATING TO THE TREATY OF MAYENCE.

James Ramsay, Major General of the kingdom of Sweden and its allies also Governor of the fortress of Hanau is constrained, with regard to the Chief-Points of the Treaty handed to him by the Hessian Ambassadors, to remark as follows :—

"Firstly, that the above-mentioned six points do not relate to the common welfare but chiefly to the person of the General himself; although he by force of his office aimed in all his actions military and civil, above all things, at the common good of the County of Hanau and especially of this fortress and its sovereign. To turn aside from such a scope and simply to deal with personal matters would cause prejudice and grievance with my superiors and disreputable rumours with friend and foe.

"Secondly, that it is apparent from the document signed by the Emperor at the Castle of Ebersdorff on September 14th of last year that the "peace-accord" concluded at Mayence on the 31st of August eodem anno was not inserted in its entirety, but only some paragraphs of it, which had been in consideration up to the 21st of August, but which had never been signed by the General.

"Thirdly, the treaty is a patched up work. The clear letter, however, showeth that certain stipulations took place as to the pardon and reconciliation of Count Philip Moritz and the eventual surrender of this town; likewise some paragraphs were agreed upon and signed and then sent to His Imp. Maj. the late Emperor ad ratificandum, which ratification took place at Regens Purgk on Dec. 5th Ao. 1636.

"Therefore the public interest requireth, that both the stipulations settled as well as the Imperial ratification concerning these first points should without any delay be brought to hand, considering that the Crown of Sweden can not rest satisfied with the present Imperial Document de dato Sept. 14th, far less accept its many discrepancies (Lit. B.).

"To this must be added, that, as may be seen both from the treaty itself and from the Salvoconduct dated Laxenburg, May 8th, 1637, this fortress was to be handed over to the *Count of Hanau,* but that in the Imperial letter of intercession to the Duke of Mecklenburg of the 4th of September, "the surrender shall take place into the hands of His *Imperial Majesty.*"

"It is likewise a grievous alteration, that the General with all his soldiers and belongings was to have a free pass and a convoy and enjoy every futherance and support, nevertheless in the forged Imperial confirmation this is tacitly omitted ; also that the hostages refer to the person of the General alone instead of the officers and soldiers on foot and horse and to all persons in the service of the Crown of Sweden and other good friends staying with him.

"Now because the foundation of the treaty is not properly established, and because common faith and truthfulness require a ' consummation' free from any blame : let the Hessian ambassadors duly co-operate that such defects be remedied and word for word, a just agreement (of the documents) be obtained. Expecting Your written communications, signatum, the 2nd of Feb., 1638."

II. DUKE BERNHARD OF WEIMAR AND RAMSAY.

Ramsay never neglected his duty towards his superior officers. He informed the Duke immediately of the treaty of Mayence ; but the latter had already heard of it through a different channel. He wrote on the 11th of Sept. 1637 :—

. . . "We have been told for certain, that you concluded a treaty with the enemy concerning the surrender of the town and fortress of Hanau. Considering that by your great industry and perseverance, you have held the place up to this time, which not only earned you immortal glory, but our own gratitude, we can fancy only, that extreme necessity and adversity compelled you to give up such an important place."

In a second letter the Duke expressed his surprise to the General, that he had obtained such favourable conditions, adding (Nov. 20th) that he had sufficient proof of Ramsay's constant and true affection for the Crown of Sweden and for the whole evangelical cause, and that he had no doubt whatever, that to his immortal honour and praise, he would persevere in it unshaken and do his best as hitherto.

In another letter the Duke recommends Ramsay to observe the paragraphs of the treaty carefully with the express order to see to it, "that all articles of the contract be fulfilled, because to promise much is nothing, the keeping of the promises is the principal thing."[1]

III. RAMSAY'S WILL.

The General, who left an extremely large fortune, exhorts his wife in the introduction to his will "to educate their son David in the fear of God," at the same time recommending her not to mourn for him longer than six weeks, and after that to marry a gentleman of good family for the best of her child. The new husband was to receive one third of the money left by him, the

[1] Wille, p. 450.

second third belonging to her and the third to their son.   In
case the latter should die without heir, the money was to go to
the General's cousin, Lord William Ramsay, and his male heirs.
A part of the interest on the property was set aside for the
support of five students of divinity.

Finally it was ordered that immediate payment should be made
for 500 pairs of shoes, bought at Elbing for the regiment.[1]

G.—Scottish Officers under Frederick the Great.

Too late to be incorporated into the text, the following
additional information regarding Scottish Officers under Frederick
the Great, chiefly derived from Charles Lowe's delightful tale,
A Fallen Star,[2] must find a place here.

Major General Grant mentioned in the text, Frederick's
favourite aide-de-camp, belonged to the Grants of Dalvey, and
was designated of Dunlugas, "an estate on the pleasant banks
of the Deveron, a few miles above the port of Banff."   At first,
being a cadet who had to push his own fortune in the world, he
took service under Elizabeth, the Empress of Russia, where his
countryman Keith procured him a commission.   After a time,
however, he exchanged it after the example of his general,
to whom he was devotedly attached, for the Prussian army.
Frederick the Great quickly discovered his great force of character, his blunt honesty[3] and his excellent capacity for hard
riding.   As the King's messenger, he performed feats of horse-
manship which seem incredible.   Shortly before the outbreak of
the Seven Years' War he covered the distance between Berlin
and Vienna and back again, including a delay of three days in the
Austrian capital, that is close on nine hundred miles, in ten days.

By these and other performances he contributed much to the
well-known readiness of the King against all surprises, and
therefore, if indirectly, to the victorious issue of the war.

One of Grant's eccentricities was his great love for his dogs.
His two intelligent Scotch collies accompanied him everywhere,
and he is said to have trained and used them for military purposes
where the services of scouts were required.

When the war was over in 1763 his grateful King made him
a Major-General and Governor of Neisse, an important fortress
on the frontier of Silesia.   But a life of peace and quiet monotony

---

[1] Wille, p. 489.   It is very doubtful if the widow ever entered into
possession of Ramsay's wealth.   The 150,000 marks deposited for him at
Amsterdam by the Imperialists, as an equivalent for the surrender of Hanau,
by some means or other found their way back into the Imperial Exchequer,
although Ramsay had distrained the money (Wille, p. 491).

[2] Downey & Co., London, 1895.   [3] See De Catt's *Memoirs*.

did ill agree with this man of daring.   He died about 1764, and lies buried in the churchyard of the Garrison Church.[1]   Of two other officers under the great Prussian King, Colonel Drummond and Quartermaster Spalding we know little more than the names.   A third one, however, named Gaudy or von Gaudy, obtained no little fame.

The Gaudys were originally Goldies or Gowdies, and hailed from Ayrshire and Dumfries-shire.   One Andrew Gaudie from Craigmuie, a parish adjacent to Craigenputtock, the temporary home of Carlyle, entered the service of Prince Ragozzi in Hungary (1641), who sent him as ambassador to Hamburg and employed him in various military capacities.   He was present in several of the later battles of the Thirty Years' War.   In 1650 he bought estates in Eastern Prussia, and in 1660 exchanged into the service of the Elector of Brandenburg as Major-General. From this Gaudy sprung quite a number of famous Prussian military leaders.   One of them is mentioned by Frederick the Great in his *Mémoires de Brandenburg* in connection with the siege of Stralsund, then occupied by the Swedes under Charles XII., as the Prussian officer who facilitated the attacking of the Swedish trenches.   It appears that Gaudy recollected having, in his school days at Stralsund, bathed in the arm of the sea near the ramparts finding it neither deep nor muddy.   To make sure of the matter, however, he sounded it in the night "and found that the Prussians might ford it, turn the left of the Swedish trenches, and thus take the enemy in flank and rear." This was successfully done, and the merit of defeating such a renowned soldier as Charles XII was due, or in part at least, due to a man of Scottish origin.

Another Gaudy, a son of the above, was attached to the staff of Field-Marshal Keith.   He was a most intelligent officer and wrote a *Diary of the Seven Years' War*, in ten folio volumes of manuscript still preserved but unpublished in the Archives of the " General Stab" at Berlin.   He also wrote treatises on fortification.

A third Gaudy was Fred. W. Leopold von Gaudy, Lieutenant-Colonel of Infantry and Knight of the Order Pour le mérite in 1809.   His son again became the famous soldier-poet, Franz von Gaudy, who has been called, though not very aptly, the " Burns and Béranger of the Fatherland rolled into one."   The simplicity and sweetness of his lyrics is still much admired in Germany.[1]

Descendants of old Gaudys are still to be met with in the Prussian Army List.

[1] See Lowe, *l.c.*, p. 364.
[2] Lowe, *A Fallen Star*, Appendix (reprinted from the *United Service Magazine*).

APPENDIX TO PART III.

THE CHURCH.

I. List of Abbots of St James' Monastery S. B. at Ratisbon.

Marianus, † 1080.

Donellus (1111-1121?).
Dermitius (1121-1149?).
Christianus (1150-1172).
Gregorius I (1172-1204).
Joannes I (1204-1211).
Matthaeus I (1211-1214).
Gregorius II (1214-1223).
Jacobus I (1223-1233).
Joannes II (1233-1240?).
Paulinus (1240?-1243).
Deocarus (1243?-1247).
Matthaeus II (1247-1250).
Jacobus II (1251-1257).
Gelasius (1257——?).
Marianus (1261-1277).
Macrobius (1277-1278?).
Christian II (1282-1287).
Macrobius II (1287-1289) " vir vere prodigus."
Matthaeus III (1290-1293).
Mauritius (1293-1296).
Marianus II (1296-1301).
Donatus I (1301-1310).
Joannes III (1310-1326).
Nicolaus (1326-1332).
Matthaeus IV (1332-1337) "dissipator."
Joannes IV (1337-1343).
Gilbertus (1343-1347).
Nicolaus II (1347-1354).
Eugenius (1354-1369).
Matthaeus V (1369-1380).
Gelasius II (1380-1384).
Matthaeus VI (1384-1396).
Philippus I (1396-1401).

Philippus II (1402-1418).
Donatus II (1418-1431).
Cormacus (1431-1436).
Alanus (1437-1442).
Benedictus (1442-1444) "multa mala fecit."
Carolus or Rovicus (1447?).
Mauritius II (deposed 1452) "prodigus."
Thaddaeus (1457).
Otto (1457-1464?).
Joannes V (1465-1479) "prodigus."
Matthaeus VII (1479-1484).
David I (1484-1499) " subdolus."
Walterus (1499-1515) "delapidator."
Joannes VI (1515-1523).
Andreas (Ruthven) (1523-1525).
David II (Cuming) (1525-1548).
Alexander (Bog) (1548-1556).
Balthasar (Dawson) (1556 1566).
Thomas Anderson (1566-1576).
Ninian Winzet (1577-1592).
Joannes VII (Whight) (1592-1623).
Benedictus Algaeus (1623-1630) " prodigus."
Alexander II (Baillie) (1640-1657).
Macarius Camerarius (1657-1672) " deposed."
Placidus Fleming (1672-1720).
Maurus Stuart (1720).
Bernard Baillie (1720-1742).
Bernard Stuart (1742-1755).
Gallus Leith (1756-1775).
Bened. Arbuthnot (1775-1820)

II. Syllabus Benefactorum Monasterii Sti. Jacobi Scotorum,
Ratisbonae, 1678.[1]

Serenissim. Elector Bavariæ, Maximil. Emanuel (†1726),	endowed the monastery with several villages and gave "mille quadringentos florinos" in 1681, 1684, '87. Two hundred in 1702.
Augustiss. Imperator Leopoldus I	donavit Placido Flaminio mille flor.
Sereniss. Princeps Wilhelmus a Hessen-Rheinfels	misit abbatem Viennam ad sollicitanda Serenissim. S. negotia et pro expensis dedit 600 fl. item pelvim argenteam et dua candelabra argent. (1701).
Illustr. Dom. Ludov. de Crecy, Regis Plenipot. ad Comitia Imperii, qui per novem annos et aliquot menses fuit in hoc monasterio (†1701),	gave embroidered vestments, etc.
Baro de Imsland (†1723)	fundavit altare Stae Annae, donavit 800 fl. pro missis, vestim. et 6369 fl. post mortem in Monast.
Ill. Dom. de Puts (†1718)	gave vestments and 1200 fl. for the boys' seminary; books and mathematical instruments, and a legacy of 3000 fl.
Ill. Dom. Jac. de Leslie (†1691)	200 Imperiales for the erection of pews.
Dom. Balthasar Fraunhoffer (†1719)	built the altar of St Dismas and endowed it with 700 fl.
Praenob. et magnus Domin. *Andreas Bauman* (†1725)	legavit multa beneficia et 250 fl. pro aedific. altare Beat. Virg. Mariae.
Bishop of Eichstetten	gave iron stoves to the value of 345 fl.
Illustr. Dom. Georgius Etheridge, eques, auratus, Seren. Jacobo II Regi a consiliis et ad comitia imperii hic Ratisbonae (1685) orator Plenipot. Discedens 1688 (?),[2]	gave political and historical books.
Dom. Leichnamschneider, Protonot. Apostol. Canonicus,	left 1000 fl.

---

[1] From the original in the Monast. S. B. at Fort Augustus.

[2] This was the famous dramatist. His life at Ratisbon, where he spent his days in gambling, protecting actresses and drinking, was little in accordance with the German dignified ideas of an ambassador. The above list shows us what became of his books after his flight from Ratisbon.

Praenob. Petrus Montmedy, Luxemburgensis (†1709). Sepultus est in Capella nostra parochiali Stae Annae prope Baptisterium, cum Epit. in pariete.	The monast. residuary legatee. 8000 fl.
Honestus et Devotus Vir Georgius Zieler, Pistor in Nieder Motzing (†1718),	For mass 300 fl.; altar cloths and 700 fl., besides a legacy of 50 fl.
Rever-diss. Dom. Albertus Ernst, Coloniensis Archidiaconus major, Senior Cathedralis Ratispon; *Comes de Wartenberg*,	statues, relics and chalices.
Rev. Praenob. Dom. Joannes Dausch, Theol. Doctor et Cathedr. Ratisp. Decanus (†1684),	50 fl. for the school and a legacy of 100 fl.
Illustr. Dom. D. Stephan Comes de Taaffe in Exercitu Caes. Colonellus (†1699),	100 Imperiales.
Admod. Rev. Doct. D. Joannes Georgius Sartorius, Canonicus (†1691),	500 Imperiales and other presents.
Perillustr. Franciscus Hay, Baro de Dalgetty († Pettaviae in Styria, 1676),	legavit 2000 Imperiales.
Perill. D. Thomas Strachan, Colon. in legione Comitis de Leslie (†1694),	100 fl. pro reparatione templi.
Die edle u. tugendhaffte Frau Maria Anna Stegerin, Wittib zu Straubing,[1]	endowed mass at the Probstei Kirche at Kehlheim in honour of the Corpus Christi Festival with 300 fl.
Not. et praec. Dom. Joannes Georgius Haas, granarius sive oeconomus ins. Collegii Eccles. S. Mariae (†1712),	for images, 50 fl.
Excell. et Ill. Dom. Robertus de Gravel, Dom. in Marli, Plenipot. Sacrae S. Majest. (†Parisiis 1689).	gave statues and 40 Imper.
Honor. Vir Joann. Matth. Eible, lupulorum mercator de Einsiedl in Bohemia,	2 masses and 50 fl.
Plur. Rev. D. Michael Adam Kerling, Parochus in Stamesried,	legavit 100 fl.
Celsissima Domina Francisca de Freidenberg, Abbat. Ratisb,	2000 fl.
Dom. Jacob. Gordon, Consiliarius Sacrae Caes. Maj. (†1787),	2000 fl. for the seminary.

[1] The noble and virtuous lady Maria Anna Steger, widow, at Straubing.

Seren. et Potent. Maximilianus Emanuel, Elector, ex hereditate *Seren.* Maximil. Philippi, patrui (†1726),	Foundations for eight youths at the seminary, 16,000 fl.
Rev. et Cels. Princeps Joannes Knöbl, Episc. Eichstettens. (†1725),	1000 fl. for annual scholarships.
Rev. D. Georgius Sigism. de Rassler, Canon ad S. Martinum, Rheinfeldiae (†1723),	2730 fl. for the maintenance of a missionary in Scotland.
Rev. Godofred. Langwert de Simmern, Episcop. praecip. nostri Semin. autor (†1741),	500 fl. for the purchase of the ground, 2200 for the building of the seminary, and legacy of 3320 fl.
Rev. Capitulum Eccles. Cathedr. Ratisb. (1682),	150 fl. annually for the seminary; abolished in 1749.
Perill. Domina Eva Elis., nobilissima Baronessa de Lewenstöck, nata de Seldner (†1717),	2000 fl. for one foundation.
Abbot of the Monast. S. B. Viennae,	150 annually for the seminary.
Praenob. D. Georg. Schwaiger, Ecclesiae Joan. Baptistae Canon. in Vilshofen ad Danubium,	for a mission in Scotland, 4000 fl.
Dom. Francisca Noyelle, Gubematrix fil. Comitis de Thierheim (†1724),	legavit 2300 fl. for a mission in Scotland.
Plur. Rev. Ericus Sadler, Kehlkeim Decanus,	legavit Seminaris 500 fl.
Dom. Christoph. Johnstone et Domina Anna Gordon, nata de Cluny (†1754),	for masses 3000 marcas Scot. = £166, 12s.

III. Catalogus Religiosorum in Monasterio S. Jacobi Scotorum Ratisbonae ab anno 1597 et deinceps professorum sub Revcrendissimo Domino D. Placido Flaminio confectus.[1]

1597, July	13.	F. Adamus *Macallus,* Edinburgensis.
1605, May	31.	„ Bened. *Alges,* Plascetensis.
1606, Aug.	15.	„ Hugo *Wallasius,* Dioc. Glascu. postea Abbas Erf.
1626, Dec.	8.	„ G. *Wedderburnus,* Dioc. Aberd.
1638, Nov.	13.	„ M. *Camerarius,* Dioc. Aberd. postea Abbas Erf. deinde Ratisb.
1650, May	15.	„ Bened. *Reith,* Aberd. † in monast. Herbipol. 1684.
1650, Sept.	18.	„ Erh. *Alexander,* Dioc. Aberd.
1655, May	6.	„ Nin. *Jhonstone,* Dioc. Aberd.
1641, March	21.	„ An. *Grajus,* de Deidon. Dioc. Brechin, † in Polonia 1965.
1663, April	15.	„ Ath. *Camerarius,* Edinb. † in Italia.

---

[1] From the original MS. in Fort Augustus.

1663, April 15.	F. Ephr. *Reid*, ex oppido Tania, Dioc. Rossens. † 1712.
1667, Feb. 2.	,, Fiacr. *Colinsonus*, Aberd. † 1686.
1667, ,, ,,	,, Hyac. *Gordon*, Dioc. Aberd. † excasu 1674.
1669, Nov. 21.	,, Plac. *Fleming*, de Capella S. Oswaldi (Kirkoswald (Ayr), Dioc. Glascu. factus sacerdos 1671, electus in Abbatem 1672. Natus 1642, Oct. 15. † 8th Jan. 1720.
1671, Oct. 18.	,, Andr. *Cooke*, de civ. et dioc. Aberd. † 1721.
1674, July 29.	,, Ehrh. *Dunbar*, de civ. et dioc. Argillensi.
1681, March 1.	,, Joan. *Dunbar*, ex opp. Neribus, dioc. Argillensi.
1682, Jan. 1.	,, Jac. *Brusius*, de civ. Clackmannan.
1682, ,, ,,	,, Jos. *Falconer*, de civ. et dioc. Edinb. † 1732.
1682, March 25.	,, *August. Gordon*, fil. Dom. Alex. Gordon in Kinquidy, Dioc. Aberd. † 1702.
1684, ,, ,,	,, *Gregor. Crighton*, de Auchingowell, Dioc. Aberd. Prior Erfurtensis. † 1748.
1687, ,, 21.	,, *Hier. Pantoune*, de civ. et dioc. Aberd. Obiit. 1719. Erfurti, S. Theol. Doctor, Prof. Publ. et Universitatis Rector Magn.
1689, Feb. 2.	,, *Columba Maclenanus*, de Stornovia, Dioc. Sod.
1691, ,, ,,	,, *Bern. Baillaeus*, de prov. Sterling, electus in abbatem. † 1743.
1692, Aug. 1.	,, *Maurus Stuart*, de Ainia, Dioc. Aberd. Abbas. † 1720. Professor in Prag, 1697.
1694, June 24.	,, *Mac. Finny*, ex Buchan.
1698, May 1.	,, *Jac.Brown*,alias Constable,Eastfortunensis. †1720.
1704, Feb. 25.	,, *Aug. Morison*, de civ. et. dioc. Aberd. † 1734.
1708, ,, ,,	,, *Ambr. Ross*, ex prov. Ross. † 1714.
1708, ,, ,,	,, *Mar. Brockie*, de civ. Edinb. Philosophiam docuit Erfurti. Dr Theol. † 1739.
1709, Nov. 30.	,, *Bonif. Leslie*, fil. Alex. Leslie de Pitcapple, Prof. ord. Erfurti. 1743 Prior Mon. Erfurt.
1709, ,, ,,	,, *Kil. Grant*, Strathpegensis, fil. Domini in Glenbrunn, docuit Phil. Erfurti.
1709, ,, ,,	,, *Plac. Hamilton*, fil. Domini in Boghead.
1720, Nov. 1.	,, *Erb. Grant*, Strathdounensis, fil. Dom. in Tambreck, Prof. Publ. in Univers. Erfurt. Missionarius in toto ducatu et aula Weimarensi ex decreto Ser. Ducis Ernesti Augusti anno 1733.
1721, ,, ,,	,, *Columb. Grant*, Strathd. fil. Domini in Ruven.
1724, Oct. 5.	,, *Maurus Grant*, ,, ,, ,, in Auchlichny.
1726, Sept. 26.	,, *Anton Stuart*, fil. Dom. in Lismurden.
1726, ,, ,,	,, *Bern. Stuart*, ,, ,, ,, Boggs.[1]
1726, ,, ,,	,, *Andr. Parkins*, fil. Isaac Parkins, ex Anglia et Annæ Wauchopia fil. Domini in Netherby, prope Edinb. † 1728.

---

[1] About him see above.

1726, Sept.   29   F. *Gallus Leith*, fil. Dom. Alex. Leith in Collithy.
                      1756 electus in abbatem.
1731,   ,, *Wilib Macdonel*, novitium induit.
1732, Feb.   24.   ,, *Andr. Gordon*, docuit Phil. Erfurte, 1737.
1734,   ,, *Jos. Rolland.*
1736, Sept.   8.   ,, *Aug. Duncan.*
1739, Oct.   4.   ,, *Joach. Gray*, natus in Fochaber, 1715.
1739, ,,   ,,   ,, *Ans. Gordon*, fil. Wilhel. de Minmor.
1742,   ,, *Joann Menzies.*
1742, Sept.   24.   ,, *Ildephonsus Kennedy.*

IV. Catalogus eorum omnium adolescentium qui ab anno MDCCXIII
advenerunt et suscepti fuere in nostrum Seminarium (Ratisbon.)

1713.

Joannes Cruickshanke, Doct. Med.
Will. Grant, major, degit in Scotiam uxoratus.
Robt. Grant, Prof. Relig.
Will Gordon, abiit in Italiam.
Will. Grant, minor, Prof. Relig.
Walter Abercromby, In Scotia Navarchia.
Joannes Leslie, Prof. Relig.
Robt. Grant, minor,   ,,
Jac. Hamilton, Abbas Herbipol.
Joann Stuart, degit in Scot. uxoratus.
Jac. Masson, abivit in Angliam.

1718.

Ludov. Grant (Strathdown), Rel. Prof.
Alex. Gordon, in Scot. maritus.
Joann. Abernethy, ad parentes rediit.
Jac. Stuart, Relig. Prof.
Georg. Lieth, Cisterciensis in Waldsassen.
Robt. Leith (Gallus), Rel. Prof.
Alex. Grant,   ,,
Alex. Stuart,   ,,
Dom. Patr. de Letterfury, qui logicam Ratisbonæ unum annum et jura civilia 2 annos Erfurti absolvit.   Vixit suis sumptibus.

1719.

Robt. Gordon.
Alex. Gordon (Dorleathers), redivit ad suos.

Joann. Henderson, Relig. Prof.
Patr. Stuart, studiis juridicis operam dedit uxorem duxit filiam Dom. de Tunberg, 1733.
Columb. Macgregor, sac. secul.
Alex. Abernethy, redivit ad suos.
Carol. Stuart, redivit in Scotiam.
Hugo Auchinleck, Prof. Rel.

1723 duo juvenes.

1731 6   ,,
1735.
Guil. Menzies, ⎫ filii Dom. de Pit-
David   ,,   ⎬ foddels, omnes
Alex.   ,,   ⎭ revocati 1738.
Jacob. Menzies, jun. frater venit
1738.
Cosm. Falconer.
Geo. Crichton.
Jas. Ravenscroft.
Thos. Kennedy, Prof. Rel.
Robt. Grant.
Joann. Macdonel.

1739.

Alex. Grant.
Alex. Gordon de Licheston.
Carolus, Alexandri pictoris fil. Edinb.
Arthur Gordon, fil. nob. Dom. Beldony.
Donaldus Macintosh, fil. patris montani (?).

1747.

Joannes Stuart, ⎫ fraters.
Jacobus   ,,   ⎭

Joannes Farquerson.
Petrus Weingardin (?).

1748.

Joannes Grant de Blair-findy, } reversi sunt.
Alex. Forsyth
Jo. Anderson de Teinet.
Car. Gordon de Beldorny.
C. Arbuthnot, Prof. Rel.

1756.

Charles Drummond, ex fam. ducum de Perth.
J. Macdonel.
Car. Fraser.
Jac. Carmichael.
Joa.   „

1764.

Jac. Hamilton, Prof. Rel.
Alex.   „   „
Alex. Macdonel.
Car.   „
Joa. Grant.
J. Duguid.

1772.

Alex. Young.
Jac. Moir.
Alex. Horn, Prof. Rel.
Car. Roy.
Dav. Drummond, Prof. Rel.
Will. Rolland.
Jac. Robertson, Prof. Rel. † 1820.

1775.

Ths. Graham, Prof. Rel.

1779.

Henry Clint.
Car. Graham.
Jac. Horn, natus 1765 at Montrose, † 1833

1784.

Petrus Sharp de Mertlach.
Ths. Moir.

1788.

Ernest Leslie } filii Dom. J. Leslie
John Leslie } de Balquhain.
Alex. Reid, in seminario mortuus.
John Deasson, Prof. Rel.

1791-2.

Robt. Macpherson.
Angus Macdonald.
Arch. Maciver, Prof. Rel., † Dean of the Cathedral at Ratisbon.

1800.

Lud. Reid.
Jac. Cruikshanks, † in Germany.
Car. Fraser.
Alex. „

1802.

Ths. Carmichael.

1817.

Jas. Macnaughton, † 1862 in America.
John Lamont, natus 1805, abiit Monachium. Observator Observatorii Regii, Prof. Astron. Munich.
Jas. Reid, reversus est in patriam.

1830.

Jac. Russel.
Alex. Scott.
Mark Diamond, Prof. Rel.
Jac. Bennet,   „
Joa. Macdonald,   „
Angus „   „

1838.

Rob. Cameron, rev. in patr. 1844 ob infirmam valet.
Joa. Stuart, missionary.
Will. „   rediit 1845.
Guil. Robertson, Prof. Rel.
Joa. Garden, red.
Guil. Hepburn, red.
Hugo Macswain, Passionist in England (1855).
Allan Macdonald, † 1840 hic.
Alex. Reid, mission. ord. red. in Scotiam (1844).

1841.

Alex. Gordon, de Upper Clachan (Enzie) rediit 1844.
Alex. Macrae, (Strathglass) rediit 1845.

Arch. Macnavish (Moydart), rediit 1845.

Col. Macdonnel, apud Inch, rediit 1845.

Dav. Macdonald (Fort William), Rel. Prof.

1845.

G. Jos. Mitchell, Aberdon. rediit 1848.

John Wiseman (Buckie), † Leith 1875.

Joa. Shaw (Gollachie), red. 1848.

Jac. Davidson,   ,,   ,,

,, Duncan,   ,,   ,,

,, Kelman (Portsoy), ,,   ,,

1852.

Joa. Miller, red. ob inf. valet.

Alex. Gall, sent home.

,, Bennet (Blairs), Rel. Prof. † 1865.

Jac. Shaw (Portsoy), red.

Joa. ,, (Buckie), Rel. Prof.

John Macdonald (Glasgow), red. 1855.

Geo. Wilson (Aberd.), Rel. Prof.

Geo. Davidson (Letterfurie), Rel. Prof.

John Macgowan (Glasgow), sent off 1855.

Joa. Carlin (Glasgow), ord. priest.

Jos. Connaghan (Glasgow), ord. priest, † 1877.

Sam. Docherty (Glasgow), † San Franciso.

Joa. Hardy (Glasgow), sent home "ob inf. val."

1855.

Joa. Macinnes (Linwood), Rel. Prof.

D. MacColl (Fort William), Rel. Prof.

D. Macintosh, Rel. Prof.

V. Letter of Queen Mary to the Emperor Rudolf II (1577).

After complaining of her sad fate the Queen continues : . . . "Sunt nonnulla monasteria in Germania ex lege et conditione in favorem Scotorum olim erecta ut in iis Scoti homines educarentur, Scotique itidem praeficerentur. Jus ipsum a nostratibus longissima possessione retentum est ab aliis proxime propter Scotorum absentiam usurpatum. Hinc a Sacra Caes. Maj. Vestra vehementer peto, ut idem jus velit ipsis Scotis tueri, et in monasteria quae sub imperio et ditione sua vacaverint, jubeat illos recipi qui pro Religione Catholica et pro fide erga me exilium aliaque omnimodo patiuntur. Imprimis illi commendo Ninianum Winzetum, Theologiae Doctorem, Confessorem meum cui non ita pridem de Ratisp. Monasterio legitime provisum est."

(State Papers, Scotland, Mary, Queen of Scots, xi. 8. King Hewison, N. Winzete's *Certane Tractates*, I. cix. f.)

VI. Diploma Rudolfi II Imperatoris in favorem Scotorum.

. . . "Cum Serenissima Princeps Domina Maria, Regina Scotorum, Consanguinea et soror nostra carissima, Oratorem suum, reverendum et devotum Joannem Leslaeum, Episcopum Rossensem, certis de rebus ad nos destinavit, inter alia Serenitatis

Suae nomine exposuit, ejusdem praedecessores, imprimis, vero
Guilielmus,[1] quondam Achaii Regis Scotiae fratrem, post multa
a se praeclare gesta, pio quodam zelo in pluribus Germaniae
locis Monasteria Ordinis S. B. solis Scotis erexisse eademque
praediis et agris opimis dotasse simulque sanxisse, ne ullus alius
nisi Scotus monachus aut Coenobiarch : ibidem admitteretur.
Secutum inde esse, ut et plerique Germaniae Principes ejusdem
Ordinis monasteria erexerint, solis Scotis conferenda.   Id
quod multa a Scotis passim per Germaniam continua successione
possessa, vel saltem Scotorum adhuc nomine appellata monasteria
abunde testentur.

Verum temporis iniquitate factum esse ut pium hoc institutum
paulatim neglectum ac complura hujusmodi monasteria aliis
quam Scotis commissa fuerint.   Cum autem hoc tempore multi
ex Scotia se offerant, qui tum more, probitate vitaeque integritate tum singulari eruditione praediti parati sint fundatorum piam
voluntatem sustinere omniaque praestare, quae ad ritus et mores
Ecclesiasticos componendos ac juventutis institutionem pertinent,
idcirco praescriptus Episcopus Rossensis tam dictae Serenissimae
Reginae quam Nationis Scoticae nomine a Nobis obnixe petit,
ut privilegiorum a longo tempore Scotis in Germania quaesitorum
conservationi nostro favore et auctoritate benigne consulere
dignaremur.   Cui tam piae petitioni cum deesse non potuerimus,
Dilectiones et Devotiones vestras . . . benigne . . hortamur
ut erga praescriptum Episcopum Ross. hac de re cum Dilec-
tionibus . . . acturum, tam benevolos vos exhibere velitis, ut
in iis, quae ad hujusmodi privilegia tuenda ac dictos Scotos in
pristinam possessionem restituendos spectant, nostram hanc
communicationem sibi haud parum profuisse intelligat, in quo
Dilect. et Devot. nobis rem gratam facturi estis . . . Datum in
arce nostra Reg. Pragae.[2]

VII. Commendatio Niniani Guilielmi, Ducis Bavariae ad Rudolphum pro recuperatione Monasterii Viennensis.

(Transl.) Your Imp. Maj. will doubtlessly remember how for
some time past, the worthy, much respected and very reverend
Abbot of S. James' Monastery at Ratisbon is trying most
anxiously, not only to recover the Scottish Monastery at Vienna
for his nation but also to fill it with good and suitable monks,
striving to redress any disorder that may have been prevalent in

[1] According to Major's chronicle (l. 2 cap. 13), William, brother
of King Achaius, built fifteen monasteries for the Scottish Benedictines
on the Continent, two of them in Cologne.

[2] Reich's Archiv at Munich, Baillie MSS. Compare K. Hewison,
l.c., I. cxi., II. 17 f.

it of late and to restore it to its old dignity; Your Imp. Maj. will also be aware that His Holiness the Pope as well as the Queen of Scotland have written on his behalf and taken the Abbot under their protection.   Y. M. will have an opportunity to grant the humble request and prayer of the foresaid Abbot; to further which I did not hesitate most submissively to pray Your I. M. to listen to him graciously and to vouchsafe, what in the end would result in the satisfaction of Y. M. and in the honour and profit of the monastery. For I have no doubt, he, the Abbot, would make great efforts and improvements in the service, the schools and other matters pertaining to the monastery, just as he did in a short time in the poor deserted monastery at Ratisbon, where he not only restored the daily religious services, but started schools out of which an important Catholic Seminary may yet grow up. Y. I. M. will also by doing so earn the gratitude of the whole Scottish Nation, the pious efforts of which on behalf of our Holy Faith have benefited our Empire so much in ancient times; and You will not be deterred by anything unjust and punishable that may have happened at Vienna in times of a general decay of ecclesiastical institutions, and which furthermore may be owing more to other nations than to the Scots. Y. I. M. has moreover all the more cause to grant the Abbot's request, as he has now been installed at Ratisbon by Imperial rescript, a monastery, which is the most renowned of all, and the mother of all Scottish Monasteries in Germany, including that at Vienna, and has so well improved it even with scanty means. I recommend the above-mentioned Abbot and myself most humbly and obediently to Y. I. Majesty's grace and good-will.

Given in my town of Munich, July 23rd, 1583.

WILLIAM, Duke of Bavaria.[1]

VIII. LIST OF SCOTTISH PUPILS AT THE JESUIT-SEMINARY OF BRAUNSBERG (Silesia) (1579-1642).[2]

Ingellus Gellonius (1579), dismissed because unfit for the clerical profession.
David Young (1580), sent home in 1583.
Andr. Jack (1582), sent to Vienna to continue his studies.

---

[1] Reich's Archiv, Munich. Cp. Hewison, l.c. II. xxiii. f. The original is difficult to decipher and not always quite clear.

[2] The list is printed as it was sent to the author by the Rev. the Regens of the Seminary at Braunsberg. Names undoubtedly Scottish have been distinguished by bolder type; the others, owing to the difficulty of deciphering, present a somewhat "unscottish" appearance.

Jonnnes Tamson (1582), died at Braunsberg in 1588.

David Lobeck (1582), returned home; juvenis petulantissimus.

Joannes Varrus (Karr?) 1584, sent to Olmütz to continue his studies.

Jacobus Anordt (?) 1585,[1] returned to his people in Scotland.

Petrus Grinnaeus (Green?), 1586, became a Jesuit and taught philosophy at Graz.

Archib. Anderlonius (1587), became a Jesuit.

David Beaton (1596), was sent "in Germaniam."

Joannes Buttery (1596), sent to Scotland in 1600, a good Catholic.

Patricius Abercrombaeus (1596), † 1611.

Wilhelmus Duglasius (1596), sent to Vilna to continue his studies, but at his own expense, "quia non fuit capax disciplinae."

Jacobus Lindsay (1596), † 1624 in Scotland as Jesuit.

Thomas Abircrombaeus (1599), went to Vilna to continue his studies.

David Kinard (1599), entered the Order.

M. Georgius (1600), educated in Denmark, became a convert, "nunc Brunsbergae exercet medicinam."

Georgius Sessaeus (Leslaeus?), 1606, † 1608.

Patricius Stichelius (1607),[2] entered the Order.

Wilhelmus Duglasius (1607), left the school and became a soldier.

Jacobus Leslaeus (1608), entered the Order at Rome, leading a blameless life.

David Setonius (1609), Syntaxista.

Jacobus Setonius ,, ,,

Thomas Duffaeus (1610), went to Pelplin,[3] but was dismissed "ob ineptitudinem."

Wilh. Abircrombaeus (1610), Rhetor. "Missus est in patriam ubi fructificavit inter catholicos."

Archib. Hegeck (Haig?), 1613, went away to enter another Order.

Alex. Ingram (1613), went away on account of illness and disobedience.

Joannes Leslaeus (1613), sent to Rome to continue his studies.

Andr. Leslaeus (1613), went to Rome ,, ,, ,, ,, and afterwards settled in Scotland as priest.

Rob. Gareochus (?) (1617),[4] went to Rome.

Thos. Camerarius (1619), a convert, sent to Rome and Scotland.

Patr. Kinart (1633), a convert; dismissed.

Alex. Minnesius (Menzies), 1641, † 1671 whilst attending the plague-stricken at Braunsberg.

Wilhelmus Minnesius (1641), Fugit.

Alexander Hajus (Hay) 1642, returned home ill.

Joannes Hajus (1642), Fugit.

---

[1] Probably Arnott. [2] Probably Stitchel.

[3] Pelplin was a monastery not far from Danzig.

[4] Probably Garioch, a district in Aberdeenshire, and a family name.

IX. Inscription on the Tombstone of Ninian Winzet.[1]
D. O. M.[2]

Ninianus Winzetus Sacro Sanctae Theologiae Doctor, vir pius
et zelosus Monasticam hic disciplinam restauravit, multaque
verbo, scripto et vitae exemplo ad aedificationem proximorum
praestitit, qui postquam huic Monasterio sexdecim annos summa
cum laude praefuisset ac successorem canonice et legitime sibi
prospexisset, tandem XXI Septembris anno Christi mill. quin-
gent. nonag. sec. aetatis vero suae septag. quarto pie et placide
obdormivit in Domino.

X. Abbot Benedictus Arbuthnot.

The tombstone of Arbuthnot, which has been removed from
the churchyard to the cloisters of the formerly Scottish Monastery of St James at Ratisbon, shows the following inscription:

In pace Christi
Sepultus heic quiescit
Ilustriss. ac Reverendiss. Dominus
Benedictus Arbuthnot,
Monasterii ad S. Jacobum Scotorum
Ratisbonae Ordinis S. Benedicti Abbas.
Natus est 5. Martii 1737.
Professus 21 Nov. 1756.
Sacerdos 14 Febr. 1761.
Abbas electus 4 Junii 1776.
Mortuus 19 Aprilis 1820.
R. I. P.
Memoriae
Viri omnibus summe venerandi,
Suis desideratissimi
Cenotaphium
in proximo S. Jacobi templo erectum
extat.

The Cenotaph mentioned above consists of a red marble-slab
on the inner wall of the church, south side. It has the following inscription:

✝

Siste viator gradum. Memoriam piam sibi merito
exposcit illustris Vir ac Revmus D.
Benedictus Arbuthnot
hujus Monasterii Abbas.

---

[1] In the Church of St James at Ratisbon. [2] Datur omnibus mori (?).

Natus fuit in Scotia die 5. mens. Martii anno MDCCXXXVII in bono paterno Rora comitatus Aberdonens; puer 11 annor. Ratisbonam venit ibique in hujus Monasterii seminario studiis humanior. absolutus vota solemnia emisit S. Benedicti regulam professus die 21 Nov. anno MDCCLVI, presbyter die 14 Febr. anno MDCCLXI ordinatus susceptam Seminarii directionem non minore diligentia ac utilitate gessit, simulque confratres atque exteros Philosophiam et Mathesin docuit per 16 fere annos, donec die 4 Junii MDCCLXXVI Abbas eligeretur. Quo in munere maxime rerum gerendar. dexteritate, miraque in tantis temporum periculis prudentia omnium, quos subditos aut superiores habuit, animos in Sui venerationem et amorem attraxit, sincera pietate, vitae integritate, morum candore, modestia et affabilitate devinctos tenuit, multimoda doctrina scriptis etiam in vulgus editis probata nominis celebritatem, quam ipse nunquam quaesivit, ab aliis meritus dignusque habitus, quem Academiae Scient. Socium eligerent. Tandem coelo maturus venerandus Senex ex hac mortali vita discessit die 19 mens. April anno MDCCCXX. sepultus in communi cemeterio extra portam S. Jacobi.

Grati animi indicem et sanctae memoriae testem isthunc lapidem posuerunt fratres desolati.[1]

XI. LIST OF ABBOTS OF THE SCOTTISH MONASTERY AT ERFURT.

1. Erhardus, at the time of Marianus, the founder.
2. Henricus I.
3. Henricus II (about 1285).
4. Wilhelmus I.
5. Philippus.
6. Nicolaus I.
7. Patricius.
8. Gelasius (about 1390).
9. Rupertus (1405-1433).
10. Thadaeus I (1433-1438).
11. Dernicius.
12. Thadaeus II (about 1450).
13. Ricardus (1458-1464).
14. Matthaeus.
15. Cornelius (1479).
16. Donatus (resigned 1485).
17. Edmundus (1485-1494).
18. Nicolaus II (1494).
19. Alanus.
20. Joannes I, fled 1507.
21. Benedictus.
22. David (about 1520).
23. Jacobus.
24. Andreas Hunter.
25. Guilielmus.
26. Johannes II Hamilton.
27. Richardus II Irwinus (until 1595).
28. Joannes Walkerus (1595-1603), from Dysart.
29. Jacobus II Winzetus.
30. Wilhelmus III Ogilvius (1613-1617).
31. Hugo Wallasius (1617-1634).
32. Alex. Baillie (1634-1646).
33. Mac. Camerarius (1646-1655).
34. Plac. Fleming (1672), Prior.
35. Hier. Panthon (1711-1719).
36. Maurus Stuart (1720).
37. Bern. Baillie.
38. Mar. Brockie, Prior 1727.
39. Greg. Crichton, Prior.
40. Bonif. Leslie, Prior.

[1] The Abbot's remains were transferred to the cloister in 1890.

XII. List of Abbots of the Scottish Monastery at Würzburg.

1. Macharius (1139-1153).[1]
2. Christian (1153-1179).[2]
3. Eugenius (†1197).
4. Gregorius (abt. 1206).
5. Matthaeus (†1215).
6. Teclanus (?) (1215-1217).
7. Elias (1217-1223).
8. Colestinus (1223-1234).
9. Gerhardus (†1242).
10. Johannes (1242-1253).
11. Johannes II (†1274).
12. Mauritius (1274-1298).
13. Joel (†1306).
14. Elias II (1318).
15. Johannes III (†1335).
16. Michaeus (1335-1341).
17. Rynaldus (about 1342).
18. Philippus I (†1361).
19. Donaldus (†1385)?
20. Henricus (about 1379).
21. Mauritius II (about 1385).
22. Timotheus (†1399).
23. Ymarus (about 1409)
24. Rutgerus (†1417).
25. Thomas I (1417-1437).
(26. Laurentius).[3]
27. Roricus (†1447).
28. Alanus (†1455).
29. Mauritius III (†1461).[4]
30. Johannes IV (†1463).
31. Otto (1463-65).
32. Thadaeus (1465-1474).

33. David (1474-1483).
34. Thomas (1483-1494).
35. Edmundus (†1497).
36. Philippus II (†1497).
37. Kilian (1504-1506). ⎫
38. Trithemius (1506-1516). ⎪
39. Matthias (†1535). ⎪
40. Erhardus Jani (†1542). ⎬ German Abbots.
41. Michael Stephan ⎪
    (†1547). ⎪
42. Reinhardus (1595). ⎭
43. Franc. Hamilton (1602-1609).
44. Guil. Ogilvie (1615-1635).
45. Robertus Forbes (1635-1637).
46. Joannes Audomarus Asloan (1638-1661).
47. Maurus Dixon (1661-1679).
48. Bernhard Maxwell (1679-1685).
49. Marianus Irvin (1685-1688).
50. Ambrosuis Cook (1689-1703), deposed.
51. Augustinus Bruce (1713-1716).
52. Maurus II Strachan (1716-1737).
53. Aug. Duffus de Fochaber (1737-1753).
54. Placidus Hamilton (1756-1786).

XIII. List of Monks at the Scottish Monastery at Würzburg.

(From about 1500-1803).

Johannes Sancton, ⎫
Johannes Macallen, ⎬ 1497.
Antonius de Hardwick, 1529.

Franciscus Hamilton, ⎫
Johannes Stuart, ⎬ 1595.
Johannes Ultonus, ⎭

---

[1] His life has been written by Ludewig and Gropp.
[2] According to Trithemius, the chronicler.
[3] There is some doubt as to Laurentius. He is called "Prelate" in a MS.
[4] Also Abbot of Ratisbon (Wieland, l.c., p. 122).

Johannes Bogg, ⎫ 1598.
Guilelmus Oginius, ⎭

Hugo,
Robertus,
Adamus,
William and Thomas, ⎬ 1615.
   (novitii),
Gabriel Wallasius,

Alex. Baillie,
Audomarus Asloan, ⎬ 1616.
Jakobus Brun,
Thos. Duffus,

Wiescemuss (?), 1618.
Silvanus Maine, 1622.
Twelve Monks in 1625.

Andreas Urquhart,
Alex. Armorgh,
Rich. Todens (Todeus),
Hugo Wallace, ⎬ 1630-35.
Andr. Maclen,
Will. Gordon,
Ben. Asloan,
Ed. Maxwell,

Thomas,
Rob. Forbes, ⎬ 1635.
Will. Maxwell,

And. Jachaeus (Jack), 1637.
Bonif. Strachan de Monte rosarum, 1659.

Maurus Dixon, ⎫ 1660.
Plac. Baillie, ⎭

Placid. Schaffdoe (English),
Ans. Dövechett („), ⎬ 1661.
Will. Dunn,

Plac. Kietus (Keith), 1662.

Alanus Crisholm
   (Chisholm), ⎬ 1665.
Bern. Maxwell,

Mich. Mackintosh,
Ninian Graham, ⎬ 1674.
Columb. Fraser,

Ninianus Ghiainus (?),[1] ⎫ 1679.
Jacob. Blair, ⎭

Aug. Bruce,
John Alexander from
   Aberdeen, an excellent
   painter,
Kilian Herris,
Greg. Seaton,
Mar. Irwin, ⎬ 1679.
Macar. Brown,
Bonif. Mackie,
Isid. Ogilvie,
Christ. Aberkrombie,
Plac. Blair,
Bern. Douglas,

Maur. Strachan, Buchan, ⎫ 1689.
Plac. Crichton, ⎭

Bened. Hay, 1701.

Gregor Cheyn, Marrensis,
Ansel Gordon, ⎬ 1713.
Kil. Macgregor, Bremar,
Mac. Somerville,

Ben. Callender, Edinb. ⎫ 1716.
Georg. Duffus, ⎭

Mar. Gordon, Banff, 1719.
Aug. Duffus de Fochaber, 1727.

Bonif. Burnet of Banchory, ⎫ 1733.
Plac. Strand de Moray, ⎭

Bern. Grant de Desky, 1737.
Ign. Gropp, 1741.
Maur. Stuart de Boggs, 1744.
Alex. Grant, 1744.
Ant. Pfirsching (a German), 1744.

Willibaldus, ⎫ 1752.
Jac. Stuart, ⎭

Bened. Mackenzie,[2] 1755.
Bern. Wilson de Edinb., 1755.

Plac. Hamilton,
Matt. Roth.
Bern. Stuart, Glamis, ⎬ 1756.
Mak. Cutts,
*Kil. Pepper, Crieff,

Thad. Roy, de Kenneth-
   mont, ⎬ 1758.
*Col. Macgowen, Balquhain,

---

[1] From Gigha, the island in Argyleshire?
[2] Comes de Sexfort = Seaforth. The title was forfeited in 1715 and not restored till 1771.

Ottmar (a German), 1760.
*Gallus Carmichael, Prior, 1785.
*Plac. Geddes, Edinb., ⎫ 1785.
*Andr. Geddes, Cairnfield, ⎭

*Maur. Macdonald, Hedrides, ⎫
*Joh. B. Anderson, ⎬ 1791.
*Ben. Ingram de Ruth (Rothes), 1791. ⎭

Those marked with an asterisk were in the Monastery in 1803, the year of its secularisation. Wieland, pp. 103-117.

XIV. Extract from the "Syllabus Benefactorum" (Würzburg).[1]

1167. *Henry of Gougrichsheim, Knight*, leaves all his property in the said village to the Monastery of the Scots. The monks on their part had to read three masses for him during the week. In the course of time Henry transferred *his two serfs or bondmen* Adalbert and his brother Burkard as well as their sister Jutta for services in the Church.

1168. *Gottfried v. Urhusen* and his wife Lucardis hand over their bondman Henry to the Scottish Monastery, who has to pay three pence annually on St James' day.

1174. *Hartroh and his son Berthold*, etc., give to the Monastery two bondmen, Gotefried and Hartmann, who are to pay 3 pence annually on St James' day, *in return for their freedom.*

1176. *Adalbard, a citizen of Würzburg*, presents 3 parts of his estate and 9 acres of vineyard to the monastery, provided his younger son Richard died childless. He also gives a stone house on the Maine, a quarter of wheat or 30 loaves annually, as well as half a tun of wine and two candles on Michaelmas-day to the Scots.

1186. *Heinrich von Altorf* and his spouse Hiltegardis liberate their bondman and all his goods on condition, that all his present and future property shall be owned by the Monastery after his death.

1216. *Gerung, a rich office-bearer* under Bishop Otto, leaves a House on the Maine to the Scottish Church for the maintenance of two lights.

1218. *Conrad of Wolfgiseshusen* transfers the ownership of his bondman Sifrid to the Monastery, in such wise as to liberate him against the annual payment of 3 pounds of wax or its value.

1287. *Heinrich Waldeber, Knight*, makes over to the Monastery his house rentable at 6 shillings annually and the orchard.

1474. *Hans Konrad of Winterhausen* and his wife, who under

[1] Wieland, *l.c.*

Abbot Thadaeus had bought for 100 gulden the third tub of grapes of 4 acres of vineyard, make this over to Abbot David and his monastery on condition that after their death a mass be said or two "as God shall direct them."

1606. *R. D. Nicolaus Greiff* legavit monasterio 400 fl. pro cujus anima singulis 4 temporibus unum sacrum celebrare tenemur cum Vigiliis defunctorum.

1636. *Antonius a Wildberg*, Cath. Eccl. Herbip. Can. legavit 5 plaustra vini et 100 flor. et 20 Malderas frumenti pro anniversario.

1721. *Ivan. Ignat. Kopp*, fusor celeberrimus, qui in vita multa bona ficit monasterio in testamento 100 flor. pro anniversario reliquit nec non 70 pond. metalli pro camp. parva ut iterum fundetur.[1]

XV. Scottish names in the Album of the University of Wittenberg (1519-1544).

Joannes Nutrison, Oct. 18, 1519.
Nicolaus Botwynni, Scotus, 1524.
D. Alexander Alesius, Scot. Edinb. Mag. Sti. Andrae, 7 Oct. 1533.
Joannes Scotus, 1539.
D. Joannes Maccabaeus, Scotus, Nov. 1540.
Gualt. Spalatinus, Scotus, 1544.
Vilhelm. Ramusius, Scotus. Artuim mag. Sti. Andr., Sept 1544.
Jacobus Balfurius, Scotus, Sept. 1544.

XVI. Catalogus Scholae Marpurgensis anno Domini MCCCCCXXVII.

DEO OPTIM. MAX. AUSPICE.

Illustrissimus simul et pietissimus princeps Philippus, Landgravius Hessiae, etc., unicus et pietatis et literarum vindex, quum quasque liberales disciplinas, partim sophistarum invidia, partim temporis difficultate, ruinam haud reparabilem minari videret, ad instaurandas eas animum appulit, et doctissimos quosque sub anno Christianae salutis MDXXVII, liberalibus stipendiis invitatos, Marpurgum vocatatque in Neacademia illa sua Trilingui recens instituta sacras literas, jus civile, utramque medicinam,

---

[1] The Monastery also derived the emoluments of a canonry at the Cathedral. They consisted in a daily supply of bread and wine, meat on Martin's day, fish on Ash-Wednesday, 2 pounds of mustard, about 14 quarters of grain, and a share of tithes. Besides this it received rent in kind from 20 villages (1560).

U

tres linguas atque adeo omnes bonas literas sinceritèr doceri jubet.

Joannes Ferrarius Montanus, juris civilis Professor et judicii Hessiae, quod curiale vocant, consiliarius, quum primum Academiae apud Marpurgum per Philippum principem recens institutae magistratum III. Kal. Junias MDXXVII iniisset, hos uti ordine scribuntur, in ejus Album, Deo Opt. Max. auspice retulit.

Then follow the names of the Professors : Lambert, Schnepf, Buschius, etc., and of the students. Amongst them are mentioned

37. Patricius Hamilton, a Lithgov. Scotus. Mag. Parisiensis.
38. Joannes Hamilton, Scotus.
39. Gilbertus Winram, Edinburgens.

In 1533 :   Petrus Banckbeus (Begbie ?), Scotus.
In 1537 :   Joan. Crom, Scotensis.[1]

XVII. Wedderburn and the German Hymns.

For the sake of comparison we subjoin the following specimens of Wedderburn's translations together with their originals :

Weisse.

1. Nun lasst uns den Leib begraben ;
Daran wir keinen Zweifel haben,
Er wird am jüngsten Tag aufstehn
Und unverweslich herfürgehn.

2. Erd ist er und von der Erden,
Wird auch zur Erd wieder werden,
Und von der Erd wieder aufstehn
Wener Gottes Posaun wird angehn.

Luther.

1. Vom Himmel hoch da Komm ich her,
Und bring euch neu und gute mähr ;
Der guten Mähr bring ich so viel ;
Davon ich singen und sagen will.

2. Euch ist ein Kindlein heut' geborn
Von einer Jungfrau auserkonn ;
Ein Kindelein, so zart und fein,
Es soll eur Freud und Wonne sein.

3. Der Sammet und die Seiden dein,
Das ist grob Heu und Windelein,
Darauf du, König, gross und reich
Herprangst als wär's dein Himmel-
reich !

Wedderburn.

1. Our brother lat us put in grave,
And na dout thairof let us have,
Bot he sall ryse on Domisday,
And have immortall lyfe for ay.

2. He is of eird and of eird maid
And maun return to eird through
deide,
Syn ryse sall fra the eird and ground
Quhen that the last trumpet sall
sound.

Wedderburn.

1. I come from heuin to tell
The best nowellis that ever befell,
To zow thir tythingis trew I bring,
And I will of them say and sing.

2. This day, to zow, is borne ane childe
Of Marie meik and Virgin milde,
That blessit bairne bening[2] and
kynde,
Sall zow reioyis[3] baith hart and
mynde.

3. The Sylk and Sandell[4] the[5] to eis,[6]
Are hay and sempill sweilling clais,
Quharint how gloris, greitist King[7]
As though in heuin war in thy
Ring.[8]

[1] Cp. Lorimer, *Life of P. Hamilton*, p. 232.
[2] benign.   [3] gladden.   [4] velvet.   [5] thee.   [6] to ease.
[7] clothes.   [8] kingdom

Nic Decius (abt. 1527).

1. Allein Gott in der Höh sei Ehr
Und Dank für seine Gnade,
Darum dass nun und nimmermehr
Uns rühren kann kein Schade.
Ein Wohlgefalln er an uns hat,
Nun ist gross Fried ohn Unterlass,
All Fehd hat nun ein Ende.

2. Wir loben, preis'n, anbeten Dich,
Für Deine Ehr wir danken,
Dass Du, Gott Vater, ewiglich
Regierst ohn' alles Wanken.
Ganz unermessn ist Deine Macht,
Fort g'schicht, was Dein Will hat
bedacht.
Wohl uns des feinen Herren!

Wedderburn.

1. Only to God on hicht be gloir
And loving be unto his grace,
Quha can condempne vs ony moir
Sen we are now at Goddis peace?
Intill his favour we are taine.[1]
Throw faith in Jesus Christ allaine
Be quhome his wraith sall end and
seace.[2]

2. We wirschip and we love and pryse
Thy Majesty and Magnitude:
That Thou, God Father, onlie wyse
Ringis[3] ower all with fortitude:
Na tung can tell Thy strength nor
mycht,[4]
Thy wordis and thochtis, all are
rycht,
And all Thy warkis just and gude.

XVIII. Melanchthon and Alesius.

Melanchthon to J. Camerarius.   (Jan. 1542?)

"Alesius, the Scot, has left the University of Frankfurt, and, although he did so against my advice, some other position must be found for him." (Corpus Reform. iv. 760.)

Melanchthon to J. Agricola.   (Cal. Feb. 1542.)

". . . as to the Scot [Alesius] I do not think that the University of Leipzig will allow him to renew the controversy. Not only have I exhorted him to give up these quarrels, but I have asked other friends also to restrain him, and they have promised to do so." (Corpus. Reform. iv. 771.)

In another letter to *Camerarius,* dated Nov. 18, 1542, the Reformer expresses a hope, that Alesius will not precipitately print every controversial matter, but restrain his "stings" (aculeos). (Corp. Reform. iv. 893.)

Melanchthon to Alesius.

"I have commissioned this Scot (the bearer) to see you in order both to hear you dispute and to tell of your native country. I expect a letter from you concerning the synod. Maccabaeus, the upright man, praises the learning, the character and piety of this James [the bearer?] (Corp. Reform. iv. 793.)

XIX. Letter of Grotius to his Friend Bernegger[5] at Strassburg.

"What Duraeus plans is difficult, especially at the present time. But other matters no less difficult have had a successful

[1] taken.   [2] cease.   [3] rulest.   [4] might.
[5] Hugo Grotius, the famous Dutch Scholar and Statesman, was born in 1583, died in 1645. Bernegger was Professor of Philology.

issue.   The striving after what is noble, even when it remains without success guarantees the fruit of a joyful conscience. . . .

I do approve of Duraeus' idea to promote the Union of those that are now disunited to the greatest detriment and an ever increasing danger.   But I also assent to what you say, that the malady has not reached the point where medicine could be administered with safety.   May the day appear at last, which after so many wounds inflicted will always appear too late.

> At nobis casso saltem delectamine
> Amare liceat, si potiri non licet."

APPENDIX TO PART IV.

STATESMAN AND SCHOLAR.

I. King Charles II to his Scotch Subjects in Poland.

Fidelibus nostris atque dilectis salutem. Nonnullorum
Vestrum ex Gente Scotica subditorum nostrorum in Regno
Polonico habitantium mercaturamque exercentium relatione
accepta, quomodo tribunus militiae Cochrovius (Cochranius)
mandati nostri obtentu ingentes pecuniae summas a vobis
exigere easque colligendi publicam potestatem a Rege Poloniae
Regio et Honorando Fratre Nostro contendere sustinuerit,
non possumus non sancte affirmare, nihil ipsum ejusmodi a
nobis in mandatis accepisse. Et quod Crafftium spectat, ad
ejus (cujus?) instantiam vos denuo ad tertiam bonorum
vestrorum et mercium partem in usus nostros erogandam
urgeri, fatemur quidem ex Batavis illum a nobis ad Regem
Poloniae expeditum fuisse, neutiquam vero potestate munitum,
a subditis nostris isthoc in regno negotiantibus publica authoritate
quicquam extorquendi. Etenim nobis de fide et observantia
Scotorum subditorum nostrorum, ut domesticorum ita ut
exterorum, ubicunque terrarum fuerint, bene securis, sic uti
haud integrum est nostris in hoc regno subditis, ulla nisi
praevio parlamenti consensu tributa imperari, ita nec exteris
invitis quicquam imponi. Ea propter exemimus et praesentibus
his ipsis exemptam Crafftio volumus omnem potestatem seu
mandati nostri, quod praetexit, authoritate ab ullo unquam
Scotorum in Regno Poloniae aut quovis in loco alio com-
morantium vel minimum exigendi, seu eum in finem a Regibus,
Principibus aut aliis magistratibus impetralem libertatem
exequendi. . .

Data insula nostra Perthana Anno 1650 regni vero nostro
secundo, die mensis Decembris nono.[1]

[1] In spite of all these insurances Lord Croffts is further employed in
diplomatic missions. See Scottish Hist. Soc. Misc. i. 201 f.

II. King Charles II to the City of Danzig.

We are informed by our trusty and well-beloved servant, Lieutenant-Generall Middleton, of the very great affection and esteeme you have shewed to Us in your reception of him, and in the good wishes you have professed to him for our successe against our rebellious subjects, and he hath likewise informed Us, that being disappointed of the present receipte of those moneys which We had hoped would have been payed to him, he should have found himselfe in very great streights, if he had not been supplyed by you with the loane of moneys, for which We render you Our hearty thankes, and doe desire you will respite the repayment of it for some time, and that you will likewise to the end he may discharge some debts he hath contracted in that Citty for Our service, further supply him with the loane of one thousand dollars; all which We doe promise you upon Our Kingly worde to cause justly to be repayed to you; and We doubte not but God will so blesse Us that We shall in a short time be able to expresse the sence We have of your affection by performing those good offices and acts of freindship to you, with which Our predecessors have alwais prosecuted that Citty, for the safety, liberty, and priviledges whereof We shall alwais be very sollicitous. And so We committ you to God's protection, who, We hope, will defend you against your enemyes. Given at Our Court at Bruxelles, etc.

The Towne of Dantzick (1657).[1]

III. Inscription on the Tomb of Erskine.

According to the Manuscript Records of the Librarian of the Cathedral at Bremen, Gerhard Meyer, the coffin of General Erskine bore the following inscription:

F. v. E.[2]

"Der Wohlgeborene Herr Herr Alexander Freyherr von Erskine, der Königl. Majest. zu Schweden Geheimbder Rath, Kriegs- und der Bremischen Etats Praesident, auch Erb-Cammerherr des Herzogthums Bremen, uf Erskeins, Schwinge, Schölisch, Rolfeshagen und Hohen Beringen Erbherr.[3]

Anno 1598 den 31st October gebohren.
1656 ,, 24th Aug. gestorben.

[1] Clarendon MSS. lv. 240. Scottish Hist. Soc. Publ. xxxi. 358 f.

[2] Freiherr von Erskine = Baronet E.

[3] Lord of the Manor. Erskine had evidently received the above-named estates as gifts from the Swedish Sovereign.

Erskine was twice married. His second wife was a widowed lady with the name of von Maltzahn, *née* von Wartensleben. Descendants are said to be still living in or about Bremen.

IV. ARTHUR JONSTON IN HEIDELBERG (1599-1601).

The title of the above named invitation for the public " disputation " is as follows :

Theoremata Physica

De Motu

Quae

D. O. M. A.

In antiquissima et celeberrima

Academia Heidelbergensi

Spectabili Dn. Decano

Theophilo Madero Philo-

los (!) et Medicin. Dr. et Physic.

Professore Ordinario,

Sub praesidio

M. Arthuri Jonstoni, Aberdo-

nensis, Scoti, Collegii Cas-

mirani Regentis

Abrahamus Eccius Geo-

goviensis Silesius

Addiem Augusti

publice in auditorio Philosophorum defendet.

Horis, locoque solitis.

Heidelbergae

Typis Vogelinianis

Anno 1601.

V. CATALOGUE OF THE WRITINGS OF DR JOHN JOHNSTON, THE POLYHISTOR (1603-1675).

Thaumatographia Naturalis, Amsterdam 1632.
Sceleton historiae Universalis, Leyden 1633. Amsterdam 1644.
Naturae constantia, Amsterdam 1634.
Enchiridion ethicum, Leyden 1634. Brieg 1658.
Horae subcisivae, seu rerum toto orbe. . . gestarum idea, Lissa
1639.
Idea universae medicinae practicae, Amsterdam 1644, 1648.
Historiae naturalis libri A. De quadrupedibus. Frankfurt a/m.

B. De piscibus et cetis.	,,	1649.
C. De avibus.	,,	1650.
D. De insectis ; de ser- pentibus et draconibus.	,,	1653.
E. De arboribus.	,,	1662.

De communione veteris ecclesiae syntagma, Amsterdam, 1658.
Polyhistor, seu rerum ab exortu universi ad nostra
       usque tempora. . . gestarum series.   Jenae 1660.
Polyhistor continuatus.   ,, 1667.
Idea hygienes recensita.   ,, 1661.
Notitia regni vegetabilis.   Leipzig 1661.
Notitia regni mineralis.   ,, 1661.
De festis Hebraeorum et Graecorum schediasma, Jenae 1670.
Syntagma universae medicinae practicae.   Breslau 1673.

Johnston's tomb in Polish-Lissa has the following inscription :
"Hic ossa composita Polyhistoris et Medici Summi Johannis
Jonstoni e generosa Scoticae familia oriundi, de Literatura sacra
et profana nonnisi praeclare meriti qui vivit annos LXXII, de-
cessit A. O. R. LXXV, suis et erudito Orbi perenne desiderium
Posteritate admirationem reliquit. Abi, Lector, et Cineribus
bene precare."[1]

VI. Agreement between Hans Kant, the Grandfather of the Philosopher, and Hans Karr, his Brother-in-law. June 4th, 1670.

". . . Whereas the late Richard Kant, father and father-in-law
of the two contracting parties respectively, in consideration of
considerable debts, the payment of which Hans Karr took upon
himself alone, did by a last disposal ordain that his son, the
above-named Hans Kant, should receive as his share of the
public-house at Werdden and all its moveables and immoveables
no more than the sum of 100 Reichsthaler, whilst Karr as the
son-in-law should retain the inn and everything pertaining to it,
and whereas the above-named Hans Kant traversed this, maintaining his right to a son's portion in full ; the contracting
parties for the sake of peace and brotherly love have agreed,
that Hans Karr should pay to Hans Kant 150 Thaler in all,
together with ten yards of linen, at five shillings a yard, in
return for which Kant resigns all and every claim to the public-
house at Werdden, its moveables and immoveables, its privileges,
rights and titles sine dolo for himself and his descendants for
ever."

A fine of ten thaler is fixed in case of breach of contract,
payable to the church at Werdden or to the Presbyterian
(Reformed) Church at Memel. Among the four witnesses, who
signed the paper, we find two Scotsmen : Wilhelm Murray and
Thoms. Sckrumsor (Scrimgeour).

[1] *Geschichte der Familie von Johnston* (History of the Family of
Johnston), 1891, p. 11 (privately printed).

VII. LIST OF SCOTTISH STUDENTS AT THE UNIVERSITY OF HELMSTÄDT
(1585-1603).

M. Joannes Johnstonus, Scotus, 1585.
M. Joannes Murdisinus (Morrison?), 1588.
M. Duncanus Liddelius, 1591.
Alexander Arbuthnot, 1591.
Gilbertus Burnat (Burnet), Scotus, Marrensis, 1591.
Joannes Skinaeus (Skene), Scotus, 1593.
Gilbertus Graoy (Gray), Scotus, 1593,

Georgius Lister, Scotus, 1593.
Duncanus Burnot (Burnet), Scotus, Abred. 1599.
Arturus Jonstanus (Jonston), Scotus, Abred. 1599.
Richardus Andersonus, Scotus, 1603.
Patricus Dunaeus, Scotus, 1603.
Joannes Cragius (Craig), Scotus, nobilis, 1605.
Georgius Forbesius, Scotus, 1606.[1]

VIII. LIST OF SCOTTISH STUDENTS AT FRANKFURT-ON-THE-ODER.

Joannes Fidelis, magister, Doctor Theolog. et Professor Franco-furd, 1547.
Andreas Lowson, Scotus, 1549.
Joannes Fidelis, egregii doctoris . . filius, 1555.
Patricius Dayrs (Dyce?), Scotus, 1576.
Duncanus Liddell, Scotus, 1579.
M. Jacobus Turnebus (Turnbull), Scotus, 1582.

M. Jacobus Helbron (Hepburn), Scotus, 1587.
M. Joannes Uddvart (Edward?),
M. Alexander Raedus (Reid), } Scoti, 1589.
M. Robertus Henrisonus, pauper Scotus, 1598.
David Lindse (Lindsay), 1656.
,, Plenderleith, nobilis Scoto-Brittannus, 1699.

IX. LIST OF SCOTTISH STUDENTS AT THE UNIVERSITY OF ROSTOCK
(1580-1615).

M. Guilhelmus Low, Scotus, Nov. 1580.
M. Johannes Johnstonus, Aug. 1584.
M. Robertus Hovaeus, Aug. 1584.
M. Archibaldus Hunterus, Scotus, Aug. 1588.
Patricius Gordoneus, Alexander Arbuthnot, } Scoti, Sept. 1589.

David Camerarius, Thomas Monguno-raeus (?), } Scoti, Aug. 1592.
Johannes Schrinaeus, Abred. Sept. 1592.
Jacobus Faber, Scotus, Feb. 1593.
Andreas Jacchaeus, Scotus, Nov. 1609.
Franciscus Gordonius, Scotus, Nov. 1615.

X. LIST OF SCOTTISH STUDENTS AT THE UNIVERSITY OF GREIFSWALD
(1519-1649).

Alexander Russael (Russel), clericus Aberdin. 1519.
Alexander Dume (?), pietate

et doctrina praestans liberalium artium magister, Divi Jacobi Pastor, 1545.[2]

---

[1] Extract from the Matriculation Rolls at Wolfenbüttel.
[2] Afterwards Professor of Theology at the University.

Alexander Sinapius (Mustard ?),
doctissimus vir, ingenuarum
artium magister, 1545.
Richardus Melving
(Melville), } Scoti,
David Pedi (Peddie), } 1546.

Robertus Henrisonus, Scotus, mag.
art. 1596.
Alexander Person (Pierson),
Scotus, 1622.
Robert Kunigem (Cunningham),
Scotus, 1649.

XI. List of Scottish Students at the University of Heidelberg
(1568-1660).

Johannes Menteyt (Menteith),
Scotus, 1568.
Guilielmus Silvius (Wood ?),
Scotus, 1570.
Olivarius Colt, Scotus, 1570.
M. Johannes Johnstonus, Scotus,
1587.
Jacobus Robertsonus, Edinbur-
gensis, 1589.
M. Robertus Uimierus, exul et
pauper, 1593.
Thomas Moranius (Moray), 1593.
M. Alexander Arbuthnot, 1594.
M. Thomas Landelus, Glascouien-
sis, 1596.[1]
David Duramensus (Durham),
Bacholdensis, 1597.[2]
M. Gualterus Donaltsonus, Abre-
donensis, 1599.
M. Arturus Jonstonus, Abredon-
ensis, 1599.
M Guilielmus Jonstonus, Scotus,
1603.
M. Andreas Aidius (Aedie),
Abredonius, 1603.

Alexander Forbosius, Scotus, 1603.
Patricius Lyndesius (Lindsay),
Scotus, 1603.
Alexander Anderson, Abredon-
iensis, 1605.
Patritius Kymerina (Cameron?),
Germanemis-Scotus, 1605.
Alexander Ramsaeus, Scotus,
Baronis de Banff filius tertio
genitus, 1606.
Patricius Dunaeus, Scotus, 1607.
Joannes Camero   „   1607.
Thomas Sincerf,   „   1609.
David Nerneus (Nairn ?), Andrea-
politanus, 1609.
Joannes Hogesius (Hog), Scotus,
1611.
Joannes Forbesius, Scotus nobilis,
1613.
Thomas Knoxius (Ramberlaeus),
Scotus, 1615.[3]
Thomas Cumingius, 1614.
Rodericus Maclennan, Scotus,
1660.

[1] "Die 15 Septembris 1596 ex senatusconsulto M. Thomas Landelus,
Glesgouiensis Scotus (jam quadragenarius et pauper), testimonium habens
a senioribus et ministro ecclesiae at Pfalzburg (et nominatim commendatus
a quadam dexteritate in curandis aegrotis), receptus fuit per hyemem in
domum Casimirianam hac lege, ne faciat medicinam (in urbe), sed
theologiae del operam."
[2] Bacholdensis = Badcall near Edderachyllis ?
[3] Ranfurly.

SUPPLEMENT.

PART I.

Page 18n. The names mentioned in [connection with the Scottish Brotherhood at *Greifswald* are:—David Gipson, Hans Leveston, Witton, Ths. Murray. It was mainly a charitable institution. In 1624 the society possessed a house in the Fischstrasse, but already in 1674 it was sold for 600 gulden and the company dissolved in consequence of the losses and ravages sustained in the Thirty Years' War. The money was handed over to the Church of St Mary. In the Stadtbuch (Burgh Records) 26, foll. 116, a Schottenstrasse is mentioned. (1557). (See Gesterding, *Beitrag zur Geschichte der Stadt Greifswald*, 1827.)

Page 50. The family of Spalding is still flourishing in Germany. The ancestor Andrew, who emigrated to Plau in Mecklenburg about 1600, became a member of the Senate; his son a Burgomaster. His grandson, Thomas, removed to Güstrow in the same country, where he likewise obtained the dignity of a " Senator." Here he and his family remained for almost two hundred years, inhabiting the same house, an old monastery of the mendicant Friars. In its gable the following verses were read :

> Die mich nicht können leiden,
> Die sollen mich meiden,
> Die mich hassen,
> Sollen mich lassen,
> Die mir nichts wollen geben,
> Sollen mich mit Gott doch lassen leben ; *i.e.*

" Those that cannot bear me, let them avoid me ; those that hate me, let them leave me alone ; those that will not give me anything, must yet with God let me live."

Other Spaldings emigrated to Pomerania. Many of them followed a professional career ;[1] others became officers.[2]

[1] We find a John David Spalding " Syndikus " of Rostock, Andreas Friedrich, founder ot the firm of G. H. Kaemmerer and a member of the Senate, in Hamburg, where a street is called after him. Another Spalding died as merchant and " Geheimer Commercienrath " at Stralsund (1860).

[2] For two hundred years we find Spaldings in the Prussian and

The most eminent of the family was Johann Joachim Spalding, born at Triebsees (Pomerania) in 1714 as the son of a clergyman. He studied divinity, and was appointed "Probst" (Archdeacon) and member of the consistorial board at Berlin (1764). Here he continued to write and to preach with much acceptance for twenty-five years. He was a great favourite with the Queen, the consort of Frederick the Great. His writings, some of which have been translated into English, bear the rationalistic stamp of his time. His piety and uprightness were acknowledged by everybody. He died in retirement at Charlottenburg in 1804. Visitors will see his bust in the Hohenzoller Museum at Berlin. His son George Ludwig also was an author. He was a member of the Academy of Sciences, and Professor at the High School. He wrote, among other works, a biography of his father.

PART II.

In Gauhen's *Adels Lexicon* are mentioned :—George Ogilvie, who settled in Germany during the Thirty Years' War and became Commandant" of the Fortress of Spielberg, near Brünn, in Moravia; George Benedict, his son, died as Polish and Saxon General and Field-Marshal in 1710; Carl Hermann, his son, was a general commanding in Bohemia and Governor of Prague (abt. 1740).

Page 112. Another Colonel Gunn was Governor of the town of Ohlau in Silesia (1638). He fortified the place, which had been destroyed by the Imperialists, with walls and moat. A Swedish garrison remained till after the Peace in 1648. Colonel John Gunn, lamented by the grateful citizens, died on the 9th of April 1649. The inscription on his tombstone in the Evangelical Church at Ohlau says of him : " Col. Johann Gunn, who laid the foundations of the fortifications of this town, was born in 1608 in the month of October. He was the descendant of a very old noble family, of the house of Golspie in the Kingdom of Scotland. He died aged forty years and six months. God grant him a peaceful rest until the joyous resurrection.

" His remains were deposited in this vault by his wife, née von Arnim, on the 14th of July, according to the custom of the nobility."

Gunn's coffin was removed in 1825 to a place near the vestry; his mail-armour is hung up in the High School; two of his rings are preserved in the church at Ohlau.[1]

German army. (See E. Spalding, *Geschichtliches*, *Urkunden der Spalding*, 1898, privately printed, 1280.)

[1] Communicated.

SUPPLEMENT.

PART IV.

STATESMAN AND SCHOLAR.

Pages 201-202. Erskine, also called Eskin or Esken in German documents, was twice married, his second wife being Lucie Christine von Wartensleben, the widow of a Baron von Maltzahn in Mecklenburg. In 1631-32 he was Swedish Plenipotentiary at Erfurt, where he gained the gratitude of the inhabitants by suggesting and actively promoting the arranging of the City Records. In Motschmann, Erfordia litterata, iv. 305, we read:

"Der Rath der Stadt Erfurt verordnete Commissarios aus seinen Mitteln, die mit den von der Universität hiezu erbetenen Personen die Privilegia, Statuten und andere hieher gehörige Documenta mussten durchgehen und über die vorseiende Restauration deliberiren; worauf dieselben dem schwedischen Rath und Residenten alhier, Alexandro von Esken, Erbherrn in Ludershagen, dessen Vorspruch und Hülfe man sich hierinne sonderlich bediente, ein Memorial unter dem 31ten August 1632 übergeben."

i.e. The Magistrates of the City of Erfurt at their own expense appointed a Commission, which together with members of the University requisitioned for the purpose, were to examine the privileges, records and other like documents, and to deliberate on their restoration if required. They then handed a Memorial to the Swedish Counsellor of State and Resident in this City, Alexander Erskine, to whose suggestion and assistance they were chiefly indebted in this matter, on the 31st of August 1632. The chief points therein were, etc., etc.

Page 312. The grandfather of Kant, the Philosopher, married a second time in 1698; and had, after an interval of seventeen years, another son in 1702. He died in 1715 and was buried according to the entry in the Register of the "Erzpriester," "on the 22nd of March with all the bells, the whole school and a hymn before his door." (Sembritzki, *Altpreuss. Monatsschrift*, Band xxxviii. 3 and 4.)

The name *Schott* or Schotte (Polish Scoda) occurs as early as 1383 in Breslau. It is frequently met with in the XVth and XVIth Centuries, especially in the eastern parts of Prussia, where the Scottish immigration was particularly numerous. Care, however, must be exercised in tracing the name Schotte back to Scottish ancestors in every case, since the German word has various other meanings. There is also a small town called Schotten in Hesse.   The name *Scott* occurs in Prussia.   One Walter Scott is a landowner and Hauptmann (captain in the army).   His ancestor emigrated towards the close of the XVIth Century from near Edinburgh and settled in Pillau.   There are now six representatives of the family in Eastern Prussia alone, four of them landowners.

The *Piersons*, who are settled in Berlin and Karlsruhe, trace their origin to one James Pierson of Balmadies, who went to Riga towards the end of the XVIIIth Century.   (See *Familien Chronik der Piersons*, privately printed.)

The family von *Mietzel* in Brandenburg derive their name from Mitchel; the von *Marshalls* from the Earl Marschal. They settled in Königsberg in the XVIIth Century.   One Samuel Marschall, a Privy Counsellor and Domdechant at Havelberg, was ennobled in 1718.   (*Märkisches Adels Lexicon.*)

INDEX.

INDEX.

A.

AARAU, 180.
Abbots of Ratisbon, 289.
Aberdeen, 6, 8, 11, 13, 18, 21 f., 28, 229, 243, 268.
Abernethy, John of, 5 n.
Achaius, King, 297 n. 1.
Agnew, Sir A., 120.
Agricola, J., 307.
Aidie, A., 231 n.
Aikenhead, P., 64.
Alesius, 165 ff., 307.
Anclam, 22.
Ancrofts, 24.
Anderson, G., 226 f., 274.
Andrew, a ship, 24.
Angus, Earl of, 16.
Arbuthnot, Abbot, 149 f., 300.
Armour, importation of, 9.
Arnisæus, 229.
Asloan, Prior, 160, 219.
Assembly, General (1587), 187.
Auchinvale, G., 228.
Augsburg, 84, 107 n., 227.

B.

BACHARACH, taking of, 83 n.
Baillie, Abbot, 146, 219.
Balon, A., 5.
Baner, General, 87, 107.
Bathory, St, 28. 72.
Bavaria, William, Duke of, 298.
Baysen, 11.
Beer, importation of, 5, 11 f., 23.
Belgrade, 119, 131.
Belleken, 5.
Berclay, D., 70.
Bergschotten, die, 129.
Bergen, 9 f.
Bernadotte, 151.
Bernhard, Duke of Weimar, 87, 93, 146, 286.
Berwick-on-Tweed, 6, 8.
Bingen, taking of, 83 n.
Birthbrieves of Aberdeen, 243 f.
  „ of Dundee, 247 f.
  „ 60.
Bobbert, C. v., 19.

Bohemia, King of, 75 f.
Bonars, 58.
Boucicault, 71 f.
Braemar, 254.
Brahe, Tycho, 222.
Brandenburg, 50, 167.
  „ Elector of, 73, 181.
  „ Markgraf of, 36.
  „ Neu-, 79.
Braunsberg (Silesia), 57, 298.
Bremen, 7, 8, 20, 242.
Breslau, 31 n., 36, 241.
Brockie, 219.
Bromberg, 35, 264
Brown, J., minister at Danzig, 189.
  „ W., 63.
Bruges, 3 n., 9, 14.
Bucquoi, 77.
Burnet, A., 89.

C.

CALVIN, 169.
Calvino-Lutheran Feud, 174 f.
Campbell, T., the poet, 150.
Carleton, 33.
Carmichael in Krakau, 48.
Carmichael, Sir Thomas Gibson, 274 n.
Caroline, Queen of Denmark, 214.
Cecil, Sir E., 72.
Chamberlain, 33.
Charles I, 40.
  „ II, 40, 309 f.
  „ V, the Emperor, 75.
Chaucer, 70.
Christina, Queen of Sweden, 179.
Clifford, 71.
Cloch, B., 70.
Cloth, Scottish, 15.
Coal, early export of, 21.
Cochlaeus, 166.
Cochrane, Sir John, 47 f., 202 f.
Coleman, Col., 128 n.
Collen, J., 13.
Comenius, 179.
Commerce with Scotland stopped, 13.
Constance, 141, 144.
Constitution of the Scottish merchants, 39 f.
Conway, General, 213.
Cook, Abbot, 160.

INDEX.

321

Gordon, Col. J. 113

",, Marianus, 162.

",, Nathaniel, 58.

",, Patrick, 33, 255.

",, Robert, 60.

",, Steelhand, 118 n.

Graham, Col., 118 n.

Grain, importation of, 24 f.

Gral, Hermann, 9.

Grant, Bernhard, 249.

",, Major, 128, 287.

Greifswald, 8, 17, 18 n., 22.

",, Scottish Students at, 313.

Grey, Sir A., 77.

Grotius, Hugo, 307.

Gunn, Sir W., 112.

",, Col. J., 316.

Gustavus Adolphus, King of Sweden, 73 f., 82 f., 175.

Gustavus Adolphus, letters of, 280 f.

H.

HAIG, Brothers, 77.

Haliburton, W., 13.

Halyburton, A., 24 n.

Halle, 79 ff.

Hamburg, 3. 6, 8, 15, 17, 21, 28, 202 f.

Hamilton, Sir A., 109 f.

",, Sir Fred., 89.

",, Sir J., 81.

",, Marquis of, 85, 104, 108 f., 282.

",, Placidus, 159 f.

",, Patrick, 163 f.

",, Col., 118 n.

Hanau, Count of, 93.

",, Siege of, 93 f.

Hansetowns, 11, 13.

Harfleur, 5.

Harris, Sir J., 208.

Heidelberg, 87, 220, 311, 314.

Helmstädt, Scottish students at, 313.

Henry IV, 4.

Henryson, 227.

Hepburn, 75, 76 ff., 82 f.

Hervie, D., 227.

Hesse-Darmstadt, Landgraf of, 95.

Hesse-Cassel, Landgraf of, 96.

",, Landgravine of, 184.

Highlanders, praise of the, 74, 129.

Hirsch, Dr Theo., 6 n., 10 n.

Hoe von Hohenegg, 177.

Hyndford, Lord, 205.

I.

IAN, Clan, 29.

Ilmenau in Thuringia, 80 n.

Independence, Scottish, lost, 30.

Ingram, B., 230.

Intrigues, Jacobite, at Ratisbon, 149.

Inverness, 8.

Irish monks, 137 f.

J.

JABLONSKI, 179.

Jackson (Dziaksen), 196.

James I, 11.

",, II, 7, 11, 229.

",, IV, 17, 244.

",, V, 22.

",, VI, 27, 31, 33, 242.

Jerichow, 226.

Jerre, Claus, 11.

Jews, 32, 35, 38 f., 55.

Johnston, A., 230, 311.

",, J., 222 f., 311 f.

Jonas, the Grite, 27.

Jülich War, 73.

Jungingen, von, 4.

Jurski, P. A., 192.

K.

KABRUHN (Cockburn), 60 ff., 269.

Kant, 12.

",, Balzer, 231 f.

",, Hans, 231, 312, 317.

",, Immanuel, 231.

",, Richard, 232.

Kaunitz, Chancellor, 131.

Keith, Earl Marshal, 120 f.

",, Field-Marshal, 120 ff.

",, the Pages, 127.

",, Sir Robert Murray, 127, 211 f.

Kerr, John, Captain, 90.

Kilchberg, 107.

Kilekanne, 6, 13, 239.

King, General, 99.

Kirkcaldy, 29.

Knape, 21.

Kneiphovia, 29.

Knox, J., 169 ff.

Kollin, battle of, 126.

Königsberg (Queenisbrig), 8, 19, 29, 31, 188, 190, 192, 229 f., 261.

Krakau, 31, 38, 49.

",, Scots in, 256.

Krämerguild, 36.

Kreuznach, taking of, 83 n.

Kriegsspiel, 127.

Krone, Deutsch-, Scots in, 55.

Krotska, battle of, 119.

Kunersdorf, battle of, 131.

X

INDEX.

Oldenburg, Countess of, 21.
Oppenheim, siege of, 82.
Orem, 49.
Orkney, Earl of, 27, 119.
Orkney, islands, 16, 20.
Osnabrück, 106.
Osten, Tideman v., 6.
Ostrowski, 56.
Oxenstierna, Chancellor, 94, 106, 176 f.

P.

PAPISTICAL GOODS, 28.
Parma, Margaret of, 18.
Pedlars, Scotch-Polish, 24, 31, 34.
Peebles, 23.
Perth, 8, 9.
Peterwardein, fortress of, 119.
Philippus, Abbot, 159.
Pilgrims, Scottish, 37 n., 117, 241.
Pirates, Frisian, 5.
  ,,   French, 10, 20, 22.
  ,,   Scottish, 4, 5 f.
Plague, the, 18 f.
Plau (in Mecklenburg), 50.
Poland, 23, 30 ff., 223, etc.
Polseyne, 16.
Pomerania, 50.
  ,,   Dukes of, 22.
Porteous in Krosna, 60.
Posen, Scots in, 54 f.
Prague, treaty of, 106.
Primogeniture, 31.
Prussia, 11 f., 14, 36 f., 51.
Prussia, Frederick William III, King of, 185.
Public Library, first in Scotland, 229.
Putzig, Scots in, 56 f.
  ,,   Trial at, 195 f.

Q.

QUEENISBRIG, see Königsberg.

R.

RAMSAY, Alex. Col., 83 n.
  ,,   Ch. A., 233,
  ,,   Sir James, 81, 90 ff., 285 f.
     Lady Isabella, 102 f.
Ratisbon, Scottish Monastery at, 138 ff.
Reay, Lord, 76 f., 91, 108, 280 f.
Reformation in Scotland, two Periods of the, 169.
Reid, Th., 229.
Rentoun, Capt., 28.
Restrictions of trade, 14 f.
Richelieu, Cardinal 89 n.

Robertson, R., Father, 151 f.
Rodan, Nic., 9.
Roe, Sir Ths., 176 f.
Romana, General, 151 f.
Ross, 12.
  ,,   Bishop, 185.
Rostock, 5, 6, 8, 11, 229.
  ,,   Scottish students at, 313.
Rousseau, 122 n.
Rowe, General, 119.
Royal Merchants in Krakau, 49.
Rudolf II, Emperor of Germany, 296.
Rügen, island of, 78.
Ruthven, Sir P., 87, 92, 107.
Rye, importation of, 12.

S.

ST ANDREWS, 8, 10, 165, 223.
St Cuthbert's geese, 16.
St Martin, 20.
St Ninian's Church, 24.
Salt, importation of, 5.
Scheele, 17.
Schieffelbein, town of, 78 f.
Schiller, 83, 113, 137 n.
Schole, H., 6.
Schönau, 12.
Schott, the name, in Germany, 317 f.
Schottenstrassen, 3 n., 18 n.
Schottland, Alt and Neu, 18 n.
Scotch Benedictines at Ratisbon, 138 ff.
  ,,   Body Guard in France, 69.
  ,,   Church at Danzig, 189 f.
  ,,   ,,   at Königsberg, 190 f.
  ,,   Regiments under Marlborough, 118 f.
Scotland, trade of, with Germany 3-31.
Scottish Debtors, 238 f.
Scots, the, driven out of Danzig, 49.
Scott, Michael, 217.
  ,,   Walter, 75.
Scottendyk, 3.
Scotus, Duns, 216.
Scrymgeour, H., 227.
Seaton, Sir John, 16.
  ,,   Col., 103.
Shipping list of Dundee, 25 f.
Sigismund, Augustus, King of Poland, 35, 40.
Simpsons at Memel, 192.
Skene, Sir J., 33.
  ,,   Baron v., 58.
Skins exported, 6, 29.
Smart, David, 28.
Soap, importation of, 23.
Spalding, 50, 315 f.
Spence, Sir J., 91 n.
Spielberg, the, 318.
Stalker, Th., 27.

Printed in Great Britain by Redwood Press Limited, Trowbridge, Wiltshire.